School of American Research
Advanced Seminar Series

DOUGLAS W. SCHWARTZ, GENERAL EDITOR

The Valley of Mexico

Advanced Seminars are made possible
by a gift in recognition of
PHILIP L. SHULTZ
for his efforts on behalf of
the School of American Research

THE VALLEY
OF MEXICO
Studies in Pre-Hispanic
Ecology and Society

EDITED BY
ERIC R. WOLF

A SCHOOL OF AMERICAN RESEARCH BOOK

UNIVERSITY OF NEW MEXICO PRESS · Albuquerque

Library of Congress Cataloging in Publication Data

Main entry under title

The Valley of Mexico

(Advanced seminar series)
Papers based on a seminar held in Santa Fe, N.M.,
Apr. 3–8, 1972.
"A School of American Research book."
Bibliography: p. 303
Includes index.
1. Indians of Mexico—Mexico, Valley of—Antiquities—
Addresses, essays, lectures. 2. Mexico, Valley of—
Antiquities—Addresses, essays, lectures. 3. Mexico—
Antiquities—Addresses, essays, lectures. 4. Human
ecology—Mexico—Mexico, Valley of—Addresses, essays,
lectures. I. Wolf, Eric Robert, 1923–
II. Series: Santa Fe, N.M. School of American
Research. Advanced seminar series.
F1219.1.M53V27   972'.004'97   75–21184
ISBN 0–8263–0398–6

To Pedro Armillas,
who led the way

Foreword

Few areas in the world of comparable size possess the richness of archaeological resources or the strength of cultural tradition that can be observed in the high, mountain-rimmed Valley of Mexico. Here the presence of the past is everywhere: in the two-thousand-year-old Cuicuilco ceremonial center, in the greatness of Teotihuacán, in the powerful Toltec statuary at Tula, and in the intriguing glimpses of Aztec Tenochtitlan seen throughout Mexico City. Added to this is a rich ethnohistorical view of Aztec life provided by Fray Bernardino de Sahagún, the Franciscan priest whose remarkable *General History of the Things of New Spain* chronicled Aztec culture in sixteenth-century Mexico. Even the stories of Moctezuma II visiting Teotihuacán for worship symbolically relate the early historic period to the very beginnings of civilization in the Valley. The importance of the past to the living is evident today at Xochimilco, where muck is still brought from the bottoms of the canals and added to the top of the gardens originally built in Aztec times, and in the great Museum of Anthropology in Mexico City, to which local people come in a steady stream to honor those who went before them.

It is natural, therefore, that a great deal of productive archaeological and ethnohistorical effort has been expended in the Valley of Mexico, and that the region has always been a focus of attempts to understand the processes leading to the rise of civilization. In his introduction to *The Valley of Mexico*, Eric Wolf reviews the historical and theoretical background, both within Mesoamerica and elsewhere, that has shaped the ideas of scholars working in the area. Carefully tracing the distinguished chain of thought linking Childe, Kluckhohn, Wittfogel, Redfield, Steward, Willey, Kirchhoff, and Armillas, Wolf nonetheless makes clear that by the late 1950s, though theory abounded concerning the reasons for the growth of civilization in the Valley of Mexico, hard evidence was in short supply.

In 1960 a group of scholars meeting at the University of Chicago set a new course of data collection to remedy this situation. Over the next twelve years an enormous field effort concentrated on a study of the origin and early development of urban civilization in the general area of the Valley of Mexico. This volume results from a seminar held at the School of American Research in 1972 to assess the results of that work and to pull from it more far-reaching conclusions relating to the original theoretical interests.

A new, neutral terminology for the chronology of Mesoamerica is presented and discussed by Price and Millon in Part 1 of *The Valley of Mexico* and is subsequently employed throughout the volume. Sanders, Parsons, and Logan next describe a powerful explanatory model for the development of civilization, dynamically interrelating population growth, food production, social differentiation, and the development of social control hierarchies. They then apply this model to the Valley of Mexico in terms of environment, settlement and population history, and agricultural development. Blanton discusses the importance of local and regional interactions involving trade as an additional element in the model. Later chapters by Millon, Diehl, and Calnek add further dimensions to an understanding of the region through detailed perspectives on the monumental city of Teotihuacán, the Valley of Mexico's relationships to the north and west throughout the prehistoric period, and ethnohistorical material available on the urbanization process at Tenochtitlan.

This volume thus provides an important contemporary interpretation of the archaeological and cultural legacy of the Valley of Mexico. Its contributors have made the results of work in this unique region more meaningful to the whole problem of the rise of civilization.

School of American Research   Douglas W. Schwartz

Contents

Contents

Figures

Maps

Tables

1
Introduction

E R I C R. W O L F

Department of Anthropology
Herbert H. Lehman College
City University of New York

Writing in 1940, Clyde Kluckhohn enraged many archaeologists working in Middle America by castigating their industrious but aimless artifact collecting, carried on without the benefit of any quickening conceptual scheme (Kluckhohn 1940:42). The field seemed to be in the firm grip of potsherd gatherers and pyramid gazers, *tepalcateros* and *piramidiotas*. Yet even then new influences were making themselves felt. Most notable were two pioneer attempts, both formulated in print in the 1930s, to combine the methods and insights of archaeology, historical geography, history, and ethnology in order to shed new light on the origins and growth of civilization. One such attempt was that of V. Gordon Childe, who wrote in 1936 that "the study of living human societies as functioning organisms has revealed to archaeologists this approach to their materials" (Childe 1936:3). It was, of course, also Childe who imparted a new direction to archaeology by conceptualizing a great body of data as the outcomes of two great revolutions in human history: the first of these was the Neolithic Revolution, ushered in by the development of food production; the second was the Urban Revolution, marked by the growth of cities and of their governing elites.

The other important figure in breaking new paths that others were to follow was Karl A. Wittfogel. In his *Wirtschaft und Gesellschaft Chinas* (1931) he interpreted the course of Chinese development in the light of Marx's concept of the Asiatic mode of production, based on the need to develop and maintain extensive systems of hydraulic agriculture. The first formulation of this concept became available to English readers in Wittfogel's *New Light on Chinese Society* (1938). Both Childe and Wittfogel, it should be noted, were Marxists and worked with the concepts and methodology of the Marxian tradition. Whatever the current status of their conceptual schemes, their overall impact and productivity in archaeology proved to be enormous.

In the United States, similarly, the 1930s witnessed the development of trends of thought that would have an important bearing on the future course of archaeology in Middle America. One of these trends, which was sociological in nature, originated with the members of the Chicago school of sociology; its representative within anthropology was Robert Redfield, who had carried out one of the first "community studies" in Tepoztlán in 1926–27. This sociological tradition emphasized the relationship between the process of differentiation in society and the coherence of understandings in men's minds, which led to Redfield's conceptual opposition between "folk ways" and "city ways," between folk culture and civilization. Another trend—one in a more materialist direction—was initiated by Julian Steward. Steward had carried out fieldwork among the Owens Valley Paiute in 1927 and 1928. Among the many publications stemming from this work, Steward's "Ecological Aspects of Southwestern Society" (1937) particularly demonstrated to archaeologists and ethnohistorians the importance of the relationships between environment, technology, settlement pattern, and social organization. The paper was rejected by the *American Anthropologist* but finally reached print overseas, in the pages of *Anthropos*.

Although Childe and Wittfogel had given a new intellectual impetus to the study of Old World civilizations, inquiry into the course of New World civilizations still followed traditional precedent. Yet here, too, there would be changes. Once again, many of them were due to the catalytic influence of Julian Steward. Under his editorship, work was begun in

Introduction

1940 on the *Handbook of South American Indians,* which eventually led to a reconceptualization of American cultural growth and development. Another step was taken in 1946 with the initiation of an integrated historical, ethnographic, and geographic study of the Virú Valley in northern Peru. Steward's influence on the strategy and interpretation of the findings was notable. One of the related studies would play an especially important part in future archaeological endeavors: it was Gordon Willey's study of settlement patterns in the Virú Valley (1953).

What about Mesoamerica? In 1946, university students in the United States were still reading Vaillant's *Aztecs of Mexico* as a synthesis of extant knowledge. Though imbued with a vision of the stylistic quality of Mesoamerican civilization, the book did not include the new ecological concerns. Yet here, too, things were beginning to change. In the early forties Paul Kirchhoff had begun to talk of Mesoamerica as an "urban" civilization (1943). Kirchhoff, also connected with the Marxian tradition, had fled to Mexico from Nazi Germany. In the course of his work he gave Mexican studies of archaeology and ethnohistory an interest in the organization of society. One of his notable contributions was "The Principles of Clanship in Human Society." Written in 1935, the paper remained available only in *samizdat* format until 1955, when it appeared in the United States in a student publication, the *Davidson Journal of Anthropology* (Kirchhoff 1959: 259–70). Kirchhoff was also responsible for disseminating in Mexico some of the writings of Wittfogel.

In 1948 Pedro Armillas's statement of a new approach to Mesoamerican prehistory appeared in his contribution to a volume on Peruvian archaeology (1948). A year later, Steward was thus able to include Mesoamerica in his consideration of cases for his "Trial Formulation of the Development of Early Civilizations" (1949). Armillas, meanwhile, following his early statement, continued his studies, contributing papers on systems of cultivation in Mesoamerica (1949); on technology, socioeconomic organization, and religion (1950); and on the importance of *chinampas* (West and Armillas 1950). Pedro Armillas was a pioneer in the truest sense of the word. Few of those who heard his discussions and presentations in the late forties and early fifties will ever forget the impact of his statements on his listeners. To him, above all, is owed the reorientation of archaeological work in the Mexican highlands.

Yet as the new interest in the interrelationships of environment, technology, settlement pattern, and sociopolitical organization gained ground, new questions were raised for which the extant data were clearly insufficient. What were the characteristics of Mesoamerican agricultural systems? What role did hydraulic agriculture play in prompting or facilitating the growth of large population centers? When was irrigation first introduced? What was the nature of these population centers? When and where did urbanism first arise? How were these urban centers provisioned? What information did the ethnohistorians have that could answer these questions? These questions guided the efforts of many investigators in the fifties (R. Millon 1954, 1957, Molíns Fábrega 1954–55, Palerm 1952, 1954, 1955, Armillas, Palerm, and Wolf 1956, Palerm and Wolf 1954–55, 1957, Sanders 1953, 1956, Wolf and Palerm 1955). These endeavors, in turn, contributed to the growing debate on the sustaining capabilities of tropical forest environments as against those of arid lands (Meggers 1954), on the role of hydraulic agriculture in the genesis and growth of civilization (Steward et al. 1955), and on the priority of the Mesoamerican lowlands over the highlands in the development of settled life and urbanism. Yet theory was clearly outrunning evidence; increasingly sophisticated trains of thought required new and more diversified data.

At the end of the fifties, certain investigators, notably William Sanders and René Millon, began to lay plans for systematic work in the Valley of Mexico, a logical area for research because the Valley had been, since early times, a core area of Mesoamerican development. Technically a basin (no river drained its waters to outside areas in pre-Hispanic times), the Valley of Mexico measures about 8,000 square kilometers from its mountain rim to its center. Located between semidesert to the north and subtropics to the south, it has had access to a varied array of resources and products, in addition to its own. The Valley's mountainous perimeter protected it from overeager intruders, yet its gateways connected it with the lands lying beyond it. A system of interconnected lakes served to link the Valley's internal shorelines.

This landscape had supported human life from the earliest times of the big-game hunters until the present day, as well as having participated in all of the major developments of Mesoamerican civilization. It was the setting for the growth of America's largest pre-Hispanic city, Teotihuacán, and the site of the Aztec city of Tenochtitlan, which the Spaniards conquered and rebuilt as the capital of their New Spain. Despite the fury of the Conquest, much pre-Hispanic documentary material had survived into modern times, together with the written observations of Spanish priests, soldiers, and officials. The museums housed vast treasures and collections of artifacts, and the Valley itself was studded with pyramids and the remains of domestic architecture. Here, then, was an area that offered the raw materials for a breakthrough in theory and data.

On 6–9 June 1960 the National Science Foundation sponsored a conference at the University of Chicago with the purpose of coordinating ongoing and future efforts in the Valley of Mexico. Robert M. Adams, Pedro Armillas, Pedro Carrasco, Michael Coe, Edward S. Deevey, Jr., William J. Mayer-Oakes, René Millon, Román Piña Chan, William T. Sanders, and Monica Bopp attended, with Eric R. Wolf acting as convener. The group recommended that future research concentrate on the northeastern part of the Valley, specifically the Valley of Teotihuacán and the vicinity of Texcoco. The arguments favoring this choice were stated in Wolf's report on the conference to the National Science Foundation:

> The Valley of Teotihuacán, containing the largest prehistoric site in Middle America, is the ideal region in which to study the origin and early development of urban civilization. The region of Texcoco, offering a unique combination of archaeological sites, native annals and conquest-period written sources, is the ideal region in which to study the later development of pre-Hispanic civilization, and the cultural processes transforming that civilization into the patterns of colonial and modern Mexico.
>
> While we advocate that future effort be concentrated in this part of the Valley, we do of course recognize that research calculated to illuminate the rise and fall of Teotihuacán or Texcoco may be carried out at other sites in the Valley of Mexico as well as outside.

A significant result of this conference was an agreement between René Millon and William T. Sanders to divide the work to be carried out in the Valley of Teotihuacán. Millon would focus on the study of the urban center, while Sanders would survey the rural portions of the Valley. The main work of surveying and mapping has been completed (R. Millon 1973, R. Millon, Drewitt, and Cowgill 1973, Sanders 1965).

In 1971 the School of American Research offered its hospitality for the holding of a seminar that could assess and discuss the work already accomplished. We are indeed fortunate that during the twelve years which have elapsed since the gathering in Chicago, not only have Millon and Sanders carried out their intended tasks, but others—working in conjunction with them or on their own—have greatly added to our knowledge of developments in the Valley. During this period Jeffrey Parsons carried out survey work in the region of Texcoco, while Richard Blanton surveyed the Ixtapalapa peninsula. Palerm plunged further into the ethnohistorical source material on hydraulic agriculture; Sanders carried out further research on agricultural systems; Richard Diehl began a renewed cycle of work at Tula. The seminar—meeting at Santa Fe, New Mexico, on 3–8 April 1972—could thus also draw on these accumulated materials. Participating in the seminar were Ignacio Bernal, Richard E. Blanton, Edward E. Calnek, George L. Cowgill, Richard A. Diehl, José Luis Lorenzo, René Millon, Ángel Palerm, Jeffrey R. Parsons, Barbara J. Price, and William T. Sanders. Eric R. Wolf was again invited to act as convener, and Sydel Silverman acted as recorder. Participants came to the meeting with statements of their findings and positions, but formal papers were prepared only after the seminar discussion. These are the papers that form the present volume. One paper, summarizing and interpreting the ethnohistorical material on hydraulic constructions in the Valley, was presented at the conference, but has appeared in book form elsewhere (Palerm 1973).

One of the pleasures of the conference was to see how much had been learned since 1960. There are now new data, and there is new theory. Systems theory, for example, has captured the imagination of the archaeologists. There has been a vast increase in the sophistication with which variables are defined and investigated: archaeologists are delving into questions of bioenergetics, demography, information theory, and computer simulation of alternative models. The use of ethnological analogues has become accepted, both to develop models as a means of clarifying particular cases and to serve the purposes of cross-cultural comparison. In all, one gains an impression of purpose, vigor, and imaginativeness which, by comparison, is sadly absent from present-day ethnology and social anthropology. But with the increase in methodological sophistication there also comes increased sophistication in argument. Some of these arguments divided participants at the conference, and the different premises and understandings underlying these arguments will be evident in the chapters that follow.

Happily there was consensus among the participants on one important issue. The seminar agreed to adopt a neutral terminology for chronological distinctions in Mesoamerican archaeology. This terminological scheme, patterned on the one developed by John Rowe (1960) for the

Introduction

Central Andes, is presented by Barbara Price in Chapter 2, followed by René Millon's comments (Chapter 3).

The second major section of the book (Chapters 4–8) consists, in part, of the ambitious efforts of William T. Sanders, Jeffrey R. Parsons, and Michael Logan to trace the course of ecological adaptation and cultural evolution in the Basin of Mexico over a period of more than two and one-half millennia. They do so in terms of a model that postulates a spiraling relation between population growth, food production, societal differentiation, and the development of societal control hierarchies (social stratification and the state). Population growth is treated as a given, and populations are seen as facing crucial options at critical points, with the outcome deciding their survival and continued maintenance and growth. Populations unable to fill new niches through fission are constrained to intensify food production. Food production, in turn, sets in motion processes of differentiation within the population, and favors the selection of populations with higher resource potential, greater societal differentiation, and better resource management over those with weaker resource potential, lower degree of differentiation, and weaker resource management. The model is clearly a variant of the Darwinian model; variations in reproductive success are secured through the differential development and organization of exosomatic means rather than through variations in genotype or phenotype.

At the conference Sanders argued that his model was not a theory, but part of a research strategy designed to test the explanatory power of the ecological approach, to see "how far" it could take him. It was not, he claimed, developed to "explain everything." Certainly the simplicity and the directness of the model are commendable, especially when one is interested in global relations and global trends. It would seem, however, that when interest turns to an analysis of the critical turning points in the spiral which connects population → technology → societal differentiation → controls, more complex models will be required (Dumond 1972b, Katz 1972, Netting 1972, Sahlins 1972).

René Millon (Chapter 10) and Edward Calnek (Chapter 12) presented a rather different approach, one that reflects in part the different types of evidence at the basis of their concerns. Sanders, Parsons, and Blanton emphasized the features of the environment, the culturally available technology, and the settlement pattern that could be read from the

7

evidence of regional surveys. In contrast Millon worked with the data of a monumental city, clearly planned to overwhelm both inhabitants and viewers with a demonstration of power rendered incarnate in layout, architecture, and decoration. Calnek, in turn, had worked with ethnohistorical sources, which permit a more refined discrimination of groups and their functions than can be gleaned from archaeological material alone. Where the purely ecological approach tends to disregard the question of meaning—and of meanings embodied in social and political organization, therefore—the urban archaeologist and the ethnohistorian are drawn inevitably into the complex problems of what Teotihuacán or Tenochtitlan are *about*, not just into questions of what they are.

Richard Blanton (Chapter 9) attempts to mediate between the two positions by suggesting that the ecological approach be extended to include exchanges of information, as well as exchanges of resources and energy. This follows the treatment of Tsembaga ritual as a regulator and transducer in an information exchange, described and analyzed by Roy A. Rappaport in his monograph on the ecology of a New Guinea population (1968), as well as in some comments by Kent Flannery (1972).

There is perhaps some aspect of Teotihuacán that lends itself to an application of information theory. It is certainly clear that Teotihuacán must have subjugated the environment, population, and technology to a heretofore unheard-of degree of coercion. It suggests a situation that Rappaport has described as the usurpation of a general-purpose system— a system whose only purpose is survival—by a partial system that subjects the general system to its single purpose. Rappaport has also argued that such a trend may lead to an "aberration of sanctity." By this he means the hypertrophy of the apparatus concerned with the issuance of meta-messages, certifying the veridity and validity of ordinary statements. Perhaps something of the kind occurred at Teotihuacán. In information terms this would involve a reduction in the improbability of messages through the operation of redundance. The greater the redundance, the fewer selective operations are required to transmit the message. From this perspective a symbolic system like that of Teotihuacán must have involved a large increase in message redundance, and an attendant decrease in flexibility.

Yet this still does not explain what Teotihuacán was *about*. Information, as communication engineers define the concept, is a measure of the number of steps taken to narrow the size of range of possible messages to the intended selective-information content. But Marshall McLuhan to the contrary notwithstanding, the message is not yet the meaning; meaning can only be defined as the selective function exercised by the message on the range of possible states of the goal complex concerned (MacKay 1964: 165). To regard Teotihuacán, therefore, merely as an information sender does not yet do justice to its complexity. Millon rightly speaks of it as a "Vatican," a repository of symbols. This requires explanation in its own terms.

Perhaps there is a hint here of the direction in which future research might go. Sanders, Parsons, and Logan seem to recognize that the organization of groups and the power either shared between them or imposed on them involves processes that possess a dynamic of their own. They have wisely chosen the term "option" to indicate that there are elements of choice involved in critical action at important turning points in development. Options for tighter organization and greater control are possible, but not assured. Indeed, some options made at such turning points may be inherently "improbable." Millon's discoveries at Teotihuacán suggest such an improbable set of events—a rapid escalation of organization and power that radically altered the ecological pattern of the surrounding countryside. This is all the more likely in that the distribution of settlements after the breakdown of Teotihuacán bears a marked resemblance to the status quo ante.

One of the possible research strategies, therefore, is to return to the detailed investigation of what can be learned from ethnohistorical sources and iconography. Such an investigation would not focus primarily on the identification of activities, personages, dynasties, and places, but on the characteristics of the native (*emic*) model for the exercise of power. A great deal has been learned about the characteristics of the Inca model through the work of such scholars as John V. Murra and R. T. Zuidema. The elements for such a specification of the Aztec model are certainly implicit in the work of Edward Calnek, including his contribution to the present volume. Greater understanding of the Toltec model will come through the contextual study of references to Toltecs and Tollan, not now seen as related ethnic populations, but as bearers of a similar mode of political order. This work will, of course, gain greatly through reference to the archaeological work now going on at Tula itself (see Chapter 10 by R. A. Diehl).

Similarly, Clara Millon's pioneering paper (C. Millon 1973) on the iconography of power at Teotihuacán and at sites influenced by Teotihuacán represents a first long step toward attempting an answer of what Teotihuacán was about. It may be of interest that Rudolf van Zantwijk has recently (1973) suggested a general political model for Mesoamerica between the thirteenth and fifteenth centuries in which he sees various principles of organization—a bipartite division conceived as a connection between male and female aspects, a tripartite principle referring to the structure of the universe, and a quadripartite principle referring to the four directions—as organizing devices for the integration of distinct ethnic groups. According to van Zantwijk (1973:25):

> In normal times each ethnic group had its own religious organization, its own social and political place within the system. The above mentioned associations of place, direction and social group and the relevant God or Gods . . . enabled each particular ethnic group to play a part in the system at a fixed time. Often the arrangement was for a certain group to be charged with military functions, another group with priesthood functions, others again with functions connected with agriculture or handicraft. Although mostly one or more ethnic groups were in charge of military and economic affairs while others controlled functions of public services, the fact that important community activities were entrusted to the various groups in turn enabled each group at some time to be at the top of a certain hierarchy.

The argument is put forward here for illustration only. Its merit lies in introducing the factors of calendric regulation and ethnic specialization into considerations of the Mesoamerican mode of politics.

The last twelve years, it is clear, have witnessed not only an enormous increase in our store of knowledge, but the development of powerful explanatory models as well. If van Zantwijk's suggestion of a general political model for Mesoamerica has any merit, it is that such a model would make possible a renewed exploration of the dialectic between *etics* and *emics* at a higher level of professional competence.

Part 1

Chronology

2

A Chronological Framework for
Cultural Development in Mesoamerica[1]

BARBARA J. PRICE
New York City

It has long been apparent that there are two distinct and complementary strategies for subdividing the culture history of an area: classification by chronological periods, and classification by developmental stages or levels of sociocultural integration. We regard chronological classification itself not as an ultimate goal of research, but as one of the necessary dimensions for the formulation and solution of archaeological problems. Like all classifications, chronological ones, employing either of these two basic strategies, have a considerable arbitrary component. Because we view classification of any sort as a means of solving a problem, the nature of the problem determines the applicability of any single classification or classification strategy.

Classification of a sequence by chronological periods requires the delimitation of defined, sequential blocks of time, regardless of cultural content in the area as a whole or in any of its subareas. The arbitrary component in this strategy is a function of the events chosen to initiate and terminate the periods. Period classification is especially useful in discussing problems of relative precocity and retardation of cultural development, in that it provides a standard independent of development itself, against which development can be measured and areas compared with each other. Classification by stages, on the other hand, is based on similarity or difference of cultural content without regard to absolute time. In this strategy arbitrariness results from the selection and weighting of the criteria of cultural content used to define each stage. Stage classification is most useful in comparing cultures at similar levels of development and in investigating the potential regularities that may inhere at various levels of complexity.

While in principle the two strategies are very different, confusion often arises in practice because they are carelessly or indiscriminately mixed. In Mesoamerica, the same terms—the familiar Preclassic (Formative), Classic, "Postclassic"—have been applied to both chronological periods and developmental stages. Information is conveyed with various qualifiers, such as "Central Mexico reaches a stage that is typologically Classic before the Maya area does," or "The Classic period of Central Mexico is typologically closer to the Postclassic of that area than it is to the Maya Classic." Even at this seminar terms such as Middle Formative and Early Classic were used in different ways by different participants at different times referring to different areas. We thus considered it advisable to retain the traditional terminology for developmental stages, but to introduce different terms entirely for a period classification. If the terminology we present may be new for Mesoamerica, it represents merely an adaptation to our data of the schema presented by Rowe (1960) for the Central Andes, and in general use by Andeanists for some ten years. The considerations that apparently impelled Rowe to formulate his terminology have led us to adapt it for Mesoamerican data. Although it is not our purpose to examine the history and varying fates of either or both classificatory strategies in world, or American, or Mesoamerican archaeology, we do recognize that this is not the first period classification attempted for the area. Our formulation, however, differs from those previously employed in Mesoamerica, as well as differing methodologically from that of Rowe.

Michael Coe (1962) employs a period classification built forward and backward from one extremely well-demarcated block of time—the Maya Initial Series, ca A.D. 300–900 (GMT correlation). He takes this as the

Classic period, and quite legitimately generalizes this block all over Meso-america, even though Long Count dates are of very limited geographic distribution. Methodologically, this parallels Rowe's reliance on the C-14 dated sequence from the Ica Valley, and his extension of this chronology to all of Peru. Sanders and Price (1968) follow Coe's periodization, with several modifications, and, like Coe, use the traditional stage terms redefined to designate periods. Porter (1972) does much the same thing—realizing the confusion, but retaining the terms largely because nearly all the rest of the Mesoamerican literature has done so. Our approach has been somewhat different.

Viewed as a whole, Mesoamerican prehistory, like that of the Central Andes, shows an alternation of phases of essentially local development of local traditions, crosscut periodically by area-wide horizon styles. We have taken this pulsation itself as the basis of our periodization, rather than specifically generalizing the sequence of any one subarea. Figure 1 presents a scheme involving seven major periods: Lithic, Initial Ceramic, Early Horizon, First Intermediate, Middle Horizon, Second Intermediate, and Late Horizon. For the subdivisions, particularly of the First and Second Intermediate periods, we have (following Rowe's precedent) relied heavily, if not exclusively, on a single local sequence, that of the Basin of Mexico.

The subdivisions of our periods, as indicated on the chart, follow two forms—one highly detailed for the Basin of Mexico master sequence, and a second, less detailed, for the rest of Mesoamerica. The detailed form follows Tolstoy (n.d.), and permits—as does Rowe's Peruvian sequence —numbered subphases, for which chronological control is excellent. Adoption of this form, and its restriction essentially to the Basin of Mexico, grew out of several conversations with Tolstoy in New York, well after the original formulation of this paper. The more generalized subdivision of major periods merely into Lower, Middle, and Upper subphases, as developed at the seminar, has been retained for the rest of Mesoamerica beyond the basin. One hopes that refinements to a degree comparable to that of the basin will be possible in the near future for other areas as well. In a pragmatic sense, moreover, the more general statement may be preferable to the more specific. Much of the Andean literature of recent years has apparently involved tinkering with chronology, in arcane debates on whether a phase begins twenty-five years earlier, or later. Al-

FIGURE 1. Mesoamerican period classification.

PERIODS		TOLSTOY CHRONOLOGY	BASIN OF MEXICO	OAXACA	PUEBLA-TEHUACÁN	MORELOS	GUERRERO
LATE HORIZON A.D. 1325–1521			Aztec III–IV	Monte Albán V			
SECOND INTERMEDIATE A.D. 750–1325	Upper A.D. 1200–1325		Aztec II Atlatongo				
	Middle A.D. 950–1200		Aztec I Mazapan		Cholulteca II		
	Lower A.D. 750–950	SI-1	Coyotlatelco Xometla Oxtoticpac	Monte Albán IV	Cholulteca I	↑	
MIDDLE HORIZON A.D. 200–750		MH-5 MH-4 MH-3 MH-2 MH-1	Metepec Late Xolalpan Early Xolalpan Late Tlamimilolpa Early Tlamimilolpa	Monte Albán IIIb Monte Albán IIIa	Cholula IV Cholula IIIa Cholula III	Xochicalco	
FIRST INTERMEDIATE 800 B.C.–A.D. 200	Upper A.D. 1–200	FI-11 FI-10	Miccaotli Tzacualli	Monte Albán II	Palo Blanco		
	Middle 300–1 B.C.	FI-9 FI-8	Patlachique-Tezoyuca Ticomán IV Cuicuilco				
	Lower 800–300 B.C.	FI-7 FI-6 FI-5 FI-4 FI-3 FI-2	Ticomán III Cuanalan Ticomán II Ticomán I Cuautepec Chimalhuacan Totolica–La Pastora Zacatenco Arbolillo Altica	Monte Albán I Guadalupe	Santa María Totomihuacan		
EARLY HORIZON 1300–800 B.C.		EH 1–4		San José Mogote		Chalcatzingo	Cave Paintings
					Las Bocas		
INITIAL CERAMIC 2500–1300 B.C.		IP	Tlatilco Tlalpan Zohapilco		Ajalpan Purrón		Puerto Marques
LITHIC 30,000–2500 B.C.	Upper 8000–2500 B.C.			Cueva Blanca	Abejas Coxcatlán El Riego		
	Middle 10,000–8000 B.C.		Tepexpan-Ixtapan	Guilá Naquitz ↓	Ajuerado ↓		
	Lower 30,000–10,000 B.C.		Tlapacoya		Valsequillo		

GULF COAST HUASTECA TAMAULIPAS	VERACRUZ-TABASCO	CHIAPAS	HIGHLAND GUATEMALA	GUATEMALA: PACIFIC COAST	LOWLAND MAYA		PERIODS	
Panuco	Cempoala	Ursina	Chinautla				LATE HORIZON A.D. 1325–1521	
		Tuxtla	Tohil		Mayapan		Upper A.D. 1200 –1325	SECOND INTERMEDIATE A.D. 750–1325
		Suchiapa			Toltec Chichen	Eznab	Middle A.D. 950 –1200	
La Salta	— Tajín III — Tajín II	Ruiz Chiapa X— Maravillas	Amatle III Amatle II		Tepeu III Tepeu II	Imix, Puuc	Lower A.D. 750 –950	
Zaquil	Tres Zapotes IV	Chiapa IX— Laguna	Amatle I (Esperanza)	Cotzumalhuapa	Tepeu I Tzakol III Tzakol II	Imix Ik Manik	MIDDLE HORIZON A.D. 200–750	
Pithaya-Eslabones	Tres Zapotes III Cerro de las Mesas III	Chiapa VIII— Jiquipilas	Aurora			Kuluk		
		Chiapa VII— Istmo	Miraflores Arenal		Tzakol I Chicanel	Cimi	Upper A.D. 1 –200	FIRST INTERMEDIATE 800 B.C.—A.D. 200
El Prisco		Chiapa VI— Horcones	Verbena			Cauac	Middle 300 –1 B.C.	
Chila	Tres Zapotes II Cerro de las Mesas II	Chiapa V— Guanacaste		Crucero	Mamom	Chuen	Lower 800 –300 B.C.	
		Chiapa IV— Francesca	Providencia	Conchas II Conchas I		Tzec		
		Chiapa III— Escalera						
Aguilar		Chiapa II— Dili	Las Charcas	Jocotal	Xe	Eb		
Ponce	Tres Zapotes I Cerro de las Mesas I						EARLY HORIZON 1300–800 B.C.	
	La Venta San Lorenzo			Cuadros Ocos				
Pavón Almagre		Chiapa I— Cotorra					INITIAL CERAMIC 2500–1300 B.C.	
							Upper 8000– 2500 B.C.	
Lerma							Middle 10,000– 8000 B.C.	LITHIC 30,000– 2500 B.C.
Diablo							Lower 30,000– 10,000 B.C.	

though such discussion is necessary and useful for certain problems, it can become somewhat arid, and can actually serve to close off discussion of other, more substantive, questions.

The suggested Lithic period was named by José Luis Lorenzo on the basis that the diagnostic lack of ceramics is the aspect contrasting most sharply with the rest of the sequence. It includes both a Paleo-Indian phase and a later phase comparable to the Archaic as that term is used by Coe and by Sanders and Price. The term "lithic," besides its greater inclusiveness, has the advantage of bearing a comparatively low burden of previous usage (unlike, specifically, "archaic"). This is the longest of the periods, and for most areas of Mesoamerica, data are scanty. Given this fact, some may question its subdivision.

The Upper Lithic period is most easily justified. If a subsistence base of hunting and gathering characterizes the Lithic period, it is in the Upper phase that this begins to change, with the experimentation with domesticates that makes this period transitional between the hunter-gatherer pattern preceding it and the economy based on agriculture that follows it in the Initial Ceramic. Subdivision of the Lower and Middle Lithic periods is perhaps more tenuous, and final disposition of this problem may well wait upon settlement of the pre-projectile-point controversy. For the present we retain the distinction. For the subsequent Initial Ceramic period the chart again shows few sites. Rowe's Initial period (to which our Initial Ceramic period corresponds) is the only one in his schema which "floats," that is, which is variable in date of onset from one area to another depending on the actual appearance of ceramics. This might ultimately be considered for Mesoamerica as well; however, the period is much better known from Peru, and at this point it makes little sense to float it for one or two sites. The appearance of ceramics is a convenient diagnostic, and is used by us as such; we are far more concerned with evidence of basic economic changes, notably in agriculture.

Our Early Horizon corresponds to the spread of influences generally known as Olmec, which appear in Mesoamerica from Guerrero through Central Mexico, Puebla, Oaxaca, Guatemala, and Salvador; it is approximately equivalent to the Middle Formative of Sanders and Price. Recent work by Coe at San Lorenzo, by Grove in Morelos and Guerrero, by Tolstoy in the Basin of Mexico, and by Flannery in Oaxaca has suggested that the principal spread of these stylistic features was actually earlier than much of the literature implies. The widely quoted dates of 800–400 B.C. from La Venta are certainly too late. Some Olmec-looking materials may indeed date from 400 B.C., and the Cycle 7 dates on some Olmecoid pieces are much later still if this calendar does have the same beginning date as the Maya Initial Series. These, however, are best regarded as epigonal, well postdating the pan-Mesoamerican influence of Olmec. In at least some areas of Mesoamerica, monumental civic architecture appears, along with evidence of nonegalitarian societies. The Early Horizon further marks the beginnings of consistent, large-scale interregional trade on an apparently regular basis involving a considerable volume and variety of goods.

The First Intermediate is marked by the disappearance of Olmec as a horizon style, and by rapid cultural development in many areas. Some regions are still acquiring an agricultural population. In others, however, particularly in the highlands of Oaxaca, Puebla, and the Basin of Mexico, the first small-scale experiments with agricultural intensification take place at the beginning of the period. By its end a fully urban center has emerged at Teotihuacán. Subdivisions of the First Intermediate are based largely, though not exclusively, on the Basin of Mexico sequence.

When used to denote a chronological period in Mesoamerica, the term "Classic" has traditionally designated the A.D. 300–900 span of the Maya Initial Series. We have broken up, in our periodization, what is more customarily presented as a unit. Rather than generalize the Maya sequence, no matter how well dated, we have instead based our Middle Horizon on the diffusion of the horizon style centered at Teotihuacán. As such our Middle Horizon includes the Middle Classic period of L. A. Parsons (1969), defined on the basis of Teotihuacán influence in the Maya area; we also include the Teotihuacán phase immediately preceding and following the horizon style proper. Although reliance on the Maya Long Count dates has proved convenient in the past, particularly so when the Lowland Maya were the recipients of cross-datable influences from elsewhere, we feel that it makes more sense to view the developments during this period from the perspective of the innovating center, rather than the recipients. We consider the spread of the horizon style itself as the most significant social, political, and economic development of the period, and reflect this view in our chronology.

It is with the Second Intermediate that specific substantive chronological problems become most acute; at present these seem to result from the current state of data, especially from the Basin of Mexico. The spatial, chronological, and perhaps functional relationships among the Coyotlatelco, Mazapan, Aztec I, and Aztec II complexes are a good deal more fluid than much of the published literature would suggest; the interpretative problems cannot be dealt with adequately until more information is available. Like the First Intermediate, this is a period characterized by the absence of a major horizon style; in the Basin of Mexico the sociopolitical organization may have been on a city-state level, but again this is unclear. What may seem most radical in this presentation is the demotion of the Tula-Toltec to an interregnum status, particularly in view of the existence of known horizon markers (notably Plumbate and Fine Orange wares). As can be seen from R. A. Diehl's work (Chapter 11), Tula, in comparison with either Teotihuacán or Tenochtitlan, does not seem an outstanding candidate to be the capital of an empire: both its civic center and its apparent total population seem unusually small. Similarly, the lack of clarity of the relationship of the supposedly Tula-affiliated Coyotlatelco and Mazapan complexes, vis-à-vis each other and vis-à-vis "Aztec I," is notable and suggestive—as is the fact that the wares generally recognized as horizon markers for this period originate outside Central Mexico altogether. The data that support most strongly the traditional intrepretation of a Toltec Empire are the massive site intrusions at Chichén Itzá, where much of the civic center shows the replacement of Puuc Maya with Tula-Toltec architecture. Various developments in the Maya area, both Highlands and Lowlands, have also been related to "Toltec" invasions or impact, but the referent of the term "Toltec" is surprisingly unclear. Considerable empirical work all over Mesoamerica is obviously required to clarify what is really happening during this period.

Tenochtitlan was founded in A.D. 1325, and this date is a convenient beginning for the Late Horizon even though the diagnostic Aztec III ceramics may occur earlier in other parts of the Basin of Mexico. The Aztec capital is in effect a single-period site (Aztec IV may be in part at least post-Conquest). Many of the components of this horizon style are technically non-Aztec, especially if ceramics alone are considered—the so-called Mixteca-Puebla style, and the Cholulteca polychromes, both of which begin earlier. At least one aspect of this style is architectural: the double-stairway, twin-temple pyramid, encountered at least as far south as Guatemala. The Late Horizon ends with the Conquest.

Chronological Framework

NOTE

1. This paper had its genesis rather by accident, in a discussion that began over lunch in terms of "Well, why not?" and the basic framework was sketched out by the end of the meal and presented for more intensive consideration. A preliminary version was circulated in June of 1972. During the winter of 1973 Paul Tolstoy informed me of a convergence—that he had been working on many of the same problems for other purposes, and had developed a similar, though not identical, scheme. A couple of meetings served to iron out major differences of terminology, on the assumption that uniformity in this area was essential. While this work has benefited considerably from his, the differing emphases of the two papers make a concurrent reading of the two quite enlightening. I do wish to thank Dr. Tolstoy for his assistance, and in one case, his tolerance.

I should further like to thank Eric Wolf, the editor of this volume, for his having drawn up the chronological chart that is the pivot of this paper.

The lag between the original development of the scheme presented here and its publication has led to the fact that it has already been used in print (Parsons 1974) prior to its appearance in this volume.

3

Chronological and Developmental Terminology: Why They Must Be Divorced

R E N É   M I L L O N

Department of Anthropology
University of Rochester

This chapter is a background statement on why and how a neutral chronological terminology for the Valley of Mexico came to be adopted by the conferees at the Santa Fe seminar on the Valley of Mexico.

Beginning with the American Anthropological Association meetings in Mexico City in 1959, I have been arguing verbally and in print against the use of a developmental terminology for chronological distinctions in Middle American archaeology (for example, Willey, Ekholm, and Millon 1964:477–78, R. Millon 1968c:214–15). At the Santa Fe conference I argued again in the same vein, insisting that chronological terminology should be of neutral value and not carry with it any developmental implications or overtones, intentionally or otherwise, as, for example, in that carried by such terms as "Formative," "Proto-Classic," and "Classic." The two kinds of classification are quite distinct conceptually and substantively.

Although there was eventual agreement on this point, there remained the twin problems of what alternative neutral terminology to adopt and whether there was any likelihood that any alternative terminology we adopted would be adopted by other Middle American archaeologists. There were at least two aspects to the latter problem. The first involved persuading Middle American archaeologists that there was, in fact, a problem with using existing developmental terminology for chronological purposes (R. Millon 1968c:214–15, 1973:50). The second aspect involved how to overcome the sheer inertia of the present classification and substitute an alternative classification that had a chance of being adopted by a significant number of Middle American archaeologists. At the Santa Fe seminar I argued that while John Rowe's terminology for Peru was a value-neutral classification (Rowe 1960, Rowe and Menzel 1967:iv–v), it probably had little chance of acceptance in Middle America, given the deeply rooted nature of the existing classification. Sanders argued that if we adopted the Rowe terminology for the Valley of Mexico in this book and continued to use it thereafter, there were enough of us sufficiently active in the field to establish its use in our future publications, thus generating a climate conducive to its gradual adoption by others. Accordingly, the Rowe terminology was adapted to the Valley of Mexico chronology at the seminar, and those at the seminar agreed to use it thereafter.

The period distinctions decided on were the Initial Period (or the Initial Ceramic Period), the Early Horizon, the First Intermediate Period, the Middle Horizon, the Second Intermediate Period, and the Late Horizon. These periods are based largely on ceramic chronology and ceramic distinctions. The period preceding the Initial Period was designated the Lithic or Pre-Ceramic Period, with internal distinctions based on lithic chronologies. The Rowe terminology was modified by naming the Intermediate Periods "First" and "Second" (the terminology still used in the chronology of Ancient Egypt), rather than "Early" and "Late"; in this way it is possible to refer to divisions within these periods as "Early," "Middle," and "Late," without becoming involved in such cumbersome terms as "Early Early Intermediate" or "Late Late Intermediate." A similar problem exists with respect to subdivisions within each of the horizons. This was left unresolved. A possible solution lies in the use of numerical or alphabetical subdivisions within each horizon.

Figure 2 shows the modified version of the Rowe chronological terminology applied to the Valley of Teotihuacán chronology. The modified terminology appears on the left in Figure 2, while the existing terminology

VALLEY OF TEOTIHUACAN CHRONOLOGY
Table of Concordances

Period	Date	Phase Names [1]		Phase Numbers [2]	Period
LATE HORIZON	A.D. 1500	Teacalco		Aztec IV	
	1400	Chimalpa		Aztec III	POST-
	1300				
	1200	Zocango		Aztec II	CLASSIC
SECOND INTERMEDIATE PERIOD	1100	Mazapan		Mazapa	
	1000				PERIOD
	900	Xometla		Coyotlatelco	———— 900 A.D.
	800	Oxtoticpac		Proto-Coyotlatelco	CLASSIC
	700	METEPEC		Teotihuacán IV	
MIDDLE HORIZON	600	XOLALPAN	Late	Teotihuacán IIIA	
	500		Early	Teotihuacán III	PERIOD
	400				
	300	TLAMIMILOLPA	Late	Teotihuacán IIA-III	———— 300 A.D.
			Early	Teotihuacán IIA	
	200	MICCAOTLI		Teotihuacán II	TERMINAL
	100	TZACUALLI	Late	Teotihuacán IA	PRE-CLASSIC
	A.D. B.C.		Early	Teotihuacán I	
	100	PATLACHIQUE	Chimalhuacán *		PERIOD
				Proto-Teotihuacán I	
FIRST INTERMEDIATE PERIOD	200	Terminal Cuanalan; Tezoyuca	Cuicuilco *		LATE
	300	Late Cuanalan	Ticoman III *		PRE-CLASSIC
	400	Middle Cuanalan	Ticoman II *		PERIOD
	500	Early Cuanalan	Ticoman I *		
	600	Chiconauhtla	Middle		MIDDLE PRE-CLASSIC
	700		Zacatenco *		PERIOD
	B.C. 800				

(Vertical label spanning A.D. 700 – B.C. 100: TEOTIHUACAN)

[1] Phase names used by personnel of Teotihuacán Mapping Project (Millon and others) and by personnel of Valley of Teotihuacán Project (Sanders and others).

[2] Phase numbers used by personnel of the Proyecto Teotihuacán, of the Instituto Nacional de Antropologia e Historia (see Acosta 1964: 58-59).

* Pre-classic phases elsewhere in the Valley of Mexico.

NOTE: The absolute chronology shown is that used by the Teotihuacán Mapping Project. Terminology for the Teotihuacán phases is based on the Armillas classification (1950) with modifications.

TEOTIHUACAN MAPPING PROJECT
UNIVERSITY OF ROCHESTER

J.A.Cerda.

RENÉ MILLON
9/64
REVISED 5/72

FIGURE 2. Valley of Teotihuacán chronology.

appears on the right. Since the Santa Fe conference Paul Tolstoy (n.d.) has adopted the modified Rowe terminology in his article on the archaeological chronology of western Mesoamerica before A.D. 900.

According to Tolstoy the most reasonable beginning date for the Early Horizon in the Valley of Mexico is about 1500 B.C., with the Initial Period beginning about 2000 B.C. or earlier. It is important to reemphasize that the chronological terminology adopted is based on ceramic chronologies. Thus, the Initial Period marks the beginning of the use of ceramics as time markers. It carries no developmental overtones. Rather, it simply represents a shift from the coarser-grained lithic chronologies of the Pre-Ceramic or Lithic Period to finer-grained ceramic chronologies.

"Horizons" represent periods when there are widespread ceramic and other cross ties in the Valley of Mexico and elsewhere in Middle America. The Early Horizon is primarily associated with the spread of Olmec and Olmec-related ceramics; the Middle Horizon, with the spread of Teotihuacán and Teotihuacán-related ceramics; and the Late Horizon, with the spread of late, fine black-on-orange ceramics, Aztec II–III, III, and IV wares (Franco 1949). The Initial Period and the First and Second Intermediate periods represent times when cross ties are much more limited than they are during horizons. The Middle Horizon starts at the beginning of or during the Early Tlamimilolpa phase at Teotihuacán, because this is when indisputable evidence of far-flung Teotihuacán cross ties begins (for example, at Altun Ha, British Honduras; see R. Millon 1973:55–56). The Middle Horizon ends during or at the close of the Metepec phase, up to or shortly before the fall of Teotihuacán, because of continuing evidence of widespread ceramic cross ties during that phase (R. Millon 1973:61, 62). If, in the future, we should find that there was a significant extension of Teotihuacán's influence in the form of cross ties much beyond the Valley of Mexico in the Miccaotli or Tzacualli phases, then the beginning of the Middle Horizon would be pushed back accordingly.

The end of the Late Horizon in the Valley of Teotihuacán, and presumably elsewhere as well, is complicated by the continuation of Aztec III and Aztec IV ceramics for a considerable period of time following the Spanish Conquest (Charlton 1972a, 1972b: 6–8, 16–19, 27–29, 30–36, 47–49, 57–61, 81–85, 118–23, 132–60, 206–7).

In Barbara Price's discussion of chronological and developmental classifications (Chapter 2), the new chronological classification is presented, but the accompanying discussion of developmental concepts and terminology carries with it many assumptions that I do not share and that I believe to be unsound, both conceptually and in terms of method. But the indispensable first step has been taken, that is, to divorce chronology from developmental or evolutionary terminology. When this is done, not only on a chronological chart but substantively in the discussion of it—something which is not done in this volume—a sorting-out process can take place that forces the archaeologist to make his developmental or evolutionary assumptions explicit. This facilitates the analysis of the problems involved in such assumptions, and, in time, may lead to a fundamental reexamination of them.

PART 2

The Valley as an Ecological System

4
The Model

MICHAEL H. LOGAN

Department of Anthropology
University of Tennessee

WILLIAM T. SANDERS

Department of Anthropology
The Pennsylvania State University

THE MODEL

Anthropologists have given considerable attention to the study of "differential evolution," or the variance in degree to which entire societies have evolved (Carneiro 1974). It is through the process of differential evolution that prehistoric and contemporary societies exhibit the vast differences in cultural level that anthropologists record and study so intensely. Unfortunately, however, most attempts to define and analyze the forces underlying differential evolution focus mainly on the effects on society of a single variable.

The model advanced in this study draws heavily on the works of several scholars concerned with differential cultural evolution, notably Boserup (1965), Steward (1955), and Wittfogel (1957). Because of its integrated approach and the use of a variety of selected concepts, this model is highly eclectic; and, although certain weaknesses are inherent

31

in such an approach, we trust that its suitability as a guide for explaining differential evolution will become apparent. The model will show the necessary components of and processual interactions in differential cultural development. That is, we will first identify those factors that are of critical importance in determining the degree to which societies evolve, and then illustrate how these factors interact to bring about culture change.

The fundamental assumption of our model is that population pressure is the primary cause of increasingly complex social and political patterns. However, rising demographic stress can result in such increased complexity only if the society's environment and technology are capable of supporting the increase in population. Research into the relationship between demographic variables and the structure or level of sociocultural systems has yielded convincing archaeological and ethnographic evidence that large, densely settled populations are socially and politically more complex than are small, less dense groups (Steward 1955, Childe 1951, Carneiro 1967, Dumond 1965, Naroll 1956). Therefore, we can conclude that when a society increases in size over time and this expansion is ongoing, locally contained, and adequately supported, then that society must develop more complex features of subsistence, economic exchange, and political integration.

Most anthropologists would agree that, as a society increases in size, it must change its structure in order to function as a social system. The unilineal stages of band, tribe, chiefdom, and state proposed by Elman Service (1971) are generalized kinds of social systems and in essence can also be considered as stages in societal size. In band and tribal societies the interaction between individuals and households is basically egalitarian, both in terms of exercise of authority and in control of basic resources. With chiefdoms or states, interpersonal relationships become unbalanced, or, as Service puts it, there is a negative reciprocity. In the case of chiefdoms this imbalance is less marked, and the ideological basis of the system is phrased in terms of kinship, a persistence of tribal principles of organization in the social structure. With highly evolved states, however, kin-based organization disappears, atrophies, or—minimally—takes on a different set of functions. Access to basic resources (such as the right to tax or to own land) is more direct, and social disequilibrium is more evident. Most pronounced is the disequilibrium in access to political power.

The Model

Each of these levels permits the integration of larger numbers of people.

The major question is why social systems evolve at all. Why should there be an evolution from tribe to chiefdom to state? Most particularly, why should individual households agree to abide by a social contract with other households in which their surplus time is put to work or appropriated by the other households? Some theorists have sought answers in terms of rising population density. Included in such arguments is the idea that social integration is closely related to the technology of communication and transportation. This line of reasoning postulates that for each technological level of communication or transportation there is a practical limit to effective social integration in terms of the size of the territory integrated; thus, the only way more people can be incorporated into a social system is by increasing the number of people per square mile. This theory, however, does not explain why, as population per unit of space increases, we do not simply have social fission,[1] that is, more societies of the same size. Why do larger social systems develop?

In any discussion of process we must keep in mind that all interacting variables are, to differing degrees, reciprocal and mutually interdependent. Such interactions should not be confused or equated with linear causality. The basic assumptions underlying our model are: (1) population increase is to be treated as given; (2) environmental and technological factors are sufficient to support and sustain the given population increase; and (3) increasingly complex patterns of social integration and political cohesion will develop as a result of the increase in population. Using these assumptions, we can summarize the model in the following way.

I. Population growth depends on certain favorable combinations of three factors:
   A. Fertility
   B. Mortality
   C. Migration
II. If the interaction of factors in I leads to population increase and subsistence stress, the group may respond by:
   A. Physical and social fission
   B. Increase in food production per unit of space by intensifying use of available resources or by exploiting newly incorporated or newly developed resources within the same physical space

III. II-A will be eliminated as a response and II-B will occur if:
  A. Environment is circumscribed and desirable resettlement locales are either occupied or nonexistent
  B. Environmental factors permit II-B
IV. If II-B does occur, this will then stimulate:
  A. Sedentary residence
  B. Differential access to both agricultural and nonagricultural resources, first within settlements and then between settlements
  C. Intrasocietal and intersocietal competition
 V. If IV-A, IV-B, and IV-C occur, then the following processes will result:
  A. Occupational specialization in nonagricultural activities
  B. Further intensification of agriculture, including specialization in agriculture in the first stages of the process
  C. Increase in economic exchange networks and the development or elaboration of managerial institutions
  D. Rank differentiation and, ultimately, class stratification
  E. Political linearization, or the emergence of more numerous, increasingly complex political controls
VI. The rate of development of II-B, IV, and V is affected by:
  A. Population size and rate of growth
  B. Size of the circumscribed area
  C. Resource variability within the circumscribed region
  D. Technological base of production and military spheres of culture
  E. Comparable events and processes occurring in nearby geographical areas
VII. The stability of, or decline in, cultural complexity will occur when:
  A. Factors in I result in a stable or diminishing population
  B. II-A is operative
  C. III-B does not permit II-B
  D. Circumscribed areas are excessively small or isolated

POPULATION GROWTH AND AGRICULTURE

The three components of population change are fertility, mortality, and migration (Wrigley 1969). All changes in population size and structure are dependent on the interactions among birth, death, and the movement of people. When this interaction leads to a continuing increase in numbers, pressures on existing resources will develop.

Responses to population pressure are numerous. The society may be forced to accept the degradation of its living standards, or controls, both biological and cultural, may be enacted to retard population growth. Neither of these responses appears to be very significant, however, since it seems that societies will not voluntarily accept a lower standard of living or practice effective fertility control. The only potentially effective methods of population control found in preindustrial societies, regularized abortion and infanticide, are seldom employed—probably because population pressure results in competition, and it is obviously disadvantageous in a competitive situation to limit manpower. Furthermore, as we shall discuss later, rising population often results in intensification of resource utilization. This requires additional labor; hence the desire of peasants in densely settled areas to have numerous children.

The two most common positive responses to population pressure are either fission or an increase in food production per unit of space. Under growing demographic stress, and when useful land is available, "fission" (the "budding" of one group from a parental stock) is perhaps the most frequent solution undertaken by preliterate peoples. This response has the distinct advantage of not requiring a change in the emergent group's social or political organization. However, as Carneiro (1970) has suggested, the factor of environmental circumscription can effectively eliminate fission as a probable response. "Circumscription" (the condition in which arable land is strongly delimited and comparatively scarce) may result from geographic factors, technological limitations, or competition among political entities. Clearly, such geographic features as vast bodies of water, mountain ranges, and deserts have long influenced the frequency and pattern of human movement. Similarly, technological limitations of transport have imposed restrictions on the movement and range of many populations. The degree of circumscription may be further increased through technological limitations on subsistence and exploitive capacities particular to any group. Here, ecological factors exercise primary constraints with regard to circumscription. Finally, competing political centers, whether tribes, chiefdoms, or states, can effectively function to obstruct migration or, instead, to direct its course. If circumscription of a population is present to a degree that cancels out fission as a primary response to rising population pressures, and if mortality and fertility remain at a level that does not reduce those pressures, then the given increase in population must be matched by an increase in food supply (Dumond 1965:311). Theoretically, the required increase in food production may be met in a number of ways: intensification of land use, technological improvements, crop specialization, hybridization and introduction of new foods, and importation of food.

Intensification of Land Use

Allan (1965) and Boserup (1965), among others, have clearly demonstrated that the shift from extensive to more intensive cultivation is a nearly universal occurrence in societies experiencing population pressure, particularly when additional agricultural land is unavailable. The term "intensification" has been used in two different ways: it can refer to the increasing frequency of crop production on a particular piece of land, or to the increasing input of labor per unit of crop land. Boserup argues that the two kinds of intensification are generally correlated, that is, intensification of land use is often accompanied by a requisite increase of labor input.

Most writers have considered extensive and intensive agriculture as two polar types or systems. They have seen extensive agriculture as more primitive, less productive, and hence likely to be replaced by intensive agriculture as the population's knowledge evolves. Since the intensification process is, at times, accompanied by technological innovations—for example, the shift from hand tools to animal-powered tools, the increased use of fertilizers, and the development of special techniques of erosion or humidity control—such innovations are cited as further evidence of the "primitive" versus the "advanced" or "civilized" status of the two systems.

Boserup argues that extensive agriculture, because of the comparative low labor input and the high yields obtained in well-fallowed fields, is a more productive system, in terms of input-output ratios, than intensive agriculture. In this sense "productivity" refers to the ratio between labor input (calculated in calorie energy, hours, or days of work) and the production or yield of crops. Thus when arable land is abundant and choice is not restricted by social or political factors, farmers elect to practice extensive cultivation, even though they are aware of intensive techniques or methods of cultivation. Intensification occurs as land availability is reduced and hence is the result of population pressure or growth.

In many cases, particularly in humid climates, intensification of land use may not be accompanied by any major innovation in tools or techniques. The less favorable input-output ratio in such cases is the product not only of increased labor input but also of a reduction in yield per unit of space (as soil fertility is reduced). This may be more than compensated for, however, by the larger percentage of land brought into production, and thus can act to relieve population pressure.

Intensification combined with special technical innovations (such as fertilization, irrigation, and terracing) may lead to an increase in yield per unit of cropped space as well and permit even denser populations. However, Boserup (1965) presents evidence to show that this is frequently accompanied by such a substantial increase in labor input that even in these cases the per capita return may be lowered. On the other hand, some technical innovations, such as the use of plows or draft animals, may increase the per capita return. The situation is complex, and the obvious conclusion is that one must carefully define such terms as "extensive," "intensive," and "productivity." Productivity, for example, may refer to input-output ratios, yield per unit of cropped space, or total yield of the agricultural land available to a social group; in each case it has different implications.

A major problem in the application of Boserup's theory to the pre-Hispanic occupation of the Basin of Mexico lies in the two basic assumptions inherent in the theory: the law of least effort, and the postulate that intensification always involves a significant decline of input-output ratio. With respect to the first assumption, we agree that in broad terms farmers do attempt to maximize returns in terms of work input. Yet the principle of least effort probably works best when crop security is high and when maintaining soil fertility is difficult. Generally this is the case in humid environments. In arid regions, where soil fertility constitutes a less serious problem and where precarious rainfall threatens crop security, the stimulus to introduce intensification practices to regulate production is very strong and may well occur early in the colonization sequence. It is also possible that this strategy, which geographers call the mini-max strategy, may in some cases be simply a variation on a maximization strategy, in the sense that regulating yields over a long period of time probably results in an overall higher average productivity.

For example, let us imagine two systems of cultivation, an extensive one in which the land is cultivated one year and rested five and an intensive one in which it is cultivated continually. Although the difference in yields between the two could be considerably less than that obtained in humid climates, we will assume that the maximum productivity is substantially higher with the extensive system of farming. Table 1 shows what the relationship between labor input and yield might be over a ten-year period.

TABLE 1

CROP YIELD BY TYPE OF CULTIVATION
OVER A TEN-YEAR PERIOD: A HYPOTHETICAL CASE

	Crop Yield (in kilos of grain per hectare)	
Year	Extensive Cultivation	Intensive Cultivation
1950	1,500	1,200
1951	1,500	1,200
1952	0	900
1953	0	800
1954	1,700	1,300
1955	300	1,000
1956	0	900
1957	0	800
1958	1,200	1,000
1959	200	500
Average	640	960

With respect to *average* yields per *hectare* of *land*, the intensive cultivation has a clear advantage over the extensive cultivation in productivity. If we assume that the *labor input* for intensive cultivation is 70 man-days per hectare and only 50 man-days for extensive cultivation, then we can make the following calculations of *per capita* productivity. Assuming that no labor was expended in cultivation (because the farmers foresaw a poor season) during years where yields were not obtained in the extensive system, that system of cultivation would yield an input-output ratio of 21.3 kilos of grain per man-day of labor. If we assume that the farmer went through the entire cycle of land preparation not knowing

38

how the year would turn out, then this reduces the kilos of grain per man-day of labor to 12.8. In arid regions, in fact, extensive cultivators very often do not plant until the rainy season is well established; in those years when rains are inadequate, the land is often left fallow. Some labor, however, is expended in working the soil to facilitate moisture storage for the next year.

The intensive system of cultivation will produce approximately 14 kilos per man-day. If we assume that at least some labor went into the preparation of those fields with extensive cultivation during the zero years, the intensive system may be more productive even at this ratio, or at least comparable. If we assume an average annual per capita consumption of 160 kilos of grain, an added disadvantage of the extensive system would be that the average yield of a hectare of land would not meet family needs, so that more land would have to be brought into production. This would increase the total labor input to approximately the level for intensive cultivation, which could be a particularly critical factor in decision making among farmers using hand tools. Finally, the paired years of no crop return would produce an intolerable stress on the family budget, particularly if we note the probability that grains could not be stored for more than two years at a time.

This problem of no crop return was probably even more serious under aboriginal conditions. In part, the high yields per time period of work that contemporary swidden farmers in humid areas achieve is due to the efficiency of steel axes and machetes. Although good field studies of the efficiency of stone tools for clearing forests are not abundant, those we do have suggest a considerably greater work requirement. Hester (1952), for example, conducted an experimental study of Yucatecan Mayan farmers who lived in a very scrubby tropical forest. His work demonstrated that it takes approximately twice as long to clear this type of forest using limestone chips as it does using modern metal machetes. In a study of Neolithic farmers in the highland New Guinea rain forest, Townsend (1969) estimated that the clearing of forest with stone tools required 5.6 times more labor than if metal tools were used. (Obviously, some tasks, such as burning, harvesting, and hauling crops, would not require extra labor input with Neolithic tools.) In conclusion, then, it can be stated that Neolithic slash and burn agriculture requires at least two to three times as much labor input per unit of land cultivated as cultivation by steel tools.

What about the intermediate levels of intensification suggested by

Boserup (1965), in which the vegetation succession is grass rather than scrub forest? The data presented in Table 2 suggest that even with metal hoes, grasses became an extremely difficult problem for hand cultivators. Our own studies of cultivation in the Basin of Mexico, in fact, point in the same direction. In the long run it requires much less labor to till land that is kept in constant cultivation than to allow the land to go fallow long enough for grass to grow and then till it, even with metal tools. With stone or wooden tools the cultivation costs of grass fallow would be considerably greater. One way of solving the problem—a solution used in some parts of Africa (Allan 1965)—is to cultivate a plot of land continuously for eight to ten years and then to let it rest for a period of perhaps eight to twenty years. The result is the equivalent of a short cycle in which between 33 and 50 percent of the land is in cultivation in any one year. With the long period of rest the trees can return, ultimately shading out the grasses before the land is to be brought back into cultivation. Whether forest regeneration is fast enough under more temperate conditions is not certain. Of course, this system will not work unless the soils are unusually fertile and can sustain a continuous cropping of eight or ten years without rest.

Clearly what we need in this context is a series of well-controlled studies of various fallowing regimes in terms of different crops, tool kits, soils, and climatic conditions. When we have this type of data, we can then apply Boserup's basic principle, the law of least effort, which would, we believe, prove to be a powerful predictive tool for understanding decisions made by farmers in their subsistence strategies, particularly when combined with a consideration of crop security.

Sanders has completed a comparative study in the Basin of Mexico of labor costs to cultivate soils of different types using plows, metal hoes, and Aztec tools. Since he was concerned primarily with the differential costs of working the soils in preparation for planting, the experiment was limited to preplanting preparation of the land. Maize cultivation today (accomplished with plows) involves the following sequence of annual activities:

barbecho (preplanting plowing of the
    soil after the fall harvest)   November–December
rastrillo (leveling the field with   immediately after the
    moldboard)   barbecho

cruzada (plowing the field in the opposite direction)	February
rastrillo (leveling the field with moldboard)	immediately after the *cruzada*
zurcada (plowing the field for planting)	April–May
siembra (planting)	April–May
primer labor (first weeding with the plow)	when crop is 10 cm high
segundar (second weeding with the plow)	when crop is 30 cm high
aterrada (hilling, done with shovels)	late summer
harvest	November

Additional labor (for example, preplanting, irrigation, work on canals and dams that provide water for the irrigation system, and terrace maintenance) may be involved in some fields. For the hand tools, we have assumed a comparable regime of activities, and we have extrapolated with data from Sanders's calculations on the preplanting working of the soil. The data are summarized in Table 2, along with comparative data from a variety of sources on different types of cultivation.

Technological Improvements

Advances in technology might involve a shift from hand tools of wood, shell, or stone to hand tools of metal and, later, to the use of draft animals. Such changes do not necessarily result in an increase in yields, but by increasing the amount of land cultivated, they may still increase the total productivity of a given area. One example would be cultivation of mid-latitude grasslands, which requires plows and draft animals for management. Another example would be the use of more efficient tools to dig wells, enabling a population to tap deeply buried water resources for irrigation. These changes might also permit a rise in per capita productivity, thereby increasing the capacity of the farmers to support non–food producers—a development which, of course, would not in itself support a larger population in the local area. Rather, it would simply change the redistribution network (unless these same non–food producers were partly supported by imported agricultural surpluses).

Examples of technical innovations that might result in greater productivity per cropped space, and possibly per capita as well, are irrigation, fertilization, or terracing. Some technological innovations involve an investment in what might be called "capital labor"—that is, the construction and maintenance of structures supplemental to the annual cost of cultivation, such as dikes, drainage ditches, irrigation canals, dams, and terracing. The adoption of such devices might often be delayed because they do require extra work input, even where per capita returns run high. Some innovations, such as large-scale drainage networks or canal systems, also might not be feasible unless the population base is large enough to carry out the required construction.

TABLE 2
INPUT-OUTPUT RATIOS FOR VARIOUS TYPES OF CULTIVATION

1. Highland Guatemala—Contemporary (humid highland environment; staple crop, maize; soils with high clay content)

Type of Land	Man-days per Hectare	Yield per Hectare (in kilo-calories)	Yield per Man-day (in kilo-calories)	Output-Input Ratio*
Huatal[a]	97	4,750,000	49,000	25:1
Pajonal (hand-tilled)[b]	172	3,750,000	21,800	11:1
Llano (hand-tilled)[c]	145	2,700,000	18,600	9:1
Llano (plowed)[d]	104	2,700,000	26,000	13:1
Rastrojo (hand-tilled)[e]	129	6,500,000	50,400	25:1
Rastrojo (plowed)[f]	90	6,500,000	72,200	36:1
Llano (hand-tilled and fertilized)[g]	168	9,000,000	53,600	27:1
Montana[h]	222	6,500,000	29,300	15:1

[a]Swidden, bush fallowing, metal tools.
[b]Grassland, long fallow, metal hoes.
[c]Grassland, short fallow, metal hoes.
[d]Grassland, short fallow, some use of hoes.
[e]Houselot, metal hoes, land fertilized from household refuse.
[f]Houselot, plows, some operations involve hoes.
[g]Grassland, short fallow, metal hoes and fertilization.
[h]Swidden, virgin forest, metal tools.

2. Highland New Guinea—Contemporary Kapauku (humid highland environment; staple crop, sweet potato; soils with high clay content)

Type of Land	Man-days per Hectare	Yield per Hectare (in kilo-calories)	Yield per Man-days (in kilo-calories)	Output-Input Ratio
Hillside bush swidden[a]	365	11,000,000	30,100	15:1
Semi-intensive—riverine terrace[b]	475	16,250,000	34,200	17:1
Intensive—riverine terrace[b]	632	18,500,000	29,300	15:1

[a]Bush fallowing, some metal tools.
[b]Primarily Neolithic tools.

3. Highland New Guinea–Tsembaga (based on kilo-calorie calculations of input rather than man-days): 16:1

4. Swidden Farmers in Lowland Mesoamerica

Type of Land	Man-days per Hectare	Yield per Hectare (in kilo-calories)	Yield per Man-days (in kilo-calories)	Output-Input Ratio
Yucatec Maya Steel tools[a]	48	3,750,000	78,100	39:1
Yucatec Maya Stone tools[a]	96	3,750,000	39,000	20:1
Petén Maya Steel tools[b]	60	4,320,000	72,000	36:1
Petén Maya Stone tools[b]	180	4,320,000	24,000	12:1
Izabal Maya Steel tools[c]	74	2,900,000	39,500	20:1
Izabal Maya Steel tools[d]	60	3,600,000	60,000	30:1
Izabal Maya Steel tools[e]	54	2,900,000	54,000	27:1
Izabal Maya Stone tools[c]	200	2,900,000	14,500	7:1
Izabal Maya Stone tools[e]	100	2,900,000	29,000	15:1
Tajin Totonac Steel tools[f]	90	5,400,000	60,000	30:1

[a]Swidden cycle—2–3 years cultivation, 12–15 years rest; scrub jungle.
[b]Swidden cycle—2–3 years cultivation, 6–8 years rest; rain forest.
[c]Swidden cycle—2–3 years cultivation, 8 years rest; rain forest.
[d]Swidden cycle—2–3 years cultivation, 4–7 years rest; secondary bush.
[e]Swidden cycle—2–3 years cultivation, 2–3 years rest; low bush.
[f]Swidden cycle—2–3 years cultivation, 12–15 years rest; rain forest.

TABLE 2 (CONT.)

5. Basin of Mexico (All calculations here do not involve substantial use of fertilizer. If a 2-to-3-year schedule of fertilization is used, all crop yields could be doubled or tripled, raising the output-input ratio considerably. Labor input includes canal irrigation and cajete planting.)

Type of Land	Man-days per Hectare	Yield per Hectare (in kilo-calories)	Yield per Man-days (in kilo-calories)	Output-Input Ratio
Metal hoes				
Clay loam	118	5,040,000	42,700	21:1
Clay loam and sod	187	5,040,000	27,000	13:1
Sandy loam to loam	60–90	3,600,000	40,000–60,000	20:1–30:1
Neolithic hoes and digging tools				
Clay loam	157	5,040,000	32,000	16:1
Clay loam and sod	239	5,040,000	21,000	11:1
Sandy loam to loam	75–113	3,600,000	32,000–48,000	16:1–24:1
Plows				
Clay loam	50	5,040,000	100,800	50:1
Sandy loam to loam	50	3,600,000	72,000	36:1

*The ratios are computed by dividing the kilo-calorie yield per man-day by 2,000 kilo-calories—the average per capita consumption of small tropical people per day. In fact, a proportion of the crop yields are cycled through domestic animals, with consequent efficiency losses. The actual consumption figure may be as high as 2,400 to 3,000 kilo-calories, depending on whether cereal or root crops are staples. In some New Guinea groups, approximately 36 percent of the root crop harvest is channeled through pigs (see Rappaport 1971). The efficiency ratio of pig raising is estimated between 2:1 and 1:1.

SOURCES: Highland Guatemala—Stadelman (1940)
Kapauku—Pospisil (1963).
Tsembaga—Rappaport (1971).
Lowland Mesoamerica—(Yucatec Maya) Steggerda (1941); (Petén Maya) Lundell (1937), U.M. Cowgill (1961, 1962); (Izabal Maya) Carter (1969); (Tajin Totonac) Kelly and Palerm (1952).
Basin of Mexico—unpublished data.

Crop Specialization

With extensive cultivation a numerically diverse subsistence inventory is the norm. Under stress of population pressure, however, a specialized or numerically reduced subsistence inventory of a few staples is the norm (Geertz 1963b). In ecosystem terminology there is a "simplification" of the system. Specialization in those food crops that give the highest yields under given technological and ecological conditions is apparently highly advantageous when population pressures exist. As Barrau (1961) has demonstrated, it is no accident that out of a basic inventory of five oceanic plant staples, the various island populations of Polynesia and Micronesia will rely on only one, two, or perhaps three of these basic foods as staples. The selectivity is defined partly by ecological factors. This process of reduction of crop variety and increasing focus on intensive cropping of a single plant is not completely understood, but apparently there is some relationship between increased labor input per unit of spaced crop and a reduction of crop variety. The process occurs even among tribal societies, as in New Guinea, and thus is apparently unrelated to market patterns. Actually, it may be a very simple matter of efficiency of labor—when the labor input reaches a certain point, it becomes more efficient to prepare a field for a single cultigen than for many.

If the population density reaches critically high levels, there is a tendency not only to produce single crops in a particular field, but to increase agricultural specialization as well. In addition to staple crops, all agricultural systems involve a variety of secondary crops. In extensive cultivation such crops are frequently intercropped with staples in a single field. Under a system of intensification, families or even entire villages may specialize in the production of a single staple or of a few secondary crops for market. This, of course, intensifies the process of economic symbiosis between social units. Decisions as to where to produce which crops are based primarily on a combination of natural and market conditions, although other cultural variables may at times override these considerations.

Hybridization and Introduction of New Foods

Improvement through hybridization and selection of food crops is and has been important in increasing yields. However, most hybrids leading to the domesticated food crops used by preliterate peoples are so old that botanists frequently debate what the original wild progenitors of a given cultigen were (Baker 1965). Therefore, it seems that hybridization was not an important determinant of food yields in preliterate societies until long after the initial crossings produced the original domesticate.

Regarding the diffusion of new crops, the introduction of the New World sweet potato in the aboriginal Polynesian subsistence economy proved to be quite significant. In New Zealand this tuber became the dominant resource among the Maori, and here, the sweet potato was more important than in any other Oceania island group (Barrau 1961).

It was of even greater significance in highland New Guinea, where the meteorological conditions were not appropriate for the effective cultivation of many tropical root crops.

Importation of Food

In societies where transportation was poorly developed, symbiosis between widely dispersed specialized food centers is of small consequence in relation to overall food production. For example, although staple foods were imported into Tenochtitlan (the Aztec capital), the maximum distance between source and destination was 150 kilometers (Barlow 1949) — and this in a highly organized state with an elaborate tax-collecting bureaucracy. It is doubtful that the average urban center, with a transportation system depending on human beasts of burden and simple boats, could be effectively supplied with basic foodstuffs through a market system whose radius exceeded 50 kilometers; the limits, in fact, were often much less. (See our model of the subsistence base for Teotihuacán presented later.) Where long distances are involved under primitive conditions, the commodities of exchange are principally valued ritual objects and, more rarely, exotic or highly valued provisions, such as protein-rich foods.

The relative importance of the previously described responses to the need to improve subsistence in any society will depend on the degree of population pressure, the environmental variability and potential, the degree of circumscription, and the original sociocultural complexities specific to that society. These, in turn, will influence the duration and intensity of increased subsistence activity. As noted earlier, intensification of land use has been the most frequent and efficient means of increasing the food resources needed to reduce population pressures.

AGRICULTURE AND ECONOMICS

Changes in subsistence patterns involve correlate changes in economic systems. This is the basic premise of Julian Steward's (1955) cultural ecology paradigm. If food production is increased primarily through intensification of land use, then the exploitation and management of resources will adjust accordingly. This adjustment stimulates changes in residence, access to resources, property rights, and competition.

Mobility in residence diminishes in proportion to intensification of land use. That is, hunters and gatherers will exhibit seasonal settlement patterns, swidden agriculturalists will become more sedentary as the period of fallowing decreases, and hydraulic farmers will be truly bound to the land (because of the smallness of individual plots and the amount of capital investment required in this agricultural pattern). Subsistence and settlement permanence, therefore, are closely related variables.

The geographic expansion of intensive agricultural practices produces disparity in resources. As the amount of arable land per capita decreases within a given circumscribed area, and technological factors remain nearly constant, differential access to resources will increase. Obviously, some groups will have access to more profitable areas than others. This is an unavoidable result of intensification.

Stricter definition of property rights will, necessarily, accompany the increase in differential access to land. As would be expected, property rights develop as a means of maintaining the preferential locales of particular groups within a limited territory. The relationship between resource accessibility and property rights is highly reciprocal; the development of each is heightened as land resources diminish and further intensification becomes necessary.

The degree of intersocietal competition between small groups over resources depends on the factors already discussed. When sedentary residence is found to be essential for maintaining a subsistence pattern that will provide sufficient food, competition over key resources will increase. By extension, intersocietal competition may also be viewed in the context of rising pressures and decreasing resources (Carneiro 1970).

Sedentary residence, differential access to goods, and competition elicit further changes in economic organization. Occupational specialization in nonagricultural activities occurs when there is sufficient surplus to free a fraction of the population from subsistence duties, but it can also occur when shortages of agricultural land force a portion of the population into non–food-producing activities. In the western highlands of Guatemala today, for example, clusters of villages are integrated into a market system centered on a market town. Farming is the prized occupation, and many villages are wholly agricultural, producing surpluses of staples for the market. In some villages, however, land is generally poor, or the land is good but population density is so high that there is insufficient land; these villages specialize in nonagricultural activities, with all or a large number of people in each village engaging in one or a few crafts.

This process may go further, so that an increasing percentage of the population in villages may become full-time nonagricultural specialists. Intensification of land use also tends to deplete all other natural resources, thus placing a greater value on specialization in nonagricultural activities. In the Basin of Mexico today, for example, peasant villages on the south shore of Lakes Chalco-Xochimilco must even purchase charcoal for fuel from other communities, and virtually all objects made from wood have to be brought in from outside.

These processes may begin very early in areas where environmental diversity is high and where key resources are highly localized. In such cases population growth simply increases the intensity of a pattern already well established. In relatively homogeneous environments, however, population growth acts like environmental diversity—even slight variations in landscape become significant, and an increasing density requires a more efficient pattern of resource utilization.

With increasing specialization a mechanism is needed for internalizing the flow of goods. One such mechanism is redistributive networks, in which foods and products are pooled into a recognized center where an authoritative individual or institution manages the exchange of material, so that farmers receive specialized products and specialists receive foods (Dalton 1964). In return for managerial services the central agent or agency takes a disproportionately large share of the profits. It is interesting to speculate that this agent, in the early stages of such a process, may be a descendant of a family or lineage that has maintained exclusive rights over particularly rich key resources. In any case, this individual's authority, institutionalized through myth and ritual, provides him with a power to demand the tribute and manage the redistribution that maintains the system. This economic system corresponds to the chiefdom level of social organization as defined by Service (1971).

ECONOMIC STRATIFICATION AND POLITICAL ORGANIZATION

Full-time specialization and redistributive networks advance the degree of ranking or stratification in the society. A few individuals or lineage groups necessarily enjoy privileged status if the economic pattern of specialization and redistribution is to function. This interaction is mutually reinforcing: because certain individuals are assigned authority over others (through mystical justifications of ancestral descent or godliness), the economic system does, in fact, prevail, and the ranking of individuals is reinforced through the functioning of the system. Obvious examples of such legitimation through myth are the origin myths of many Polynesian chiefs and the magical powers of *mana,* which only the chiefs control. There is, in all probability, a close statistical correlation between major increases of energy with cultural systems and the emergence of new institutions to manage this increased energy, as well as a practical limit for the capacity of a chiefdom-type organization to manage energy transfers of a certain volume. Ultimately, special institutions are required to resolve this problem. They may take the form of a market or of a much more bureaucratic system of centralized redistribution.

With increases in specialization and competition, and with the need for expansion in redistributive networks, increasingly complex and institutionalized political controls arise. When surplus potentials can support a larger and more diversified class of specialists, the need for enlarged redistributive networks also increases. The enlargement of networks has a consolidating effect on the system, and the power of the managerial center becomes more absolute. According to H. T. Odum (1971), the greater the amount of energy that circulates through points in a system, the more complex and subtle the web of interrelationships becomes, and the social positions in a system undergo qualitative changes in functions.

With the emergence of numerous special-interest groups, most of which are based on economic specialization, traditional kin-based methods of social control and dispute arbitration break down, and more formal means of political authority become imperative. In this case, the economic interdependence of a given population provides a powerful stimulus for individuals to accept a social contract involving asymmetrical political and economic interrelationships.

Wholly aside from the symbiosis between economically unlike communities or groups within communities, competition itself, exacerbated by rising population pressure, may play a very significant role in political evolution. Minimally, this pressure could be a simple increase in personal disputes (both on the intracommunity and intercommunity level); maximally, it could involve quarrels over primary resources such as agricultural land. As both Netting (1972) and Carneiro (1967) have pointed out, the possible number of conflicts rises at a geometric rate in proportion to population increase. Netting, in his study of sacred power and political evolu-

49

tion in Nigeria (1972), notes that the increase in such conflicts may reach such an intolerable level (possibly this too is predictable in a mathematical way) that groups and individuals ultimately prove willing to surrender some autonomy to a mediator. Frequently this mediator is already a prestigious individual (in the African cases, a rainmaker priest). Since gifts are made to the mediator, he builds up a fund of economic as well as political power, and the last step necessary to produce a structural change is to make the position hereditary (if, in fact, it was not already so). The emergence of a chiefdom is associated with such a structural change.

A major question in Netting's formulation is whether a more coercive, asymmetrical social system could evolve through this type of process. However, more urgent stresses would probably be required.

The reduction of available land because of overpopulation may be a primary catalyst for intrasocietal competition. Such competition may be heightened further by soil erosion and land degradation through overcultivation. Increasingly complex political controls are prerequisites for effective exploitation in the presence of diminishing resources. In a recent paper Sanders (1971) has suggested this as a major process that led to state formation in the Valley of Guatemala. During the Terminal Formative (200 B.C.–A.D. 200) the population was large enough to stimulate occupation, not only of the deep, productive soils of the valley floor, but also of the neighboring piedmont and higher slopes of the valley. By Late Classic times (A.D. 700–1000) the slopes were severely eroded, forcing the population to abandon them and retreat to the deep soil areas below. Sanders suggests that this movement led to a patron-client type of social interaction between the holders of land on the valley floor and those on the slopes above.

Carrying the process to a higher organizational level, this would lead to intersocietal competition, warfare, conquest and—in the absence of the potential for fission—to incorporation and exploitation of conquered groups. This, in essence, is Carneiro's (1970) theory of the origin of the state. We do not quarrel with his formulation, but we do note that these processes can only operate and produce the results envisaged if, at some point during the curve of population growth and agricultural intensification, there is an awareness that resources are not inexhaustible and that there is a "limited good." Otherwise the process of intensification would simply lead to the allocation of smaller and smaller parcels of land per capita to more and more people, and the result would be a relatively self-sufficient, food-producing population living in small, politically autonomous communities with no significant change in the social or economic structure. This, in fact, may occur in some regions of the world, as Geertz (1963b) has pointed out in his discussion of agricultural involution in Indonesia. What normally seems to happen is that at a certain point in population growth, people recognize the relationships between resources and population. A strict definition of property rights emerges, and some person[s] or group[s] achieve control over more agricultural resources than they themselves need; this group then generates surpluses through patron-client labor relationships to finance or underwrite the redistribution system.

An interesting outcome of this process is a change in the status of at least some craft specialists. We have already noted the origin of the craftsmen—they are persons who become specialists because they lack agricultural land. As the system of class stratification becomes more marked, and as certain persons at the top are able to demand a higher share of the energy of the system, this energy may be used to underwrite the subsistence of a class of elite craftsmen who enjoy unusually high status within the system. This, in turn, has repercussions on the system of stratification apart from simply adding another element to it: leaders may then consolidate their prestige and power through redistribution down through the system of the products of the elite craftsmen.

FURTHER CONSIDERATIONS

Basically, then, our model is one of a population reaching carrying capacity, and, in the process, engendering population pressure and competition, both intrasocietal and intersocietal. The flexibility in agricultural systems so well described by Boserup (1965) and elaborated on by numerous other writers has caused considerable discussion among anthropologists in recent years as to the usefulness of the concept of carrying capacity. Thus it is necessary to discuss briefly the term as we use it.

"Carrying capacity" is usually defined as the maximal population size an area can sustain without long-range deleterious effects on the environment. The problem lies with the phrase "long-range deleterious effects," which is often used to mean that an irreversible process of deterioration is set in motion that either converts agricultural land into wasteland or reduces the capacity of the land to support a human population. It is not clear, however, how often this process actually occurs in human affairs, and hence the accuracy of this definition is questionable. If, however, "carrying capacity" is used to mean simply that point beyond which there is a reduction in productivity per area planted, then the concept can be easily adapted to Boserup's theory of intensification of land use.

Since we use the term in the latter sense, we must examine its relevance to such theoretical concepts as population pressure, competition, and cultural evolution. Our theoretical position involves certain assumptions—that patterns of land use, work input, and techniques of cultivation always become traditionalized in a particular culture and, in turn, are functionally interrelated with the institutions and ideology of the culture; that cultures are systems in nature and that they also act to preserve existing systems.

All of this means that the initial responses to population pressure will be to preserve the system; wherever space is available, physical and/or social fission will usually occur. If physical space is not available, a population is faced with two choices: stabilization of the existing system by stringent population controls, or innovations leading to the appearance of a new system. Our theoretical position is that few environments completely limit innovations in cultural systems; thus, the creation of a new system is a more common response.

A major theoretical point is the specific quantitative aspect of responses to rising population. How nearly does a population, in terms of a given system, approach carrying capacity before responses are triggered? In a recent paper Hassan (1973) points out that when no possibilities of increasing food supply are available, populations tend to stabilize at 50 to 80 percent of carrying capacity. Fission as a response to population pressure may occur at as low as 30 percent of carrying capacity. It would seem, therefore, that even at 30 percent the people recognize the limited good, and that at 50 to 80 percent regulatory mechanisms are set in motion to stabilize population.

The theoretical argument presented here is in the context of an environmental situation and cultural technology that permit a substantial increase in food production. Because of the principle of least effort we would expect a population to use an extensive system of cultivation first because of the more favorable input-output ratio. When 30 percent of carrying capacity is reached, spatial fission will occur. When 50 to 80 percent of carrying capacity is reached, innovations in the form of more intensive agricultural practices will occur; in response to these changes, alterations in the social institutions and their underlying ideology will follow. The new resource utilization systems will then permit further population growth, or the process may engender several cycles of change until some absolute level of carrying capacity is achieved in terms of technological and environmental limitations. As new systems evolve, they, in turn, become self-conserving, and the process of population growth continues, an approximation of carrying capacity is reached, and change to a new system occurs.

Another assumption in our theoretical position is that the principle of least effort applies not only to agricultural systems but to social systems as well. Human populations tend to organize themselves in the most economical means possible. If we combine these principles with an additional one—that transportation and communication technology limit the size of physical territory that can be effectively organized (see page 33)— then the interrelations between population size, population density, population pressure, carrying capacity, and social organization seem clear.

THE RATE OF SOCIAL EVOLUTION

The rate of sociocultural change within a population depends on numerous factors, the most important of which is the rate of population growth. As Dumond (1965:302) points out, population growth is not a simple cause of cultural change, but rather is both a cause and an effect of that change. In groups experiencing geographical or political circumscription, population growth is a very significant variable. We suggest that, as the rate of population growth increases, correlate factors involving subsistence and social organization will change proportionately. The rate of growth is an important aspect of the temporal, spatial, and numerical aspects of population pressure.

The rate of increase in population density, in the absence of biocultural controls regulating growth, will be faster in small, circumscribed areas than in large ones (Vayda and Rappaport 1963). Populations residing in small areas, therefore, would be expected to experience a given level of pressure more rapidly than those living in larger areas. Furthermore, *absolute* geographic space may not be the crucial factor affecting the rapidity of rising population pressures. Rather, *specific* environmental conditions are of primary importance. Within any area only a percentage of the land—depending on the interactions of technology, institutions, and environment—is useful for agriculture. If the percentage is relatively low in proportion to the number of occupants, intensification of land use will necessarily arise if the population is to be supported. Therefore, population pressures influencing changes in the subsistence pattern from extensive to intensive practices would be expected to occur more rapidly in areas with a low percentage of cultivable land. On the other hand, because of their greater total population capacity, large areas should in time permit much more complex levels of maximum sociopolitical evolution.

Internal variability of a circumscribed area can, as we have noted previously, influence the rapidity with which population pressure occurs by delimiting the amount of area that is of use to any one technological activity. Ecological variability is also an important variable affecting the rate of cultural development in other contexts. A diversified area is more likely to have particularly rich zones capable of sustaining agricultural intensification of specific crops, thus more adequately fulfilling the needs of the population than is generally true in areas where agricultural potential is reduced through homogeneity.

Environmental diversity, or the lack of it, also produces a great disparity in population density, and this, in turn, would have two major effects. In terms of intersocietal competition it would provide an explanation for military success. More importantly, it could account for the stability of the system of stratification that emerged after the conquest. (This factor would also act in much the same way within an existing society.)

We would also argue that in environments that vary strikingly in agricultural productivity and in which other resources are highly localized, the pressure toward the formation of large, internally complex societies is considerable, even when population density is light or moderate. This is because of the facility with which overall productive efficiency can be improved through subregional specialization, and the necessarily higher levels of coordination that such intraregional specialization requires.

It is perhaps in this connection that Wittfogel's hydraulic theory (1957) is most useful when applied to areas with small irrigation systems. (We say "small" because we see the relationship between political power and water control in large systems as unequivocal.) The difference in crop security and productivity between irrigated and nonirrigated land offers the sharpest contrast possible. When one adds to this the internal needs of an irrigation system in water allocation, construction, maintenance, and resolution of disputes, then the effect of such a system in sociopolitical dynamics would seem obvious.

Without getting involved in the complex debate on the relationship between irrigation and the emergence of the state, we would also argue that if the chiefdom type of organization preceded irrigation in a particular area, population pressure would eventually stimulate the chief to organize the population for the construction of large-scale irrigation systems. This progression may well have been the catalyst that transformed the position of chief to that of king. Even if states were founded in an area before the introduction of irrigation systems, the development of such systems would undoubtedly consolidate the power of the ruling class and enhance the stratification system.

Geographic variability also favors the development of specialization. High-quality stone and clay for the manufacturing of implements and containers may occur exclusively in one locale, but these items can be traded for exotic foods grown only in another locale. Where variability exists, particular requirements for specialization in foods and products are greatly reduced when compared with areas lacking marked zoning.

Sanders (1970) has pointed out the distribution of a number of key resources in the Teotihuacán Valley for the needs of the peasant level of a society. Major superficial deposits of basalt, which provided raw materials for grinding stones, are found in several extensive areas, particularly within the Middle Horizon city. A fairly extensive deposit of obsidian for chipped stone tools occurs southeast of Otumba at the upper edge of the Valley; pottery clays occur in the middle Valley near San Sebastián; reeds for baskets were abundant in the area around the springs; and salt could be obtained from the immediate lakeshore. At least in First Intermediate times the nearby slopes were covered with pine forests, so that wood was abundant. The only major deficiencies in the Valley's resources were lime, for cooking and construction, and aquatic protein foods, since the portion of Lake Texcoco fronting on the Valley was poor in lake food resources. During the First Intermediate period, however, game was probably abundant throughout the Valley. As the population grew in Middle Horizon times, some resources, such as game and wood, must have been seriously depleted, while others, such as obsidian and salt, no longer sufficed for the needs of a greatly expanded population.

The interrelationships between the processes discussed here are reciprocal, with numerous feedback loops, to such a degree that the question of cause and effect really issues in a "chicken and egg" type of debate. For example, one could argue that increasing craft specialization results in corresponding increases in subsocietal differentiation, thus stimulating social stratification. On the other hand, stratification stimulates craft specialization because the upper class, with its greater concentration of wealth, is able to sponsor craft specialists. Another factor that stimulates specialization is technological evolution, since it increases the productivity of specialists, thus expanding their clientele.

In summary, where environmental diversity is considerable, where population density and technological level are high, and where degradation of the environment is advanced, the stimulus toward stratified societies is maximal.

THE BASIN OF MEXICO SURVEY

One of the major decisions of the Chicago National Science Foundation Conference was to conduct a settlement survey of the Basin of Mexico, a project that was initiated in 1960 with the Teotihuacán Valley project directed by William T. Sanders, and continued in 1962 with the Teotihuacán Mapping project, directed by René Millon. Sanders's project included a survey of the Valley of Teotihuacán, while Millon surveyed the Classic city itself. The fieldwork phase of the Teotihuacán Valley project, which lasted from 1960 to 1964, included studies of contemporary settlement patterns and agriculture, settlement surveys of pre-Hispanic sites, and excavations of a number of sites to resolve specific problems encountered in survey and ethnohistoric studies of the sixteenth-century postcontact populations. The project provided a solid base, in terms of method and theoretical orientation, for surveys of the remainder of the Basin and enabled the subsequent surveys to be completed with minimal cost in time and money.

With the termination of the Teotihuacán Valley project, Jeffrey Parsons, one of the graduate students on the project, elaborated plans to finish the Basin of Mexico survey. He divided the Basin into a number of regions comparable in size to the Teotihuacán Valley (Map 1). They were named the Texcoco, Ixtapalapa, Chalco, Xochimilco, Tacuba, Cuauhtitlán, Tezoyuca, and Zumpango regions. In 1965 Parsons returned to the Valley of Teotihuacán and completed surveys on a number of vacant

56

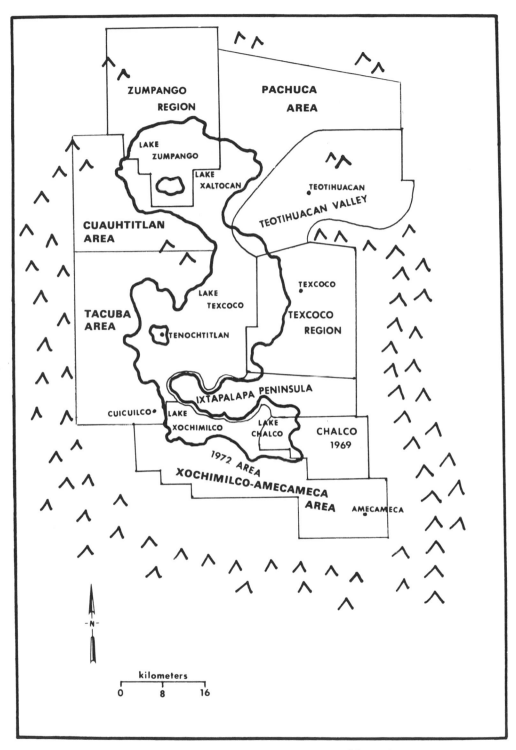

MAP 1. The Valley of Mexico, showing separate survey areas. Mountain ranges are depicted schematically.

areas. Between 1968 and 1972 he and one of his students, Richard Blanton, were occupied in settlement surveys of the Texcoco, Ixtapalapa, Chalco, and Xochimilco regions; in 1973 Parsons completed the Zumpango region. Sanders returned in 1972 to conduct a study of peasant ecology in the Texcoco region; in 1974 he completed the surveys of two of the three remaining regions of the Basin: the Cuautitlán and Tacuba regions. In Chapters 5–8 we will use the theoretical model we have presented to interpret archaeological data derived from these regional surveys.

NOTE

1. One point should be stressed here. The term "fission" has been used to describe different processes that sometimes, but not necessarily, go hand in hand. It may refer to simple physical fission, in which a segment of a village splits off, migrates to a new locality, and forms a new village, all the while maintaining social ties with the mother village; both communities also maintain their ties to a larger social order. Social fission thus refers to a process of splitting off of one segment of the social system and the founding of a new autonomous society. The latter is always accompanied by physical fission, but the reverse is not necessarily the case.

5

The Natural Environment of the Basin of Mexico

W I L L I A M T. S A N D E R S

Department of Anthropology
The Pennsylvania State University

The Basin of Mexico is a great elevated plain surrounded on three sides by high mountain walls (to the east by the Sierra Nevada, to the west by the Sierra Las Cruces, and to the south by the Sierra Ajusco); the northern border of the Basin consists of a series of low, discontinuous ranges of hills. The mountain walls reach a maximum elevation of slightly below 6,000 meters in the southeast with the two snow-capped volcanoes of Ixtaccihuatl and Popocatepetl. Within the three ranges numerous peaks have elevations in the 3,000-to-4,000-meter band, while the Basin floor is approximately 2,236 meters above sea level. The Basin's total surface area is approximately 8,000 square kilometers, and it extends about 120 kilometers (north to south) by 70 kilometers (east to west).

Before the construction of the "Gran Canal," the Basin was a closed hydrographic unit. Springs, meltwater from snowfields, and runoff from the summer rains all flowed into the center of the Basin, draining into a series of lakes that traversed the Basin floor in a nearly continuous chain from north to south. The colonial documents refer sometimes to three and at times to as many as six lakes (based on such artificial divisions as dikes). During some years, however, the lakes formed a single sheet of water, located at varying elevations. To the north was Lake Xaltocan (or Lakes Xaltocan-Zumpango; in the center, Lake Texcoco (or Lakes Mexico-Texcoco); and to the south, Lake Xochimilco (or Lakes Chalco-Xochimilco).

Lake Xochimilco was located three meters higher than Lake Texcoco and drained into it. Because of this outlet, which apparently functioned all year, and because of the presence of numerous springs along the southern shore, the water was fresh and covered by floating vegetation "so thick one could walk on it." Lake Texcoco, being the lowest lake and the ultimate destination of all drainage, was extremely saline, Lake Xaltocan was also higher than Lake Texcoco, but since it drained into Lake Texcoco only seasonally it was more saline than Lake Xochimilco (except for small areas near local springs).

In the nineteenth century the lakes covered an average area of approximately 1,000 square kilometers, or one-eighth of the Basin's surface. The average contour of the Lake Texcoco shoreline measured 2,240 meters, although this varied from season to season and from year to year. Generally, the lakes were shallow, varying in depth from 1 to 3 meters. During the dry seasons they frequently shrank in surface area so that canoe traffic from lake to lake was interrupted for short periods.

Today the various water sources feed into hundreds of permanent and seasonal streams that ultimately enter the lake system. The seasonal streams have cut canyonlike beds, called barrancas, and the drainage from rainfall is extraordinarily vigorous and destructive.

The Basin presents a unique combination of favorable and unfavorable circumstances for a maize-based agricultural economy. The annual rainfall varies from a minimum of 450 millimeters on the northern plains to 1,500 millimeters on the middle slopes of the southern ranges. Since approximately 80 percent of the rainfall occurs between June 1 and October 1, and since this period is the thermal summer season, conditions are optimal for maize. In addition, the soils are generally fertile, and a high percentage have ideal texture for cultivation, particularly for an agricultural system based on hand-powered tools of wood and stone. There are, however, several major obstacles to intensive cultivation of the area.

The most serious problem is the winter frost season. Generally the frosts are severe between November 1 and February 1, but they frequently begin in October and occasionally last well into February. Historic frosts have produced crop disasters as early as September and as late as May. In pre-Hispanic times the problem was particularly acute, since no native cultigens were adapted to the frost season. Minimally, this meant a single cropping season and very careful planning of agricultural activities.

Rain falls in a typical monsoon pattern, with scattered showers from November 1 to May 1, increasing to several substantial showers in May. Rainfall is usually consistent and regular between June 1 and mid September, but it declines rapidly during the balance of September and October. The average rainfall (Map 2) in the Basin varies from 450 millimeters in the north to 800 millimeters in the south on the Basin floor. (On the neighboring slopes in each sector averages are approximately 50 percent higher.) Even in the drier portions of the Basin, however, the average amount of rainfall—because of its seasonal concentration—is adequate for maize production. These figures are averages, though, and in some years rainfall is inadequate in the drier areas.

Although the rainy season has never failed completely (at least not since meteorological stations were established in the region near the end of the nineteenth century), the beginning of the rainy season is frequently delayed until mid June. Midseason droughts lasting up to several weeks are by no means rare, and in the central and northern portions of the Basin rainfall is highly variable from year to year, frequently falling below the requirement for a good maize crop. For example, we have a sixty-year record of rainfall at the Tacuba station, a relatively favorable locality, in which the rainfall dropped below 500 millimeters fifteen times.

The Basin's staple crop has been and continues to be maize. Although the most productive varieties require a six-month growing season, there are faster growing, less productive varieties that mature in four months. Because maize originated at elevations lower than those in the Basin of Mexico, it has little resistance to frost and is particularly vulnerable at the critical phases of germination and ear formation—two stages when moisture requirements are high. The major problem, therefore, is the relative timing of the rains and frosts; a late rainy season and early frosts are fatal for the maize crop. The frost-rainfall problem varies considerably in significance from area to area within the Basin, however. Above 2,700 meters, an area that constitutes 15 percent of the total land surface, the frost season is so prolonged that maize cannot be grown except in a few

61

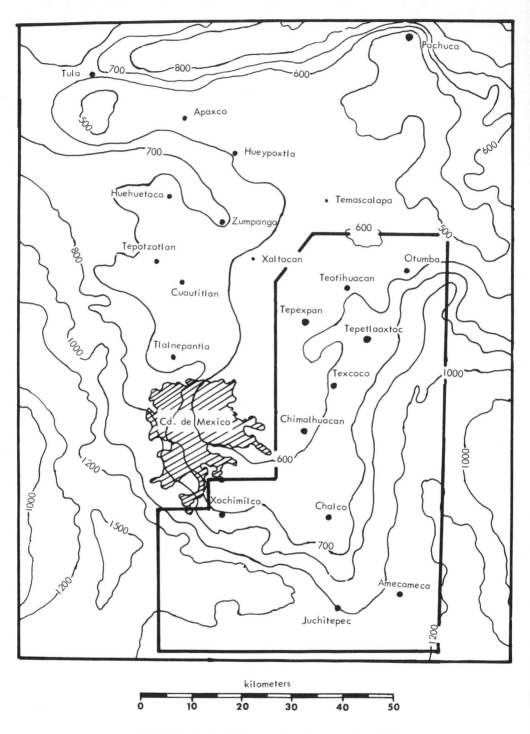

MAP 2. Basin of Mexico, showing annual rainfall.

localized warm spots. Within the elevation band where maize can be grown (2,240–2,700 meters), the frost-rainfall problem is most severe in the Upper Piedmont (2,500–2,700 meters) and the Outer Lakeshore Plain (2,250–2,300 meters)—two areas which together make up 40 percent of the surface area. The problem is less severe in the south, where the precipitation is both more abundant and more regular. Of the remaining 45 percent of the Basin, 20 percent lies below 2,250 meters (two-thirds of this was lake, and the rest a narrow band along the lakeshore, which we will call the Inner Lakeshore Plain); the other 25 percent lies between 2,300–2,500 meters, an area referred to here as the Lower Piedmont. Both the Inner Lakeshore Plain and the Lower Piedmont are relatively free of the frost problem. (See Map 3.)

A third major problem of cultivation is the relatively high percentage of land that is susceptible to erosion—65 percent of the agricultural land in the Basin. Fourth, in the early phase of colonization, an additional problem was drainage in the lower lying areas. Approximately 3,200 kilometers of land surface (lake bed, 1,000 square kilometers; Inner Lakeshore Plain, 600 square kilometers; Outer Lakeshore Plain, 1,600 square kilometers) lie below 2,300 meters. Excluding the lakes we estimate that all of the Inner Plain and at least half of the Outer Plain (excluding most of the northern Outer Plain) was an area of high water table and hence characterized by drainage problems.

Under ideal conditions the first substantial showers begin in April and early May, permitting planting and seed germination; the ears are fully developed by September, and the few frosts that occur in October will not damage the crop. Actually, the decline of rainfall in October and November is ideal for the final maturation of the crop. In the drier portions of the Basin such ideal conditions probably occur only two years out of five, and, of course, these areas frequently lack sufficient rainfall. In the south, not only is rainfall higher on the average but its variability is less prejudicial to crops. The problem of timing is less critical too, since adequate moisture for early planting occurs in most years. To aggravate further the problems in the center and north of the Basin, however, the soil mantle erodes because of the more torrential character of rainfall and the sparser natural vegetation. Since the Conquest and consequent introduction of grazing animals, large areas of the Piedmont have lost much of their soil, resulting in a thin soil layer that does not retain sufficient moisture. The maintenance of a fairly deep soil profile—ideally in excess of one meter—is therefore another consideration.

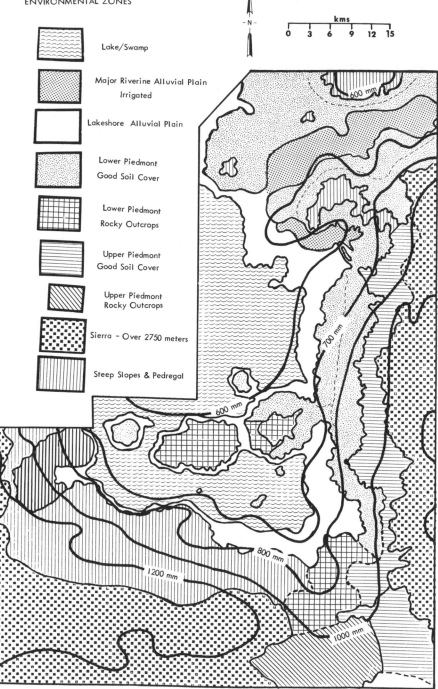

ENVIRONMENTAL ZONES

Lake/Swamp

Major Riverine Alluvial Plain
Irrigated

Lakeshore Alluvial Plain

Lower Piedmont
Good Soil Cover

Lower Piedmont
Rocky Outcrops

Upper Piedmont
Good Soil Cover

Upper Piedmont
Rocky Outcrops

Sierra – Over 2750 meters

Steep Slopes & Pedregal

MAP 3. Survey area, showing ecological zones.

In pre-Hispanic cultivation two other problems must have been of primary concern: soil texture during the period of initial colonization and soil fertility in times of population pressure. Most soil maps classify soils of the central and southern parts of the Basin (within the strip of agricultural exploitations) as "Chernozems," and those of the north as "Chesnut." Both are associated with subhumid to semiarid climates, both fit into a major soil grouping called "soils of calcification," and both generally have great natural fertility. The overall impression is that local differences in soil types within the 2,240-to-2,700-meter contour are minor in relation to agricultural productivity. Of greater importance are variations in soil depth and texture—characteristics that are most closely related to the problems of water conservation and friability.

Because of variations in intensity of erosion or angle of slope, soil depth varies considerably and has a striking effect on agricultural productivity, particularly in the drier central and northern Basin. The least productive part of the Basin is undoubtedly the north; because the mean annual rainfall is lowest and because erosion has reduced the thickness of the soil mantle, maize cultivation is exceedingly precarious in that area. Soil texture is another critical factor. Although loamy, friable, loose-textured soils are the most common and ideal for agriculture, they are extremely susceptible to erosion. Other soil types occur in localized areas in the Basin: sandy soils are found in eroded slopes where the finer soil particles have been washed out, and clay-textured soils are especially common near the lakeshore. Above 2,600 to 2,800 meters podzol soils predominate, but they are notoriously poor for agriculture, a factor further limiting upward agricultural expansion.

With hand tools of stone and wood for tillage sandy-textured soils would seem to be ideal, but lack of moisture would present a problem. Clearly, some kind of compromise would have to be struck between soil workability and the need for humidity retention; thus, sandy loams or loams would seem to be the preferred soil type, not a high-clay-content soil that was probably unworkable with pre-Hispanic tools. Regarding the problem of maintaining soil fertility, the loam-textured soils would again represent a kind of compromise—too sandy a soil would not have sufficient cation exchange capacity to maintain soil fertility. Our soil samples from the Texcoco area suggest that while the natural process of cation exchange of bases in the loams and clays is substantial, the major problem is the replacement of nitrogen and organic matter. Since the

Spanish Conquest the primary source of these elements has been animal fertilizers, a resource in very short supply in pre-Hispanic times. In most systems of agriculture where domestic animals are few in number and small in size, the solution lies in fallowing, a process whereby a successional stage of the natural ecosystem is allowed to reoccupy the field for a specified period of years.

To reconstruct the natural vegetation of the Basin would be difficult, since at least 4,000 years of agricultural exploitation have completely removed it from the belt of peasant occupation. However, small areas of relatively unaltered vegetation can be used as a guide. There was probably a gradual shift from broadleaf forest in the south to xerophytic or scrub forest in the north. Between 2,600 and 4,500 meters coniferous forest was the dominant vegetation, above that were strips of alpine meadows or tundra, and finally, in the southeast, snowfields. With respect to human occupation and land use two important points should be stressed. The permanent removal of the vegetation between 2,240 and 2,700 meters (in contrast to the tropical lowlands of Mesoamerica) presented no serious obstacle to the Mesoamerican farmer, even with his primitive technology. Above 2,600 to 2,800 meters the pre-Hispanic population had an easily available source of forest products for construction, household technology, transportation, and medicine.

On the basis of documentary Aztec archaeological data and ethnographic data from the contemporary population, we know that the many and very real agricultural problems were and are effectively met. But the various solutions clearly involved enormous differences in labor input and crop output.

Today the major solution to the frost-rainfall problem is preplanting irrigation—in other words, to irrigate the land and plant it before the rainy season begins. Although the southern portion of the Basin has a relatively high annual rainfall, this technique is useful even in this area. Preplanting irrigation, however, is particularly effective in the central and northern portions of the Basin, where most of the soils, because of their loamy texture, have an unusually high water retention capacity. Here, preplanting irrigation can be begun as early as January or February and the succeeding planting delayed as late as May. The ideal arrangement, in terms of seed germination and early plant growth, is to irrigate in March or April and plant in April or early May. After planting, the crop growth can then depend entirely on natural rainfall. The preplanting irrigation season, therefore, can be as long as four to five months, thus allowing a small amount of water to be very widely distributed.

Furthermore, because of the micro-variability of the temperature and rainfall regime within the Basin, the ideal dates for planting vary from February to March in the Upper Piedmont (theoretically there is considerable risk in planting this early in the Upper Piedmont because of the long frost season, but early fall frosts are a much greater threat than the spring frosts), to March and April in the Outer Plain, to April and May in the Lower Piedmont and Inner Plain. An irrigation system based on water sources in the Sierra and following the attitudinal gradients could therefore be effectively organized to irrigate lands from the heights to the Basin floor. The same system could be used to resolve the problems of a midseason drought, but in a much more limited way, since only a fraction of the lands could be provided with water during a short period. It should be pointed out, however, that rainfall is highly localized in the Basin so that one area may have a highly favorable rainfall-temperature regime in a particular year while another suffers a disaster, even though the two are only 15 to 20 kilometers apart. As a result, it would be unlikely that drought phases would be generalized in timing and duration over the entire area served by a large irrigation system.

In the Alluvial Plain, where the water table is high and the major initial problem is drainage, the solution is simple: construct a network of drainage ditches linked to the natural waterways of the area. These networks would range in size from those serving the lands of an entire village or several villages to ditches on the peripheries of or within the holdings of a single family. As the water table is lowered, the same canal system can serve for permanent or floodwater irrigation.

In sloping terrain the main solution to the problem of soil erosion is the construction of retaining walls around the fields. On low gradients simple earth embankments will serve, while on steeper slopes terraces faced with stone or blocks of tepetate or some volcanic conglomerate are used. Additional defense can be provided by planting maguey, nopal, or, sometimes, fruit trees, along the defensive works and even in widely spaced rows parallel to the slope within the field. Terraces, of course, retain not only the soil but also the moisture; in addition, to further improve the moisture level in the soil, the terraces could be connected with floodwater or permanent irrigation systems.

6

Settlement and Population History of the Basin of Mexico

JEFFREY R. PARSONS

Museum of Anthropology
University of Michigan

INTRODUCTION

Critical to our evaluation of the model is our ability to estimate over-all population size and settlement distribution during the various phases of occupation of the Basin of Mexico. In the course of making population estimates from the physical remains of prehistoric occupation, we have encountered many problems and made several assumptions. To evaluate our demographic reconstructions adequately, the reader should be aware of these problems and assumptions. We stress beforehand that the formulation of population estimates is hardly a straightforward process. We acknowledge lacunae in our data and crudity in our method. However, we have some confidence that our population profiles have real utility in a relative sense—that is, while less confidence should be attached to our absolute figures (which must be considered as carefully considered guesses), we are somewhat more certain of the relative values. For example, we feel assured that a population estimate of, say, 30,000 people for one period represents about one-half the population of another period, which we estimate roughly to be 60,000.

A critical factor in estimating a particular prehistoric population from settlement pattern data is understanding the settlement system in which the population was participating (Struever 1968, 1971). And central to describing a prehistoric settlement system is the specification of functional attributes of occupational loci. The assessment of function is a major operation in itself, which, if done adequately, requires intensive sampling at many sites and sophisticated analysis of artifactual material (Hill 1970). Our surveys up to this point have provided good data only for gross chronology, settlement size and relative occupational density, relative architectural complexity, site location regarding major natural and cultural features, and changing configurations of these variables over time. Although this is a very significant body of data, it still does not provide an adequate basis for inferring the kinds of activities performed at different sites, the categories of people who occupied these sites, and the character of the occupation itself. Thus we cannot always say whether sites of a particular time period represent permanent habitations, seasonal occupations, or permanent but short-term occupations which may be merely the remains of activities spatially disassociated from residences. (See, for example, our discussion below of the rural settlement during the Middle Horizon.)

Chronology is another major problem for any kind of prehistoric demography. In our case we do not yet have a regional artifact chronology that can be used to delineate time periods much shorter than 200 to 300 years, with the exception of the Teotihuacán Valley. Therefore, for much of the Basin, our perspective on the reconstructions and settlement patterns for each period constitutes a composite view of all occupational activity over a period of six to ten human generations. This creates a situation in which we cannot really differentiate between one extreme (in which all sites assigned to a particular time period are thought to have been occupied continuously for that entire period) or the other (in which only a few sites of any given time period are said to have been inhabited at any particular point within the time period, with site locations shifting rather frequently). Neither can we know with certainty what part of the total surface area of any site was occupied at any given point in time. What we do know, however, is the spatial distribution of a series of population units over definable units of time.

Furthermore, a change in settlement system within one of our relatively long periods could result in our lumping together sites that were participating in more than one settlement system. This would badly obscure both earlier and later systems, thereby producing a misleading population estimate. Similarly, there could have been a major change in the settlement system within one time period, or from one period to the next, so that many more sites were actually produced with no significant growth of regional population. In addition, a change in the settlement system could have occurred so that the number of sites increased while the overall population declined—a situation which we might interpret to mean that there had been a population increase. Conversely, it is quite possible that a change in the settlement system could produce fewer sites from one period to the next, although the regional population was actually expanding. Our population estimates would thus probably be the reverse of what actually occurred.

In making population estimates, we generally have only two variables to work with: the area of occupational debris on the ground surface (in some periods mainly potsherds), and the relative density of the debris. Architectural remains sometimes occur, but only in some areas; furthermore, only during some phases does their preservation permit an estimation of population based on a housemound size and number. Most sites are practically level, if not uneven and irregular, with no way to determine the location of former structures. In our survey, the surface area was obtained by a planimeter measurement after the site had been plotted on a base map. (Sites were not defined or measured in the field.) It was only after we had plotted our field observations (noted on survey airphotos) on a large sheet of tracing paper and completed our ceramic analysis for each occupational locus that we could define a particular site. In most cases, it is fairly obvious where one should draw a site border on the regional map: occupational debris fades off quickly beyond a certain point. However, there are some cases, especially in the Late Horizon, where widely dispersed occupation makes the drawing of site borders a difficult and arbitrary process. Our estimate of a settlement's surface area, therefore, is not a precisely determined figure.

Our estimation of occupational density is done on a subjective basis. In most cases, with a little experience, a member of our survey can visually estimate several different levels of relative sherd density as he walks over the ground. Any two observers, however, may have somewhat different

71

impressions of sherd densities; furthermore, there is a great decrease in the reliability of simple visual estimation for specific time periods at multi-component sites. We are probably justified in assuming that the effects of alluviation, erosion, and plowing on our surface impressions are fairly uniform for most sites. One major exception to this might be on the flat plain around the edge of a lake, where alluviation has been considerable and where sites are more likely to have been buried or partly obscured than elsewhere. Another would be situations where small sites in the higher areas have been completely removed by sheet or gully erosion.

In converting occupational density on sites to population estimates, we have used density figures calculated for modern peasant settlements in central Mexico, where most of the inhabitants are engaged in relatively traditional agriculture (Sanders 1965:50). At sites where surface sherd densities are consistently in the heavier ranges of our visual scale, we have used density figures of 2,500 to 5,000 people per square kilometer (25 to 50 per hectare), which characterize Sanders's "High Density Compact Village" settlement type. At sites where the density of surface sherds is consistently in the lighter ranges of our visual scale, we have been guided by density figures for the "Compact Low Density Village" (10 to 25 per hectare), "Scattered Village" (5 to 10 per hectare), and "Compact Ranchería" (2 to 3 per hectare) settlement types that Sanders defined. Naturally, this system is most applicable to a settlement system in which all sites are fully occupied on a year-round basis, and naturally, departures from it will produce errors in population estimates in direct proportion to the degree of departure. As yet, we have not attempted to quantify the relationship between population density and sherd density, which would involve deducing, from ethnographically established guidelines, the number of pots a household would be expected to have used and broken over time.

Three considerations suggest that this procedure for estimating prehistoric populations is reasonable. First, in a very few cases, we feel that practically all structures associated with an archaeological site can still be identified and counted on the ground surface. In these cases, assuming that all the structures were residential in function, we computed the sites' populations by multiplying the numbers of mounds by a range of figures for average household size. The outcome has been within the range we would have estimated on the basis of area and sherd density alone. Second, we have subjectively compared refuse density of contemporary villages with pre-Hispanic sites, with favorable results. And third, Sanders et al. (1970), in an intensive survey based on documentary sources, calculated the population in the Basin of Mexico during the Late Horizon; their figures correspond well with maximal calculations made independently from archaeological data alone in the Texcoco and Chalco areas. In fact, Sanders's maximum population figures from documentary sources are approximately 20 percent higher than J. R. Parsons's maximum figures based on survey.

Another problem in estimating population lies in our inability to separate sherd density and relative length of occupation within one of our ceramic phases. Conceivably, a site could be occupied by a few hundred people for a long, continuous period within one of our chronological phases. This could produce a density of surface pottery that would probably look much more substantial than, say, in a case where the same number of people had occupied a site area of about the same size for a significantly shorter period within one of our chronological phases. Our population estimates for the former case would substantially exceed those for the latter, although, in actuality, both sites represent the same number of people, at least during a part of the phase.

Detailed discussions of our survey methodology appear in J. R. Parsons's monographs for the Texcoco Region (1971b:16–24) and Blanton's study of the Ixtapalapa region (1972b:16–21). We are quite sure that we located nearly all the significant residential sites from the Early Horizon through the Late Horizon in the areas surveyed. We are equally confident that the absence of those few sites that we may have overlooked does not appreciably affect the magnitude or postulated implications of our population estimations. This confidence is somewhat less for the area of deep alluvial soils around the edges of the lake system.

Another potential problem concerns the possible differential recovery of sites in a settlement system characterized by nucleated occupation versus a system that is highly dispersed. While most sites are very small—for example, less than 50 meters in diameter—and show no surface mounding, a substantial number of occupation loci may have been missed. Therefore our population estimates for highly dispersed settlement systems are probably more subject to significant error than our estimates for nucleated systems. This problem is particularly acute in calculating the size of the Middle Horizon and Second Intermediate: Phase 2 rural population.

73

In addition to all these considerations, we have included a "survey factor" of 20 percent in our population estimates. After making our calculations directly from the archaeological remains, we added 20 percent to our estimates to allow for the discrepancy between documentary versus archaeological calculations in the Conquest period population estimates.

An assumption basic to all our demographic reconstructions is that there is no significant chronological overlap of the principal ceramic types and complexes we have used to define our time periods (J. R. Parsons 1971b). One final note: at the time this chapter was written, our population estimates were not yet complete for the 1972 survey area in the southern Basin, nor for the 1973 surveys in the northwestern portion of the Basin. Thus, for these latter areas we lacked specific population figures, although the general trends for each period were apparent.

Early Horizon (ca. 1500–900 B.C.)

The Early Horizon period is a time of extremely sparse occupation. In fact, the only substantial site in our survey area is a village of about 9 hectares, located on the east side of the Tlapacoya Peninsula on the northeast shore of Lake Chalco. There are two small hamlets along the north shore of Lakes Chalco-Xochimilco, about 8 to 10 kilometers west of Tlapacoya, and another small hamlet on the south shore of Lake Texcoco on the opposite side of the Ixtapalapa Peninsula. In 1972 two small hamlets were located a few kilometers east of Amecameca at about 2,550 meters. The total population represented by all these sites probably did not exceed a thousand persons. (See Map 4.)

To our knowledge there is only one additional known Early Horizon occupation of any consequence in the Basin of Mexico: Tlatilco, a substantial site of unknown dimensions, located on the lower western piedmont of Lake Texcoco (Piña Chan 1958). Although this site may well be larger and more complex than any contemporary occupation we have located in the southeastern Basin, it almost certainly had fewer than 1,000 inhabitants.

Except for two tiny hamlets in the high Amecameca subvalley, then, all known Early Horizon occupation is restricted to low ground near the lakeshore. The great majority of the population apparently resided at two substantial village communities at Tlapacoya and Tlatilco. The small hamlet sites we have located may well represent seasonal or temporary

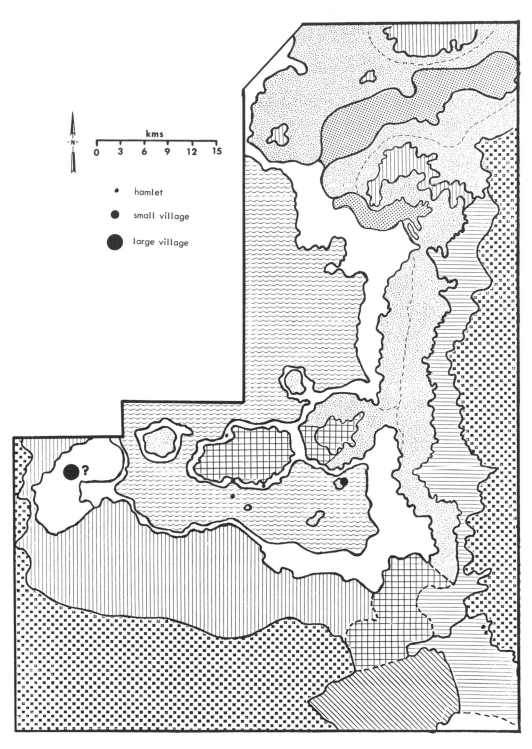

MAP 4. Survey area, showing Early Horizon settlements.

occupations, associated with the exploitation of lacustrine or mountain resources by people who lived at Tlapacoya and Tlatilco. The total population of our survey area probably did not exceed a thousand people at any given time in the Early Horizon period. Several hundred additional people, possibly as many as a thousand, probably resided at Tlatilco outside of the survey area. In addition, there may have been a substantial village site at Cuicuilco, again near the lakeshore.

First Intermediate: Phase 1 (ca. 900–500 B.C.)

Phase 1 of the First Intermediate saw a great population expansion from the preceding Early Horizon times, although population still remained at a low level compared with later periods. The zone of greatest population density and size remained very clearly the southern Basin, where two fairly consistent patterns are apparent. First, spaced rather evenly around the shoreline of Lakes Chalco-Xochimilco are six nucleated settlements between 10 and 58 hectares in area. (Another similar site is found at Chimalhuacán in the southeast corner of Lake Texcoco.) Second, there are four sites of comparable size on the Lower Piedmont east of Lake Chalco. Most of these sites are separated by distances of 8 to 10 kilometers of essentially unoccupied ground. Within the area east of Lake Chalco this spacing is reduced to about 3 to 4 kilometers. Low mounds can be detected on several of these sites, but there are probably domestic structures, and there are no indications of public or monumental architecture. With one exception, these sites lie between 2,240 and 2,300 meters. (See Map 5.)

The Cuicuilco site in the southwest corner of the Basin of Mexico (just outside our survey area) is best known for its First Intermediate: Phases 2 and 3 occupation, although indications of earlier occupation have been noted there (Heizer and Bennyhoff 1958). We suspect that there is a substantial First Intermediate: Phase 1 occupation here (and perhaps even some substantial Early Horizon), for two reasons: (1) before the volcanic eruption that destroyed the site and covered much of the local region, this would have been an area quite analogous, in terms of productive potential, to the region east and southeast of Lake Chalco; and (2) Cuicuilco lies about 10 kilometers distance from the next known First Intermediate: Phase 1 site to the east, and thus would fit the general spacing for sites in the southern Basin of Mexico.

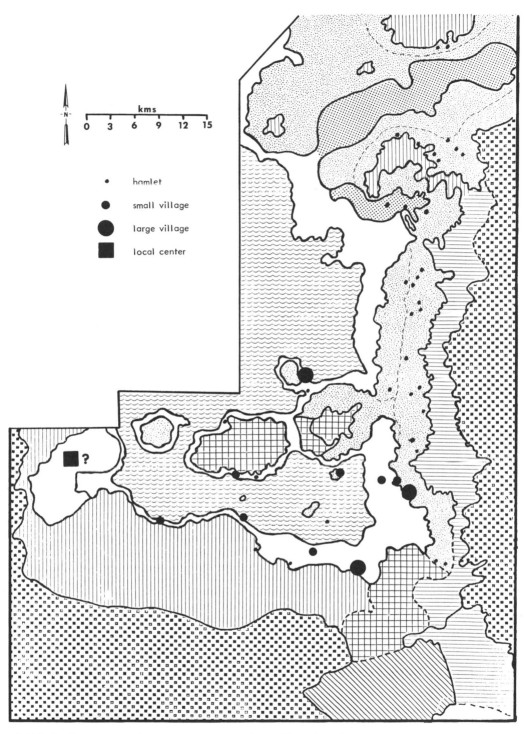

MAP 5. Survey area, showing First Intermediate: Phase 1 settlements.

In the central and northern portions of our survey area, the First Intermediate: Phase 1 occupation is quite different. Here we have found only hamlets (at least twenty-five), seldom measuring more than a few hectares in area; there is a complete absence of architectural remains here, although occupational debris is generally substantial. Most of these small sites are well up in the Piedmont at 2,350 meters. We suspect that a fairly substantial site may exist under the nucleated ancient and modern settlement in the vicinity of the springs at San Juan Teotihuacán—it is a unique zone of cultivable high water table that should have been appropriate for subsistence during this phase. Known sites in the Teotihuacán Valley indicate that this region is the most sparsely occupied within our survey area at this time. The hamlets in the Texcoco-Teotihuacán area appear to occur in at least seven discrete clusters.

First Intermediate: Phase 2 (ca. 500–200 B.C.)

Two features stand out in the First Intermediate: Phase 2 occupation in our survey area: (1) there is a very considerable expansion and intensification of occupation, and (2) there is, for the first time, substantial occupation of some zones which up to this point had been essentially without settlement. Although the overall rate of increase is much less than the roughly twentyfold expansion between Early Horizon and First Intermediate: Phase 1 times, there is still a four- or fivefold increase between Phase 1 and Phase 2 over most of our survey area. (See Map 6 for Phase 2 data.)

The southern Basin remains the zone of maximum population size and density. Here there are about fifteen very substantial nucleated sites, several of which exceed 100 hectares in area. In two or three of these large sites are remains of what appear to be modest temple platforms or other public architecture. We also have evidence of a major population shift away from the immediate lakeshore toward the Lower Piedmont during this period. If we exclude Cuicuilco (which is located approximately between the Lower Piedmont and the lakeshore) from this analysis, six out of the eight surveyed settlements, each with populations exceeding 1,000 persons, were located in the Lower Piedmont.

In the Texcoco area the population is located primarily on the Lower Piedmont, with two clusters of settlements on the lakeshore. The survey

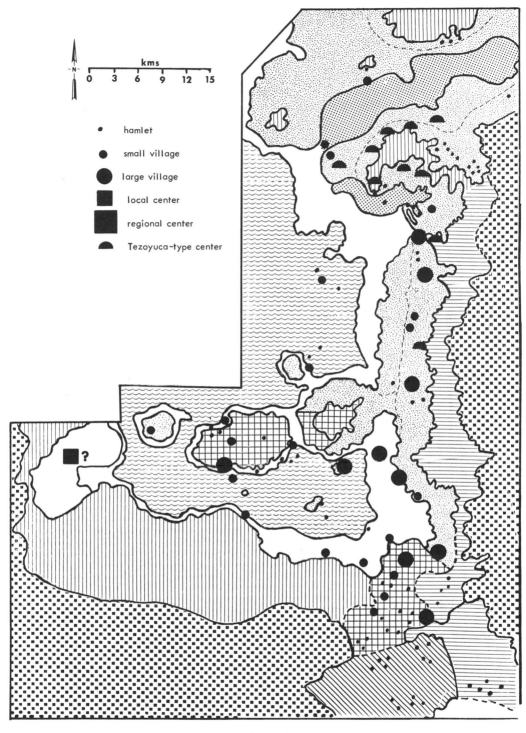

MAP 6. Survey area, showing First Intermediate: Phase 2 settlements.

included 2 sites, each about 30 to 40 hectares in size, with estimated populations of 600 to 1,800 people as well as another site, measuring 100 hectares, with an estimated population of 1,700 to 3,500 people. In the latter site there may be a small temple platform. The remaining 23 sites are all hamlets and small villages. From what we have learned, the overall population size and density, the size of the community, and complexity of sociopolitical structure is clearly of a much lower order than that in the far south; just as clearly, however, the Texcoco population was considerably larger than that in the Teotihuacán Valley.

Occupation in the Teotihuacán Valley appears marginal when compared with the central and southern sites, but it does include three suprahamlet-sized communities (small villages of perhaps 200 to 500 inhabitants) and at least twenty-five hamlets.

The spacing between these large Phase 2 sites is considerably more varied and less regular than that for Phase 1. Around the Lakes Chalco-Xochimilco heartland in the south, intersite distances (spacing between large sites) range from 1 to 5 kilometers. Further north the spacing tends to be greater.

We understand very little of Cuicuilco, a site that may well have been the largest center in the Basin of Mexico in the First Intermediate: Phase 2. Because of an overlay of volcanic lava and modern urbanization, we cannot study the site and environs of Cuicuilco, and this is one of our greatest handicaps in understanding the early demography in the southern Basin; the fact that the area is likely to remain forever beyond our reach is most distressing. Cuicuilco did, however, have a strong regional impact in First Intermediate: Phase 2 times, as is suggested by our failure to find any substantial occupation along the southern shore of Lake Xochimilco. At least one large Phase 1 site exists in this region, and sites of later periods are common. The apparent lack of occupation in the Lake Xochimilco area during Phase 2 may be related to a rapid population nucleation and concentration at Cuicuilco.

Three new zones were occupied for the first time in Phase 2: (1) the poorly drained eastern shore of Lake Texcoco, (2) the higher Piedmont southeast of Lake Chalco along the pass leading up to the high Amecameca subvalley, and (3) the Alluvial Plain in the Teotihuacán Valley, where the three largest communities in that area are located. In the first two zones, sites are often fairly numerous but small—seldom more than a few hectares in surface area—with no visible architectural remains. Expansion into higher ground in the southern Basin did not include the rugged piedmont directly south of the lake system—a large area that would remain empty and show no significant pre-Hispanic occupation before Late Horizon times. The contorted topography and heavy rock rubble undoubtedly restricted the agricultural productivity of the higher piedmont, especially in the absence of terracing, which most modern cultivators find essential for meeting crop yields. The great contrast in occupational history between this rugged southern piedmont and the smooth piedmont formed on older geological deposits on the eastern side of the Basin of Mexico clearly indicates the great disparity in subsistence value between these two regions through most of the pre-Hispanic cultural sequence.

First Intermediate: Phase 3 (ca. 200 B.C.–A.D. 100)

For Phase 3 we are especially plagued with problems of ceramic chronology. Three basic ceramic complexes may fall into this general time span: (1) Tezoyuca (Sanders 1965, M. West 1965), which seems to be concentrated around the edges of the Patlachique Range in the southern Teotihuacán Valley and the northern Texcoco region; (2) Patlachique (Sanders 1965, J. R. Parsons 1971a, 1971b), which is widely distributed over our entire survey area; and (3) Tzacualli (Sanders 1965, J. R. Parsons 1971a, 1971b, R. Millon, Drewitt, and Bennyhoff 1965), which is apparently restricted to the northeastern portion of the Basin but which is difficult to separate from Patlachique in our badly weathered surface samples. We will not attempt to deal with these ceramic problems now, but most of the observations we will make here apply best to the Patlachique phase. In earlier reports (Sanders 1965, J. R. Parsons 1971a, 1971b) Tezoyuca was considered as a contemporary regional variant of the Patlachique; now, however, we suspect that it may overlap in time mainly with the Phase 2 Cuanalan/Ticomán assemblage, thus dating from 300–200 B.C. Apparently Tzacualli falls primarily into the first century A.D., an especially critical era regarding the formation of the Teotihuacán urban system. Unfortunately, however, we do not have good control of regional demography during this phase.

The First Intermediate: Phase 3 is characterized by some very basic departures from the demographic patterns of the preceding periods. It is a complex phase, with considerable regional variation and differentiation in occupation. During this period there were two major regional centers at opposite corners of the Basin of Mexico: Teotihuacán in the northeast, and Cuicuilco, some 60 kilometers to the southwest. The size and occupational characteristics of Cuicuilco remain poorly understood; however R. Millon's (1972) work indicates that Teotihuacán covered an area of about 600 hectares and contained perhaps 10,000 people. There is also good evidence for craft workshops and ceremonial-civic architecture of modest dimensions at Teotihuacán. As for Cuicuilco, it may well have been a roughly similar size and character, although its major temple platforms seem to be larger than any contemporary architecture at Teotihuacán. There are no other known centers anywhere in our survey area or elsewhere in the Basin that even remotely approach the size and complexity of Teotihuacán and Cuicuilco during the First Intermediate: Phase 3.

Within our survey area five main settlement pattern categories can be distinguished for Phase 3. The first settlement pattern, which is concentrated around the eastern and southern edges of Lake Chalco, has its core area in the Lower Piedmont, at the juncture of the broad Lakeshore Plain and Lower Piedmont zones east of the lake. In this latter zone are a half-dozen large, nucleated sites (most of which had also been occupied in Phase 2 times), with several approaching or exceeding 100 hectares in size. Large, nucleated sites up to 70 hectares in area extend along the lowermost flank of the Lower Piedmont along the south shore of the lake as far west as Atlapulco, but these are much more widely spaced than those further east. Small sites up to 15 hectares in area are numerous, but monumental architecture seems to be absent or very poorly developed throughout the general area. It is within this region of our survey area, however, that we found the highest population size and density anywhere in Phase 3 times —a continuation of the situation during Phases 1 and 2.

The second settlement pattern can be distinguished in two marginal regions of the Basin of Mexico: (1) the high Amecameca subvalley in the far southeastern corner of our survey area, and (2) the dry northwestern corner of the Basin of Mexico, north of Lake Zumpango. Here we found only scattered small sites, with only very few approaching 10 to 15 hectares in area. Most sites are considerably less than 5 hectares, and architecture is totally absent. In the northern region the Phase 3 sites represent the earliest significant occupation of the region.

The third settlement pattern—found on the Ixtapalapa Peninsula—has very few sites. Most occupation here is concentrated in several substantial sites, up to 40 hectares in area, located well up in the rugged piedmont. One of these sites contains abundant platform mounds standing up to 7 meters high (Blanton 1972b). This settlement pattern is unique within our survey area in that it represents an apparent demographic decline and abandonment of large areas of the Ixtapalapa Peninsula from Phase 2 times. Almost everywhere else the transition from Phase 2 to Phase 3 saw population stability, as in the southeast, or a rather impressive population expansion, as in the Texcoco and Teotihuacán regions.

The Texcoco region, east of Lake Texcoco, is a fourth settlement pattern. Here we discerned four settlement clusters, each including a hilltop site with modest monumental architecture (most of which seems to have predominantly Tezoyuca ceramics). We also located a large nucleated settlement (up to 100 hectares) on the Lower Piedmont, with a small civic center and abundant small sites scattered rather widely over the entire area. The four settlement clusters are evenly spaced, and each contained roughly 5,000 inhabitants.

In the Teotihuacán Valley—the fifth settlement system—about half the population was concentrated on the center of Teotihuacán itself. The remaining half was widely distributed in a variety of much smaller settlements, primarily on the Lower Piedmont.

In summary, the First Intermediate: Phase 3 presents a diversified patterning of settlement. Except for the Ixtapalapa Peninsula, the general overall impression is one of maximum population density for the overall First Intermediate period, with a marked concentration of settlement on the Lower Piedmont, as well as considerable variation in settlement types, ranging from tiny hamlets to sizable communities, some of which had incipient urban characteristics. (See Map 7.) The five major settlement patterns just presented suggest that we can expect a certain amount of regional variability in the natural and sociocultural factors that have produced these very different settlement configurations. Although there is substantial population growth from the Phase 2 base, the rate of increase is quite variable within our survey area: there is only a slight expansion in the southern Basin, while the northern area sees four- or fivefold increase.

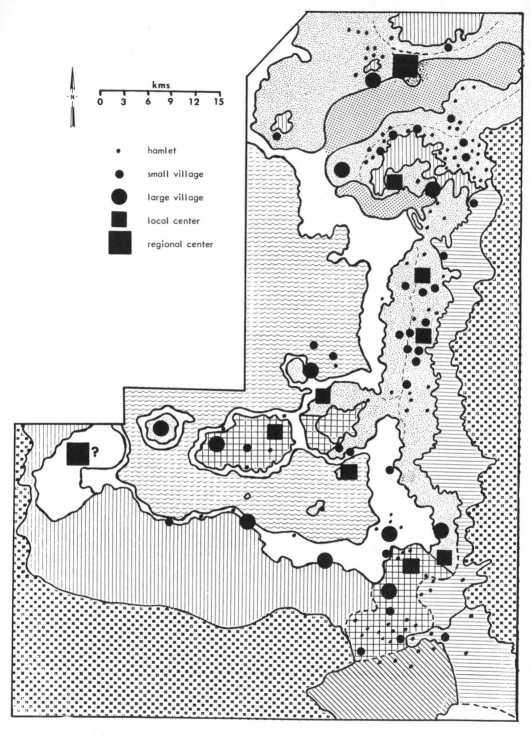

MAP 7. Survey area, showing First Intermediate: Phase 3 Settlements.

> *First Intermediate:* Phase 4 (ca. A.D. 100–400)
> *Middle Horizon* (ca. A.D. 400–700)

The first century A.D. was a critical period in the Basin of Mexico. During this time (the Tzacualli phase), Teotihuacán grew rapidly to become a massive urban center extending over about 20 square kilometers, with a population estimated at between 30,000 and 50,000 (R. Millon 1973:93). Then, while Teotihuacán's surface extent changed only slightly, its population spiraled upward, until, by A.D. 500, it numbered well over 100,000. R. Millon and his co-workers have documented the great architectural and functional variability within Teotihuacán's urban zone (R. Millon 1970b, 1973, Spence 1967a). However, because of problems with ceramic chronology, we are unable to discuss regional settlement patterning or demographic patterns for the critical first century A.D. in any meaningful way. Rather, we will try to describe the Middle Horizon settlement pattern in our survey area and compare this to the First Intermediate: Phase 3 (Patlachique phase). We will discuss this long period as a unit, since present indications are that settlement, at least outside of the Teotihuacán Valley, was relatively stable, that is, most of our sites seem to have similar occupations during both early and late phases of this period.

Within the Teotihuacán Valley virtually all of the population resided within the urban center itself. Most of the significant rural occupation was restricted to a few relatively small communities well up into the Lower Piedmont, aligned along extensions of the city's major east-west and south avenues. Sanders's excavations at one rural site (Sanders 1967), several kilometers west of Teotihuacán, suggest that maguey cultivation and pulque production may have been the primary activities there. In fact, Sanders (1965, 1967) has suggested a settlement system in which the few rural communities in the Teotihuacán Valley performed special functions, such as maguey production in marginal areas, while most of the urban inhabitants intensively cultivated the irrigated Alluvial Plain. These hypotheses have yet to be adequately tested. One clear exception is a large concentration of small towns and large villages on the north slope of Cerro Gordo, outside the Valley proper.

A delineation of occupational patterns south of the Teotihuacán Valley has illuminated some aspects of Teotihuacán's urbanization and regional influences within its own heartland. Everywhere in our survey area outside of the Teotihuacán Valley, the Middle Horizon settlement pattern

85

consists of numerous small sites, usually hamlets or villages. Most are smaller than 10 hectares, although a few range between 15 and 25 hectares. Monumental architecture is generally lacking. While there is no apparent patterning or structuring of site location, most of the sites are situated in the Lower Piedmont in locations comparable to the First Intermediate: Phase 3 sites; however, there are some sites in nearly every natural zone. The high Amecameca subvalley remains marginal, and the rugged southern piedmont is still virtually unoccupied.

Only two or three sites deviate from this general pattern: one, Tx-EC-32 (Portesuelo), covers about 60 to 80 hectares (J. R. Parsons 1971b), and another, Ix-EC-37 (on the flank of Cerro de la Estrella at the western end of the Ixtapalapa Peninsula), is about the same size (Blanton 1972b). The occupation at both sites is badly obscured by much heavier later material, but we believe that these are small local centers (with at most a few thousand inhabitants) that contain some very modest ceremonial-civic architecture.

A third site is a substantial ceremonial complex located on a low hill overlooking the Papalotla floodplain. Although it lacks an attached residential area, it may have served as an administrative center for the integration of economic activities in the northern and central portions of the Texcoco area.

Particularly impressive is the demographic depression in relation to the preceding phase. This depression, which characterizes Middle Horizon occupation everywhere south of the Teotihuacán Valley, is most marked in the two general areas of heaviest First Intermediate: Phase 3 occupation: (1) in the Texcoco region, where we estimate a decline from almost 20,000 people to substantially fewer than 5,000, and (2) in the broad Piedmont east of Lake Chalco, where a Middle Horizon population of perhaps 2,000 compares with a First Intermediate: Phase 3 figure of probably close to 20,000. On the Ixtapalapa Peninsula the Middle Horizon population appears to be roughly half of the figure of 6,000 to 7,000 for the preceding phase. In the more marginal area south of Lakes Chalco-Xochimilco, a decline of about 50 percent also seems likely.

The only exception to this general pattern of population decline is found in the northwestern corner of the Basin of Mexico, where our 1973 surveys in the Zumpango region clearly indicate a substantial population increase in the Middle Horizon. Here, the very sparse occupation of the First Intermediate: Phase 3 expanded substantially, and Middle Horizon sites are found throughout this section of our survey area. Despite this considerable increase, however, Middle Horizon occupation in the Zumpango Region is very similar to what we have found elsewhere in the Basin of Mexico outside the Teotihuacán Valley: a uniform scattering of small sites, few exceeding the 5 to 10 hectare range, with very limited architectural remains.

Even at this stage in our investigation, it seems apparent that in comparing First Intermediate: Phase 3 and Middle Horizon occupations in our survey area, we are dealing with profoundly different settlement systems, even though we still do not completely understand what those systems are. We saw that the regional Phase 3 system was characterized by a three- or four-level settlement hierarchy: (1) two very large sites of several hundred hectares, each having abundant monumental architecture, at opposite corners of the Basin of Mexico; (2) numerous middle-level centers measuring between 40 and 100 hectares, with those in the Texcoco area having noticeable ceremonial-civic architecture, while those in the southeast do not; (3) hilltop sites with modest ceremonial-civic architecture; and (4) numerous smaller sites of variable size.

By contrast, the Middle Horizon system (see Map 8) is exceedingly top-heavy, with one huge center at least forty times larger than any other contemporary community. The next level in the Middle Horizon settlement hierarchy is represented by only two sites within our survey area, both apparently modest local centers of 60 to 80 hectares. There is a substantial Middle Horizon site of unknown dimensions at Atzcapotzalco on the western shore of Lake Texcoco, outside our survey area. Today this location is wholly covered by modern urbanization, but investigations several decades ago by Vaillant (Mayer-Oakes 1960:175) suggest that it may have been roughly comparable to the two other local centers in our survey area. Below this sparsely represented second tier in the Middle Horizon system lies a presently undifferentiated level of numerous small villages and hamlets. Further analysis within this group may detect an additional level of a few sites in the 15-to-25-hectare range.

A significant part of the rapid population growth and urbanization at Teotihuacán itself, in the first centuries of the Christian era, was probably caused by a large-scale influx of people into Teotihuacán from over a large area, but most particularly from the Texcoco district. At the moment, all indications are that most of the Basin of Mexico was profoundly affected by the migrations, and that provincial populations were substantially de-

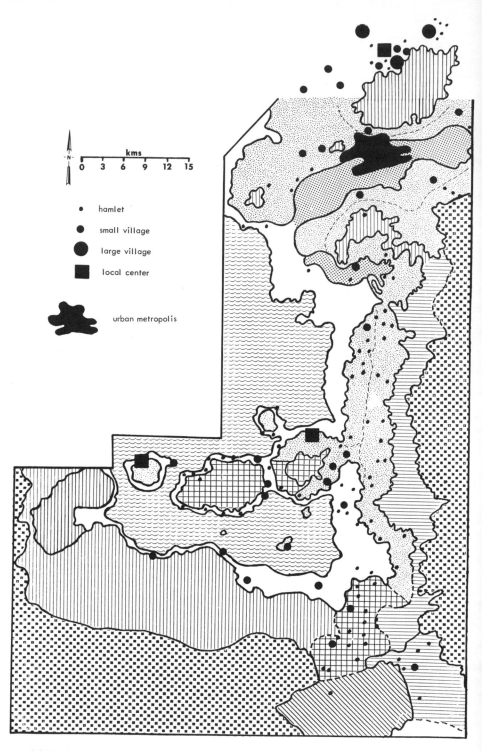

MAP 8. Survey area, showing Middle Horizon settlements.

pleted as the urban center expanded. We cannot now infer the causal factors or sociopolitical mechanisms that structured this remarkable demographic process, but judging from architectural features of Tzacualli-phase Teotihuacán (first century A.D.), the ideology of integration was predominantly religious.

By whatever means the process was effected, the extreme population nucleation and rural population depression also seem to have characterized the First Intermediate: Phase 3–Middle Horizon transition in the adjacent Tlaxcala-Puebla region, where a few large centers were also emerging (Dumond 1972a). From this, we can infer that much of central Mexico was participating in the same general processes which so transformed the terminal phase of the First Intermediate period. Even further afield, Adams (1972) has shown that in Uruk and elsewhere in southern Mesopotamia, there was a marked regional depression of rural settlement in the early third millennium B.C. and a rapid growth of large urban centers. This material indicates that extreme population concentration was adaptive, though not necessarily for the same reasons, in the consolidation of some primary state systems wherever they developed.

There is an additional dimension of Teotihuacán's rise to dominance: the initial spurt of Teotihuacán's rapid growth and florescence correlates closely with the abrupt demise, by volcanic destruction, of Cuicuilco (Teotihuacán's main competitor in the Basin) at some point shortly after the beginning of the Christian era. Thus, Teotihuacán's dominance of the Basin of Mexico in the first century A.D. may have been caused, in part, not only by the sudden destruction of Cuicuilco, but also by the loss of much of its productive potential.

Second Intermediate: Phase 1 (ca. A.D. 700–900)

The eighth and ninth centuries of the Christian era witnessed a transformation of regional settlement patterning in the Basin as profound as that which occurred between the First Intermediate and the Middle Horizon periods. A consistent pattern is now discernible within our survey area for the Second Intermediate: Phase 1. Teotihuacán itself rapidly declined to a fraction of its former size (Sanders 1965), an event that was apparently accompanied by burning and abandonment of at least part of the site's central core area (R. F. Millon 1972:109). Several large nucleated settlements began to develop around the edges of the Alluvial Plain in the lower, irrigable section of the Teotihuacán Valley where Middle Horizon occupation had been sparse (Sanders 1965). We also know that there was substantial Second Intermediate: Phase 1 occupation around the northwestern shore of Lake Texcoco, outside our survey area (Rattray 1966, Tozzer 1921). It was perhaps, the largest such concentration in the Basin: Coyotlatelco, Pueblo Perdido, and Tenayo—all of considerable size—were located here.

Immediately south of the Teotihuacán Valley there was a sudden growth of six large, nucleated sites, each measuring between 100 and 400 hectares in area. At least four of these sites contain substantial ceremonial-civic architecture in the form of temple platforms up to 10 meters high. All of these centers developed from much smaller Middle Horizon sites—such as Portesuelo, Cerro de la Estrella, and Xico—on the same location. The six large sites are widely spaced and occur in four clusters: (1) a closely spaced pair (TX-ET-4, TX-ET-7) north of the Rio Papalotla totaling about 380 hectares and containing perhaps 15,000 people; (2) another such pair west of Chalco with a total area of roughly 200 hectares and a total population of about 7,000 people; (3) a single community at Portesuelo (TX-ET-18) covering more than 400 hectares and inhabited by perhaps 10,000 people; and (4) a single large site at Cerro de la Estrella (IX-ET-13) measuring about 170 hectares with an estimated population of about 4,500. These four settlement clusters are separated by 20-to-30-kilometer intervals of very limited occupation, consisting of small, widely spaced hamlets and small villages. (See Map 9).

Phase 1 shows a very obvious orientation toward low-lying ground. In the south there is a marked clustering around the lakeshore, while in the Texcoco region occupation is concentrated near the lower edge of the Lower Piedmont adjacent to the floodplains of the two major stream systems. Settlement at higher elevations is present but quite limited. The only area that shows a significant proliferation of small sites is the shoreline of the Ixtapalapa Peninsula.

Our 1973 surveys in the northwestern Basin of Mexico have indicated a somewhat comparable settlement pattern here. A single large nucleated site of about 40 or 50 hectares occupies one end of a huge flat-topped mesa that rises steeply to nearly 300 meters above the main Valley floor. We found large platform mounds up to 5 meters high at this site, along with a distinct plaza complex. Elsewhere in the Zumpango region, occupation

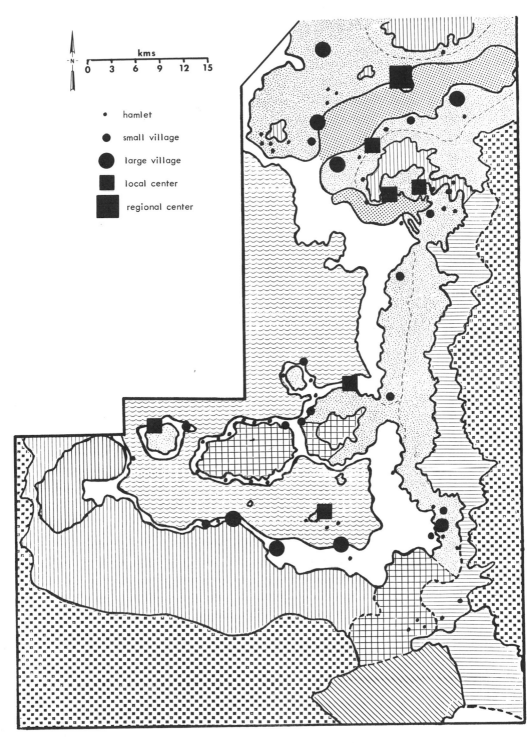

MAP 9.   Survey area, showing Second Intermediate: Phase 1 settlements.

of this period is restricted to scattered small sites, where architectural remains are absent.

The settlement pattern data suggest that as the power and prestige of Teotihuacán disintegrated after A.D. 7òo, the regional population of the Teotihuacán Valley declined to a point (about 40,000 people—Sanders 1965) roughly in keeping with the local productive capacity of the lower Valley. Large blocks of population sloughed off from the decaying Teotihuacán center and spread out into the most productive zones of the sparsely occupied remainder of the Basin. Once we know more about demography at the newly developing centers like Tula and Cholula, we might see substantial population inputs from Teotihuacán into these urban centers at about this time. This seems particularly likely since our overall population estimates in our survey area for the Second Intermediate: Phase 2 fall significantly below those of the Middle Horizon. The centrifugal forces that are so abundantly manifest in the Second Intermediate: Phase 1 settlement patterning make it quite clear that the mechanisms which had maintained the top-heavy Middle Horizon settlement system for some 600 years quickly ceased to operate after about A.D. 700.

The settlement in our survey area still had a nucleated aspect, with almost all population south of the Teotihuacán Valley concentrated in a half-dozen substantial sites. The relatively even spacing of these occupational loci suggests a fairly equivalent apportionment of resources, with each locus having access to a surrounding radius of roughly 10 to 15 kilometers. The decidedly nucleated aspect of this system may reflect a number of factors: (1) a holdover, on a miniature scale, of some organizational mechanism from the preceding Middle Horizon; (2) a series of constraints emanating from one or more new power centers outside the survey area (for example, Tula, Cholula, Xochicalco); or (3) an intensely competitive hostile situation favoring nucleated settlement.

If we assume a substantial population residing in the area west of Lake Texcoco, as indicated by Rattray's studies (1966, 1972), we seem to have at least three great settlement clusters: the Ixtapalapa Peninsula, including the Chalco and Portesuelo clusters; the Teotihuacán Valley, including the Papalotla cluster; and the Tacuba area. This arrangement probably represents some kind of ethnic or political alignments. However, we are not suggesting that each of these clusters was politically centralized, since the almost equal size of some of the large settlements within them would argue against this.

It is clear that in order to understand the full implications of our Second Intermediate: Phase 1 settlement data, we are going to have to look further afield than was necessary in the case of the First Intermediate: Phase 3 or Middle Horizon. When considered in isolation, the Second Intermediate: Phase 1 settlement pattern in our survey area is more difficult to understand than the First Intermediate: Phase 3. As a result, we must expand our minimal unit of regional analysis to take into account the many new complicating factors created by the long existence of Teotihuacán's large state operation. We need to know what is happening in terms of regional demography at the newly emerging centers (such as Cholula, Xochicalco, and Tula) for the later Middle Horizon and Second Intermediate: Phase 1.

Second Intermediate: Phase 2 (ca. A.D. 900–1150)

The single most outstanding settlement feature of the Second Intermediate: Phase 2 is its dispersion. (See Map 10.) Large nucleated sites are virtually absent, with substantial sites occurring only at Xico Island in eastern Lake Chalco, at Portesuelo (TX-LT-53) in the southern Texcoco region, at Teotihuacán itself, and at a few other localities around the edge of the Alluvial Plain in the Teotihuacán Valley. All of these were centers in Phase 1 times, but they were apparently of much larger size. Apart from these small local centers, then, settlement is extremely dispersed and widely scattered over the entire survey area. Villages and hamlets comprise the vast majority of site types—in fact, our surveys have revealed at least 250 sites in this phase. The largest Phase 2 sites, except for Portesuelo and Xico, are in the Teotihuacán Valley. The small sites occur in virtually all environmental zones, including even the Alluvial Plain in the Texcoco area.

Overall there seems to be a substantial demographic depression in relation to the preceding phase. However, this apparent depression varies considerably within our survey area. In the Teotihuacán Valley, population is reduced by roughly one-fourth. In the Texcoco region the data suggest a depression by about two-thirds. In the southern Basin of Mexico the Phase 2 population seems to be maintained at about the Phase 1 level. Thus while there is a very substantial population loss in the central portion of our survey area, there is relatively little change for the northern

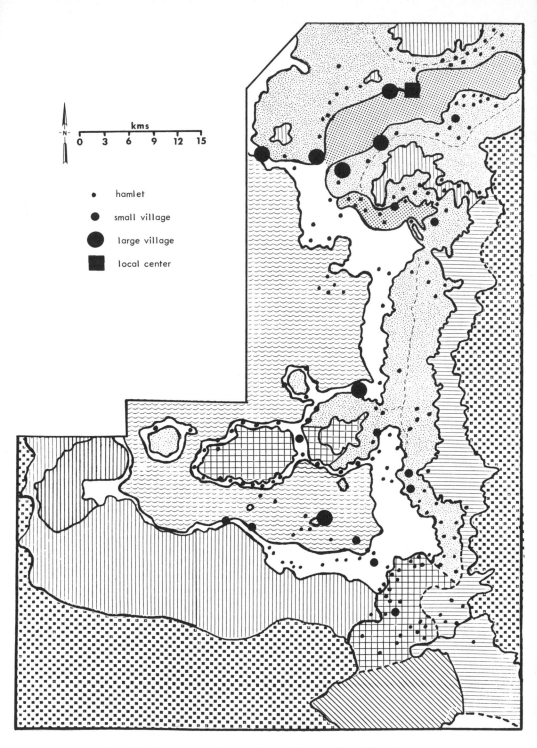

MAP 10.   Survey area, showing Second Intermediate: Phase 2 settlements.

and southern areas. All of these conclusions, we should point out, are subject to revision, especially when one considers the difficulty of estimating population during periods characterized by such a dispersed settlement pattern.

Once again we find it difficult to understand these settlement data in the absence of regional demographic information from the areas of Tula, Cholula, Xochicalco, and the western Basin of Mexico. Why did demographic depression occur at such different rates in our survey area? If the substantial population losses we noted in our central survey area are valid, it is apparent that these losses were not being entirely absorbed in the adjacent sections of our survey area. Thus, we might expect to see significant population inputs for this period at Tula, Cholula, Xochicalco, and elsewhere outside our survey area. We are also presently at a loss to explain the extreme dispersion of Phase 2 occupation (see Chapter 8).

Our 1973 surveys in the northwestern Basin of Mexico have provided some additional insight into these problems. The northwestern sector saw a substantial population increase between Phases 1 and 2 of the Second Intermediate period. The Phase 2 sites are numerous, and often large and nucleated (including two that approach or exceed 100 hectares). In addition, sizable platform mounds are common at many sites. The Zumpango region is unique within our survey area—only here does the Second Intermediate: Phase 2 occupation rival the size and complexity of that of the subsequent Late Horizon. Apparently whatever population reduction occurred in the south was more than compensated for by increases in the far north. It is probably significant that our 1973 survey area abuts directly onto the immediate heartland of Tula itself.

Second Intermediate: Phase 3 and Late Horizon (A.D. 1200–1520)

It has sometimes been assumed that the ceramic complex characterized by Aztec I (Culhuacán) Black-on-Orange pottery (Griffin and Espejo 1947) is partly contemporary with the Second Intermediate: Phase 2 Mazapan complex (J. R. Parsons 1970). Moreover, several writers, ourselves included, have felt that the Aztec I assemblage was a southern Basin of Mexico tradition whose origins are closely tied in with the Cholula ceramic tradition. Likewise, the Mazapan complex has been considered a northern Basin of Mexico tradition, closely linked with Tula. In our recent regional surveys in the southern Basin, however, we have noted a very distinct Second Intermediate: Phase 2 ceramic complex, with many good Mazapan markers, existing as far south as our investigations have extended. Even more telling, Muller (1970:139–40) reports an abundance of standard Mazapan ceramic markers from her Cholulteca II phase at Cholula. On the other hand, we have found that while Aztec I material is quite common in the southern Basin, Aztec II Black-on-Orange (Tenayuca variant) is scarce here. Conversely, Aztec II Black-on-Orange is abundant in the central Basin of Mexico, where Aztec I is practically absent. The dividing line between Aztec I and Aztec II pottery seems to be roughly the Ixtapalapa Peninsula.

Some additional complexities have arisen as a result of our 1973 surveys in the northwestern Basin of Mexico. Here the Mazapan ceramic complex (Second Intermediate: Phase 2) is everywhere succeeded by the Aztec III assemblage (Tenochtitlan variant). Only at Xaltocan, an island site in Lakes Xaltocan-Zumpango, is Aztec II pottery present in quantity. Elsewhere in the Zumpango region only a few pieces of Aztec II material have been noted. Recent surveys around Tula and its immediate sustaining area show a corresponding low frequency of Aztec II in that area. Thus, we have an unusual situation: in the southern part of our survey area (from the Ixtapalapa Peninsula southward), we apparently have a Mazapan–Aztec I–Aztec III sequence, with abundant Aztec II material only at Culhuacán (at the western end of the Ixtapalapa Peninsula); in the central sector of our survey area (between Xaltocan on the north and Ixtapalapa on the south), we have a Mazapan–Aztec II–Aztec III sequence. In the northwestern part of our survey area, we have found a Mazapan–Aztec III succession.

In summary, the data suggest that the Mazapan assemblage (in several closely related regional variants) is chronologically antecedent to all variants of the Aztec ceramic complex in most of the Basin of Mexico. The Aztec I assemblage (except in very small quantities) is very clearly restricted to the southern Basin. The Aztec II assemblage seems to be restricted to the central and north-central sectors. The Aztec III assemblage is present, and very uniform, over the entire Basin. Thus, in defining occupations and estimating populations for the Second Intermediate: Phase 3, we should probably use the Aztec I assemblage in our southern survey area, the Aztec II assemblage in the central and north-central survey area, and perhaps some late subphase of the Mazapan assemblage (which has not yet been defined) in the northwest. The alternative to this procedure is to have the entire Zumpango region virtually without population during the Second Intermediate: Phase 3, and a huge population loss before rapid recovery in the Late Horizon.

Our demographic reconstructions for the Second Intermediate: Phase 3 are most secure for the Basin's central area, between Xaltocan and Ixtapalapa. Here there is a very substantial population expansion and population nucleation from the dispersed Second Intermediate: Phase 2 base. Modest urban communities abruptly appear at Ixtapalapa, Chimalhuacán, Coatlínchan, Huexotla, Cuanalan, and Teotihuacán. Of these, only Teotihuacán had a substantial Second Intermediate: Phase 2 occupation. However, throughout this sector of our survey area, many Second Intermediate: Phase 2 hamlets developed into large Phase 3 villages.

For the southern survey area there is less apparent growth during Phase 3 in relation to Phase 2. Many small scattered Phase 2 sites in the Piedmont were abandoned, but there was considerable nucleation and growth at small urban centers at Culhuacán, Chalco, and Xico (only Xico had a substantial Phase 2 occupation). Although our population estimates for the southern area are not yet complete, it appears that from Phase 2 to Phase 3 there may have been a slight population increase, most of which is explained by the development of nucleated centers around the edges of Lake Chalco. Such lakeside concentration of occupation suggests that chinampa agriculture first developed on a fairly large scale during Phase 3 times. The Lake Chalco occupation is the only point within our survey area where settlement data suggest an expansion of agriculture into new niches during the Second Intermediate: Phase 3.

The Phase 2 to Phase 3 transition in the Zumpango region of the northwestern Basin remains unclear. If Phase 3 occupation is actually represented there by a still unrecognized late subphase of the Mazapan assemblage, then the apparent Phase 2 occupation may be somewhat smaller than what we have suggested. Such a situation might also mean that Phase 2 and Phase 3 occupations in this northwestern area did not differ greatly. This tentative reconstruction seems preferable to equating the near absence of Aztec II pottery in this region with a very low population level.

Urbanization and population expansion progressed at an accelerating rate during the Late Horizon (see Map 11). New urban centers appeared, generally along the lakeshore, but also on the interior Piedmont.

Although some Aztec II occupation occurred at Texcoco, most of the occupation there was late. J. R. Parsons (1971b) estimates that Late Horizon Texcoco covered approximately 450 hectares and had a population of between 12,000 and 25,000 people. Sanders's (1970) independent evaluation of the sixteenth-century documentary sources would suggest that the higher figure is correct. Besides the size of the town, Parsons also reports additional archeological evidence of major developments in the level of political organization, with a new type of site (also reported in the documentary literature), the "royal retreat." The archaeological examples of this are TX-A-6 on the lakeshore near Atenco and, of course, the archaeological remains of the famous gardens of Nezahualcoyotl at Texcotzingo (TX-A-62).

The major population cluster for the Late Horizon, however, was the dual city of Tenochtitlan-Tlatelolco and the vast complex of smaller towns and villages on the neighboring lakeshore. Sanders's documentary estimates would suggest a total population in this area of approximately 300,000 people.

During the Late Horizon rural occupation expanded at a phenomenal rate, especially in the northern two-thirds of our survey area. Previously marginal niches, such as the Upper Piedmont and some parts of the Lakeshore Plain, now have abundant occupation. Much of the Chalco-Xochimilco lakebed has been totally transformed into chinampa plots with sophisticated hydraulic controls (Palerm 1973, Armillas 1971). We strongly suspect that for the first time similar large-scale drainage had also transformed much of the swampy eastern shoreland of Lake Texcoco into productive agricultural land.

Charlton's (1972b) work with Colonial ceramics indicates that some material which we have considered as Late Horizon may actually date to the century after the Spanish contact. This may eventually require some downward revision of our estimated Aztec population, but almost certainly not to an extent that would affect the general validity of our present interpretations and impressions.

One final observation on Late Horizon population concerns the contrast between settlement patterns and rate of population expansion be-

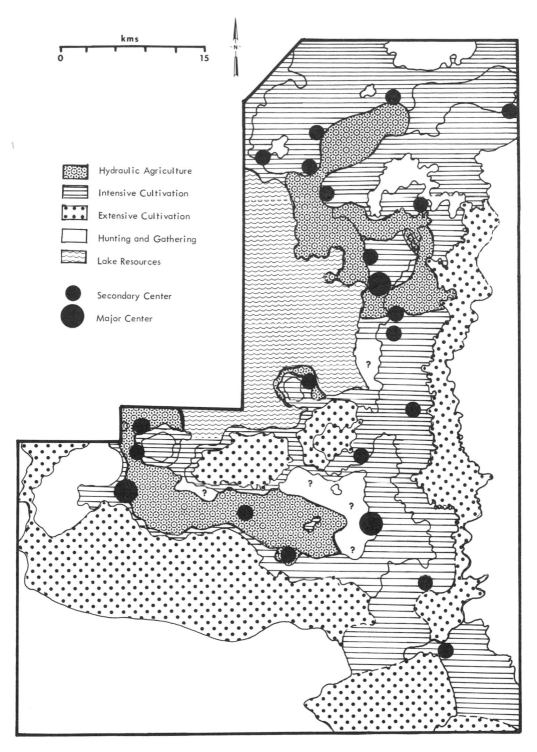

MAP 11. Survey area, showing Late Horizon urban communities.

tween the southern third and the northern two-thirds of our survey area. In the northern section (the Teotihuacán Valley, Texcoco region) Aztec rural occupation is characterized by densely sown but dispersed housemounds. In the south rural occupation is much less substantial, and individual housemounds are seldom apparent on the ground surface, except in the lakebed chinampa district. Our estimates of overall population for the northern area far exceed those of the southern regions, and these estimates of population distribution, based on site survey, agree strikingly with Sanders' (1970) reconstruction of population distribution for the sixteenth century.

7

The Agricultural History
of the Basin of Mexico

WILLIAM T. SANDERS

Department of Anthropology
The Pennsylvania State University

INTRODUCTION

In Chapter 5 we discussed the natural environment of the Basin and the features that were particularly relevant to the problems of an agricultural population with a maize-based crop complex. The major features may be summarized as follows:

(1) The soils are not only easily cultivated using Neolithic tools, but they are generally fertile and capable of sustained cultivation with modest application of simple soil restoration techniques (that is, animal and vegetable fertilizers, crop rotation, short-phase fallowing, intercropping, floodwater and permanent irrigation, and terracing). There is, however, a high percentage of sloping terrain where soils are markedly susceptible to erosion, and constant effort is required to control this destructive process.

(2) The plant cover is fragile and easily controlled with simple tools.

(3) The rainfall-temperature regime is favorable to maize cultivation

only in the south. In the central and northern parts of the Basin the combination of early frosts and retarded rains, plus internal droughts, makes maize production difficult and crop loss frequent.

(4) In a number of areas, local permanent water resources are available for permanent irrigation, and the numerous barrancas provide water for floodwater irrigation. Such systems, however, require intensive land use, heavy expenditures of labor per man, and suprafamily (and often supracommunity) cooperation to maintain, construct, and operate.

(5) Since the summer rains generally provide adequate moisture in areas with moderately deep to deep soils, the primary need is preplanting irrigation. Using this method, the farmer can get a head start on the rainy season, and the plants have more time to grow before the fall frosts. Even in areas of permanent irrigation, however, most of the humidity for plant growth comes from rainfall—which means that a small amount of irrigation water goes a long way. Mexican agronomers call this system *medio riego*.

(6) The lakes were a tremendously significant resource for the pre-Hispanic and Colonial populations. Not only did they provide a natural highway system for a people lacking beasts of burden, but they also linked all parts of the Basin—in fact, most of the major population centers in 1519 were located near lakeshores. In addition, the lakes were important sources of protein foods for a population with few domestic animals, and they provided other products, especially salt. The freshwater Lake Xochimilco was nearly covered by artificial, island-like gardens called chinampas, which were the most intensively cultivated and productive lands in Mesoamerica; the chinampas provided much of the surplus foods needed to support the urban communities in 1519.

(7) Internally, there is considerable variability in geographical characteristics within the Basin, a condition that stimulated local specialization and trade. Variations in vegetation, topography, soil depth, water resources, amount and distribution of rainfall, and elevation and spatial position regarding mountain passes and lakeshores, along with the distributions of specialized resources (for example, salt, clay, obsidian, lumber, lime, and stone) all acted as factors promoting this specialization and trade.

Finally, ranges of small hills within the Basin tend to isolate parts of it into smaller topographic and hydrographic units.

In this chapter we will explain the means by which the pre-Hispanic populations adapted to these environmental features, with particular focus on water and soil conservation systems. It was only by using such systems as permanent and floodwater irrigation, swamp reclamation, and terracing that the urban civilization achieved the population base needed to support itself.

CANAL IRRIGATION

Types of Irrigation

Today, the basic irrigation pattern in the Basin is one in which water is conducted directly from sources to the agricultural field, and storage techniques are relatively rare and undeveloped. This system is a distinctly inefficient use of a resource. The technology is generally simple. It involves the use of dams of earth and rock, brush, or masonry, as well as simple ditches excavated into the soil layers or the tepetate subsoil. According to the nature of the water source, two types of irrigation exist: permanent spring-based irrigation and floodwater irrigation.

The floodwater system may, at times, be unreliable. For example, most of the natural drainage of the Basin is seasonal, and a stream will frequently flow for only a few hours during and after a heavy rain shower. In the southeast, where rainfall is heavier and where meltwater from the glaciers of Popocatepetl and Iztaccíhuatl adds to the flow, streams may be permanent or flow for several months of the year, but these conditions occur precisely where irrigation is least needed to ensure crop production. A number of springs, however, do occur in areas where irrigation either markedly improves productivity or is necessary for dependable cropping. The largest concentration is at San Juan Teotihuacán, where 80 to 100 springs are located within an area of a few square kilometers; and in the 1920s these springs provided an annual average flow of approximately 1,000 liters per second. Additional major sources occur above Texcoco, at the junction of the Upper Piedmont with the Sierra (34 springs with a total output, in the 1920s, of 423 liters per second); along the lakeside edge of Cerro Chimalhuacán; at the sources of the Rio Cuauhtitlán; and above Coyoacán. The major sources of the water needed to maintain Lakes Chalco and Xochimilco at adequate levels for chinampa cultivation during the dry season were numerous springs strung along the south edge of the lakes.

All of the springs just mentioned were sources for Late Horizon irrigation systems. The Texcoco and Coyoacán systems provided water for terraces on the Piedmont, as well as for lands on the Lakeshore Plain; the Teotihuacán and Cuauhtitlán systems provided water almost entirely for irrigating the Alluvial Plain.

The second type of irrigation in the Basin draws on numerous floodwaters from the barrancas. Floodwater irrigation can be described in terms of two basic subtypes, one in the plains and the other on the Piedmont. Today, much of the Piedmont is badly scarred by sheet and gulley erosion; too, there is an enormous volume of runoff that ultimately reaches the major portions of the river systems in the Alluvial Plain. In a number of areas, large terrace complexes constructed on the Piedmont trap the runoff from the steeper slopes above them. Some of these arrangements are rather ingenious and sophisticated. In the Cerro Gordo, north slope area, for example, terraces are laid out in vertical strips separated by floodwater canals. The floodwater from above the terrace is directed into the canal, and each terrace has a small earth bank projecting into the canal to divert the stream. In addition, the terraces are not only equipped with ditches to break the force of the water where it enters, but they have lateral as well as lower earth defense walls. Because of the reduced area covered by these terraces today, much of the Piedmont runoff reaches the major tributaries in the Alluvial Plain, where it is available for floodwater irrigation of the deep soils in the plain. A series of masonry dams with wooden gates have been constructed across the streams on the plain. When the gates are closed, the water is backed up into a large pond and immediately diverted by canals to the fields. When fields served by the canal have been irrigated, the gates are opened and the water is allowed to flow down to the next dam. Large barrancas in the middle portion of the Teotihuacán Valley plain may have four or five dams built along their lengths.

The Demographic Potential of Irrigation in the Basin of Mexico

Recently there have been a number of criticisms of the value of Wittfogel's (1957) theoretical concepts as applied to irrigation in the Basin of Mexico. Basically, the criticism is that the irrigation systems were too small and able to supply only a fraction of the food supply; thus, they neither required complex bureaucratic management nor stimulated conflict and competition. In this section we will offer a counter-argument to these criticisms.

With respect to permanent spring-based irrigation, we have detailed data on two of the systems—on the San Juan Teotihuacán springs and the Texcoco Piedmont springs. The San Juan springs system is apparently dying, according to evidence which shows that the output of water has steadily declined over the past fifty years. In the 1920s Gamio et al. (1922) estimated the flow of water at the springs to be 1,000 liters per second. In 1956 Sanders found the springs to have a flow of 580 liters (according to the federal water regulations); at the time the springs regulated 3,652 hectares of land. R. Millon, Hall, and Díaz (1962), in a study dating from the 1960s, estimated the flow of water at only 540 liters. Finally, a recent publication shows that the output since then has dropped to below 500 liters per second (Comisión Hidrológica de la Cuenca del Valle de México 1968). (Current data also show greater month-to-month variability than previously.)

The major cause of the declining output of the San Juan springs in the twentieth century has been the perforation of artesian wells, both within the Valley of Teotihuacán and in the bed of Lake Texcoco. Between 1519 and 1920, enormous amounts of land eroded in the Valley as a result of population decline from disease, as well as the abandonment of agricultural lands on the Piedmont and their conversion to grazing lands. What effect this erosion has had is unknown, but there may have been even more water in the system in 1519 than in 1920. Too, the long period of occupation from the First Intermediate: Phase 1 to the Late Horizon witnessed a continuous process of deforestation, which certainly must have affected the drainage in the area to a great degree. (See Map 12, showing the twentieth-century irrigation system in the Teotihuacán Valley.)

Other permanent water resources on a smaller scale were probably available in First Intermediate times; some may still have been functioning as late as the apogee of Teotihuacán. Mooser, in fact, has postulated the existence of a series of springs within the archaeological zone in Middle Horizon times that provided an additional flow of 100 to 200 liters per second (Lorenzo 1968).

What this means is that the Late Horizon irrigation system could have been at least 1.7 times larger than the recent system, and the Middle Horizon system approximately twice as large and capable of serving a total

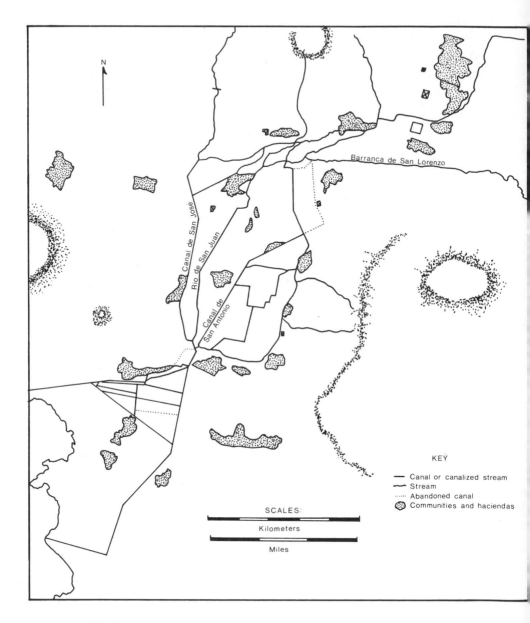

MAP 12.   Irrigation system, contemporary Teotihuacán Valley.

of 7,200 hectares of land. There is direct evidence for the larger size of the Late Horizon system, which we shall discuss in a later section.

In the Texcoco Piedmont 31 springs were still functioning in the 1920s (see Table 3). The springs are grouped not in terms of the present routing of the canal system but in terms of the natural drainage of the area before canalization. (See also Map 13, which shows the spring locations and the structure of the twentieth-century irrigation system in the Texcoco area.)

What is the agricultural significance of the two systems? On the basis of our studies of the contemporary system, an average yield of 1,400 kilos of maize, with minimal or no use of animal fertilizer, is a reasonable calculation. If we assume somewhat lower productivity, because less well-

TABLE 3

TEXCOCO SPRINGS OF THE 1920S

Irrigation System	Water Flow (in liters per second)	Irrigable Area (in hectares)
Rio Papalotla		
Cluster 1 (Springs 1–6)	280	—
Cluster 2 (Springs 10–13)	23	—
Total	303	1,818
Rio Jalapango		
Cluster 1 (Springs 7–9)	30	—
Cluster 2 (Springs 32–34)	38–48	—
Total	68–78	408–462
Rio Coxcacuaco		
Cluster 1 (Springs 14–24)	35	—
Cluster 2 (Springs 25–27)	8	—
Cluster 3 (Spring 28)	4	—
Cluster 4	5	—
Total	52	300
Grand Total	423–433	2,526–2,580

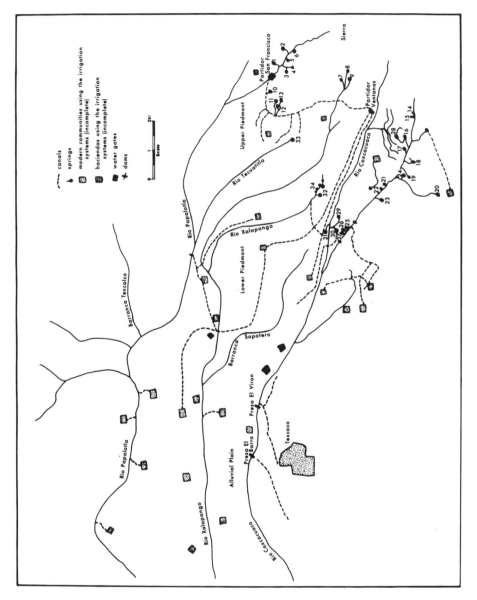

MAP 13. Irrigation system, contemporary Texcoco Piedmont.

developed varieties of maize may have been used in the Middle Horizon period, this figure might be lowered to 1,050 kilos.

In many peasant communities in Mexico and Guatemala today, maize makes up approximately 80 percent of the diet. Because of the very high population density during Late Horizon times, we will assume a comparable reliance, if not on maize alone, at least on the combination of maize and amaranth, the two basic grains available in the area. What little data we have on amaranth suggest comparable requirements of moisture, temperature, and productivity per unit of land, so we can simply combine the two to an overall grain equivalent. For the Middle Horizon and earlier phases, the dependence on maize was probably much less, considering the abundance of wild food resources in the area. We thus suggest the two dietary models shown in Table 4 as possibly representing the pre-Hispanic situation.

TABLE 4

MODELS OF PRE-HISPANIC DIETARY HABITS

	Maize-Amaranth	Beans	Pulque	Misc. Plants	Misc. Animals
Model 1 (Late Horizon)	80%	10%	4%	4%	2%
Model 2 (Middle Horizon and earlier)	65%	10%	4%	10%	11%

On the basis of the studies of contemporary peasant diet, and correlating the data with respect to weight, size, age, and sex variability, the average per capita consumption in pre-Hispanic times was probably about 2,000 kilo-calories per day. If 80 percent of the food supply was derived from maize, then the average annual per capita consumption would be 160 kilos. If 60 percent was derived from maize, then the average annual per capita consumption would be 128 kilos.

Another variable to be considered is the percentage of irrigated land that would be devoted to maize production as opposed to other crops. On the basis of patterns of land use in the Teotihuacán Valley today (where land is devoted either to maize or to a humidity-demanding commercial crop like alfalfa), one could argue for 100 percent maize utilization. However, we have prepared two models, one calculated at 100 percent and the other at a 65 percent dependence on maize (Table 5).

TABLE 5

COMPARATIVE DEMOGRAPHIC CAPACITY—IRRIGATION SYSTEMS IN THE TEOTIHUACÁN VALLEY–TEXCOCO PIEDMONT

| | | 65% Dependence on Maize | | | |
| | | 100% Planted in Maize | | 65% Planted in Maize | |
System	Land Area (in hectares)	1,400 kg per hectare	1,050 kg per hectare	1,400 kg per hectare	1,050 kg per hectare
Contemporary Teotihuacán system	3,600	39,600	28,800	25,740	18,720
Middle Horizon, Teotihuacán system	7,200	79,200	57,600	49,480	37,440
Middle Horizon, both systems	9,700	116,700	77,600	69,355	50,440

| | | 80% Dependence on Maize | | | |
| | | 100% Planted in Maize | | 65% Planted in Maize | |
System	Land Area (in hectares)	1,400 kg per hectare	1,000 kg per hectare	1,400 kg per hectare	1,000 kg per hectare
Contemporary Teotihuacán system	3,600	32,400	21,600	21,060	14,040
Middle Horizon, Teotihuacán system	7,200	64,800	43,200	42,120	28,080
Middle Horizon, both systems	9,700	87,300	60,200	56,745	39,130

Citing a sixteenth-century source, Palerm (1961b) reports that the Coyoacán system served the needs of 23,000 vasallos. It is not clear what the term vasallos refers to, but it obviously was a major system, at least comparable to the Texcoco Piedmont complex. Although we lack quantitative data on the Cuauhtitlán system (in terms of the sixteenth-century population of the district), it must have been minimally comparable to the Texcoco or Coyoacán complex. All of this means that the various spring-based canal systems in the Basin could have provided the basic caloric requirements for a maximum of 150,000 people, or 12 percent of the calculated Late Horizon population of the Basin. This calculation assumes a 100 percent use of irrigated land for maize, with a 65 percent calorie intake from maize and an average yield of 1,400 kilos per hectare. It also assumes that irrigation resources in the Teotihuacán Valley and Texcoco Piedmont were at least comparable to those in the 1920s.

We have already stressed the inefficiency of the irrigation system. If we calculate the 1950 flow of water from the San Juan springs, it was 18 million cubic meters. According to recent agronomic studies in the Basin of Mexico, a single preplanting irrigation of maize on most soils requires approximately 1,200 cubic meters of water. Theoretically, then, this water, if it were all stored in reservoirs for redistribution, could be used to irrigate 15,000 hectares of land rather than the 3,652 hectares actually irrigated. As the system works today, it can be used effectively only from 1 February to 1 June—that is, one-third of the year, which reduces the irrigable area to 5,000 hectares. The difference between the actual area irrigated (3,652 hectares) and 5,000 hectares is presumably loss due to filtration and evaporation.

This low level of efficiency is even more evident when one considers the use of floodwaters. In 1922 Gamio and his coworkers estimated the total cubic volume of an annual rainfall in the lower portion of the Teotihuacán Valley (an area of 370 square kilometers) to be 220 million cubic meters. Of this they estimated that 30 percent evaporated, 50 percent was absorbed into the soil and subsoil, and 20 percent—or 44 million cubic meters—flowed into the barranca system. Gamio concluded that if the barranca flow and the water from the springs were used, even under the existing system of relatively inefficient use of water resources, at least 10,000 hectares of land could be irrigated. In fact, if all this water were held in reservoirs and fed into fields with a closed piping system, theoretically this potential could be enormously expanded to irrigate over 50,000 hectares of land. Considering the fact that the Basin of Mexico is approximately 7,000 to 8,000 square kilometers in size, the total runoff into the barranca system is enormous. Just how much of this potential was actually tapped by the pre-Hispanic population is a major research problem, and our relevant hard data are admittedly few. At any rate, it seems obvious not only that the irrigation resources of the area were considerable, but that they could have played a significant role in the evolution of pre-Hispanic cultivation.

Late Horizon Irrigation

Palerm (1955) and Palerm and Wolf (1961b, 1961c, 1961d), have summarized the documentary data on permanent irrigation systems in the Basin of Mexico at the moment of the Spanish Conquest. The evidence is convincing that all of the major resources were fully utilized.

What of the survey area, and particularly the Texcotzingo–Teotihuacán systems? According to the data from the *Relaciones Geográficas*, the Teotihuacán system, which extended from the springs all the way to the lakeshore, was at least as extensive as the contemporary one. Quoting from the 1579 *Relación de Tecciztlán* (Paso y Troncoso 1905b):

4. Esta asentada la cauesera de aculma en un llano, al pie de una loma alta, es raso no tiene nengun fuente, pasa per el dicho pueblo el rio que dizen San Juan, dividido en tres asequias de agua con quien riegan gran pedazo de tierra casi una legua en largo e medio en ancho; es fertil de pastos y de mantenimyentos.

19. Pasa por el dicho pueblo de aculma el rrio que llama de San Juan, partido en quatro asequias, lleuara cada una de ellos dos bueyes de agua, rriegase an ella un legua de tierra.

4. . . . beben las naturales de jagueyes, acepto la Cabecera ques abuindosa de agua, tiene muchos fuentes an poco trecho de que procede un rio grande en la qual tienen las naturales un molino, rieganse con el agua del dicho rio dos leguas de tierra, que toda su corriente hasta entrar en la laguna, pasando per los pueblos de aculma, tepexpa y tequisistlan, termino con tescuco; es tierra abundosa do pasto y mantenimyentos.

3. El temple de tequisistlan es frio y umido por estar asentado serca de la laguna grande entre asequias de agua.

19. Pasa par la parte de leuante del dico pueblo de tequisistlan el rio que llama de San Juan, en una asequia onda dos tiros del dicho pueblo; rriegan con el casi medio legua de tierra.

3. El temple y calidad de la cauesera de tepexpa es frio y umydo por estar asentado en baxo la mayor parte del, y entre asequias de agua. . . .

19. No thiene rrio ny fuente, solo pasa por el pueblo el rrio que llaman de San Juan, deuidido en dos asequias de agua, con que se rriega distancia de media legua de tierra del dicho pueblo de tepexpa.

Agricultural History

From the "Abecedario de las visitas" (Paso y Troncoso 1905a), dating from the 1540s, we have a description of the town of Tepecha: "Este pueblo esta asentado en un cerillo, tiene poca tierra de regadio, tiene en largo ochocientas brazas de largo y Seiscientos y Catorze en ancho, que son mill y dozientas brazas."

The total population utilizing the Teotihuacán system in 1580 was, we estimate, only 8,000 persons. The town and nearby village of Atlatongo possessed approximately 1,200 hectares of irrigated land at that time, with 1,500 tributaries—in other words, 0.8 hectares per tributary. This would amount to approximately 2.4 hectares per extended family of eight persons, a reasonable holding in terms of our estimates of labor costs and crop yields. The fact that communities as far below the springs as Tequistlán were using the system suggests that it was built for a much more substantial population. Our calculation of the population of the same area at the time of the Conquest is approximately 24,000 people, with 7,300 tributaries. Supposing that in all of the villages utilizing the system, the average household held 0.8 hectares, as in 1580, then that 5,840 hectares were under irrigation in 1519. These figures also suggest the production of a substantial surplus. If we estimate the average yield per hectare as 1,400 kilos, then the total production of this land would be 8,176,000 kilos, enough to supply a population of 51,000 people with their daily maize requirements. These figures check very well with our experimental studies of work input and productivity, and they demonstrate the unusual significance of the irrigated land in the Valley in terms of the support of large urban communities.

Floodwater Irrigation

When we started the Teotihuacán Valley project, we assumed that floodwater irrigation was of pre-Hispanic date. Our assumption was correct—the Teotihuacán Valley survey demonstrated conclusively that the terrace type of floodwater irrigation was, in fact, of major significance in Aztec times. The floodwater system of the Alluvial Plain of the middle Valley, however, is probably of recent origin. Its effectiveness is based essentially on the eroded condition of the adjacent Piedmont, since much of the runoff for the system is supplied from this area. But if the Piedmont had been intensively cultivated and terraced, a considerably reduced runoff would have been available for the lower ends of the barranca system, and the availability of water for floodwater irrigation of the plain would have been much less than today. The Atlatongo system excavated by R. Millon, however, does show some floodwater irrigation of the lower end of the Piedmont. In addition, floodwater irrigation and terracing were a diagnostic practice in the Texcoco Piedmont during the Late Horizon, as Parsons's (1971b) survey data indicate. Map 14 shows the contemporary floodwater dam system in the Valley.

Pre–Late Horizon Irrigation

In our study of pre–Late Horizon times, we had to rely wholly on archaeological data, with the result that what we present here must be considered highly tentative. We knew that defunct canal and dam systems in the Teotihuacán Valley are numerous, but that few can be securely dated; most of those that can are Late Horizon. When we began the Teotihuacán Valley survey, we planned to date most defunct hydraulic systems by simple spatial proximity of primary canals to settlements. We expected to find a number of settlements of a particular time period not only in close physical association with primary canals, but also with specific evidence of spatial relationships between house remains and branch canals.

With respect to overall field strategy we decided to follow a lead suggested by René Millon (1957) in his analysis of a small floodwater system north of Atlatongo, on the Piedmont. Millon argued that the population would first have utilized the big permanent lower Valley system because of its dependable water supply; only at a later date would the people have harnessed the more marginal floodwater sources. If we could date the marginal systems, therefore, it would provide us with a minimal antiquity for the main system. This approach was most attractive, since the technical problems of trying to locate and excavate ancient settlements and canal systems in the deep soil plain were many and complicated. Furthermore, the principal canals in the main system, which probably have not shifted position since they were first utilized, have been periodically sedimented and dredged, thus presenting enormous problems for stratigraphic control. We would have been forced to locate secondary or tertiary canals of the system that would relate to landholding units, which obviously

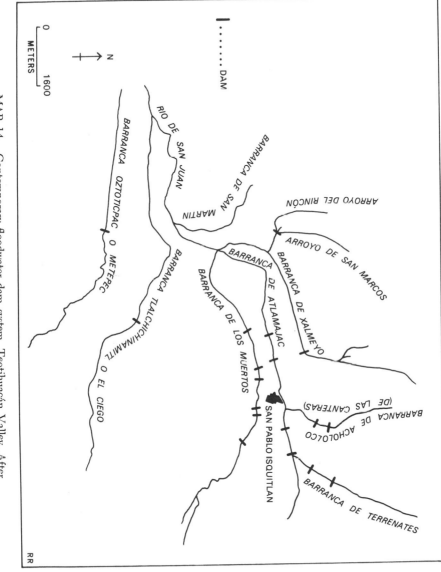

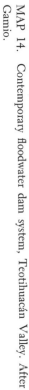

MAP 14. Contemporary floodwater dam system, Teotihuacán Valley. After Gamio.

would change from period to period. This is a virtuously hopeless task without sophisticated aerial photography.

One problem with Millon's assumption is the possibility that some of the smaller systems might have had permanent water supplies in the past. Hence, they might have been utilized before the main system, which would have involved a considerably greater input of manpower resources to build and maintain. This would be particularly true if the smaller systems served areas of higher, better drained, and fertile soils, where the cost of cultivation would be minimal.

The Piedmont seemed an ideal area to search for small, marginal systems, since erosion would have exposed any ditch systems cut into the tepetate and conceivably would have left some remains of dams along the streams. The major problem lay in the strategy of associational dating. Late Horizon occupation is everywhere, and since virtually all the pre–Late Horizon sites have Late Horizon occupations as well, the dating of an abandoned hydraulic work is always difficult. The fact that the Late Horizon witnessed the peak population for the Valley only intensifies the problem. As we have already noted, Late Horizon Piedmont-settlement is of the type that enables us easily to date terraces and in some cases their associated canals. In general, pre–Late Horizon settlements were comparable to those found today—compact settlements with the agricultural land lying almost entirely outside the settlement. On the Piedmont, therefore, the neat house-to-terrace-to-branch-canal type of associational dating cannot be used. Furthermore, most of the systems were so small that they served a single settlement, and the longer ones were preserved only in fragments. Thus the technique of dating by settlement alignment to canal was generally not possible. Finally, to complicate the problem, many of the systems have gone through multiple uses and modifications, including uses by the contemporary population.

Millon's (1957) excavation of one of these systems exemplifies the problem, and he does suggest a possible pre–Late Horizon use of the system. However, an indirect but more equivocal method of estimating the use of hydraulic resources is to study population history in small local areas. In other words, the closer a pre-Hispanic population size within a small area (say, 10 to 20 square kilometers) approximates the modern size, then the greater the likelihood that a comparable system of land use was in vogue. There are, of course, numerous technical problems in reconstructing population size from archaeological data.

116

Agricultural History

With respect to the permanent irrigation of the Alluvial Plain, the problem is, as we have pointed out, acute. Several lines of data suggest strongly that the lower Valley system dates at least as far back as the Middle Horizon, and possibly as early as First Intermediate: Phase 4 times (Tzacualli). First, the city covered about 20 square kilometers at its peak and was traversed by a network of natural tributaries, as well as by the San Juan River itself. This entire network was canalized and accommodated to the rather rigid plan of the city, suggesting large-scale manipulation of water systems by the Teotihuacanos. Second, the location of the city at the head of the spring system (and, as Mooser [Lorenzo 1968] postulates, some springs were entirely within the city) in a comparable position to the Late Horizon town is highly suggestive. Third, the Tepantitla murals show canals and small rectangular gardens, structured like the chinampa-like fields that are found today near the springs. Finally, the size of Teotihuacán, even before Millon's survey increased the figure to over 100,000 people, suggested intensive use of agricultural resources.

Millon's latest surveys (Millon, Drewitt, and Cowgill 1973) have located a system of reservoirs and canals that would have served the needs of the urban population, again confirming the fact that the Teotihuacán population did engage in hydraulic works on a large scale. The Middle Horizon settlement pattern—in which the bulk of the farming population apparently lived in the city and traveled back and forth to outlying fields—of course complicates the problem of dating canal systems. The modern, Second Intermediate: Phase 1 and, to a certain extent, the Late Horizon populations formed a series of settlements along the edges of the Alluvial Plain and an additional string of settlements down the center. Although we did not locate any Middle Horizon settlements, we did find suggestions of use of the irrigation system in the form of light concentrations of Middle Horizon pottery along several of the major canals.

The strongest argument for the use of an irrigation system, however, lies in our pollen graphs from El Tular (see Fig. 3), a small spring near Atlatongo, and from Cuanalan, at the lower end of the irrigation system. Our reasoning was that in the area around the springs, before the construction of the irrigation system, there must have been a vegetation adapted to swampy conditions. Today this area of high water table has been converted to a system of chinampas, which covers a maximum of only 100 hectares. Since the El Tular spring is located well down valley

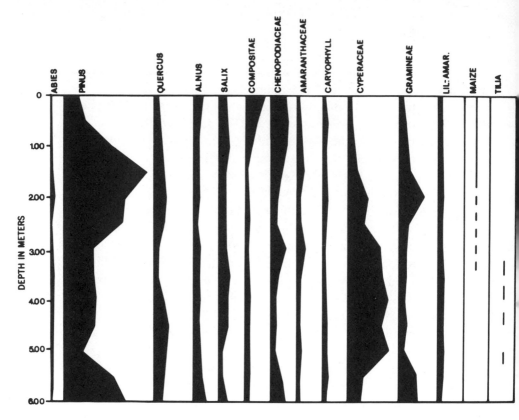

FIGURE 3.   Pollen diagram 1, El Tular.

from the contemporary high-water-table area, the pollen profile suggests
that this environmental niche was once considerably larger, perhaps having a maximal extent of about 1,000 hectares.

Particularly significant in the graph is the behavior of a group of plants
called cyperacea, or sedges, which live under swampy conditions. In the
lower levels of the graph (from 3 to 6 meters below the surface), cyperacea make up 30 percent of the pollen sample, leading us to conclude that
sedges were undoubtedly the dominant plants all over the spring area
before its drainage for irrigation. At the 3-to-2.5-meter level the percentage
suddenly and dramatically drops to perhaps 7 percent of the total sample,
then gradually declines to reach a low point of 3 percent in the upper-
most level. The most likely explanation for such a reduction is artificial
drainage of the swamps. El Tular is a small spring located 2.5 kilometers
down valley from the main cluster of springs at San Juan, indicating that
the drainage project had evolved to include land at least that far down

valley. Following the initial reduction, the rest of the profile shows a steady decline in moisture around the springs up to the time of the Spanish Conquest—a reflection of further change and expansion of the irrigation system down valley.

By comparing the pollen profile from El Tular with one taken at Cuanalan, which can be directly correlated with the First Intermediate: Phase 2 occupation there, we have been able to relate the El Tular graph to the history of settlement in the Valley. The rapid reduction of sedge pollen at El Tular apparently dates from the Patlachique phase, thus strikingly agreeing with the known history of settlement in the Valley. Also supporting this explanation is the fact that maize pollen appears slightly before the time of the sudden reduction of the frequency of sedges.

Our impression is that much of the intensively cultivated land in the Teotihuacán Valley in the First Intermediate: Phase 3 was probably similar in morphology to the chinampas presently found near the San Juan springs. Today, because of the overall desiccation of the Valley, only 100 hectares of land can be cultivated intensively. During Phase 3 and the succeeding Phase 4, and even into the Middle Horizon, the area of high water table could have been considerably greater.

In summary, therefore, our data suggest (1) an inception of chinampa cultivation in the spring area and possible irrigation down valley in the vicinity of Cuanalan during the First Intermediate: Phase 2; (2) a striking expansion of chinampa cultivation in First Intermediate: Phase 3 times; and (3) a rapid expansion, possibly to the maximal size of the main irrigation system, down valley during Tzacualli times (First Intermediate: Phase 4), and most certainly by Tlamimilolpa times (Early Middle Horizon). (The specifics of the system will be covered in detail in the following section.)

North of Cerro Gordo there is an ancient canal system that can, with some assurance, be dated as pre-Aztec, probably pre-Toltec (see Map 15). It begins with a major tributary barranca that flows between Cerros Ahuatepec and Tezqueme. Below the hills the barranca goes north for a distance of approximately one kilometer, then swings to the west and, after an additional kilometer, joins another major barranca that begins between Cerro Tezqueme and Cerro Tlacuache Grande. All drainage in this area ultimately flows into a main stream called the Barranca de Tecorral, which runs below the village of Maquixco Alto. Between Cerros

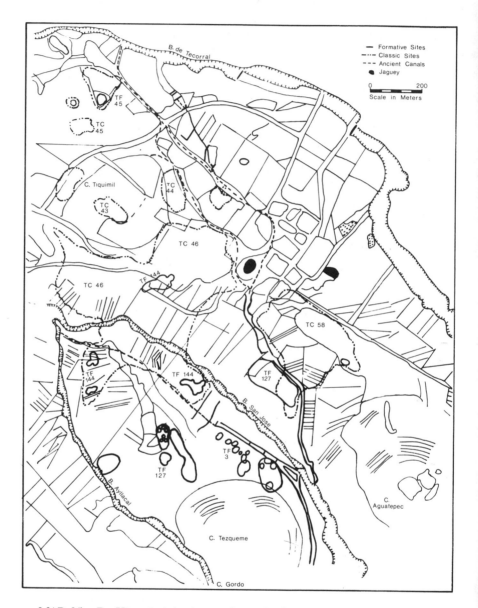

MAP 15. Pre-Hispanic irrigation on Cerro Gordo, North Slope.

Ahuatepec and Tezqueme, the barranca has a depth of nearly 20 meters and is 40 to 60 meters wide. At this point a canal intake (the west canal) departs from the barranca and runs parallel to it. The canal can be traced for a distance of 500 meters before it vanishes in an extensive area of tepetate wash. On aerial photographs (but not on the ground) it can be traced across the wash until it joins another barranca east of Cerro Teclalo. Since the canal, for a distance of 100 meters from the intake, is 2 to 4 meters deep, it could only have functioned as a canal when the barranca was a shallow stream. There must have been a dam across the stream when the canal was functioning, but the lateral erosion that occurred when the stream widened has destroyed any traces of it. Following the downcutting of the barranca, the canal apparently continued to function as a natural drainage tract; today it is 10 to 20 meters wide and has an undulating plan. It appears, therefore, more like a barranca than a canal—in fact, it is considered and treated as such by the contemporary peasants, who have constructed a series of check dams within it. The lower portion of the canal, that is, the portion where it shifts direction, runs along the southern or upper edge of the big Middle Horizon village site TC 46. Below the last check dam and before entering the tepetate area, the canal widens and decreases in depth.

A second canal (the east canal) departs from the same barranca between Cerros Ahuatepec and Tezqueme, but on the opposite side and at a point 100 meters upstream from the west canal. It flows northeast and is easily traced for a distance of 800 meters to the upper edge of the village of Maquixco Alto. For the first 500 meters the east canal appears as a narrow, shallow trench that could still function today if the barranca had not incised its bed so deeply. It then enters a wide, deeply scarred wash between two functional modern-Aztec terrace systems. At the point where the canal enters the village, it has deeply incised its bed.

Two large contemporary check dams have been constructed within the east canal bed and, as in the case of the west canal, it looks more like a small barranca than a canal. Below the check dam the water enters a great tepetate wash area near the village jaguey, to which some of the drainage is diverted. Below the jaguey the drainage diverges to follow two tracts, each presently serving as a village street road. We are convinced that these streets are old canal beds that became floodwater drainage tracts after they ceased to function as permanent canals. Today, they are utilized not only as streets, but also as floodwater canals for the terraces in the west and northwest edge of the village. The lower one is of particular interest. It flows 150 meters northeast and makes a sharp turn to the northwest, where it flows for 300 meters. It then angles across several modern fields. In passing across one field, the canal has incised its bed deeply—in fact, two contemporary check dams have been constructed over it. The canal, cut down into the tepetate, can be seen, distinctly, running under the check dam wall. In its course through the fields it is 280 meters long. Once out of the fields, the canal appears as a shallow barranca running between a set of contemporary terraces on the west and a large unterraced field on the east; it then enters the Barranca de Tecorral. This last stretch is 250 meters long. The total length of the lower canal is a little over 2 kilometers.

After leaving the jaguey area, the upper canal parallels the lower, with the distance between the two varying from 100 to 150 meters. It flows about 800 meters, then enters the same barranca as the lower canal, but downstream. Sections of it, as in the case of the upper canal, serve as contemporary village roads and floodwater drainage tracts; the lower portion is still used to supply the set of terraces noted above in our description of the upper canal. The terraces are bordered on both sides by the two ancient canals.

The entire drainage pattern is easily traced on aerial photos, particularly on large-scale photos. With respect to morphology, the canals are clearly nonfunctional over most of their lengths in terms of the present-day terrace-floodwater systems. In fact, as we pointed out, they are treated as barrancas. It is equally obvious that they are not natural, since they flow diagonally and connect parts of the natural stream systems.

The present system of cultivation in the Maquixco Alto area is described in detail by Charlton (Sanders et al. 1970). Basically, it involves the construction of sets of vertical terraces separated by shallow floodwater canals. Water is diverted from the canals into each terrace by small earth embankments that enter the canal; the system is self-flooding.

The older portions of the contemporary systems are in part remnants of the Aztec system, which functioned in much the same way. Although a great deal of the old system has been obliterated by erosion, its remnants are visible everywhere. In some cases, the contemporary villages are recolonizing these eroded areas and building new systems that are morphologically identical with the old ones.

The ancient canal system we have described is quite different in character, since the canals led water directly from major streams and were presumably filled by means of a dam built across the barranca. In this respect, the system is more like the floodwater irrigation system of the Alluvial Plain in the middle Valley or the permanent system in the lower Valley. It could only have worked at a time when the barrancas were shallow, narrow, and semipermanent or permanent streams. Not only is the system morphologically different from the Aztec and contemporary systems, but, to judge from Colonial documents pertaining to the area, many of the deep barrancas were already formed in Aztec times. The canals therefore must be pre-Aztec. Assuming this to be the case, the precise dating remains the major problem.

Second Intermediate: Phase 2 occupation is considerable in the area; in fact, the upper part of the east canal flows through the center of TT 36, and the lower part through the largest Phase 2 site in the area, TT 35. There are Second Intermediate: Phase 2 sites associated with the west canal.

By far the most massive occupation of the area served by the two canals is that of the Middle Horizon. The east canal runs along the southwest edge of TC 58, a densely settled village site measuring 8 hectares. Flowing along the northeast edge of TC 46, a huge village of 25 hectares, is the lower part of the canal, with each of its lower branches running past two Middle Horizon hamlets, TC 64 and TC 45. Immediately before the canals enter the Barranca de Tecorral, the upper branch flows by the cluster of Middle Horizon hamlets TC 63, 60, 62, and 61. The lower portion of the west canal flows along the entire south edge of the large village site TC 46.

In view of the very heavy Middle Horizon occupation of the area and the closeness of the canal system to it, the canals probably date from this period. There is, however, a good possibility that they date from as early as First Intermediate: Phase 4 times, since at least five Phase 4 hamlets have been found within a short distance of the canal system (TF 3, 72, 144, 127, and 202).

In the Texcoco Piedmont springs region, the evidence for pre–Late Horizon irrigation is even more inferential. However, the First Intermediate: Phase 1 and Middle Horizon sites tend to cluster either in areas served by the Late Horizon–recent irrigation systems or at the lower edge of Chimalhuacán Hill, where the combination of a high water table, springs, and the climatic effects of the nearby lake would prove an ideal setting for an agricultural community. A point needs to be made here regarding the feasibility of simple canal systems in pre–Late Horizon times. Several writers—Charlton (1972a) and J. R. Parsons (1971b), for example—have argued that irrigation in the Texcoco Piedmont would require public works comparable in size and scale to the known Late Horizon aqueducts. Since there is no evidence for pre–Late Horizon construction on such a scale, irrigation would not have been feasible. In fact, most of the modern system is a combination of the use of natural waterways and artificial canals, with only a fraction of it involving the use of large aqueducts (in one case, one of the Late Horizon aqueducts is still in use). There are numerous possible routes for artificial canals, and today over half of the system flows through natural waterways.

Even more important, the barranca system as seen in the area today is probably the product of deforestation and erosion. We suspect that during the First Intermediate and the Middle Horizon, the drainage pattern consisted of small, shallow streams into which the spring flow drained. If this was the case, then communities situated in the Lower Piedmont would have been able to tap directly into the nearby streams, and irrigation canals would have involved simply constructed ditches a few hundred meters in length.

Tentative Reconstruction of the History of Canal Irrigation in the Texcoco-Teotihuacán Area

The following reconstruction is admittedly based on spotty and often equivocal supporting data, and perhaps should be considered a model for future testing rather than a conclusion. However, it does fit the settlement history as we now understand it.

The First Intermediate: Phase 1 is the first instance of a genuine agricultural occupation in the Texcoco-Teotihuacán area. With the exception of a large village site on the lower lakeside flank of Cerro Chimalhuacán, the occupation consisted of a series of hamlets within the 2,300-to-2,500-meter contour. There is no convincing evidence for agricultural terracing or irrigation at this time. The succeeding Phase 2 of the First Intermediate witnessed a continuation of the same ecological preference for the Lower Piedmont, with a few notable examples. Most settlements were hamlet-size, but there were several villages—three at the upper edge of the Lower Piedmont in the Texcoco area (TX-LF-9, 12, and 22), and two smaller villages on the edge of the Alluvial Plain in the Teotihuacán Valley. One of the Teotihuacán villages lies within the pseudo-chinampa area, and the other is well down valley where the lower valley plain joins the delta plain. Two of the Texcoco villages are located within the area included in the Late Horizon and modern irrigation system with its permanent spring sources. In all probability, the first experiments in hydraulic agriculture in our area occurred at the two Teotihuacán Valley sites and in the Texcoco Piedmont.

However, it was probably during the First Intermediate: Phase 3 that canal irrigation first developed, at least in the Texcoco sector. Assuming that the drainage through the Upper Piedmont consisted of small, shallow streams, then three (and possibly four) spring clusters were the source of water for a series of small feeder canals between the rivers and the nearby fields. All three irrigation systems are closely correlated with the clusters of population during Phase 2 and Phase 3. A fourth population cluster occurred at the base of Chimalhuacán Hill, where a chinampa-like pattern along the edge of the hill was the possible agricultural system. Only one cluster of settlements is unrelated to any contemporary hydraulic resource.

In the Teotihuacán Valley the two First Intermediate: Phase 2 settlements (at the spring and down valley) both went through a period of explosive growth, particularly the spring settlement. We have postulated the maximal expansion of the chinampa-like cultivation system at this time, possibly including an area as large as 1,000 hectares of land. R. Millon (1973) has estimated that the First Intermediate: Phase 3 town numbered 10,000 people, the largest settlement at this time in the Basin of Mexico except Cuicuilco. The large village site located down valley had an estimated population of 500 to 1,000 people and may have been based upon small-scale canal irrigation from the Rio de San Juan.

Throughout the first century of the First Intermediate: Phase 3, we postulate the existence of a series of small hydraulic cores capable of providing the maize requirement for populations varying from 1,000 to 10,000 people. We also see the area at this time as divided into a number of competing polities, with populations varying from a few thousand in the Texcoco area to 15,000 to 20,000 in the Teotihuacán Valley. In the Teotihuacán Valley, at least half of the people were living in hamlets scattered through the hilly flanks of the Valley, the same area in which population was concentrated in the earlier periods.

During the First Intermediate: Phase 4 and the Middle Horizon, the situation changed dramatically. First, virtually the entire First Intermediate: Phase 3 population that we postulated as using the Texcoco Piedmont irrigation system was reduced to a fraction of its former size. Extrapolating from J. R. Parsons's (1971b) estimates, we would suggest a decline from possibly 10,000 people at the inception of the Middle period to perhaps as low as 1,000 by the end of it. On the other hand, the population in the far southern portion of the Texcoco area held its own or decreased only slightly.

Second, in the Teotihuacán Valley, almost all the small settlements above 2,300 meters were abandoned, as well as the large First Intermediate: Phase 3 village at the lower end of the Valley. Within 200 years, the Phase 3 town at the springs exploded into a community of nearly 45,000 people, growing to 125,000 people within a period of 700 years. The bulk of the population of the Valley—at least 85 percent—resided in this one center, with the balance scattered along the peripheral portions of the Valley on the Lower Piedmont. This process of population growth evidently correlated with the final reduction of vegetation in the area of the springs and was undoubtedly related to a major expansion of the main irrigation system and other marginal irrigation systems in the Valley.

Because of the critical problems of transporting bulk goods for basic foodstuffs, the relatively low ratio of energy input to output in cultivation, and the added security provided by irrigation—all in the context of a system based only on human energy—we are offering here an energy system model for Middle Horizon Teotihuacán. First, we are assuming that all land potentially irrigable from the Teotihuacán springs (1,100–1,200 liters per second minimally) was cultivated, irrigated, and directly controlled by the city's population. For the Texcoco Piedmont area we are assuming that the hydrographic pattern had changed only slightly since the First Intermediate period; the techniques of irrigation by short feeder canals from the natural drainage were simply expanded. This would mean a minimal flow of 303 liters per second for the Papalotla River. Geographically, the Papalotla irrigation system is as close to Teotihuacán as is the lower end of the Teotihuacán system itself, and the Teotihuacanos would have had direct access and presumably control of such lands. (In 1972 we walked by a somewhat circuitous route from Tepetltaoxtoc to Oxtotipac in approximately three hours.) The thinness of occupation and scarcity of residential sites in the area compared with the previous phase further suggests that this was indeed the case. In fact, the substantial reduction of population, even in the area served by the Xalapango and Coxcacuaco systems, would also indicate that at least some of the land served by these systems was cultivated by the Teotihuacán population. Another possibility is that the water from the springs that served these systems was diverted by artificial canals into the headwaters of the Papalotla system and used to expand it. (This should, of course, be detectable by intensive archaeological surveys.)

We see the sequence of events as follows: Because of its greater size the Teotihuacán polity emerged as the dominant political system in the area. The Texcoco population was incorporated into the larger Teotihuacán state, either voluntarily or involuntarily. This would account for a sizable amount of the population growth that occurred during the First Intermediate: Phase 4 times. With this augmented population it was possible—and also necessary—to expand the irrigation system. Thus, the First Intermediate: Phase 3 irrigation system in the Lower Piedmont not only continued to function, but, in all probability, the descendants of the earlier populations utilizing the system continued to exercise ownership rights over the same lands after their removal to Teotihuacán.

Full use of the water from the springs at the Teotihuacán and the Papalotla systems (1,403–1,503 liters per second) would result in a virtually continuous zone of irrigated land broken only in the center by the Patlachique range. For our model, then, we will assume that all of the land served by the two systems was farmed by residents of Teotihuacán and that the bulk of the population cultivated land from the two systems. We will also assume that the Xalapango-Coxcacuaco was used primarily by the local resident population, at least during the first half of the Middle Horizon. Our calculations yield a figure of 8,818 to 9,418 hectares of irrigated land available for cultivation. On the basis of R. Millon's (1970b) statements about occupational specialization at Teotihuacán, and allowing for a fairly large professional ruling class, we estimate that farmers or part-time farmers made up approximately two-thirds of the total population of the city, or about 85,000 people. The settlement pattern data indicate that the population was organized into a series of large residential groups, most of which probably had a kinlike structure. These groups ranged in size from 30 to 80 people, with perhaps a modal size of approximately 50 persons. This means that there were perhaps 1,700 corporate land-using groups within the city. The average irrigated landholding for these groups would have been 5.2 to 5.4 hectares.

Assuming that the quantity of land was held in proportion to the population size of the corporate group, and that all irrigated fields were planted in maize, this would be approximately 7,280 to 7,500 kilos of maize per household (calculated at 1,400 kilos per hectare yield). If 65 percent of the caloric intake were derived from maize, then each household would need approximately 6,400 kilos per year; if 80 percent, then 8,000 kilos. In the first case, each household could even have produced a surplus of maize; in the second case, the amount would almost have provided the daily requirements. We suspect, in fact, that landholdings were highly variable in size and unevenly distributed. Many lands were probably held by the ruling nonfarming class, and the farming population may even have stood in a kind of tenant-patron relationship to the nonfarmers. One fact our calculations do show, however, is that the productivity of the irrigated land must have been a critical factor in the evolution and maintenance of the Middle Horizon city. Furthermore, although the irrigated land clearly could not have accounted for the complete energy requirements of the city, it could have supplied a substantial percentage of it, feeding perhaps as much as five-sixths of the total population of the city by drawing on surplus productivity from the two southern canal systems. With respect to the total energy requirements of the nearby rural population as well as the city, we have designed a model that attempts to show the relationships between the basic energy requirements and the sources of all types of nutriments (basic grains, animal proteins, and other plant foods) in terms of commuting distance to the city.

For the Toltec period (Second Intermediate: Phases 1 and 2), the sequence of demographic and settlement events suggests a number of continuities and changes in the pattern. These changes, in fact, offer strong support for our previous Middle Horizon models. The most significant overall occurrence was the rapid decline of Teotihuacán as a major population center, an event that also coincided with a rapid dispersal of the population into the countryside. The dispersal, however, was not sufficient to account for all of the city's population loss. We would estimate a total population of no more than 60,000 in the Texcoco-Teotihuacán region as compared with the probable figure of about 150,000 residing in the same area at the peak of the Middle Horizon. Even if we assume that much of the population loss affected the upper and middle social strata— people who moved on to new urban centers and markets—the conclusion seems inescapable that even the agricultural population declined to at least 50 percent of its former numbers. Of particular interest is the fact that all of the remaining population clustered around two areas: the middle Papalotla Alluvial Plain in the south, and the edge of the lower Valley Alluvial Plain in the Teotihuacán Valley in the north. In other words, the people retrenched to the two major areas of irrigated land.

The small Middle Horizon population that presumably utilized the Coxcacuaco and Jalapango springs virtually disappeared. The decline in that area actually began, as we noted, during the Teotihuacán period, and it is tempting to blame this loss on the deforestation of the Upper Piedmont and possible barranca down-cutting that would have made maintenance of the canal system increasingly costly. In Aztec and contemporary times, the only part of the Piedmont that did not present striking topographic and hydrographic problems in canal routing was the Papalotla portion. Also of interest is the unusual stability of population in the south Texcoco Piedmont, where settlement was not only substantial in overall size, but even in terms of specific community locations. The events in the Second Intermediate: Phase 3 would seem to fit rather neatly our model of the hydraulic core-periphery concept for Middle Horizon Teotihuacán.

Sanders views the Second Intermediate: Phase 2 (Late Toltec) in the Teotihuacán Valley as one of population expansion, while J. R. Parsons sees a decline in the Texcoco area. In both cases, the pattern is a definite population decline in large nucleated centers and a rapid process of ruralization of population—in other words, a dispersion into hamlets as the basic settlement unit. In the Teotihuacán Valley, the heavy concentration around the Alluvial Plain continued but was accompanied by a major expansion into all of the marginal areas of the Valley. The distribution equaled that of Late Horizon times but on a much lower level of intensity. In the Texcoco area, the northern or Papalotla sector and the Portesuelo sector in the far south show a striking continuity in population size and zonal distribution, only experiencing the noted shift of settlement type from large nucleated communities into hamlets. Of particular interest is the fact that the central sector population was reestablished, but unlike the earlier period it was now strung along the riverine floodplains in the Lakeshore Plains, not on the Piedmont, suggesting continuing problems in the utilization of the Upper and Middle Piedmont areas. (For the Late Horizon period, we have, as noted previously, considerable archaeological and documentary data, which have been summarized in full in the preceding section.)

TERRACING

With the possible exception of TF 8 (a First Intermediate: Phase 1 and Phase 2 hamlet) in the Teotihuacán Valley, the earliest evidence of terracing in the survey area is that associated with the Patlachique and Tezoyuca ceramic complexes. Nearly all the large villages and centers of this time period are found on the Piedmont or summit of foothills, and all of them show evidence of terracing. In the Patlachique-phase sites, where such terracing is extensive, the amount of refuse on the terraces suggests that most of the surface area of each terrace was in cultivation, since the area occupied by the residential structures was proportionately very small. For this reason, Patlachique settlements tend to be quite dispersed and, in fact, are comparable to contemporary villages—scattered and compact, but low density. That terraces are present within the village's residential area also suggests an infield-outfield type of cultivation and the continuing use of terracing during the First Intermediate: Phase 4, Middle Horizon, and Second Intermediate: Phase 1. The settlement pattern of these phases, with most of the rural population living in fairly large, densely nucleated settlements, makes dating otherwise very difficult. There is also scattered evidence of terracing throughout the Teotihuacán Valley during the Second Intermediate: Phase 2, when settlement was dispersed.

For the Late Horizon, the evidence is conclusive, and we would estimate that virtually all the areas defined as the Lower or Upper Piedmont (throughout the northern and central portions of the survey area) were covered with bancal or stone terraces. The Late Horizon rural settlement pattern consists of houses directly associated with terraces. In terms of the specific topographic situation, settlement within the terraced areas varied in plan and layout. The Teotihuacán Valley, for example, has a linear northeast-southwest plan; running down the center of the valley is a strip of alluvial plain bordered on each side by gently sloping piedmonts, which are flanked in turn by steep-sided hills. The northern range consists of a series of separate elevations, whereas the southern range, the Patlachique, is a solid phalanx of hills. There is virtually a continuous strip settlement along the Lower Piedmont on both sides of the Valley, but along the north flank the strip completely encircles the hills.

The topographic layout differs considerably in the Texcoco area, where there are very wide north-south zones, ranging from the Lakeshore to the flat Alluvial Plain, on to the Lower Piedmont, and finally to the Upper Piedmont and the Sierra. Both of the zones that we have defined as the Lower and Upper Piedmont are covered by a continuous blanket of dispersed housemounds and terraces, with only occasional ceremonial centers breaking the continuity of what looks essentially like a single, large, rural community. The only area where the settlement pattern compares with that in the Teotihuacán Valley is on the Piedmont along the southern flank of the Patlachique Range.

In the far southern portions of the Basin, there seems to be very little evidence of terracing until Late Horizon times, but, of course, many of the elevated portions were virtually uninhabited until this period. Even in Late Horizon times, terracing was limited to the Milpa Alta zone; in the Tlalmanalco-Amecameca zones, it was almost nonexistent. In part, this lack of development may have been due to the more humid climate and heavier vegetation, with a consequent decline in the erosive power of the rains. It is also possible that the more humid climate there posed a much more serious problem in the maintenance of soil fertility, and hence the extra labor involved in terrace construction may not have been worth the effort. Unfortunately, we lack studies of contemporary agriculture in the area to establish this point.

DRAINAGE AGRICULTURE

Large areas along the lakeshore consisted of swampy land that could have been cultivated only with a considerable outlay of labor on the part of the individual farmer. Cultivation here most probably involved rather complex, large-scale drainage projects that would have required a considerable degree of political organization.

One of the most extensive areas of this type of terrain in the Basin of Mexico lies east of Lake Texcoco. The area was virtually unoccupied throughout the First Intermediate and Middle Horizon periods. The reasons seem clear: drainage problems, more severe frosts, lower rainfall, and heavier soils. Theoretically, the plain would not be cultivated until

131

the supply of land became short, and this, in fact, is what the population profile suggests. On the other hand, once these problems were resolved, the Alluvial Plain had enormous agricultural potential; the high water table would ameliorate the problems of lower rainfall and more severe frosts; the soils are more fertile than on the adjacent Piedmont, and erosion, of course, is no problem.

Except for a few First Intermediate: Phase 2 and 3 sites on the lakeshore, the initial substantial occupation of the Lakeshore Plain in the Texcoco region took place during the Second Intermediate: Phase 2. It is interesting that this occurred in linear strips along major riverine flood plains in the northern and central sectors, presumably because of the double combination of more friable soils and the high water table. By the time of the Spanish Conquest, all of the northern and central portions of the plain had been brought under cultivation. The major question concerns the process by which this was achieved. Studies of contemporary agriculture at Atenco and Tocuila by Sanders (unpublished) have provided some interesting clues in this regard.

Today the plain is traversed by a network of canals that depart from the rivers in the area and either drain back into the main river or enter other streams. This system was in full use fifty years ago when the haciendas were at their apogee and had multiple functions—to provide adequate drainage and floodwater for irrigation, and to bring silt to fields to enrich the soil. At that time, the water table was within a few meters of the surface, at least in the Inner Lakeshore Plain section. Since 1930, however, the water table has dropped dramatically all over the area to 10 to 20 meters below the surface, and drainage is no longer a consideration or a problem. Today, those sections of the system that still function are used primarily for irrigation and to flush salt from the desiccated lakebed.

Although the nineteenth-century haciendas remodeled and built parts of the system, there are numerous references to the major canals in the sixteenth-century literature (Palerm 1961b), verifying that much of the system is Late Horizon in date. At the time of the Aztec colonization, the plain was narrower because of the greater extent of the lake; too, the water table conditions of 1920 around the two contemporary lakeshore communities were probably generalized over much of the plain. The major problem in colonization would have been drainage. Once drained, the same canals could have functioned to bring floodwaters to the fields for irrigation. Even more important, with the floodwaters came coarser sediments, which changed the texture of the soil and made it amenable to tillage with simple, wooden digging tools. Sanders is still in the process of tabulating the data, but at least 30 and possibly 50 percent of the lands of Atenco could be classified as loams rather than clays, apparently the result of this process. An added bonus would be annual increments of fertility, permitting intensive cropping. The lack of major watercourses in the southern plain probably explains the dearth of Late Horizon sites in the area.

Another major area of comparable soil and moisture conditions occurs east of Lake Chalco, where, according to the settlement history, drainage problems were not resolved. On the other hand, the smaller plains south of Lakes Chalco-Xochimilco were occupied as early as First Intermediate: Phase 1 times. By the Late Horizon, this entire southern strip was apparently completely and continuously cultivated. Of interest here is the fact that a major river system—the Rio Amecameca—crosses the plain with a very heavy sediment load, the heaviest of any river in the Basin of Mexico. Presumably, the process of alluviation here, because of the volume of water and soil transported, not only produces a more friable soil over a larger area, but reduces drainage problems as well.

Using the lakes themselves, a prehistoric population undertook the most staggering and impressive drainage project of all. Before summarizing Armillas's recent evaluation of the system, a quote from Sanders (1965:44) indicates our conception of the system at that time.

> This system, called chinampa cultivation, is probably the most intensive and productive kind of agriculture practiced in the New World in pre-Hispanic times. The main characteristic of the system, as practiced in the south, includes the construction of artificial islands within freshwater lakes. These islands are built of alternate layers of mud scooped from the lake bottom and vegetation collected from the surface. After the island has reached a height of a few inches above the lake surface, huejote trees are planted along the edge to retain the soil. The islands are usually in the form of long, narrow rectangles which facilitate bucket irrigation and natural inward seepage of water from the lake. The soil is very rich in organic matter, porous, very dark in color, and land use is extraordinarily intensive; no chinampas are rested for more than three to four months of the year. By the use of seedbeds a continuous succession of crops, in all stages of growth (mostly vegetables for the Mexico City market) may be seen on a single chinampa. To maintain such a demanding cycle of

cropping, fertilizers, in the form of fresh mud and floating vegetation, are periodically added to the chinampa. Crops are irrigated by scooping or splashing water onto the chinampa from canoes or by poles and buckets from the chinampa itself. All preparation of the soil is done by hand tools.

As the system was expanded, most of the surfaces of Lake Chalco-Xochimilco and Lake Mexico (a part of Lake Texcoco dyked off from the main lake) were reduced from open lake into a network of chinampas and canals. An added advantage of this system is that produce could be loaded from chinampas into canoes and poled directly to the urban markets along the lakeshores or in towns within the lake, such as Aztec Tenochtitlan and colonial Mexico City. The growth of urban centers in and on the lakes in the Aztec period was, in part, correlated with the evolution of this system of agriculture.

Armillas's (1971) recent surveys of the chinampa area demonstrate that although some chinampas may have been constructed as Sanders described, the process of chinampa formation as a whole was very different from that which was previously thought. First, he points out, the lake bottom was shaped like an "exceedingly shallow saucer" and confined by a low bank around almost the entire perimeter, with the exception of the east. The break of angle of this bank was 2,240 meters above sea level, and most of the elevation readings of the lakebed itself were between 2,238 and 2,239 meters, with a few spots as low as 2,236 meters. Even allowing for a certain amount of subsidence since the Conquest, the overall depth of the lake apparently did not exceed 1 to 2 meters over most of its surface area. During the dry season, the area would resemble a vast swamp of varying hydrological conditions, interspersed with localized deep ponds and areas of high ground. Of interest is the fact that the deep pools were never converted to cultivation and are present on maps of the area throughout Colonial and Republican periods.

Armillas believes that chinampa formation was facilitated by the construction of a vast network of drainage ditches, which gradually reduced the water content of the soil to the point where cultivation was possible. In addition, his survey data suggest that the process of colonization proceeded from natural islands and offshore peninsulas on the mainland. The major ditches, used to drain the area, were also utilized as transportation arteries; ultimately large dikes were constructed to further regulate the water distribution, most probably to restrict flooding during the rainy season. The extraordinary regularity of the chinampa plots revealed in

Armillas's surveys indicates some kind of centralized direction or planning. Although some of the offshore and island communities date before the Late Horizon, the evidence is strong that the bulk of the area was colonized at that time and that most probably this colonization was planned by a central government. This could have been carried out by local states such as Tlahuac, Mixquic, or Xochimilco, but some of it may actually have been organized by the Tenochca themselves.

The process of fertilization described by Sanders would elevate the chinampas somewhat more and reduce the danger of flooding. Since it takes a considerable period of time before the vegetation consolidates in the soil, the cross section of a chinampa would suggest artificial construction, and, in essence, the upper portions of the profiles of these plots were artificial. Small, localized areas of chinampas apparently were found in Lake Texcoco at the base of Cerro Chimalhuacan and in Lake Xaltocan (in the community of Xaltocan), where local springs provided enough fresh, new water to reduce the salinity of the two lakes.

In the fifteenth century, the Tenochca of Tenochtitlan converted the western one-third of Lake Texcoco into a freshwater lake by constructing a network of dikes equipped with sluice gates. This also brought fresh water from the nearby mountains into the dike basins to convert them more rapidly to fresh water, opening much of this area for chinampa cultivation. Palerm (1973) discusses the structure of the system in more detail.

Armillas (1971) estimates that the southern lake chinampa zone covered an area of 12,000 hectares, of which 9,000 hectares were usable agricultural land and 3,000 hectares involved bodies of open water, canals, and islands. According to Sanders's (1965) estimate of the productivity of maize in the southern area, this system could support approximately 171,000 people with a per capita maize consumption of 160 kilos. The total population supported by the system may have been as high as 200,000, but it is difficult to estimate since we have very few data on the size of the northern chinampa areas. If we add to this the population of the Texcoco plain, then at least 300,000 people could have been supported by drainage or swamp reclamation agriculture. In fact, at least some of the chinampas were dedicated to specialized truck gardening for the market system, comparable to recent uses of the same area.

Drainage agriculture—to use the broader term—probably began very early in the history of the Basin, among those communities located at the lakeshores. This means it may have begun as early as Early Horizon. It was only during the Late Horizon, however, that this system of agriculture came to involve enormous expanses of land. The sole area of major previous historical significance regarding drainage agriculture was the zone around the Teotihuacán springs, which was apparently connected in its development with the emergence of the First Intermediate: Phase 3 town of Teotihuacán.

ESTIMATING CARRYING CAPACITY—THE TEXCOCO AREA AS A TEST OF METHODOLOGY

We will concentrate first on the Texcoco area as a test case since we have a detailed settlement history of the area and considerable controlled data from contemporary ecology, the latter collected expressly to elucidate the settlement history. At the time of agricultural colonization, the landscape must have borne a very different appearance than it does today. We would define three major ecozones: the Alluvial Plain (2,240–2,300 meters), the Piedmont (2,300–2,700 meters), and the Sierra (2,700–5,000 meters). The Alluvial Plain may be subdivided into two major divisions, the Inner Lakeshore Plain and the Outer Lakeshore Plain.

The presence of Lake Texcoco no doubt resulted in a water table considerably closer to the surface within a few kilometers of the lakeshore, thus creating the Inner Plain. It was an area in which the frequency of frost was reduced because of the high water content of the soil and the presence of the lake. However, that portion of the Inner Plain closest to the average lake level would have suffered frequent seasonal inundations from the lake, thus making the soils heavily impregnated with salt. It would be useful, therefore, to subdivide the Inner Plain into a salt-free band and a salt-endangered band. For both the Inner and Outer Plains, a further distinction should be made between riverine floodplains that traverse it and interfluve areas free of such flooding, since the flooding would have striking effects on soil texture, moisture, and fertility.

The Piedmont should be subdivided into a lower and upper division, the border running approximately at the 2,500-meter contour line. The Upper Piedmont would have a steeper average slope angle, thinner soils, and a much more severe frost season. Recent soil surveys also show that many of the soils found in the area are vertisols or heavy clays.

Agricultural History

For the time of initial colonization, we would reconstruct the vegetation as follows: A coniferous forest covered the Sierra and Upper Piedmont, while the primary cover on the Lower Piedmont was a broadleaf forest dominated by oak. Conditions on the Plain must have been highly variable, with cypress, capulin, and other moisture-loving trees along the rivers; oak forests on the well-drained interfluves, interspersed with meadows; hydrophytic vegetation over most of the Inner Lakeshore Plain; and salt bush and grass in the immediate offshore areas. All of the area would have had a substantial soil mantle—on the basis of contemporary remnants, it might have measured up to 50 to 60 centimeters, even in moderate-slope areas of the Upper Piedmont. A major difference between the past and present situation is that the band of springs now found at the Upper Piedmont's Sierra junction very probably included many more springs at the time the Basin was colonized, resulting in a much greater output of water. We would also suggest that the upper courses of the major streams of the area were once shallow brooks. With the extra spring output and retarded drainage of precipitation, they probably held water throughout the year, or at least for prolonged periods of time. On the basis of this reconstruction along with previous discussion of problems of pre-Hispanic adaptation to the area, we have compiled a table that reflects the differences in the agricultural potential of the Texcoco area's various ecological zones (Table 6).

The Patlachique-Tezoyuca phase (First Intermediate: Phase 3) is the first phase for which we have definite evidence of site ranking or stratification, which suggests a centralized political system in the survey area. Can we apply our population growth-pressure-competition paradigm to explain this development? If we compare J. R. Parsons's (1971b) calculated First Intermediate: Phase 3 population (10,070 to 20,200) with his estimates of Late Horizon times (57,585 to 116,395 people), then it would seem that the Phase 3 population was so much less than that of the Late Horizon as to negate the value of a model based on competition over land resources. If we examine the actual distribution of sites, however, another picture emerges. In the northern and central sectors, virtually all of the sites are not only found in the Lower Piedmont, but are at the upper portion of it. If we argue that farmers normally do not cultivate land beyond a 2-to-3 kilometer radius of their homes—and this seems to be the consistent pattern—then agricultural activities were restricted to a very small fraction of the area. Any discussion of population pressure must therefore

TABLE 6
AGRONOMIC POTENTIAL OF ECOLOGICAL ZONES IN THE TEXCOCO REGION

Ecological Zone	Soil Fertility	Soil Texture	Soil Depth	Susceptibility to Erosion	Frost Problems	Rainfall Conditions	Drainage	Special Problems
Inner Lakeshore Plain								
Interfluve — Salinized		Clay Clay-Loam	Deep	None	Moderate	Poor	High water table	Salt Drainage
Interfluve — Salt-Free	High	Clay Clay-Loam	Deep	None	Moderate	Poor	High water table	Drainage Heavy soil
Riverine Flood Plain	Very high	Loam Sandy-Loam	Deep	None	Moderate	Poor	High water table	Occasional flooding
Outer Lakeshore Plain								
Riverine Flood Plain	Very high	Loam Sandy-Loam	Deep	None	Severe	Poor	High water table	Occasional flooding
Interfluve	High	Clay Clay-Loam	Deep	None	Severe	Poor	Moderately high water table	Heavy soils Localized sod

Lower Piedmont	Moderate	Sandy-Loam Loam Clay-Loam	Moderate	Moderate	Moderate	Fair	Rapid drainage Small, semipermanent, possibly permanent brooks	Generally good conditions
Upper Piedmont	Low to moderate	Clay-Loam Clay	Shallow to moderate	Moderate to high	Severe	Good	Rapid drainage Small, semipermanent, possibly permanent brooks	Frosts, heavy soils Erosion severe Fertility problems
Sierra	Low	Loam Sandy-Loam	Shallow	High	Cultivation impossible	Excellent	Abundant, rapid runoff Deeply incised streams Numerous springs	Nonagricultural resource

consider that zone as the critical agricultural resource. The fact that settlement was restricted to a specific band in the Lower Piedmont during the entire First Intermediate and Middle Horizon periods further strengthens this argument. The process of colonization seems to involve selection of a particular ecozone, followed by intensification of use rather than niche expansion.

What were some of the variables that were responsible for this selectivity? In terms of the total combination of factors, the Lower Piedmont was clearly a highly favorable niche: it had fertile, friable, and moderately deep soils, with a low-to-moderate susceptibility to erosion; the most favorable frost regime; moderately high rainfall; and abundant surface drainage. The Upper Piedmont, on the other hand, not only had poorer general soil conditions in terms of soil depth, texture, and fertility, but it presented a more serious problem as far as erosion was concerned. If we had detailed empirical data on input/output ratios for cultivation in this area, then we could probably demonstrate that niche intensification in the Lower Piedmont would be a more productive response to population growth than niche diversification. There may, however, have been even more imperative reasons for the lack of expansion into the Upper Piedmont, such as the absence of varieties of maize adaptable to the short growing season. The avoidance of the Alluvial Plain may have been due to a combination of several sets of factors, related to the increased cost of cultivation and greater risk (which, in the long run, mean the same thing, since a series of crop losses would reduce the average yield). Again, there may also have been a more imperative reason for the retardation of colonization: the labor requirements for large-scale drainage and floodwater canal systems. Even in the Early Intermediate: Phase 3, the polities were very small in size and probably insufficiently centralized to command the labor for large-scale public works of this type. The archaeological settlement data suggest that large-scale colonization did not occur until Late Horizon times, and probably not until Texcoco had established hegemony over the entire area. If we accept this reasoning, then we can consider the Lower Piedmont as the major agricultural resource for the First Intermediate period and test our population pressure hypothesis with this consideration.

In testing our hypothesis, we will follow the procedure suggested by William Allan (1965) in his classic study, *The African Husbandman*. One of Allan's principles is that in order to estimate carrying capacity, one must measure three components: the cultivable land factor, the land use factor, and the cultivation factor. Our study (as stated previously) will concentrate on what we consider to be the prime agricultural resource in the First Intermediate period—the Lower Piedmont, an ecological zone that includes approximately 13,000 hectares of land. However, since the strip of First Intermediate: Phase 3 settlement is densely concentrated in just the upper half of this ecozone, the key agricultural resource on the Piedmont is really only 7,000 hectares. Residences, waterways, local hills and rock outcrops, areas of naturally thin soil, and borders between fields would reduce the amount of agricultural land somewhat further, so that the actual surface of cultivated land in this strip could not have exceeded 5,000 hectares.

This assessment of agricultural resources refers specifically to the central and southern sectors of the Lower Piedmont. A somewhat different situation exists in the northern strip. Here, although the sites are numerous, large, and dense and are concentrated in a position comparable to those in the central and southern regions, the northern Piedmont itself is so narrow in proportion to population size that some other agricultural resource must have been used. We suspect that much of the nearby Papalotla floodplain was cultivated as well—a suspicion that is strengthened by the presence of First Intermediate: Phase 1 and 2 villages and hamlets within the floodplain. We do not have data to calculate the size of the floodplain, but it included minimally 1,500 hectares of land, and possibly as much as 2,500 hectares. Of all the rivers in the Texcoco area, the Papalotla has the greatest flow of floodwater, as well as the greatest sediment load (see Table 7). It is also a permanent stream, since the big San Francisco springs drain naturally into it (with a flow, in the 1920s, of 300 liters per second), and it has the most extensive floodplain.[1] Our calculations of the cultivable land factor in the First Intermediate: Phase 3 are shown in Table 8. According to the table, the total significant agricultural resources in the Lower Piedmont are 10,200–11,000 hectares of land. A few small sites do occur in the Upper Piedmont and lakeshore zone, but these were probably special resource sites.

A more difficult problem is posed by the assessment of the land use factor, that is, the cycle of cultivation and resting. Today, virtually all land is cropped annually, and no planned fallowing is practiced—a reflection of the extreme pressure on the land currently available. Theoretically, the entire range of fallowing systems defined by Boserup (1965) could have been

TABLE 7

VOLUME OF WATER AND SILT IN SUSPENSION PER YEAR
OF RIVERS IN THE BASIN OF MEXICO

River	Station	Period of Observation	Average Volume of Water (in thousands of cubic meters)	Average Volume of Sediment (in thousands of cubic meters)	Average Percent of Sediment per Volume
Rio Hondo	Molinito	1961–66	19,994	56.518	0.2827
Rio de los Remedios	Molino Blanco	1961–66	73,076	249.756	0.3418
Rio Tepetlaxco	Salitre	1961–66	2,270	22.365	0.9852
Rio Magdalena	Desv. Alta	1962–66	5,145	5.670	0.1102
Rio Ameca	San Luis Mo II	1965–66	7,329	77.969	1.0639
Rio Teotihuacán	Tepexpan	1962–66	3,197*	7.525	0.2354
Rio Papalotla	LaGrande	1962–66	7,727	55.280	0.7154
Rio Xalapango	Atenco	1961–66	1,468	8.203	0.5588
Rio Coxcacuaco	San Andres	1961–66	2,997	26.214	0.8747
Rio Texcoco	Texcoco	1961–66	1,842	11.077	0.6014
Rio Chapingo	Chapingo	1961–66	1,687	18.834	1.1164
Rio San Bernardino	San Mateo	1961–66	2,290	21.416	0.9352
Rio Santa Monica	Tejocote	1961–66	2,088	19.955	0.9557
Rio Cuauhtitlán	Huehuetoca	1965–66	112,114†	97.209	0.0867

*This figure does not include water draining from the springs at San Juan Teotihuacán
—approximately 18,000,000 cubic meters per year.
†Some of this figure is artificial drainage from Mexico City.

TABLE 8

CULTIVABLE LAND FACTOR—FIRST INTERMEDIATE:
PHASE 3

Type of Land	Total Land Surface (in hectares)	Agricultural Land (in hectares)
First-class land		
Lower Piedmont	7,000	5,000
Papalotla floodplain	1,500–2,500	1,200–2,000
Second-class land		
Lower Piedmont	6,000	4,000
Total	14,500–15,500	10,200–11,000

practiced in pre-Hispanic times. In fact, because of the factors we discussed in connection with Neolithic technology, we would tend to reduce these choices considerably.

Many of the soils in the Lower Piedmont could sustain continuous maize cropping without irrigation or fertilization, but maize yields stabilize at very low levels (500 to 600 kilos per hectare according to a study conducted by the Chapingo School of Agriculture). With irrigation and very modest additions of fertilizers (that is, within the capacities of pre-Hispanic cultivators), these average yields could have been raised to 1,000 kilos on the Piedmont, and up to 1,400 kilos in the riverine floodplains. Most informants today who have a good supply of animal fertilizers apply them every three years. With ideal rainfall conditions or with irrigation, this schedule would raise yields to three to five times the base levels.

Most studies of agriculture in highland Mexico (see Palerm 1961a, for example) suggest that if little or no fertilizer is used, a fallowing regime of 1:1, 2:1, or 1:2 is sufficient to maintain yields well above the base level potential. The range relates to variations in soil fertility. Scattered data from our Basin of Mexico study suggest a similar situation. In the poorer, limestone-based soils of Huehuetenango, Guatemala, the cycle of fallowing is comparable but apparently unstable, and over several decades it ultimately produces a degraded soil-vegetation association called *llano* (Stadelman 1940). In Huehuetenango, the ratio of yields on degraded soils to soils recently brought into cultivation to freshly tilled forest lands is approximately 1:1.8:2.6.

We would suggest that during the First Intermediate period, most of the land was alternately cultivated and fallowed, possibly with a longer cycling pattern in the earlier periods and a reduction to a 1:1 or 1:2 cycle by Phase 3 times. For the Late Horizon period, a variety of systems were probably in use, and, as we have pointed out, all ecozones were utilized. Table 9, highly tentative though it is, indicates the potential of various methods of cultivation in all of Texcoco's ecological zones for the Late Horizon period. We have made the assumption, based on fairly reliable data, that floodwater or spring-based irrigation not only regularizes yields and hence raises average productivity by reducing losses, but also adds enough nutrients to the soil to eliminate the need for fallowing. We have included in Table 9 three other categories of land that we know were present in Late Horizon times, *calmil*, or "houselot" lands, where house-

TABLE 9
TYPES OF LATE HORIZON CULTIVATION IN THE
TEXCOCO AREA

Type of Cultivation	Average Yield of Cropped Fields (in kilograms per hectare)	Land Use Factor		Average Yield per Hectare of Agricultural Land (in kilograms)
Calmil	1,400	Annual	1	1,400
Alluvial Plain— permanent irrigation	1,400	Annual	1	1,400
Piedmont—permanent irrigation	1,000	Annual	1	1,000
Alluvial Plain— floodwater irrigation	1,000	Annual	1	1,000
Piedmont—floodwater terraces	800	Annual	1	800
Riverine floodplain	1,200	Annual	1	1,200
Naturally humid land	1,400	1:1	2	700
Chinampa	3,000*	Annual	1	3,000
Pseudo-chinampa	2,000	Annual	1	2,000
Temporal—Alluvial Plain	1,000	1:1	2	500
Temporal—Piedmont	400–800	1:1	2	200–400
Bush fallowing	1,400	1:4	5	280

*Minimum yield

hold refuse provided exceptionally rich nutrients for the soil; chinampa cultivation from the southern part of the Basin; and the pseudo-chinampas from the Teotihuacán Valley.

Before completing our analysis of the First Intermediate: Phase 3 land use factor, we must digress momentarily to discuss the cultivation factor. By "cultivation factor," Allan meant the amount of land actually planted in crops in a particular year that was needed to sustain a particular family or person. The word "sustain," however, is ambiguous. Allan's method of calculation was empirical, based on family economic aspirations in a variety of cases drawn from Africa. The meaning of "sustain," therefore, varies from group to group. In some cases, for example, the group may be completely isolated, without access to markets, and possess an essentially egalitarian internal structure; hence a family will only plant as much land as needed to provide actual subsistence. In other areas, the family might produce a substantial surplus above subsistence needs to pay taxes to an elite, or sell its crops through a market system. We are concerned here not with the redistribution of food throughout a social system, but simply with the total amount of food that could be produced by the system. We will, therefore, establish a cultivation factor that refers only to the *subsistence* needs of an average family.

For this we need to know two things: the relative ratio of maize yields during the First Intermediate: Phase 3 as compared with Late Horizon and contemporary maize, and the percentage of the diet that was based upon maize. In the absence of any quantifiable substantive information, we will offer two models for the percentage of maize in the diet. With one model we will assume that 80 percent of the caloric intake is derived from maize, a figure comparable to that of poorer peasant families today, and probably very close to peasant consumption during the Late Horizon. Considering the fact that the First Intermediate: Phase 3 population utilized only a small percentage of the total area for agriculture, there must have been abundant fishing and hunting-and-gathering resources; we therefore offer a second model, in which only 65 percent of the food intake was maize. Estimating a daily average consumption of approximately 2,000 kilo-calories (a reasonable estimate for all ages in a peasant population in which the average weight and stature is that of the Central Mexican), the average per capita intake of maize would then amount to 160 and 128 kilos respectively.

On the basis of MacNeish's research on Tamaulipas and Tehuacan (1964), and Flannery's in Oaxaca (1968b), it is clear that First Intermediate maize must have been considerably less productive per plant than Late Horizon or contemporary maize. Flannery (1967, 1973) and more recently Kirkby (1973) have stressed this point in several papers, although Flannery may have considerably underestimated the productivity of maize in the earlier periods. His calculations are based only on the comparison of ear size, and he has suggested that the Early Horizon fields may have yielded as little as 200 to 250 kilos of maize per hectare. This figure seems too low. Based upon Allan's (1965) data from Africa and Stadelman's (1940) data from Highland Guatemala, it can be argued that the *average* farmer would have to receive at least double these yields on the *average* before the energy input-output returns would be worth the effort. With Neolithic tools, the extra labor required would make even the 400-to-500 kilo level somewhat marginal; thus we suggest that the achievement of sedentary residence in the Early Horizon is related to this degree of productivity taken as a minimum.

This suggestion is based on the consideration that small ear size is associated with small total plant size, and since smaller plants would demand fewer soil nutrients and less water, they could be planted closer together. There is also evidence from the study of teocentli and from Mangelsdorf's experimental work in the laboratory (Mangelsdorf, MacNeish, and Galinat 1966) that the more primitive varieties of maize produced higher numbers of ears per plant. In the absence of empirical data, we will assume that the productivity of Early Horizon maize was about one-half that of contemporary maize under the same soil and moisture conditions. MacNeish's (1964) Tehuacán research suggests that essentially modern varieties of criollo maize were present by A.D. 600–700, a theory that is also supported by the spacing of maize hills in the preserved pre-Hispanic fields near Nealtica, Puebla (Seele 1973). We will therefore estimate the productivity of First Intermediate: Phase 3 maize at about three-fourths of those varieties.

On the basis of these data and using our two models of maize consumption, the yields and cultivation factors shown in Table 10 may be established for an extended family of seven persons—the average size in the mid sixteenth century (see Sanders 1971).

We are now in a position to estimate the carrying capacity of the First Intermediate period. If we assume forest fallowing on the Lower Piedmont as the primary system for Phases 1 and 2, then the capacity of the area could be evaluated as follows: For the 5,000 hectares of first-class land, assuming a cultivation factor of 1.1 and a land use factor of 5, we calculate that the average extended family of seven requires 5.5 hectares of agricultural land. This implies adequate holdings to provide maize for approximately 909 families, or 6,363 people. The 4,000 hectares of second-class Piedmont land, with a cultivation factor of 1.9 and a land use factor of 5, would yield 9.5 hectares of land per family, or sufficient land for 421 families (2,947 persons). The total population amounts to 9,310. This assumes that all agricultural land is planted in maize or an equivalent grain like amaranth. Although some cultigens in the diet, such as beans, squash, and maguey, were intercropped with maize, some land was probably utilized entirely for other crops so that these figures should be considered maximal. J. R. Parsons's estimate (1971b) of the Phase 2 population is 3,860 to 9,000 people, with approximately 500 to 1,000 residing

TABLE 10
YIELDS AND CULTIVATION FACTORS FOR A MID-SIXTEENTH-CENTURY FAMILY

Cultivation/ Type of System	Post-First Intermediate: Phase 3		First Intermediate: Phase 3		First Intermediate: Phase 1–2		Early Horizon	
	Yield*	Cultivation Factor†	Yield*	Cultivation Factor†	Yield*	Cultivation Factor†	Yield*	Cultivation Factor†
Alluvial Plain (permanent irrigation)	1,400	0.8	1,050	0.86	875	1.1	700	1.3
Piedmont (permanent irrigation)	1,000	1.1	750	1.2	625	1.5	500	1.8
Alluvial Plain (floodwater irrigation)	1,000	1.1	750	1.2	625	1.5	500	1.8
Piedmont (floodwater terracing)	800	1.4	600	1.5	500	1.9	400	2.25
Tierra de Humedad	1,400	0.8	1,050	0.86	875	1.1	700	1.3
Tierra de Humedad (riverine)	1,200	0.95	900	1.03	750	1.3	600	1.55
Chinampa	3,000	0.37	2,250	0.4	1,875	0.5	1,500	0.6
Pseudo-chinampa	2,000	0.55	1,500	0.6	1,250	0.75	1,000	0.9
Alluvial Plain (temporal)	1,000	1.1	750	1.2	625	1.6	500	1.8
Piedmont (temporal)	400–800	1.4–2.8	300–600	1.5–3.0	250–500	1.9–3.8	200–400	2.5–5.0
Bush Fallowing (good land)	1,400	0.8	1,050	0.86	875	1.1	700	1.3
Bush Fallowing (poor land)	800	1.4	600	1.5	500	1.9	400	2.25

*In kilograms per hectare.
†In hectares.

in the Papalotla floodplain and on the shore of the lake at Chimalhuacán. If we subtract these figures, the estimate comes to 3,360 to 8,000 on the Piedmont proper. Because of the survey preservation factor noted earlier, we would raise the overall total for the area to about 11,000 maximum and thus raise the total for the Piedmont to about 9,800 people. The data suggest that maximum carrying capacity using bush fallow would have been reached by Phase 2 times.

For phase 3 we will begin by assuming no significant utilization of fertilizers, no irrigation, and as short a fallowing system as possible. For the Lower Piedmont the cultivation factor on the better lands would be 1.5 hectares and the land use factor would be 2, yielding a total of 3.0 hectares per extended family. The 5,000 hectares would then provide enough land for 1,666 families or 11,662 people. The marginal lands with a cultivation factor of 3.0 and a land use of 6.0 furnished enough land to supply 667 families, or 4,669 people—a grand total of 16,331. We suggest that at this time the Papalotla alluvial floodplain was heavily utilized, with at least 1,000 hectares under cultivation. To calculate the carrying capacity of this area, we will use an estimated yield midway between that of the floodwater irrigated plain and naturally humid lands, since portions of it probably would be Tierra de Humedad. This would provide a cultivation factor of perhaps 1.0 and a land use factor of 1.0 as well, since the natural flooding of the river would maintain soil fertility—which means a capacity of 1,000 families, or 7,000 people. The total capacity, then, of the various systems of agriculture according to our First Intermediate: Phase 3 model sustains 23,331 persons. Parsons's estimate (1971b) of a population of the area in Phase 3 times is from 10,070 to 20,200. Again extrapolating for the preservation factor, we would provide a maximum estimate of the Phase 3 population of 24,000. Thus if the maximal figures are close to the actual population of the area, a situation of extreme land pressures is suggested.

In fact, the pressures on the land may have been even greater than we have assumed in the preceding discussion. On the basis of the settlement pattern data, it is clear that the lower portions of the Lower Piedmont were only sparingly used. We think the answer here lies in labor-input cost, even with the conditions of relatively friable soils. The average extended family would have to put three hectares of land in crops each year, with a manpower of only two to two and one-half workers. We suggest that as the population increased, instead of moving to more marginal lands to avoid the labor cost of increased cultivation, the shift was to further intensification of the land already cultivated, probably involving the use of springs for permanent irrigation. The cultivation factor for irrigated Piedmont would be 1.2 and the land use factor 1.2; in other words, output would increase with only a minimal amount of additional labor. There would be some added input of labor, of course, with the construction and maintenance of the canal system. In the case of the Papalotla floodplain, the use of irrigation would not substantially decrease the cultivation factor, but the expansion of the area of cultivation for this type of ecological niche would, of course, affect total productivity.

At any rate, whether we postulate an expansion of cultivation into marginal areas or an intensification of the use of the better land, it is clear that our population pressure model does apply to the Texcoco area in Phase 3 times (see Fig. 4). The fact that no really substantial increase of the cultivable land factor occurred in the succeeding 1,000 years of occupation, together with the lack of expansion into new ecological niches, demonstrates that the carrying capacity of the area was, in fact, reached in First Intermediate: Phase 3 times.

The calculated maximal population of 24,000 is still considerably less than that in the Late Horizon for the Lower Piedmont. How was this larger Late Horizon population supported? J. R. Parsons (1971b) has postulated the following distribution of the Late Horizon period population: Upper Piedmont, 15,635; Lower Piedmont, 73,230; and Lakeshore Plain, 27,530. These figures, however, need recalculation. Parsons assigns the population of the three towns of Huexotla, Coatlíchan, and Chimalhuacán to the Lower Piedmont when, in fact, these three communities lie at the very edge of the Lower Piedmont, where the population could have cultivated both the Lower Piedmont and the Alluvial Plain. He also classifies a large portion of the northern section of the Alluvial Plain (the Papalotla floodplain) as Piedmont. If we correct for these factors, then the Aztec population residing in the Papalotla floodplain and the Lower Piedmont is reduced to about 33,000. Correcting for the survey factor, this would be about 40,000 or approximately 167 percent of the population of the First Intermediate: Phase 3 period. Considering that maize was then probably 50 percent more productive, the Aztec capacity of the area using the same techniques (i.e., no irrigation) would be 36,000 people. However, since we have assumed a higher per capita maize consumption by the Aztec population—160 kilos during Phase 3 versus 128 during the earlier

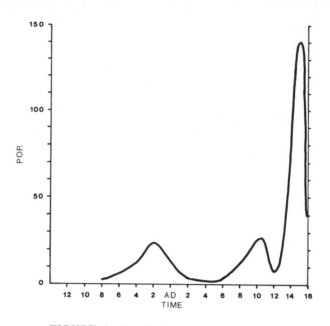

FIGURE 4. Population curve, Texcoco region.

phase—the actual population capacity would drop to 80 percent, or 29,000 persons. The only way the Aztec population could have supported so many people would have been through full use of permanent irrigation as well as floodwater irrigation, thereby making possible continuous cultivation and regularizing production of most fields. In fact, this is what the data from the sixteenth century suggest. Some communities, particularly those utilizing the irrigation system, may have devoted much of their land to garden crops and obtained staples from the market in the Alluvial Plain towns. This is, in fact, the contemporary pattern and would at least double the demographic potential of the area. At any rate, what these comparisons do show is that the First Intermediate: Phase 3 population was dense enough to have generated severe population pressures and perhaps triggered the development of hydraulic agriculture; both processes could have stimulated centralized political control. If cultivation was more extensive in the First Intermediate: Phase 2 times, then there could have been pressures even at that time which would have generated village fission and conflicts over territory, at the very least.

With respect to the total carrying capacity of the Basin of Mexico, we will now attempt to apply our methodology to the balance of the survey areas. We have excellent control with respect to agricultural models for the Teotihuacán Valley, which are virtually identical to those used for the Texcoco area. The only exception is the large area of high water table near the San Juan springs, where a kind of chinampa cultivation is in use today, what we have referred to as "pseudo-chinampa" in Tables 9 and 10.

Our weakest control is for the Ixtapalapa-Chalco-Amecameca-Xochimilco areas, the southern third of the Basin. Sanders's 1953 study of the chinampas and temporal lands of San Gregorio Atlapulco contains all the data we have on contemporary cultivation in that zone. This is unfortunate, since the southern Basin is climatically and geologically very distinctive and its whole pattern of agriculture is likely to have been unusual. Maize cultivation, for example, posed special problems there. First, a much higher percentage of the area lies above the 2,700-meter contour—the Sierra ecozone—and was hence unusable for agriculture. Second, a high percentage of the land on the Lower and Upper Piedmont, south of Lakes Chalco-Xochimilco, is a recent volcanic formation. J. R. Parsons's surveys show that this area was unoccupied until Late Horizon times, and this is the only part of the Basin of Mexico where the contemporary rural population exceeds the Aztec. At the Santa Fe seminar, José Luis Lorenzo pointed out that it was probably a volcanic wasteland comparable to the San Ángel Pedregal throughout much of the pre-Hispanic history of the area. In addition, many areas that do have a respectable soil cover and are intensively cultivated today are above the 2,400-meter contour and hence are located in the less favorable temperature regime of the Upper Piedmont. Finally, there is also an extensive area of older volcanic topography that presents intermediate conditions: Blanton's Cerro Pino and Lomas y Hoyas zone in the Ixtapalapa Peninsula and another large area near Juchitepec in the southeastern corner of the Basin. Within these areas there are zones with adequate soil cover below 2,700 meters, but we estimate that probably not more than 50 to 70 percent of the land could be used.

Climatic conditions are much more favorable in the south than in the Texcoco-Teotihuacán areas, since rainfall is substantially heavier—comparable, in fact, to that in much of highland Guatemala. The frost-rainfall schedule therefore poses a much less critical problem, even at lower elevations. Also, because of the abundant drainage, a high percentage of the Lakeshore Plain would have riverine deposits, and the soils would be more easily available to a Neolithic peasantry. The water table would be generally higher, however, and drainage problems would complicate the situation. At any rate, one would not expect large hydraulic works other than drainage-type systems, and, of course, virtually the entire lake surface was colonized and converted into chinampas in Late Horizon times. Considering the enormous capacity of chinampa cultivation and the colonization of the Milpa Alta volcanic region, we would expect that the Late Horizon population considerably exceeded that of any earlier time period. One area, however—the San Ángel Pedregal, which was a major agricultural resource during the First Intermediate period—became a rocky wasteland after the eruption of Xitle and has remained so until the present day.

The key agricultural zone of the Chalco-Tlalmanalco-Amecameca areas was the Lower Piedmont, east of Chalco, which is nothing more than a southern extension of the same zone in the Texcoco area, with the added advantage of increased rainfall. In this area, however, it diminishes to a band only two and one-half to three kilometers wide. See the survey maps for the First Intermediate period for this area and the ones that follow.

A second major area of settlement existed around Tlalmanalco, in the transitional volcanic zone, where large areas of exposed rock formation are interspersed with areas of relatively deep soil. Marginal settlement also occurred in the First Intermediate period in the Upper Piedmont, around Amecameca, suggesting population pressure. In addition, several significant settlements during this period were located on the Lakeshore Plain, within the riverine floodplains, a niche comparable to the settlement in the Papalotla floodplain of the Texcoco area. In fact, one of the two largest Phase 1 settlements is located here, indicating that the area was colonized early in the sequence. As has been pointed out, this appears to have been the preferred niche during the Early Horizon and First Intermediate: Phase 1; not until Phases 2 and 3 did the demographic balance shift to the Lower Piedmont. In summary, the key agricultural resources in the Chalco-Tlalmanalco-Amecameca area seem to have been located in the Lower Piedmont, wherever soil was deep enough to permit cultivation and in certain areas along the Lakeshore Plain, where the soils were friable and easily worked. Figure 5 shows the population curve for the Chalco region.

During First Intermediate times the only agricultural resource in the Xochimilco area was the Lower Piedmont and adjacent Lakeshore Plain in the vicinity of the town of Xochimilco, the area today referred to as the Pedregal de San Ángel. Since the end of the period, it has no longer

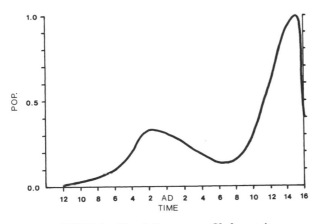

FIGURE 5. Population curve, Chalco region.

served as an agricultural resource. The presence of the Pedregal makes it very difficult to estimate the specific agricultural characteristics of this area or its population history. What is clear is that the area was colonized possibly as early as Early Horizon, but definitely by First Intermediate: Phase 1 times. Not only was the population large enough to construct a small civic center—the only one then in existence in the Basin of Mexico —but the largest settlements in Phases 2 and 3 were found here as well. In short, although the Xochimilco area is a small, reduced zone, it clearly was a key area in terms of First Intermediate period occupation of the Basin of Mexico. Figure 6 shows the Xochimilco region population curve.

The Ixtapalapa region is unique in that the most favorable ecological zone for settlement during the First Intermediate period, the Lower Piedmont, was restricted to a very small area, including the slopes of Cerro de Estrella and a part of the Portezuelo Range. Much of the elevated ground of the peninsula is much too rocky for effective cultivation. Furthermore, the Alluvial Plain is narrow everywhere and probably had a very high water table. Although this would present drainage problems, it would also provide an unusually favorable niche with respect to the frost regime. In our calculations of carrying capacity in Ixtapalapa, we will consider the Lakeshore Plain as a key resource as well. The population was rather dense, presumably because of the attractiveness of aquatic products on both sides, the saltwater lake to the north and the freshwater lake to the south. Figure 7 shows the Ixtapalapa population curve.

In the Teotihuacán Valley all of the basic ecological factors were similar to those in the Texcoco area, but the actual settlement configuration is less easily explained or summarized. As a result of our survey, it is

153

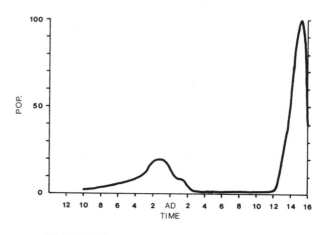

FIGURE 6. Population curve, Xochimilco region.

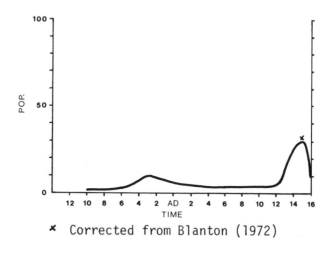

✗ Corrected from Blanton (1972)

FIGURE 7. Population curve, Ixtapalapa region.

clear that the favorite niche for settlement during the First Intermediate period was, in fact, the Lower Piedmont, particularly its upper sections, close to the flanking ranges, or high hills, where runoff would be unusually abundant. Virtually all the Phase 1 sites are located in this setting. During Phase 2 times sites were much more numerous and located in the same ecological zone, but a substantial number of people, at least 20 percent of the population, were living in the Alluvial Plain, half in the area of the San Juan springs, and the balance at Cuanalan, down valley. (We have explained the San Juan settlement as possibly related to the inception of pseudo-chinampa cultivation in the high water table area near the springs.) By Phase 3 times at least 50 percent of the population of the valley was living in a large town on the Lower Piedmont immediately above the springs—the nucleus of the growth of the great Middle Horizon metropolis. In part, this situation might be related to soil erosion in the Piedmont. Many of the Lower Piedmont sites are on much more steeply sloping terrain than that of the Texcoco area, and it is conceivable that erosion was a serious problem. However, the fact that the population shift was initiated as early as Phase 2, when the Piedmont population was far below the levels reached in Phase 3 times, suggests that the shift was not really related to land pressures. Perhaps the greater risk of crop loss from frost and droughts in this northern area provided a stronger stimulus to a more efficient system of adaptation. At any rate, our conclusion is that the key land resources during the First Intermediate period were the Lower Piedmont, at positions of abundant off-slope drainage, and the high water table area near the springs. See Figure 8 for the Teotihuacán First Intermediate: Phase 3 population curve. The Basin of Mexico curve is shown in Figure 9.

Instead of proceeding with a detailed manipulation of data for these areas as we did for Texcoco, we shall simply assess the population by time phase and calculate to what degree the population had reached carrying capacity in terms of our models of agricultural systems. These data are summarized in Table 11.

If we take the various ranges of carrying capacities and survey estimates, then the following assessment could be made. By either First Intermediate: Phase 2 or 3 times, the population of the Ixtapalapa region had reached from 30 to 85 percent of carrying capacity, the Chalco region 40 to 130 percent, the Cuicuilco area 30 to 165 percent, the Teotihuacán Valley 65 percent, the Texcoco region 50 to 100 percent. These percent-

TABLE 11
FIRST INTERMEDIATE: PHASE 3 CARRYING CAPACITY

Region	Surface Area (in square kilometers)	Cultivable Land Factor (in hectares)	Land Use Factor	Cultivation Factor* (in hectares)	Carrying Capacity†	Survey Estimate Phase 2	Survey Estimate Phase 3
Ixtapalapa							
Lakeshore Plain							
High water table	15	1,000	2	1.03	3,295		
Moderate water table	15	1,125	2	1.20	3,276		
Lower Piedmont	63	4,200	2	1.5–3.0	4,900–9,800		
					11,471–16,371	4,800–9,600‡	4,560–8,400‡
Chalco							
Class A land							
Lower Piedmont	111	7,400	2	1.5–3.0	8,631–17,269		
Lower Piedmont-rocky	90	4,500	2	1.5–3.0	5,250–10,500		
Riverine plain	20	2,010	1	1.03	13,657		
Class B land							
Lakeshore Plain (interfluve)	MARGINAL USE						
Upper Piedmont							
					27,538–41,426	12,000–24,000	18,000–36,000

Xochimilco-Alluvial Plain	50	4,000				
or El Pedregal						
Model 1—Unirrigated						
High water table		1,000	2	1.03	3,295	
Mid water table		3,000	2	1.20	8,750	
					12,045	
Model 2—50% irrigated						
Irrigated		1,500	1	0.85	12,808	Depends on
Unirrigated		1,500	2	1.20	4,375	size
High water table		1,000	2	1.03	3,295	of
					20,478	Cuicuilco
Model 3—80% irrigated						(10,000–20,000?)
Irrigated		3,000	1	0.86	25,616	
High water table		1,000	2	1.03	3,295	
					28,911	
Teotihuacán Valley						
Class A land						
Lower Piedmont (upper)	100	6,666	2	1.5	15,554	
Upper Piedmont (lower)	40	2,000	2	2.0	3,500	
Pseudo-chinampa	10	1,000	1	0.6	11,662	
Class B land						
Lower Piedmont (lower)			MARGINAL USE			6,000§
					30,716	22,000§

*Cultivation factor is·for an extended family of seven persons.

†Carrying capacity = $\dfrac{\text{cultivable land factor}}{\text{land use factor}} \div \text{cultivation factor} \times 7$.

‡Blanton (1972b) with 20% added for preservation factor.

§Sanders (1965) and R. Millon (1970b) with additional 20% preservation factor for rural sites.

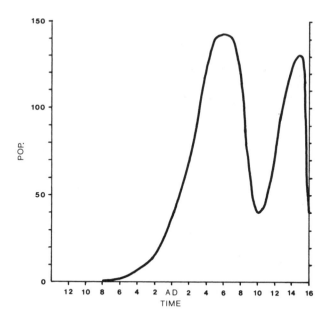

FIGURE 8. Population curve, Teotihuacán Valley region.

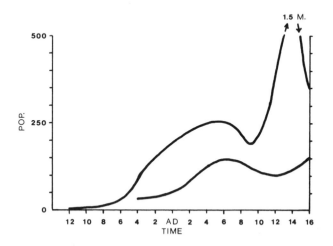

FIGURE 9. Population curve, Basin of Mexico and Tula region.

ages could be increased appreciably if we use Kirkby's (1973) lower yields for maize and include some calculation of crop production for domestic animals. At any rate, the data strongly suggest that population pressure played a significant role in the emergence of intra- and intercommunity ranking by the end of the First Intermediate period—the time when archaeological evidence also suggests such ranking.

NOTE

1. As noted previously, most of the soils in the plain have a high clay content, making them difficult to cultivate with primitive hand tools. The exception would be the floodplain of the rivers in which the soils contain a considerable percentage of coarse materials. It is no surprise, therefore, that colonization of the Alluvial Plain was initiated in a riverine floodplain.

8

Summary and Conclusions

WILLIAM T. SANDERS

Department of Anthropology
The Pennsylvania State University

JEFFREY R. PARSONS

Museum of Anthropology
University of Michigan

MICHAEL H. LOGAN

Department of Anthropology
University of Tennessee

The following is a reconstruction of ecological adaptation during the period from 1500 B.C. to A.D. 1521. We have detailed descriptive data on settlement variability, settlement location, and civic architecture. On the basis of these data, we can make carefully controlled inferences about degrees of political control and centralization, land use preferences, and, in some phases, internal societal differentiation. We can also present reasonable estimates of population sizes for each of the areas by time phases, but there is a series of problems that can only be solved through tighter chronological control and testing by excavation. Furthermore, we know something about the location of key resources other than agricultural land, local specialization, and distribution networks, although these data are deficient. Finally, our direct data on agricultural systems are thin, except, of course, for the Late Horizon.

Most of our reconstruction consists of a series of specific models based on the assumptions derived from Boserup's (1965) general model. In the construction of these models, we have used scattered direct data from the pre–Late Horizon periods, as well as inferences about the presence or absence of certain techniques of land use intensification (floodwater irrigation on terraces and in the plain, perennial irrigation, and drainage cultivation) from the settlement data and population reconstructions.

In defense of these reconstructions, it should be pointed out that the environment of the Basin of Mexico puts severe restrictions on alternatives. If the population estimates are reasonable, it is difficult to see how the dense First Intermediate: Phase 3 and Middle Horizon populations could have been supported without the development of humidity and erosion controls. The close coincidences in settlement location between Late Horizon and pre–Late Horizon sites regarding water resources offer further indirect support for our reconstruction. With these considerations in mind, we will now summarize the cultural history of the Basin.

It is clear from the work of MacNeish (1964) in Puebla and Flannery in Oaxaca (1967–68; see Flannery n.d.) that domesticated maize was present at a very early date immediately south of the Basin of Mexico, in dry highland regions at intermediate elevations that apparently were the habitat of the wild variant of maize. The archaeological data also indicate that the human population was denser and that rank-based social systems developed earlier in this region than in the Basin of Mexico.

The ceramics of the Early Horizon in the Basin of Mexico are virtually identical with those in the intermediate highlands of Morelos. A reasonable hypothesis, then, is that the first sedentary farmer-potters to settle the Basin of Mexico were migrants from Morelos, just over the Ajusco Range to the south. A wide, low pass connects the two areas above Amecameca in the southeast corner of the Basin. Assuming this hypothesis to be correct, we would expect to find our earliest settlements in the southern portion of the Basin and to find a denser settlement there than elsewhere during early pre-Hispanic settlement history. We would also expect that Boserup's (1965) extensive-to-intensive-cultivation model would be particularly applicable to the history of the agricultural utilization of that area, since the southeastern portion of the Basin has heavier rainfall, and hence crop security based on rainfall alone is higher.

With the exception of three hamlets, all sites in the southern Basin represent substantial villages on the shore of Lakes Chalco and Xochimilco. Presumably the combination of lake resources with well-drained but dependable moisture in the soil for cultivation was the primary factor in settlement distribution. The major exception to this pattern is the Tlatilco village site on the Lower Piedmont, west of Lake Texcoco and outside of our survey area. We might point out in this connection, however, that the west side of Lake Texcoco has somewhat higher rainfall than the east and in this regard is perhaps more comparable to the southern Basin, although the evidence for irrigation both at Cuicuilco in the southwest and at Coyoacán does indicate that crop security was still a problem in this portion of the Basin.

Of interest also is the fact that two of the sites, Tlatilco and Tlapacoya, do exhibit evidence of marked social ranking in their earliest components. Considering the lack of evidence of significant ranking in the succeeding First Intermediate: Phase 1, when populations were considerably larger, this fact suggests a contradiction in our model. We would, however, point out a rather close parallel with the process of fission and migration in Polynesia, where a dissident group, under the leadership of a junior member of the chiefly lineage, would often leave an island and colonize uninhabited islands nearby. For a short period the colonizing group would maintain a chiefdom structure, but within a few decades or centuries of initial colonization, because of the abundance of land and resultant potential for further fission, the power of the chief would decline rapidly and a more egalitarian society would result—an interesting case of cultural devolution. An excellent specific case is that of the Maori in New Zealand (a very large island and settled late), where an essentially egalitarian society persisted until European contact. Perhaps the initial penetration of the Basin of Mexico occurred as a result of fission from one of the highly developed Morelos chiefdoms.

Why was the Basin initially colonized? According to the study of San Lorenzo by Cobean et al. (1971), obsidian from the Basin of Mexico was one of the prime objects needed and obtained by the Olmecs of the South Gulf Coast during the Early Horizon. M. D. Coe and others, notably Grove (1968a), have argued that centers like Chalcatzingo in Morelos were parts of a widespread trade network. Prior to the actual colonization of the Basin, obsidian from the Otumba area apparently filtered into this trade network of Morelos chiefdoms. We presume that at this time it was quarried and delivered to the exchange network by hunting and gathering bands living in the northern area. The penetration by people from Morelos may well have occurred as an attempt to consolidate and better control this trade resource.

In the succeeding First Intermediate: Phase 1 a series of striking changes occurred. On Map 5 we have traced population distribution during this phase that we believe to be the product of village fission. The major events were a filling in of the southern area and a colonization of the lower Texcoco Piedmont as far north as the southern rampart of the Teotihuacán Valley. A few isolated hamlets occur on the north side of the Teotihuacán Valley, but no settlements have been reported to the north of the survey area. In support of Boserup's extensive-intensive cultivation paradigm (1965) is the fact that the settlements were small and widely spaced and that the colonization of this large area was completed within the first two hundred years of the First Intermediate: Phase 1.

The First Intermediate: Phase 1 represents a tremendous demographic expansion. From a tiny Early Horizon base the population probably grew to at least ten thousand people within the survey area, distributed in a dozen substantial villages around the edges of the southern lake system. The relative density of this occupation and a distinct tendency toward regular spacing of sites around the lakeshore suggest that this prime niche might have been approaching a limit conditioned both by subsistence technology and by the organizational mechanisms available for regional sociopolitical integration. The observed fragmentation of face-to-face residential groups in simple egalitarian societies at levels above a few hundred persons seems relevant here (see, for example, Lee 1972; Forge 1972; Woodburn 1972). This fragmentation apparently occurs primarily because of the inability of egalitarian systems to resolve intragroup conflicts, which multiply rapidly at population levels much above a few hundred individuals. In the chiefdom situation, the presence of high-ranking individuals who would have some authority to resolve certain conflicts would raise this maximal limit significantly. We are presently unaware of any ethnographically observed maximal limit for face-to-face residential groups that might be operative for chiefdom systems, but the largest stable Polynesian chiefdom reported by Sahlins involves populations below ten thousand persons (Sahlins 1958). It may be of interest to note that our largest sites suggest nucleated residential groups of roughly two thousand persons—the upper level of most tribes. The predominant intersite spacing of 8 to 10 kilometers for substantial sites may reflect the general inability of polities in the Basin of Mexico at this time to resolve intercommunity conflict for regional population densities much higher than about twenty-five persons per square kilometer.

Summary and Conclusions

The First Intermediate: Phase 2 is a period of massive population growth and expansion into new niches throughout most of our survey area. Whatever the principal restraints in Phase 1 times (in terms of the size of face-to-face residential groups and regional population density), it is apparent that they are no longer operative. This probably implies considerable change in political structure between the two phases. There are several nucleated Phase 2 communities exceeding four thousand people, and overall population density is everywhere some four times as high as that of the preceding phase. Nevertheless, our settlement data evidence no clear dominance hierarchy. There are a half-dozen sites in the 70-to-100-hectare range, all of which show some evidence of civic construction. No single center, however, can be designated as regionally dominant on the basis of what we now know, with the possible exception of Cuicuilco. There are strong suggestions that at this time this center was becoming significantly larger than other contemporary centers and exercising political influence in a different way, most notably by the concentration of regional population into a rapidly expanding urban core.

The southern heartland around the shoreline of Lake Chalco-Xochimilco continued to be the focus of major occupation. The growth of sites in the northern two-thirds of our survey area, however, and the general expansion of small sites into higher ground throughout the eastern side of the Basin of Mexico suggest that subsistence was more secure in these new regions than in the previous periods. Improved water-control techniques and improved varieties of plant cultigens may have been involved in this expansion. The presence of sites on the marshy eastern shore of Lake Texcoco, far from any cultivable land, suggests the exploitation of lacustrine resources on a scale that may imply the beginning of local redistributive networks and symbiotic relationships between agriculturalists and lakeside hunters, gatherers, or salt collectors.

In summary, the initial precocity of the southern area of the Basin was maintained throughout Phases 1 and 2. The population distribution during the First Intermediate: Phase 2 shows a gradation of density, community size, and degree of political centralization from south to north, with the only large political center, Cuicuilco, occurring in the southern portion of the Basin. Recent surveys by Parsons in the northwestern part of the Basin dramatically confirm this patterning. He reports only one Phase 2 site and no Phase 1 sites in a test area measuring 400 square kilometers.

Several sites in the southeast are either large villages or small towns with small-scale ceremonial architecture; Cuicuilco, of course, was probably a real town with massive ceremonial constructions. In the Texcoco area, the pattern is one of substantial villages, one of which may have had small ceremonial platforms. The Teotihuacán Valley, on the other hand, was an area primarily of hamlet-size settlements.

If Palerm and Wolf's identification of the ditch at Cuicuilco is correct (1961d), then it appears that the growth of that center may, in fact, be related to intensification of cultivation and inception of hydraulic agriculture. We estimate the capacity of the Cuicuilco area without irrigation to be eight to ten thousand persons, a figure which could be increased to twenty-two to twenty-six thousand if the entire plain was irrigated. Considering our lack of control on the settlement size of Cuicuilco, either model could apply.

In Phase 3 of the First Intermediate period, the demographic and cultural preeminence of the south begins to decline. Although the largest settlement in the Basin of Mexico was probably still located at Cuicuilco, ceremonial architecture and several townlike settlements occur in the Texcoco Piedmont area, where population had increased. The population estimates are too imprecise to assert positively that canal irrigation was functioning at this time, but some kind of intensification of land use obviously occurred to support the population increase calculated by J. R. Parsons. The distribution of site clusters, as we pointed out, does tie in very closely with the position of the springs and the area irrigated by the Late Horizon canal systems.

At any rate, even if we use the lower estimates of the population for each of the phases and areas, it is clear that the population was denser and earlier in the south—a fact directly related to the appearance of political centers. Furthermore, we need not have population reaching carrying capacity to produce land pressure, so even Parsons's lower figures would support our theoretical argument.

In our calculations of carrying capacity, furthermore, we have assumed free access to agricultural land, both intrasocietal and intersocietal. In fact, the spacing of settlement clusters in Early Intermediate: Phase 3 times suggests hostility between clusters; the presence of intervening areas of "no-man's-land" would probably aggravate the problem. Under these conditions one would expect that the reduction of the land resource available per capita would produce considerable intrasocietal competition and variability in landholdings, a process that in turn would stimulate political centralization and ranking.

The dense settlement east of Lake Chalco is probably related to the high productive potential of this relatively humid area under natural rainfall cultivation. Within this region there is little indication that any one site was locally predominant. This relatively egalitarian arrangement may be related to the apparent lack of any inherent selection or stimulus for stratification in a subsistence mode dominated by rainfall cultivation. In marked contrast to the northern part of our survey area, the southeastern portion shows a remarkable continuity in population size and settlement patterning between Phases 2 and 3. In fact, Phase 3 in the southeast seems to be little more than the expansion of a basically Phase 2 settlement system.

The very different situation in the Teotihuacán Valley—where there is a single very dominant site and many much smaller secondary settlements of roughly equivalent status—may be related to the selection and stimulus for social stratification inherent in the implementation and operation of a valley-wide canal irrigation system. The great population expansion and very marked change in regional settlement patterning within the Teotihuacán Valley relative to the preceding phase strongly suggest some very basic organizational changes in the area during the last few centuries B.C. Comparable changes are not at all apparent in the southeastern region of the Basin of Mexico, where there is much greater demographic and settlement pattern stability between the First Intermediate: Phase 2 and Phase 3. It is very tempting to see this marked north-south difference as related to the implementation of new canal irrigation systems during Phase 3 times in the north and a continued dependence on long-established rainfall cultivation in the south. It should one day be possible to demonstrate conclusively that the operation of such a hydraulic system had by this point become a critical factor in the emergence of the town of Teotihuacán. As Millon, Drewitt, and Cowgill (1973) have emphasized, this hydraulic argument should be considered together with the close proximity of Teotihuacán to the two major obsidian sources in Mesoamerica.

The unique settlement configuration of the Texcoco region is seen as a product of its close juxtaposition to the Teotihuacán system, where a nascent state polity was emerging and consolidating itself (Earle 1971). If we are correct, further testing in this region should indicate relatively closer ties to Teotihuacán than to settlements farther to the south, where a comparable structuring of settlement location is not apparent.

The demographic depression and unusual settlement distribution of the Ixtapalapa Peninsula may be primarily related to the peninsula's position as a buffer zone between competitive emergent state polities at Cuicuilco and Teotihuacán. The wholesale abandonment of land occupied in Phase 2 and the restriction of major sites to highly defensible locations suggest that the relationship between Cuicuilco and Teotihuacán in Phase 3 times was dominated in overt hostility. Several Phase 3 sites in the peninsula are on hilltop locations.

The clearly marginal role of the southern Piedmont and the Amecameca subvalley during Phases 2 and 3 suggests that there was little stimulus to utilize land over 2,400 meters or to invest labor in terracing and clearing fields in rugged areas. The direct correlation between (1) the narrow Lakeshore Plain, the rugged Piedmont, high elevation, and limited occupation and (2) the wide Lakeshore Plain, the broad, smooth Piedmont, low elevation, and demographic optimum clearly indicates the orientation and priorities of First Intermediate period subsistence in the southern Basin of Mexico.

In the case of the Teotihuacán Valley, a major breakthrough in ecological adaptation apparently occurred with the drainage of the spring area for chinampa cultivation. We say "apparently" because our only corroborative data are the location of the Early Intermediate: Phase 3 town and the evidence from the pollen profiles. This event resulted in a complete reversal of demographic trends in the succeeding Early Intermediate: Phase 4 (Tzacualli-Miccaotli phase) and the Middle Horizon (Tlamimilolpa-Xolapan phases).

Up until First Intermediate: Phase 4 times, the history of population, settlement, and political centralization (and, inferentially, agricultural systems) seems to fit our theoretical position rather well. One major deficiency of the data is in the area of economic specialization, which, predictably, should increase with time. We also need more detailed archaeological data on the matter of social differentiation within the Early Intermediate: Phase 3 polities, as reflected in either houses or burials. Here data are admittedly weak. Such data, of course, cannot be directly derived from regional surveys of the type described but would require either extensive excavations or intensive surveys of the type conducted by René

Millon at Teotihuacán. First Intermediate: Phase 3 resource utilization is summarized in Map 16.

The final phases of the First Intermediate period witnessed, as we pointed out, a series of spectacular changes in the culture of the Basin, most particularly the extraordinary growth of Teotihuacán from a town to a metropolis. Our estimates show a total population increase in the survey area between the First Intermediate: Phase 3 and the Middle Horizon (from 105,000 to 150,000, taking Parsons's [1971a, 1971b] maximal population estimates, or our reassessment of them, 130,000 to 180,000). This is essentially because of the remarkable growth of population at Teotihuacán itself, since there is good evidence of population reduction in most of the survey area. The population reduction is most severe in areas immediately adjacent to the Teotihuacán Valley and least evident in the southern portion of the Basin. In the Texcoco area the northern and central sectors suffer reductions of perhaps 90 percent of the occupation, while the southern sector plus Ixtapalapa, Chalco, and Amecameca suffered a reduction of perhaps 60 percent, according to Parsons's calculations, or 40 percent with the reassessment of his figures presented in Table 12. The data suggest that a substantial amount of the growth of Teotihuacán was fed by a massive population movement from the hinterland and that virtually all of the population in the northern and central sectors of the Texcoco area moved into the city. In the case of Xochimilco, the population loss was virtually total after the eruption of Xitle and the consequent removal of the only favorable niche for cultivation in the entire southwest area.

Furthermore, the Middle Horizon sites reported by Parsons are all rather peculiar when compared with earlier sites in the same area. We do have evidence of substantial rural settlement in peripheral locations of the Teotihuacán Valley during the Middle Horizon period for comparison. These sites look like small editions of Teotihuacán itself, in that they exhibit densely nucleated residential areas, substantial ceremonial architecture, large multifamily houses constructed of masonry, and virtually the entire range of artifact types found at Teotihuacán. In contrast, the Middle Horizon sites outside the Teotihuacán Valley generally have very thin occupations, in terms of concentration of artifact materials, and no evidence of substantial architecture; even some of the ceramic samples show peculiar gaps when compared to samples from the Teotihuacán Valley.

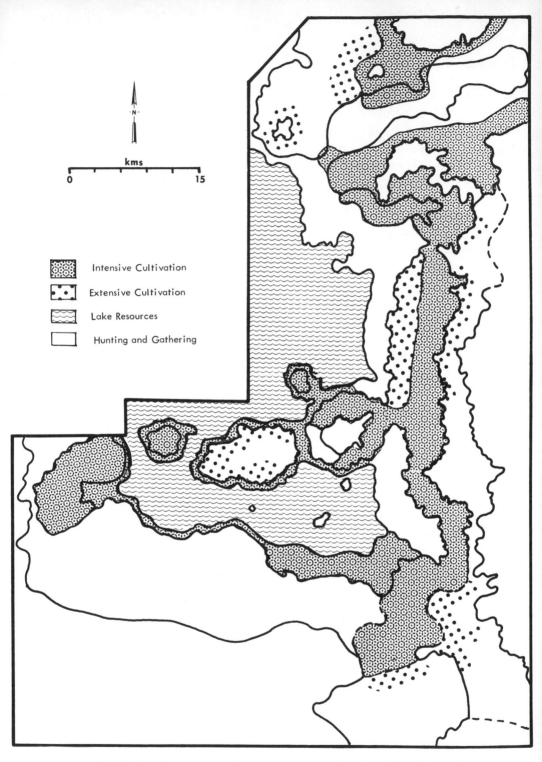

MAP 16. Survey area, showing resource utilization, First Intermediate: Phase 3.

Summary and Conclusions

What we suspect is that some of these sites were exploitation sites for particular resources and that the occupational debris found there represents either seasonal occupation or year-round residence by special exploitation groups sent out from Teotihuacán itself.

While we have no direct evidence of what kinds of specialized activities took place at Middle Horizon sites, two good possibilities suggest themselves at this point: (1) the production of salt around the edges of saline Lake Texcoco; and (2) the production of lime—to be used for stucco, in cement, and for food preparation—in the northernmost Basin, where the only substantial lime deposits in the region are located.

A very tempting ethnographic model here is that of Yoruba towns in Nigeria, where large lineage groups reside in compounds within the town, own land outside the community, and also practice various kinds of craft and mercantile activities within it. Entire nuclear families or single individuals are sent to the outlying farms either to reside throughout the year (to tend valuable commercial crops like cacao) or to pay a series of visits during the year (to tend subsistence crops). What we are suggesting is that perhaps the large corporate groups that were housed in the compounds at Teotihuacán owned special resource sites outside the Teotihuacán Valley and sent members of the household to exploit these resources periodically or to occupy them on an annual or seasonal basis. In his estimates of the population of Teotihuacán, René Millon based his calculations on the amount of probably roofed-over space found in the compounds. Using this kind of calculation, his maximum figure is 200,000 people. We suspect that at certain months of the year—when exploitation groups were not functioning, and when the cycle of ceremonial activities reached its peak of intensity—the population of the city may well have reached this level (not including foreign visitors). During most of the year, however, it probably had a resident population of 125,000, as Millon suggests (1970a, 1970b), with the balance of the people residing in the exploitation sites.

The situation was probably even more complex than this outline suggests. Some sites were probably occupied only for a short term, others for seasons or larger portions of the year; still others perhaps served as permanent administrative centers, for example, Ixtapalapa (Ix-EC-37), Cerro Portezuelo (Tx-EC-32), and Papalotla within the survey area and others, like Azcaputzalco and the much smaller site at Tultepec, outside of it.

On the basis of recent studies by René Millon (Millon, Drewitt, and Cowgill 1973, Millon 1967b, 1970b), there is abundant evidence of major changes in the entire institutional structure of Teotihuacán between the First Intermediate and Middle Horizon periods; these changes parallel those in population and settlement systems during the same time span. First of all, the scale of public architecture at Teotihuacán is vastly greater than anything occurring in the First Intermediate period, implying a much more thorough and politically explicit control of surplus labor. Evidence not only of ranking but of social stratification is clear and unequivocal in housing, tombs, and portable technology. The Ciudadela, with its enormous interior space and great size, was apparently the royal palace. Evidence of residences in direct association with the Temples of the Sun and Moon suggests the presence of a professional priesthood. Craft specialization and even subspecialization in manufacturing and commercial activities suggest intense economic differentiation, as do the physical vastness of the apparent marketplace and its central location. Further evidence of internal social differentiation is the presence of ethnic ghettos within the city. In short, the evidence for social differentiation through differential access to economic resources and control of political power suggests a major breakthrough or change in institutions between First Intermediate and the Middle Horizon—a change from a chiefdom-type organization to the state.

The settlement and socioeconomic system we have hypothesized, we believe, was only made possible by a pattern in which the bulk of the food supply was drawn from a radius of 20 kilometers from the city, and this could only have been the case assuming our model of maximal use of hydraulic agriculture. Much of the Basin was, in essence, a nonagricultural resource area, although crops were undoubtedly grown all over it to support the exploitation groups. Our model of the subsistence base of the city is summarized in Table 12.

The irrigable land within the 20 kilometer radius could have provided two-thirds of the total population of the city and its satellite villages and hamlets with maize if all irrigated land were planted in maize and if we assume an average yield of 1,400 kilograms per hectare with a per capita consumption of maize accounting for 65 percent of the daily caloric intake. If the yield were decreased to 1,050 kilograms per hectare and 80 percent of the caloric intake were derived from maize, the population figures would be lowered to approximately 40 percent. If we assume a pattern whereby only 65 percent of the land would be devoted to maize, then the population figures would have to be reduced further to about one-

TABLE 12

SUBSISTENCE BASE OF MIDDLE HORIZON TEOTIHUACÁN

Radius (in kilometers)	Area (in square kilometers)	Irrigable Land (in hectares)	Population Range Based on 100% Planted in Maize	Irrigated Land 65% Planted in Maize (in hectares)
10	310	3,000	18,000– 33,000	11,700–21,450
15	707	9,000	15,000– 99,000	35,100–64,350
20	1,255	9,700	58,200–106,700	37,830–72,355

third. When the unirrigated land is included it is clear that all of the food supply of the Middle Horizon city could easily have been derived from the area we have suggested as directly dependent upon the city and between 33 and 65 percent of the maize supply from the irrigable land. Map 17 shows Middle Horizon resource utilization.

Undoubtedly, as Millon has argued, a major factor that gave stability to this pattern of increasing nucleation and concentration of activities at Teotihuacán over a 700-year period was the city's growing role in external trade. The relationship probably involved feedback between urbanism and commerce, since the settlement pattern and social structure of Teotihuacán with its large compounds as units of production and distribution probably gave the city a competitive edge over other centers in the overall Mesoamerican trading network.

We see these changes as a rather extreme response to a variety of stimuli. One of these would be the intense competition for living space among the dozen or so Intermediate Period: Phase 3 chiefdoms in the Basin. The two most powerful chiefdoms were Teotihuacán, with a probable maximal population of 20,000, and Cuicuilco, possibly as large. The other polities ranged in size from 3,000 to 6,000 people. At some point in First Intermediate: Phase 4 times a single event, the Xitle eruption, wiped out the Cuicuilco chiefdom and upset what was probably a well-balanced power system.

A major question here, and one which can only be answered with tighter chronological control, is whether Teotihuacán exercised some kind of suzerainty over the northern and central Texcoco districts prior to the cataclysmic destruction of Cuicuilco. If so, then the rapid process of nucleation at Teotihuacán during First Intermediate: Phase 4 times could be explained as a response to a highly competitive political setting. Heizer

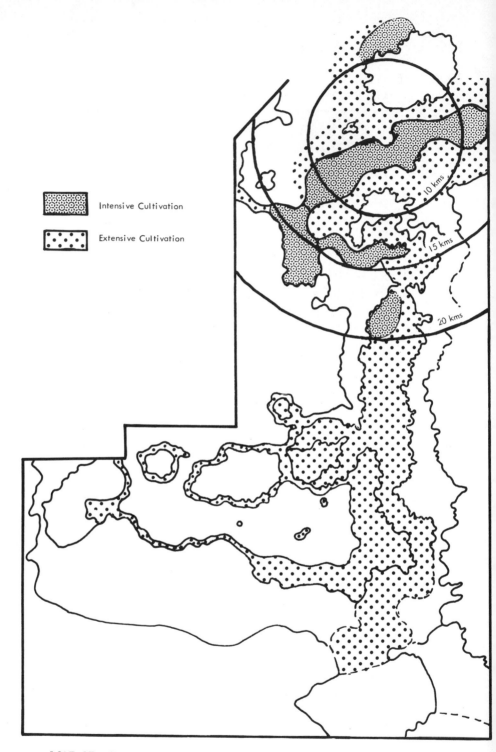

Intensive Cultivation

Extensive Cultivation

10 kms

15 kms

20 kms

MAP 17. Survey area, showing resource utilization, Middle Horizon.

and Bennyhoff (1958) do report a few Tzacualli trade sherds at Cuicuilco which would support this reconstruction.

A tentative reconstruction of events leading up to Teotihuacán's dominance in the affairs of the Basin of Mexico might be as follows:

1. An initial phase during First Intermediate: Phase 3 times in which the town of Teotihuacán controlled only the Teotihuacán Valley, possibly with a network of military alliances with the smaller Texcoco chiefdoms.

2. A phase of conquest by Teotihuacán of the northern and central Texcoco chiefdoms, but without nucleation, during First Intermediate: Phase 4 or very late Phase 3 times.

3. A phase of rapid nucleation of population drawn from the conquered territory and consequent meteoric growth of the population of the city of Teotihuacán. This would be associated with the collapse of Cuicuilco and integration of the entire Basin of Mexico into a single political and economic system, either early in Phase 4 times or in about the middle of Phase 4 (during what has been referred to as the Miccaotli phase).

4. The Tlamimilolpa-Xolalpan phases, or Middle Horizon, are characterized by a doubling of population at Teotihuacán itself and by further expansion of Teotihuacán's role in Mesoamerican affairs generally. Accompanying this expanded role, which apparently was primarily economic in nature, was the rapid process of increasing urbanization of life at Teotihuacán as described by René Millon (1967b, 1970b, Millon, Drewitt, and Cowgill 1973).

Blanton (1972a) has pointed out the striking similarity between the First Intermediate: Phase 3 and Second Intermediate: Phase 1 periods, on the one hand, and between Middle Horizon–Second Intermediate: Phase 2 settlement systems on the other, suggesting comparable political situations. The collapse of Teotihuacán was followed by the appearance of a series of centers similar in size to each other. Both in terms of the order of magnitude of the size of centers and of their respective sustaining areas, these were very similar to the politically organized districts of the First Intermediate: Phase 3. This suggests a comparable pattern of political fragmentation and competition. There were also differences, however, between the two settlement systems in that the Second Intermediate: Phase 1 centers were somewhat larger and denser. They also show considerably larger scale civic architecture, suggesting differences in social structure if not in degree of political fragmentation.

In the Teotihuacán Valley, the pattern of a number of small polities is also found, although Teotihuacán itself was probably larger than any other center. It was probably, however, not larger by more than a factor of four or five. The situation may be compared with that obtaining in the Valley in Late Horizon times, prior to its incorporation into the Texcoco state. The town of Teotihuacán was then larger, more prestigious, and possessed of the largest market in the Valley, but did not directly rule over the other towns in the area. The only political control on the part of other towns at that time was exercised in relationship to irrigation. The ruler of Teotihuacán owned the springs and collected rent for the use of the water from rulers from downstream states such as Acolman, Tezoyuca, and Tepexpan. This alignment of large nucleated settlements at the edge of the lower valley of the Alluvial Plain in the Teotihuacán Valley and the position of the largest town at the spring in Second Intermediate: Phase 2 times also strongly supports our previous reconstruction, which holds that there was a large-scale irrigation system in the valley in Middle Horizon times.

In the succeeding Late Intermediate: Phase 2 (the Mazapan phase) there are striking parallels with the Middle Horizon settlement system. First of all, over much of the Basin, there is a shift from the population concentrated in large nucleated settlements to dispersion over a great number of small villages and hamlets. Even the local centers of administration are strikingly smaller and denser in settlement when compared to those in Phase 1. The centers, however, in most cases occupied the same localities.

A major movement of population, possibly much of it from Teotihuacán, and hence representing an urban-to-urban movement, occurred to the north of the Basin of Mexico at the site of Tula, the capital of a major new political system. Recent surveys by Diehl (personal communication) assign a probable population maximum of 50,000 to 60,000 people to the Late Toltec city. The smaller size of Tula is interesting, considering the greater abundance of small settlements in the sustaining area compared to the Middle Horizon. Apparently the process of nucleation at Teotihuacán was more complete than in the case of Tula. If we include the Tula area in our calculations, the total population of the Basin in Late Intermediate: Phase 2 would not differ substantially from that in Middle Horizon times and would perhaps be substantially larger. It was certainly larger than in Phase 1 times. Contrary to a recent paper by Dumond and Muller

(1972), who have suggested that the two periods of political centralization were periods of population reduction or stability, we would estimate that the population in the two periods of centralization was appreciably larger than during the preceding periods of decentralization.

With respect to the Second Intermediate: Phase 2, this conclusion is based upon the inclusion of the Tula area in the calculations, and upon the fact that in many of the local areas of the Basin proper the period was one of substantial niche expansion. We cannot conceive of this happening under conditions of overall population reduction. This analysis points up the problem of understanding the population history of areas without reference to areas adjacent to them and to the political fortunes of centers. The important point here is that a large enough region must be included in the survey to account for temporary local dislocations and movements of population. Our inclusion of the Tula area is predicated upon the evidence from ethnohistory of the close cultural and social ties maintained by that area with the Basin of Mexico during Toltec and Aztec times.

Our recent surveys in the northwestern Basin, in the 400-square-kilometer test area noted above, show a substantial Late Toltec population, including two large towns. There is a strong suggestion in these data that the demographic balance shifted strongly northward at this time and that a substantial proportion of the people lived in the northern half of the Basin. This, of course, strengthens even further our contention that this phase was marked not by overall population decline but probably by general population increase. The Early Aztec settlement replicates that of the First Intermediate: Phase 3 and Second Intermediate: Phase 1 occupations on a much larger scale and involves a much larger population, larger central communities, and considerable niche expansion, particularly in the use of the Alluvial Plain in the Texcoco area and of swampy zones in and around Lakes Chalco-Xochimilco. If we estimate the Second Intermediate: Phase 1 population in the survey area at close to 90,000, then the Early Aztec must have been at least double that size, and this massive increase must be understood as the result of improvement in the subsistence system. For the entire Basin and Tula area, the population may well have reached a figure that substantially exceeded the two previous periods of political centralization (Second Intermediate: Phase 2 and Middle Horizon).

The basis for the remarkable demographic growth during Late Horizon times in the Basin of Mexico is not wholly clear to us at this time. We can only note here that this recovery correlates directly with (1) the return of major pan-Mesoamerican power centers to this area after an interval of some 500 years following the collapse of Teotihuacán; and (2) major development in the subsistence base, such as chinampa cultivation, intensified use of existing agricultural land, and expansion into new niches, particularly in the Upper Piedmont, the southern volcanic area, and into the Texcoco plain. It was also a period of expansion in floodwater irrigation. Undoubtedly many or all of these processes began or accelerated during the Early Aztec period. The result was an extremely efficient overall exploitation of resources within the Basin of Mexico, apparently made possible by intensive regional specialization and redistribution through a multicentered market system in which the lake system provided the principal transportation arteries (see Sanders and Price 1968). That the Late Horizon population of the Basin of Mexico far exceeded that of the Middle Horizon is thus not difficult to understand. Middle Horizon settlement data indicate little orientation toward the lake system. Thus Teotihuacán probably lacked effective utilization of the only efficient long-distance transportation artery in central Mexico. With its extreme concentration of a great proportion of consumers and producers in a single locality and its lopsided regional settlement hierarchy, the Middle Horizon system could thus make only very inefficient use of the productive potential of the entire Basin of Mexico. The major questions posed by these considerations are why the elaboration of agricultural technology and niche expansion was delayed so long and why population varied so little during the long period from 200 B.C. to A.D. 1200.

Appendix: Comment on Sanders, Parsons, and Logan

RICHARD E. BLANTON
Department of Anthropology
Hunter College
City University of New York

I find myself in disagreement with the views on human population dynamics expressed in the chapters by Sanders, Parsons, and Logan. In my view, we know very little about the roles of population variables in sociocultural change and adaptation. Surely our knowledge is not so secure or sophisticated that we may assume that human populations will tend to grow. Also, it is by no means clear to me why population growth or population pressure would necessarily lead to evolutionary change—numerous other responses to these conditions are at least as likely to occur.

Recently I have presented an argument (Blanton 1975) regarding human population growth which is nearly the opposite of that presented in Chapters 4–8. I postulated that population growth may be largely an epiphenomenon that only occurs in the context of certain specifiable circumstances, and that population growth may be more a product than a cause of sociocultural evolution. Specifically, I argued that population growth is one of several possible responses to a situation where there is increased demand for labor power in a society. While the theory cannot be fully described here, in essence it is as follows: evolving societies that become more complex in the sense of containing more parts, subparts, and ties between parts must increasingly capture more energy and materials from their environments.

Most of the increases in energy and material demands of evolving societies are related to the necessity for expanding the capacity for information processing, storage, and analysis (Flannery 1972:411, Maruyama 1963:174, J. G. Miller 1965:195). Particularly for preindustrial and nonindustrial societies, this may mean that producers may be required to work more—they may be required to step up agricultural productivity and do more corvée labor, for example. This could have implications in terms of population dynamics, because producers may decide that an appropriate strategy, in the light of increasing demands placed on them, is to have a large family. According to the demographer Kasarda, if ". . . the economy is of the household unit type where the family itself is the exclusive unit of production, the compulsion to have a large number of children is strong. Since the household unit's major source of labor-power is the family members, its strength as a producing unit varies with its size. . . . Large numbers of children are desired . . . because they are economic necessities" (Kasarda 1971:308). The result of decisions to have large families could be overall population growth in the society.

This approach to the explanation of human population growth is not new. In fact, it has been applied for some time in connection with industrializing and colonial societies by economists under the rubric of "demand-for-labor" analysis (Coontz 1968). White (1973) has adopted this method to explain colonial population growth in Java (see also Geertz 1963a:69 and Polgar 1971:5). The advantage of such an approach in the analysis of human population dynamics is that it is not necessary to assume that human populations will tend to grow. Instead, it should be possible to *explain* instances of growth by referring to the dynamics of the society in question. It follows from this argument that in explaining the dynamics of societies, we should look for causal factors other than population growth and related populational processes.

9

The Role of Symbiosis in Adaptation
and Sociocultural Change
in the Valley of Mexico

RICHARD E. BLANTON

Department of Anthropology
Hunter College
City University of New York

This chapter will of necessity be short, because there is little evidence on the nature of symbiotic networks in the pre-Hispanic Valley of Mexico, and even less on the role of symbiosis in the Valley's sociocultural evolution—a process that is so apparent in the archaeological records.[1] Almost no evidence exists to substantiate the role of symbiosis in the Valley, in spite of the fact that abundant descriptive information regarding trade and occupational specialization has recently become available (largely resulting from work carried on by the Valley of Mexico project, as well as from other sources). This information is particularly abundant for the Late Horizon (Sanders 1952, 1956, 1965, Sanders and Price 1968, J. R. Parsons 1971b, in press, M. H. Parsons 1972a, 1972b, Charlton 1969, Blanton 1972b, Chapman 1957), but some data are available for earlier periods as well. For example, René Millon (1973) located roughly 500 workshops at Teotihuacán and found barrios where foreign merchants may have lived. Sanders (1967), in excavating at TC-8 in the Teotihuacán Valley, uncovered a village which he thinks specialized in the production of maguey products for consumption in Teotihuacán. Full documentation of this evidence for local and long-distance trade will not be attempted here. Rather, I will look at the settlement pattern data for the eastern Valley of Mexico and at the useful excavated data here and for certain other places in Meso-america; from this I will draw inferences regarding the nature and impact of symbiosis on Valley populations at different points in time, and suggest kinds of research that could be carried out to test the hypotheses generated.

ECOLOGY

It is necessary to digress briefly here to discuss ecology in general. This is important for two reasons. First, symbiosis is a topic within the realm of ecology, and the methods and purposes of a discussion of symbiosis cannot be stated apart from a description of the methods and goals of the larger topic. Second, there seemed to be some confusion among certain members of the Valley of Mexico seminar regarding the nature and scope of ecological studies, both by those who conduct ecologically oriented studies and by those who criticize these endeavors. These critics seem to be reacting to ecological work, best exemplified by Sanders and Price (1968), which has been almost exclusively oriented toward understanding environment, subsistence, trade, and population growth. In contrast, René Millon (1973) points out that certain aspects of cultural systems removed from this techno-environmental-population core have been unduly neglected, particularly those aspects of systems that have to do with the "sacred."

This debate sounds much like that recently discussed by Kent Flannery, who argues that the differences between "ecologists" and what he calls "humanists" would not have to exist if a broader view of ecology were adopted (1972:400):

> To read what the "ecologists" write, one would think that civilized peoples only ate, excreted, and reproduced; to read what the human-ists write, one would think civilizations were above all three and de-voted all their energy to the arts. In this paper I will argue that the humanists must cease thinking ecology "dehumanizes" history, and ecologists must cease to regard art, religion, and ideology as mere "epiphenomena" without causal significance. In an ecosystem ap-

proach to the analysis of human societies everything which transmits information is within the province of ecology.

Populations do, in fact, exchange material, energy, *and* information with their environments—and the "environment" of a human population includes other human populations with which it articulates. As Rappaport (1968) has shown, ritual among the Tsembaga of Highland New Guinea serves to transmit information between populations regarding the state of certain variables, as well as regulating matter and energy exchanges between these populations and the local and regional environments (see also Vayda and Rappaport 1967).

Cultural ecologists clearly should pay more attention to analogous features of more complex societies. For example, pilgrimages to Teotihuacán, exchange activities and rituals there, and the construction and maintenance of large monuments may all have had importance in information exchanges or regulation of material exchanges for local and regional populations in the Teotihuacán empire. For example, constructing and maintaining a building as large as the Pyramid of the Sun surely transmitted information to local members and members of other populations regarding the state of certain variables in the Teotihuacán system—such as the amount and dependability of surplus food and labor available, or the viability of the central administration.

SYMBIOSIS

Sanders and Price (1968:188) define symbiosis as " . . . the economic interdependence of social and physical population units in a given region to the advantage of all." In my view this definition should be refined. As Eugene Odum (1971:212) points out, symbiosis literally means "living together"; whether or not the association is mutually beneficial is not stated. Symbiosis in plant and animal ecology refers to situations where distinct populations of species interact in ways that affect one or both. However, the nature of the interaction is not specified by the general term. The symbiotic relationship, for example, may be negative, as in parasitism; commensal, where one population is benefited, but the other remains unaffected; protocooperative, in which both populations benefit but the association is not required; or mutualistic, in which both populations require the association for their continued survival. It should be worthwhile to retain this generalized usage of "symbiosis" in anthropology since whether "economic interdependence of social and physical population units" is mutually beneficial or not in each case cannot be assumed a priori. The exact nature of the symbiotic relations within and between populations must be specified.

While I argue that anthropologists should borrow, and not change, the terminology dealing with symbiosis from plant and animal ecology, I should point out that the symbiotic relationships which concern anthropologists are different from those which nonanthropological ecologists study. Symbiosis in plant and animal ecology refers to interactions between different species, that is, interactions between groups whose boundaries are defined genetically. These kinds of symbiosis, of course, exist in ecosystems containing cultural systems, but they are not usually included in the analysis of symbiosis in anthropology. What normally concern anthropologists are interactions within and between human groups where the boundaries are defined socioculturally and linguistically. In most cases these interactions involve trade or exchange of products, although there are exceptions. An isolated incidence of trade at a given point in time, for example, need not imply a symbiotic relationship. In addition, there are a variety of situations involving interaction between groups which cannot be described as trade, but which should be described as symbiotic. For example, an exchange relationship between the center of an empire and a conquered population may constitute a mutualistic symbiotic relationship if the center depends on tribute exacted, while the tribute-paying group in turn depends on central grain stores in times of local crop failures, or relies on the central administration to maintain trade routes militarily.

Because symbiotic relations between groups not involving exchanges of materials are difficult to detect and analyze archaeologically, symbiosis, as used here, will refer to situations where interactions between groups involve exchange or trade. Two such classes of exchange or trade relations exist in primitive societies. One, which involves exchange across cultural-linguistic boundaries, will be referred to as "regional symbiosis," because the concern is with regional, as well as with local systems (see Rappaport 1968:226). Materials exchanged in regional symbiotic networks are often high-status, durable goods (and sometimes food and other mundane items) that can be transported rather easily over long distances. This variety of exchange involves crossing cultural-linguistic boundaries, so that special "boundary mechanisms" are normally necessary. In primitive cultural systems such exchanges rarely involve face-to-face encounters between random members of populations. Rather, certain individuals—often "trade partners" who are usually high-ranking individuals—act as group representatives (Sahlins 1972:298, Harding 1967:243, 248 passim), although other exchange mechanisms, such as "blind trade," also exist. Blind trade, in fact, may persist when states interact with primitive groups (Herodotus 1954:307). For archaic states, ports-of-trade (and sometimes fairs) serve as boundary mechanisms (Chapman 1957, Arnold 1957).

The second class of exchange or trade relations existing in primitive societies involves local systems, and will be referred to as "local symbiosis." Relevant here are such things as reciprocity, redistribution, and local markets. The two varieties of symbiosis, regional and local, are not always completely separable. In many cases goods obtained in regional networks become available in local systems through redistribution or markets. A good example of a product exchanged through both classes of symbiotic networks in Mesoamerican cultural systems was obsidian (L. A. Parsons and Price 1971).

CHRONOLOGICAL REVIEW OF SYMBIOTIC NETWORKS IN THE VALLEY OF MEXICO

The Early Horizon (Ixtapaluca Phase)

Little is known about the Early Horizon period in the Valley of Mexico. No complete villages, or even complete houses, have been excavated and documented; in fact, only a total of eight sites have been located— Tlatilco, Ayotla, Ix-EF-2 and 3, and four new localities recently located by Jeffrey and Mary Parsons (1971a, 1973) (two in the lakebed of Lake Chalco, south of Tlaltenco, and two near Amecameca, at about 2,600 meters). Only recently (Tolstoy and Paradis 1970) have the ceramics of this phase been described. The striking feature of the assemblages is that they contain vessels and figurines virtually identical with some found in contemporary assemblages in other parts of Mesoamerica, and they are characterized, in part, by the presence of Olmec motifs. Pottery and figurines of this genre have been described in the Cuadros phase of the Pacific Coast of Guatemala, (M. D. Coe and Flannery 1967), the Chicharras and San Lorenzo phases at San Lorenzo Tenochtitlan (M. D. Coe 1969), the La Juana phase in Morelos (Grove 1970), the Chiapa I phase in the Grijalva Depression (Dixon 1959), the Ajalpan phase in the Tehuacán Valley (MacNeish 1962), and in the San José phase in the Valley of Oaxaca (Flannery 1970).

The widespread occurrence of materials of this type, along with evidence of long-distance movement of such goods as jade, serpentine, magnetite mirrors, and obsidian, suggests that there was much contact between at least some Mesoamerican populations during the Early Horizon. The exact nature of this contact remains poorly understood today, despite an impressive amount of research and writing surrounding the "Olmec problem" during the last few years (M. D. Coe 1965, 1968, Benson 1968, Bernal 1968, Wicke 1971).

Flannery and Schoenwetter (1970) suggest that an Early Horizon trade network, or series of trade networks, existed which involved the movement of high-status items, as well as food, between populations. Participation by a population in a trade network of this type can be adaptive, they point out, because

> given the erratic rainfall of semi-arid regions like Oaxaca [or the Valley of Mexico], unusually good years—and hence maize surpluses—are unpredictable. One way of "banking" unpredictable maize surpluses (as an alternative to storage) is to convert them into imperishable trade goods which can be used either (1) as "wealth" in times of shortage, or (2) as part of a ritual exchange system, used to establish reciprocal obligations between neighboring peoples. Such exchange systems help to "even out" the differences between good and bad years by circulating foodstuffs and trade goods between regions with different crop cycles (Flannery and Schoenwetter 1970: 148–50).

The term "interaction sphere," first used by Joseph Caldwell (1964), can be used to denote situations such as this where small, undoubtedly politically autonomous groups engage in protocooperative or mutualistic symbiotic relationships, involving exchanges in "wealth," food, and perhaps personnel.

Regarding the spread of Olmec motifs, Flannery (1968b) has also pointed out that as highland cultural systems became increasingly hierarchically organized, high-ranking individuals may have borrowed some of the attributes of a powerful supernatural system to enhance their own prestige and influence. This may help to explain the widespread popularity of Olmec iconography. Yet another point to consider in this context may be the possible sanctification of the goods exchanged. In order for an interaction sphere of this type to operate effectively, trade goods or "wealth" must be readily exchangeable across cultural and linguistic boundaries. Items may be exchangeable because they are made of valuable, nonlocal materials (such as jade) and/or because their production requires much labor and skill. However, to sanctify trade items by investing them with symbols pertaining to a powerful supernatural system gives them a value far beyond their intrinsic worth. The holder of such an item may feel that possessing it gives him some kind of supernatural power; all of this assures that the items will be readily exchangeable.

Perhaps the most important consequence of the Olmec interaction sphere, touched on by Flannery (1968b), is that it may have speeded up the already-existing process of centralization in Mesoamerican societies, since high-ranking individuals could enhance their own prestige and power by borrowing some of the attributes of a powerful supernatural system. The impact of such an interaction sphere on the processes of sociocultural change among local groups may also have operated on a more general level. Populations capable of participating regularly in such a trade network would have had adaptive advantages over populations not able to participate. There may have been a variety of reasons why some populations were better able to take part in the Olmec interaction sphere than others, but the most important may have been related to hierarchical organization, or the degree of centralization of power. In other words, the interaction sphere was an aspect of the cultural environment of Mesoamerican populations in which there was positive selective pressure for centralization. Systems with highly centralized organizations were better adapted because high-ranking individuals could maintain restricted access to valuable raw materials (such as magnetite or obsidian sources), at the expense of other populations, and these same individuals would have had the resources to underwrite and organize the part-time or full-time craft specialists who prepared the raw materials for exchange. Head men or chiefs in such systems could also have maintained trade partners over a wide region more effectively than individual cultivators. In the portion of the Valley of Oaxaca that he studied, Flannery (1968b) found that most long-distance trade items, such as magnetite and ilmenite mirrors, were found on one site only, at San José Mogote, even though other sites were closer to the sources; furthermore, their distribution on this one site suggests that their production and trade were directed by high-ranking individuals.

Exactly how the Valley of Mexico populations fitted into the proposed Olmec interaction sphere is unclear and will remain so until excavations and systemic surface collections are carried out comparable to Flannery's at San José Mogote. It is likely, however, that at least some people in the Valley supplied obsidian to the trade network. Some Teotihuacán Valley obsidian from the Early Horizon is present in deposits as far away as San Lorenzo Tenochtitlan (M. D. Coe and Cobean 1970). In a recent study of Formative Mesoamerican exchange networks, Jane Wheeler Pires-Ferreira (1973) has defined what she calls the "Barranca de los Estetes Exchange Network," named after the obsidian flows located near the village of Otumba in the Teotihuacán Valley. She was able to trace the distribution of obsidian from this flow, as well as from other Mesoamerican obsidian flows, by analyzing obsidian samples (using sodium and manganese neutron activation analysis [Gordus et al. 1967]) from sites dating to the Early Horizon. Barranca de los Estetes obsidian is densest in the Central Highlands region, but the obsidian that Pires-Ferreira sampled from sites of this period in the Valley of Oaxaca contained 36.5 percent obsidian from this source. Furthermore, in the sites in Morelos, Oaxaca, and in the Gulf Coastal region where Barranca de los Estetes obsidian is found, the obsidian is almost always in the form of blades—very few cores have been found. In all probability, then, Barranca de los Estetes obsidian was being worked into blades in the Valley of Mexico prior to export (Pires-Ferreira 1973).

The Lower First Intermediate (Zacatenco Phase)

The widespread similarities in ceramic assemblages and continued evidence for trade in high-status items during the Lower First Intermediate period in Mesoamerica suggest the continuation of an interaction sphere. Locally in the Valley of Mexico, however, sociocultural changes were in process that culminated during the Middle First Intermediate period. These changes included population growth (from eight Early Horizon sites to over forty known Lower First Intermediate sites), and occupation of a wider range of environmental zones than had occurred during the Early Horizon. All Early Horizon sites, except the two located by J. R.

Parsons near Amecameca, are located on or near the Lakeshore Plain environmental zone.

> *Middle First Intermediate* (Ticoman and
> Patlachique-Tezoyuca phases)

During this period there were important changes in the cultural systems of the Valley of Mexico (Sanders 1965, J. R. Parsons 1971b, Blanton 1972a, 1972b). These changes included (1) rapid population growth, involving growth of some existing communities, as well as the formation of new communities; (2) the appearance of a more pronounced hierarchy of communities, ranging from at least one community, Cuicuilco, which may have covered several square kilometers, to middle-range communities such as Tlapacoya (Ix-LF-2, Ix-TF-4), which covered about 65 hectares, to small hamlets and villages lacking civic architecture; (3) the beginning of construction of truly large-scale monumental architecture; and (4) the occupation of a wide range of environmental zones, a process that had started during the Lower First Intermediate but that was even more pronounced during this period. What all this means in terms of changes in local and regional symbiotic networks cannot be known because of the paucity of excavation, but several things can be inferred from the settlement pattern data, as well as from the scant excavated data. In my view the occupation of a wide range of environmental zones suggests that local symbiosis was more important than it had been earlier.

J. R. Parsons (1971b) found three Ticoman sites in the Texcoco region, located in what must have been saline, marshy swamp adjacent to Lake Texcoco, where agriculture would not have been feasible. He suggests that these communities engaged in the specialized exploitation of lacustrine resources. In the Ixtapalapa Peninsula region some new communities were founded in portions of the Piedmont—an area where soils are thin, where maize agriculture based on rainfall is undependable, where no streams or springs suitable for irrigation exist, and where there would have been no easy access to such lake products as fish, wildfowl, and salt. On the other hand, these communities would have been well situated for the specialized production of nopal and maguey, and some had ready access to the products of the Sierra.

It may be that the abrupt sociopolitical changes during the Middle First Intermediate period can be tied, in part, to this inferred intensification of local symbiosis. Part of the power and prestige of the local chiefs may still have been due to their participation in an interaction sphere, yet their positions of power could have been further enhanced if they increasingly controlled, and perhaps even encouraged, local symbiotic networks by serving as pivots for redistributive systems (Sahlins 1960, Harding 1967:250). Such individuals probably lived in large, dominant communities, and had the resources to underwrite the construction of large-scale monumental architecture.

Upper First Intermediate (Tzacualli phase)–Late Horizon (Aztec III-IV phase)

Anthropologists generally agree that from Upper First Intermediate through Late Horizon times, populations in the Valley were dominated, for the first time, by states—an event that was first manifested by the explosive expansion of Teotihuacán (during the Tzacualli phase) and the simultaneous decline of centers such as Tlapacoya (Blanton 1972b:58–59). According to Sanders and Price (1968) symbiosis, among other things, was a key causal variable in the growth of such highly centralized systems. Such complex environments as the "symbiotic region" including the Central Plateau and central Veracruz, they argue, engendered specialization of production and exchange between zones. Under these conditions, they point out, there is strong selective pressure for the development of large, powerful sociopolitical units, such as states, to regulate and control these symbiotic relationships.

To date, however, not one researcher working in the Valley of Mexico has oriented an archaeological research project to the generation and testing of hypotheses regarding the proposed cause-effect interrelationships of symbiosis and state origins. In fact, to my knowledge, only one such project has been carried out in an area where pristine states evolved, namely, in Southwest Asia. There, Henry Wright and Gregory Johnson (1975) have attempted to test hypotheses specifically linking symbiosis and the rise of the state. The theoretical basis of their research rests on the postulates of information processing. All cultural systems, of course, process information, but simple cultural systems do this on a generalized level—because relatively little information has to be processed and few decisions need to be made, no body of specialized decision-makers is necessary. If one or more subsystems of a cultural system expand in size and/or complexity, however, the information flow may exceed the system's "channel capacity," in which case the simple decision-making apparatus may become insufficient. Under these conditions decision-making specialists may be appointed to aid ranking individuals in such tasks as processing information, making decisions, and carrying out orders. As a result, not only would the number of decision-makers increase, but there would also be more specialization among the decision makers themselves. The state (which Wright and Johnson define as a society with a segregated, specialized "control mechanism" that specializes in decision making) may be the eventual outcome of such a process of expansion and increasing specialization of the body of decision-makers.

From this theoretical base a hypothesis can be generated: an increase in the intensity or complexity of symbiotic relations within or among groups in a region might force ranking figures to appoint and support increasing numbers of specialized assistants, leading eventually to state development. To test this hypothesis, Wright (Wright and Johnson 1975) carried out excavations at a local center in the Deh Luran plain, Farukhabad, which lies midway between Susa and Uruk, two large centers that were important during the time of early state formation in Southwest Asia. Wright reasoned that he would be able to monitor a shift in the intensity of regional symbiosis by excavating a site on the traditional route between these two main centers, especially since the site seems to have been a distribution point for a local resource, bitumen. While Wright's conclusions must be considered tentative—given the usual problem of trying to excavate a representative sample when the site is large and complex and the archaeologist's resources are minimal—they are suggestive. His evidence indicates that interregional exchange in prestate times was minimal, but that it increased significantly *after* state origins in the region. Something, or things other than an increase in the intensity of regional symbiosis, then, had a causal role in state formation.

Johnson may have found one of those other factors (Wright and Johnson 1975). Based on his analysis of shifts in settlement pattern, workshop location, and distribution of workshop products, he suggests that the organization of local exchange underwent major changes during and just before state development in the same area. Specifically, ceramic workshops became centralized in a few centers, rather than remaining scattered in small settlements. The settlement pattern shifts noted by Johnson support the idea that some centers were becoming important in local exchange, since the emerging settlement patterns also closely conform to those predicted by classical central place theory (Christaller 1966).

The exact relationship between the shift in organization of local symbiosis and the formation of states hypothesized by Wright and Johnson is complex and need not be repeated here. The important point for our purposes is that in at least one small portion of Southwest Asia, symbiosis, at least on a local level, may have had some role in the origin of the state. Research like this will be required to assess the suggested, but never demonstrated, role of symbiosis in the rise of the state in central Mexico.

Whatever the cause-effect interrelationships between symbiosis and the rise of the state, it is clear that once states had evolved in the Valley of Mexico, there were fundamental changes in local and regional symbiotic networks. Interaction spheres were no doubt replaced as states gained the organizational abilities and resource bases that enabled them to conquer large regions and directly control the movement of goods. At Kaminaljuyú, for example, there is evidence that Teotihuacán was able to take direct control of an important trade route which must have involved at least obsidian, cacao, and jade (Sanders and Price 1968, L. A. Parsons and Price 1971). Teotihuacán's "merchants' barrios" described by René Millon (1973) suggest a kind of exchange relationship or interaction between regional populations different from the trade partners and other border mechanisms that typify exchange relations between simpler societies.

On the level of local symbiosis, redistributive-reciprocal exchange relations were probably superseded by market exchange, which made possible exchange on a much larger scale. More goods could be moved quickly and dependably, involving many more people. René Millon believes that he has located the central Teotihuacán marketplace, the "Great Compound." It is widely accepted that such phenomena were present during the Late Horizon: markets (Díaz del Castillo 1910:70–75, Cortés 1963: 72–73), military control of regions with desirable products, such as the cacao-producing region of Xoconuxco (Barlow 1949), and ports-of-trade (Chapman 1957) were important mechanisms of interstate exchange.

The settlement pattern data for the Upper First Intermediate through the Late Horizon periods from the eastern Valley of Mexico enable me to go beyond these statements of the probable form of symbiotic networks, which, with the exception of the Late Horizon, are mostly derived by analogy with ethnographically known primitive states. As I have pointed out previously (Blanton 1972a, 1972b), two patterns of settlement configuration are discernible during this broad period when states dominated Valley populations. During the Middle Horizon and the Middle Second Intermediate periods, rural Valley settlements were mostly small, dispersed villages, and population densities were low. These periods saw the Valley being dominated by large urban centers: Teotihuacán during the Middle Horizon, and Tula, Hidalgo, during Middle Second Intermediate.

The Lower Second Intermediate period, however, was different. Following the decline of Teotihuacán, population densities increased in the Texcoco and the Ixtapalapa Peninsula regions, and this was probably true Valley-wide, with the exception of the Teotihuacán Valley, where population densities decreased as the urban center declined. A large portion of the Valley population lived in a widely scattered series of urban centers such as Azcapotzalco, Cerro Tenayo, Cerro de la Estrella, Portezuelo, and Xico. In those areas of the Valley that have been surveyed, large unused areas like "shatter zones" separate the major centers. This settlement pattern surely reflects the fact that this was a time of political fragmentation, or "Balkanization." It is not likely that one large center dominated Valley affairs (Blanton 1972a, 1972b, Dumond and Muller 1972).

The Late Horizon situation is strongly analogous to that of the Lower Second Intermediate. Admittedly, Tenochtitlan largely dominated the Valley in many spheres by the time of the Conquest, but probably not to the extent that Teotihuacán once had. During the Late Horizon, a series of urban centers, each of which retained considerable autonomy, were widely scattered throughout the Valley. Judging from the rapidity with which such centers as Texcoco, Chalco, and Xochimilco joined the side of the Spaniards, Tenochtitlan's domination of the Valley was surely only ephemeral. Historical accounts of the several centuries preceding the Conquest describe "Balkanization" and competition between local centers (Ixtlilxochitl 1952).

What can be inferred from these data regarding the nature of changes through time in symbiotic networks is problematical, but I have already (1972a, 1972b) suggested the following. As Teotihuacán emerged during the Tzacualli phase, it militarily dominated, then eliminated local centers that had once been the foci of local symbiotic networks. The new centers that developed—for example, Portezuelo (J. R. Parsons 1971b:60–61) and Cerro de la Estrella (Blanton 1972b:79)—were relatively small, with populations of at most 1,000 or so; as far as we can tell from surface evidence alone, they were architecturally simple, that is, they were little more than large villages. One Late Horizon site—Azcapotzalco, in the western Valley—may have been large and important, but it has now been completely destroyed by the urban expansion of modern Mexico City. Descriptions of the site before its destruction, however, do not indicate that it was anywhere near as impressive as Teotihuacán.

Obviously, then, the most important market and production center in the Valley of Mexico was Teotihuacán. Villages close to it were surely keyed into its market system, as Sanders's (1967) excavations at TC-8 demonstrate. Outside the Teotihuacán Valley, however, Classic villages may have been too far removed from the urban center to participate actively in the market. They may thus have been relatively self-sufficient. Little or no evidence of craft specialization has been found on Middle Horizon sites outside the Teotihuacán Valley. This apparent decrease in the importance of local symbiosis may, in part, explain the population declines of the Middle Horizon in the rural Valley of Mexico, since active participation in such networks is adaptive in regions such as this, where agricultural production is unpredictable, and where necessary products are in some cases discretely and widely distributed.

In regard to local symbiosis the Late Horizon, in my view, was very different from the Middle Horizon. Besides the main market at Tenochtitlan-Tlatelolco, the Valley witnessed the growth, in Late Horizon times, of a series of local urban centers that functioned in part, as foci of local symbiotic networks. Apparently a large portion of the Valley population participated in these local market systems. Even if we lacked the ethnohistoric and early colonial literature that demonstrates the importance of craft specialization and exchange, the situation would still be clear. Surface evidence for specialization on Late Horizon sites is common (M. H. Parsons 1972a, 1972b, J. R. Parsons n.d.a, Spence and Parsons 1972, Charlton 1969, Blanton 1972b), and a wide range of environmental zones was occupied, including marginal environments where little could have been produced but maguey and nopal.

What I am arguing for here is a market dynamic in the Valley, such that, for political and perhaps other reasons, the organization of markets changed through time. At some times rural peasants were intensively engaged in market systems and at other times less so, and this cycle, in turn, had demographic impact on the region as a whole. That symbiosis and population variables are systematically interrelated seems clear. For example, in the Valley of Oaxaca today, production of craft items for the market is, for some peasants, an alternative strategy to agriculture during lean years (Cook 1970:786, S. Lees, personal communication). Local agricultural failures can be compensated for in several ways, but one important strategy, at least among some groups, is the stepped-up production of items to be sold in the market. The market, then, is a mechanism for "evening out" unpredictable harvests. If the market system were to change so that participation in it no longer served as a viable alternative strategy during lean years, this would surely have demographic impact, producing, for instance, emigration, or a lower birth rate during lean years because of nutritional stress, or both.

THE "RANK-SIZE RULE"

The qualitative differences between the Middle Horizon and the Middle Second Intermediate period, on the one hand, and the Late Horizon, on the other, can be clarified when the rank-size distributions for the three periods are shown graphically (Figs. 10–12). Rank-size relationships were first noted by geographers interested in locational analysis, "central place theory," and the like (see, for example, Haggett 1966). Establishing the rank-size distribution of communities in a region is done by plotting the rank of centers (based on population, where rank 1 is the largest center) on one axis and the population size on the other axis, on double-log paper. The rank-size distribution for a region is referred to as "log-normal" if it corresponds to the so-called rank-size rule, which may be written as $Pn \cdot Pl(n)^{-1}$, where "Pn is the population of the nth town in the series 1,2,3 . . . n in which all towns in a region are arranged in descending order by population, and Pl is the population of the biggest town" (Haggett 1966:101). For Figures 10–12 log-normal was calculated from the size of the rank 1 center.

To plot the rank-size distributions for the pre-Hispanic Valley of Mexico, I used population estimates from J. R. Parsons (1971a, 1971b) for the Chalco and Texcoco regions, and from Blanton (1972b) for the Ixtapalapa Peninsula region (from which I omitted the Late Horizon city Ixtapalapa, which is today virtually completely destroyed, so that no accurate estimate of its population can be given). Added to this was René Millon's latest estimate of the population of Teotihuacán at its height

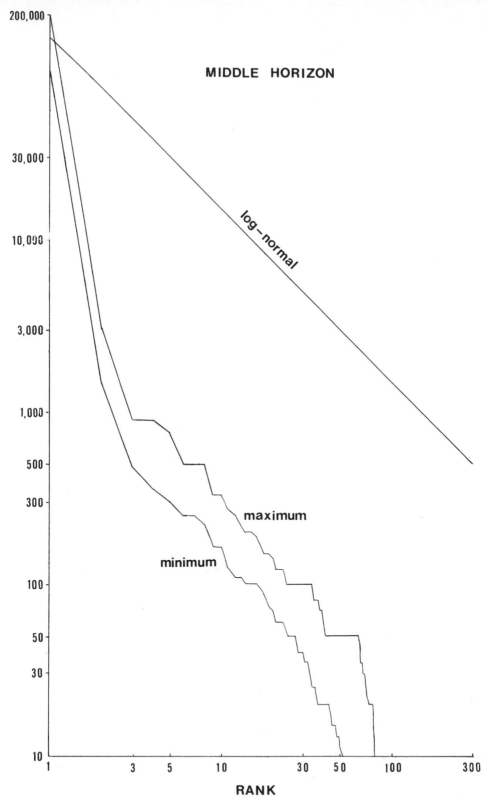

FIGURE 10. Rank-size distribution: Middle Horizon.

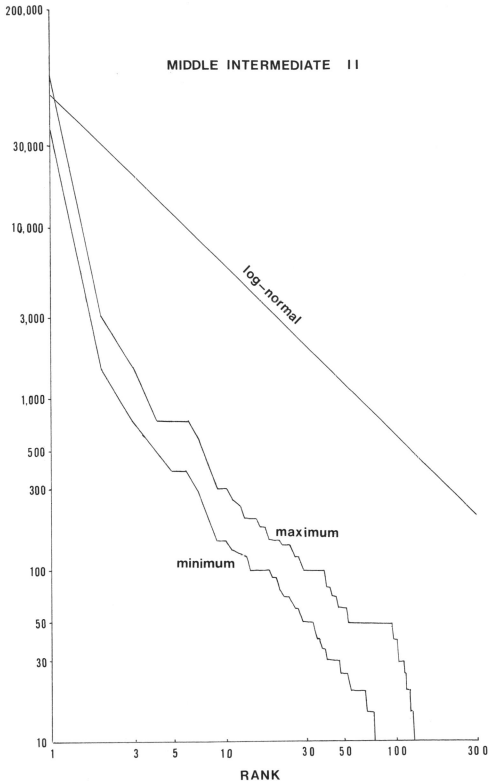

FIGURE 11. Rank-size distribution: Middle Second Intermediate.

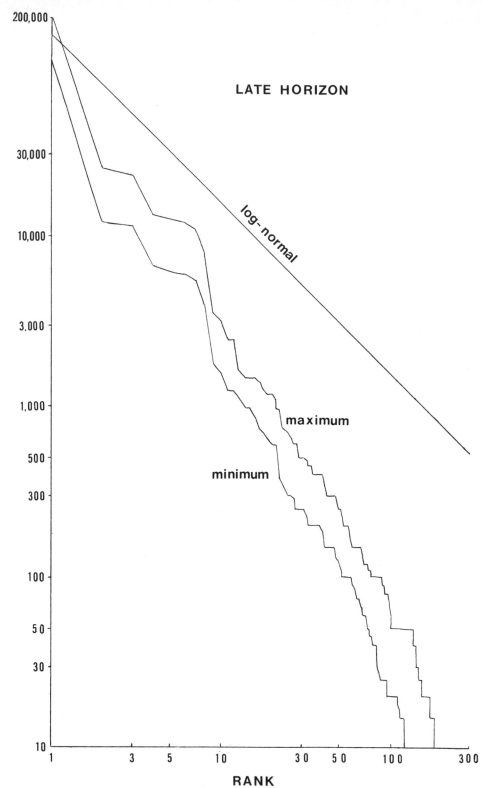

FIGURE 12. Rank-size distribution: Late Horizon.

(personal communication), and an estimate for Tenochtitlan from Edward Calnek (personal communication). For the Middle Second Intermediate period, I added the latest estimate for the population of Tula (Diehl, personal communication) to the Valley data, because, as I have argued, it is likely that Tula dominated Valley affairs at that time.

Because all the communities in the Valley have not yet been mapped, these rank-size graphs are not truly representative—and there is the further possibility that not all Middle Horizon sites were contemporary with Teotihuacán at its height (in A.D. 600). I argue that while future surveys will alter the number of communities, the basic shape of the rank-size lines for each period will remain essentially the same. In other words, if we continue to find numerous small Middle Horizon hamlets and villages but no large centers, then there will continue to be a large drop from the rank 1 center to the second-, third-, and fourth-ranking centers (and the same will be true for the Middle Second Intermediate). In contrast, many Late Horizon local urban centers (such as Coyoacán, Tlacopan, Azcapotzalco, Cuauhtitlan, and Xochimilco) have not yet been mapped, and Ixtapalapa, which could not be mapped, was not included on the graph. These centers will tend to fill out the area of the Late Horizon graph just below the rank 1 center.

The "rank-size rule" is not really a rule at all. Rather, it describes fairly accurately the size relationships of communities in some regions, for example, the United States (Berry 1967: Fig. 4.1). Other regions do not show the log-normal distribution but why this is so has never been fully explained by geographers. Note that the Late Horizon rank-size distribution fairly closely approximates log-normal (especially since the second- and third-ranking centers are nearly as large as predicted according to the formula), while the Middle Horizon and Middle Second Intermediate periods deviate considerably from log-normal. The reasons for such deviations are not now fully clear, but similar situations do exist. For example, some modern regions deviate from log-normal because they are dominated by large "primate cities," such as the Argentine capital, Buenos Aires. Cesar Vapnarsky (1969), a geographer, has explained this deviation by referring to the degree of "closure" of Argentina's economic system. According to geographers, the closure of an economic system is the extent to which economic interactions in the system are completed there (Feldt 1965). Closure can be expressed as a quotient varying between 0 and 1. If the system has no articulation with the outside world, closure is 1; but if all economic transactions terminated or begun in the system are completed outside it, then closure is 0.

Vapnarsky suggests a relationship between the degree of primacy of the main centers in a region and the degree of closure of the economic system in that region, that is, " . . . the lower the degree of closure, the higher is expected to be the degree of primacy of the city which establishes the main link between the given area and the external world" (1969:585). Buenos Aires, he points out, grew largely because it was the main national link to Europe, both in the exportation of agricultural products and the importation of manufactured goods.

Argentina may be a reasonable analogy for the situation in the Valley of Mexico during the Middle Horizon and the Middle Second Intermediate period. Teotihuacán's large size can only be understood if it is viewed not simply as the key center of craft specialization and exchange for the Valley of Mexico, but also as the center of a large, regional symbiotic network and center of a large empire. The Culhua Mexica, on the other hand, unable so completely to conquer local Valley polities, could not maintain an imperial apparatus as elaborate as the one that had been maintained during the Middle Horizon. And as we know, the Culhua Mexican "empire" was brittle indeed, and conquered groups sent tribute only because of threats of reprisal for nonpayment. No conquered city in this empire was completely rebuilt in the style of the capital, as Kaminaljuyú, Matacapan, and perhaps others had been during the Middle Horizon. As far as material culture goes, there is little evidence (with only a few exceptions) of the Aztec presence outside the Valley of Mexico.

The rank-size graphs suggest that the degree of closure of the Middle Second Intermediate period was like that of the Middle Horizon. However, other similarities also exist between the Middle Horizon and the Middle Second Intermediate periods. L. A. Parsons and Price (1971) point out that Chichén Itza may have had the same kind of relationship with Tula that Kaminaljuyú enjoyed with Teotihuacán—which suggests that the two capitals organized their relationships with distant populations along the same lines. In addition, the rank-size curves for the Valley of Mexico for these two periods are very similar in form. First, as has already been noted, the second- and third-ranking communities are small in comparison with the main centers. Second, there are steps or jumps in both curves at about population size 300 to 1,000, and at about population size 25 to 50. The latter step is also present to a certain extent on the

Late Horizon graph, indicating that villages with 25 to 50 people were relatively common during all three periods. All of this suggests that during the Middle Horizon and the Middle Second Intermediate periods, there were "empires" focused in the Valley of Mexico region and organized along the same lines. Perhaps the descendents of the Teotihuacán elite tried to reestablish an empire at Tula, Hidalgo, after a period of political fragmentation (the Early First Intermediate period), employing the same organizational paradigm that had been used at Teotihuacán.

CONCLUSION

Although we have made important progress during the last ten years or so, the latest existing evidence from the Valley of Mexico regarding symbiosis is quite inadequate to allow more than speculation on the role of symbiosis in adaptation and sociocultural change during the pre-Hispanic period. This situation can only be changed if future research is oriented toward specific problems. How was exchange organized? Who produced goods, who underwrote production, who controlled exchange? Who had access to trade goods, and what was the status of producers and controllers of exchange? How much was produced and exchanged? How much did this vary from system to system and through time? Was production a full-time or a part-time activity? How can redistributive systems be distinguished archaeologically from market systems? When did markets first appear?

Excavations of whole houses, and even whole communities, will be required to deal with problems such as these, but in some cases simple systematic surface collecting projects, such as Flannery's work at San José Mogote, can contribute valuable evidence.

NOTE

1. I thank Dan DeMicco, graduate student at Hunter College, City University of New York, who prepared the rank-size graphs. Helpful comments on this and an earlier version came from Daniel Bates, Susan Lees, Dudley Varner, Kent Flannery, Gregory Johnson, Jeffrey Parsons, and Marcus Winter.

Part 3

Urban Society

10
Social Relations in Ancient Teotihuacán

RENÉ MILLON

Department of Anthropology
University of Rochester

The ancient city of Teotihuacán, the subject of this chapter,[1] was located in the valley of the same name, in the northeastern quadrant of the Basin of Mexico. Gaining in importance shortly before the onset of the Christian era, it came to exercise strong influence over large populations and wide areas, to decline again around A.D. 750.

This chapter draws on the evidence contained in the Teotihuacán map and on some of what has been learned from it to date. Map 18 represents the ancient city as we think it looked around A.D. 600, during the latter part of the Middle Horizon (see Fig. 15 and Chapter 3). Figures 13 and 14 show plans of residential structures in Teotihuacán. Map 19 is a topographic map of the area shown in Map 18. Two colleagues have been collaborating with me in the preparation and completion of the map: Bruce Drewitt of the University of Toronto and George Cowgill of Brandeis University. The first volume of our researches has already been published—the volume on the map itself (R. Millon 1973, Millon, Drewitt, and Cowgill 1973).

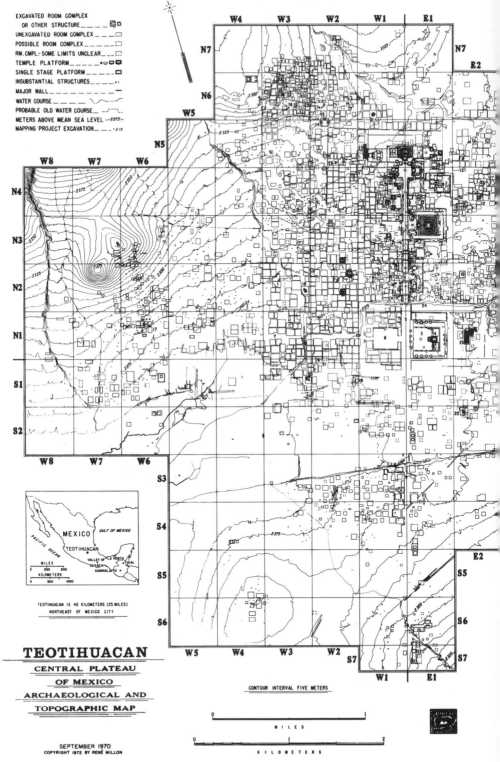

MAP 18. Ancient Teotihuacán. Most buildings shown are unexcavated one-story apartment compounds.

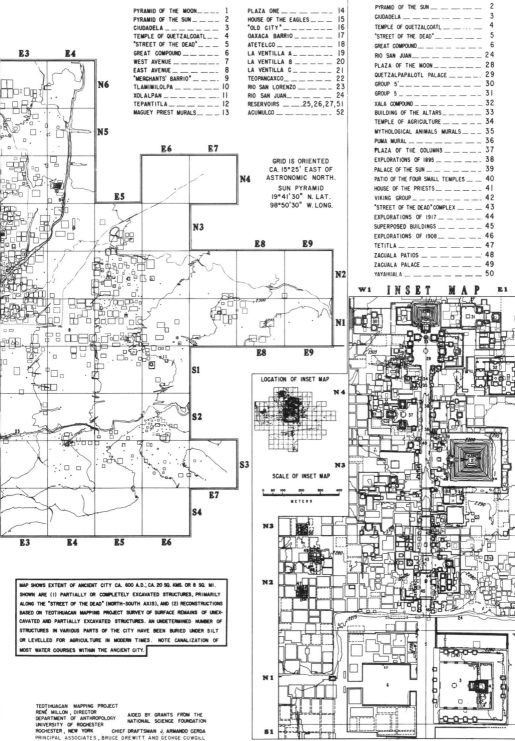

K E Y

PYRAMID OF THE MOON — 1
PYRAMID OF THE SUN — 2
CIUDADELA — 3
TEMPLE OF QUETZALCOATL — 4
"STREET OF THE DEAD" — 5
GREAT COMPOUND — 6
WEST AVENUE — 7
EAST AVENUE — 8
"MERCHANTS' BARRIO" — 9
TLAMIMILOLPA — 10
XOLALPAN — 11
TEPANTITLA — 12
MAGUEY PRIEST MURALS — 13

PLAZA ONE — 14
HOUSE OF THE EAGLES — 15
"OLD CITY" — 16
OAXACA BARRIO — 17
ATETELCO — 18
LA VENTILLA A — 19
LA VENTILLA B — 20
LA VENTILLA C — 21
TEOPANCAXCO — 22
RIO SAN LORENZO — 23
RIO SAN JUAN — 24
RESERVOIRS — 25,26,27,51
ACUMULCO — 52

GRID IS ORIENTED
CA. 15°25' EAST OF
ASTRONOMIC NORTH.

SUN PYRAMID
19°41'30" N. LAT.
98°50'30" W. LONG.

KEY TO INSET MAP

PYRAMID OF THE MOON — 1
PYRAMID OF THE SUN — 2
CIUDADELA — 3
TEMPLE OF QUETZALCOATL — 4
"STREET OF THE DEAD" — 5
GREAT COMPOUND — 6
RIO SAN JUAN — 24
PLAZA OF THE MOON — 28
QUETZALPAPALOTL PALACE — 29
GROUP 5' — 30
GROUP 5 — 31
XALA COMPOUND — 32
BUILDING OF THE ALTARS — 33
TEMPLE OF AGRICULTURE — 34
MYTHOLOGICAL ANIMALS MURALS — 35
PUMA MURAL — 36
PLAZA OF THE COLUMNS — 37
EXPLORATIONS OF 1895 — 38
PALACE OF THE SUN — 39
PATIO OF THE FOUR SMALL TEMPLES — 40
HOUSE OF THE PRIESTS — 41
VIKING GROUP — 42
"STREET OF THE DEAD" COMPLEX — 43
EXPLORATIONS OF 1917 — 44
SUPERPOSED BUILDINGS — 45
EXPLORATIONS OF 1908 — 46
TETITLA — 47
ZACUALA PATIOS — 48
ZACUALA PALACE — 49
YAYAHUALA — 50

INSET MAP

LOCATION OF INSET MAP

SCALE OF INSET MAP
0   50   100   200   300   400
METERS

MAP SHOWS EXTENT OF ANCIENT CITY CA. 600 A.D.; CA. 20 SQ. KMS. OR 8 SQ. MI.
SHOWN ARE (1) PARTIALLY OR COMPLETELY EXCAVATED STRUCTURES, PRIMARILY
ALONG THE "STREET OF THE DEAD" (NORTH-SOUTH AXIS), AND (2) RECONSTRUCTIONS
BASED ON TEOTIHUACAN MAPPING PROJECT SURVEY OF SURFACE REMAINS OF UNEX-
CAVATED AND PARTIALLY EXCAVATED STRUCTURES. AN UNDETERMINED NUMBER OF
STRUCTURES IN VARIOUS PARTS OF THE CITY HAVE BEEN BURIED UNDER SILT
OR LEVELLED FOR AGRICULTURE IN MODERN TIMES. NOTE CANALIZATION OF
MOST WATER COURSES WITHIN THE ANCIENT CITY.

TEOTIHUACAN MAPPING PROJECT
RENÉ MILLON, DIRECTOR
DEPARTMENT OF ANTHROPOLOGY   AIDED BY GRANTS FROM THE
UNIVERSITY OF ROCHESTER   NATIONAL SCIENCE FOUNDATION
ROCHESTER, NEW YORK   CHIEF DRAFTSMAN J. ARMANDO CERDA
PRINCIPAL ASSOCIATES, BRUCE DREWITT AND GEORGE COWGILL

TEOTIHUACAN

ESTADO DE MEXICO

MEXICO

TOPOGRAPHIC MAP

SEPTEMBER 1970
COPYRIGHT 1972 BY RENÉ MILLON

CONTOUR INTERVAL ONE METER

MILES

KILOMETERS

TEOTIHUACAN IS 40 KILOMETERS (25 MILES)
NORTHEAST OF MEXICO CITY

MAP 19. Photogrammetric map of the region of ancient Teotihuacán, prepared from a reduced mosaic of the topographic sheets used in the field to produce Map 18. The grid system of 500-meter squares is oriented to the "Street of the Dead," the north-south axis of the ancient city (ca. 15°25' east of north).

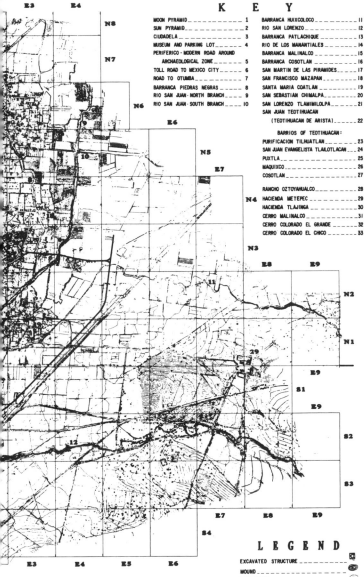

K E Y

MOON PYRAMID _ _ _ _ _ _ _ _ _ 1
SUN PYRAMID _ _ _ _ _ _ _ _ _ 2
CIUDADELA _ _ _ _ _ _ _ _ _ _ 3
MUSEUM AND PARKING LOT _ _ _ _ _ 4
PERIFERICO - MODERN ROAD AROUND
    ARCHAEOLOGICAL ZONE _ _ _ _ _ 5
TOLL ROAD TO MEXICO CITY _ _ _ _ 6
ROAD TO OTUMBA _ _ _ _ _ _ _ 7
BARRANCA PIEDRAS NEGRAS _ _ _ _ 8
RIO SAN JUAN - NORTH BRANCH _ _ _ 9
RIO SAN JUAN - SOUTH BRANCH _ _ _ 10

BARRANCA HUIXCOLOCO _ _ _ _ _ _ 11
RIO SAN LORENZO _ _ _ _ _ _ _ 12
BARRANCA PATLACHIQUE _ _ _ _ _ 13
RIO DE LOS MANANTIALES _ _ _ _ _ 14
BARRANCA MALINALCO _ _ _ _ _ _ 15
BARRANCA COSOTLAN _ _ _ _ _ _ 16
SAN MARTIN DE LAS PIRAMIDES _ _ _ 17
SAN FRANCISCO MAZAPAN _ _ _ _ _ 18
SANTA MARIA COATLAN _ _ _ _ _ _ 19
SAN SEBASTIAN CHIMALPA _ _ _ _ _ 20
SAN LORENZO TLAMIMILOLPA _ _ _ _ 21
SAN JUAN TEOTIHUACAN
    (TEOTIHUACAN DE ARISTA) _ _ _ _ 22

BARRIOS OF TEOTIHUACAN:

PURIFICACION TILHUATLAN _ _ _ _ _ 23
SAN JUAN EVANGELISTA TLAILOTLACAN _ 24
PUXTLA _ _ _ _ _ _ _ _ _ _ _ 25
MAQUIXCO _ _ _ _ _ _ _ _ _ _ 26
COSOTLAN _ _ _ _ _ _ _ _ _ _ 27

RANCHO OZTOYAHUALCO _ _ _ _ _ _ 28
HACIENDA METEPEC _ _ _ _ _ _ _ 29
HACIENDA TLAJINGA _ _ _ _ _ _ _ 30
CERRO MALINALCO _ _ _ _ _ _ _ 31
CERRO COLORADO EL GRANDE _ _ _ _ 32
CERRO COLORADO EL CHICO _ _ _ _ _ 33

L E G E N D

EXCAVATED STRUCTURE _ _ _ _ _ _ _
MOUND _ _ _ _ _ _ _ _ _ _ _ _
LOW MOUND _ _ _ _ _ _ _ _ _ _
DEPRESSION _ _ _ _ _ _ _ _ _ _
MODERN BUILDING _ _ _ _ _ _ _ _
VEGETATION _ _ _ _ _ _ _ _ _ _
ROAD _ _ _ _ _ _ _ _ _ _ _ _
PATH OR TRAIL _ _ _ _ _ _ _ _ _
WATER COURSE _ _ _ _ _ _ _ _ _
RAILROAD _ _ _ _ _ _ _ _ _ _ _
HIGH VOLTAGE POWER LINE _ _ _ _ _
POWER, TELEPHONE AND TELEGRAPH LINES _ _

THIS MAP IS A MOSAIC MADE FROM REDUCTIONS OF THE MACHINE-DRAWN,
PHOTOGRAMMETRIC PENCIL SHEETS WHICH WERE NOT ORIGINALLY INTENDED
FOR PUBLICATION AS SUCH. IT CONTAINS A NUMBER OF MINOR DIS-
CREPANCIES AND PROBLEMATIC REPRESENTATIONS, MOST OF WHICH ARE
RESOLVED ON THE FINAL 1:2 000 DRAWINGS IN VOLUME 1 OF THE PROJECT
REPORTS. IT IS PUBLISHED IN THIS FORM IN THE BELIEF THAT ITS
USEFULNESS OUTWEIGHS ITS DEFICIENCIES. FEATURES ARE SHOWN AS
THEY EXISTED IN MARCH, 1962, BEFORE MOST OF THE EXCAVATIONS OF
MEXICO'S INSTITUTO NACIONAL DE ANTROPOLOGIA E HISTORIA (INAH).
EXCEPTIONS ARE THE ROAD AROUND THE ARCHAEOLOGICAL ZONE AND THE
HIGHWAYS CONSTRUCTED SINCE 1962.

TEOTIHUACAN MAPPING PROJECT
RENÉ MILLON, DIRECTOR
DEPARTMENT OF ANTHROPOLOGY
UNIVERSITY OF ROCHESTER
ROCHESTER, NEW YORK
PRINCIPAL ASSOCIATES,
  BRUCE DREWITT AND GEORGE COWGILL
AIDED BY GRANTS FROM THE
NATIONAL SCIENCE FOUNDATION

GRID IS ORIENTED
CA. 15°25' EAST OF
ASTRONOMIC NORTH.

SUN PYRAMID
19°41'30" N. LAT.
98°50'30" W. LONG.
CHIEF DRAFTSMAN J. ARMANDO CERDA

ELEVATION AT ZERO POINT OF GRID SYSTEM
CA. 2 276 METERS ABOVE MEAN SEA LEVEL.

PHOTOGRAMMETRIC MANUSCRIPT MAP PREPARED BY
CIA. MEXICANA AEROFOTO, S.A., MEXICO, D. F.
AND HUNTING MAPPING, INC., ROCHESTER, N. Y.
(NOW LOCKWOOD MAPPING).

TEOTIHUACAN APARTMENT COMPOUNDS

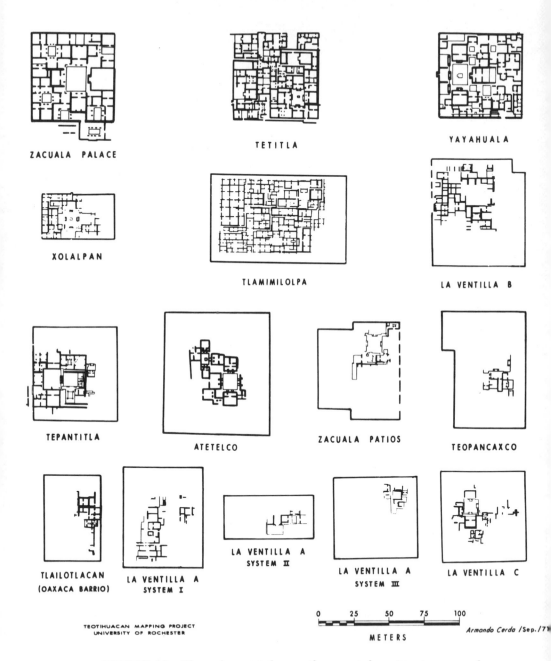

ZACUALA PALACE

TETITLA

YAYAHUALA

XOLALPAN

TLAMIMILOLPA

LA VENTILLA B

TEPANTITLA

ATETELCO

ZACUALA PATIOS

TEOPANCAXCO

TLAILOTLACAN
(OAXACA BARRIO)

LA VENTILLA A
SYSTEM I

LA VENTILLA A
SYSTEM II

LA VENTILLA A
SYSTEM III

LA VENTILLA C

TEOTIHUACAN MAPPING PROJECT
UNIVERSITY OF ROCHESTER

0   25   50   75   100
METERS

Armando Cerda /Sep./7?

FIGURE 13. Plans of excavated or partly excavated apartment compounds in Teotihuacán drawn to the same scale. In the case of partly excavated compounds, the locations of most exterior walls are approximate.

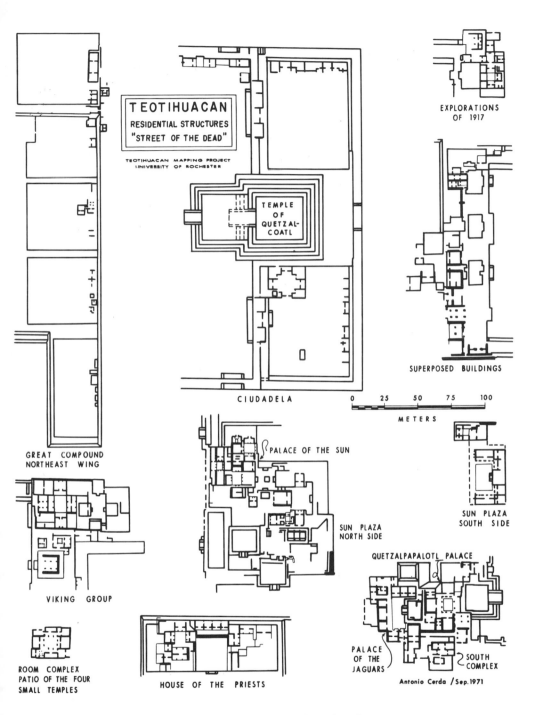

TEOTIHUACAN

RESIDENTIAL STRUCTURES
"STREET OF THE DEAD"

TEOTIHUACAN MAPPING PROJECT
UNIVERSITY OF ROCHESTER

TEMPLE
OF
QUETZAL-
COATL

EXPLORATIONS
OF 1917

SUPERPOSED BUILDINGS

CIUDADELA

0   25   50   75   100

METERS

GREAT COMPOUND
NORTHEAST WING

PALACE OF THE SUN

SUN PLAZA
SOUTH SIDE

VIKING GROUP

SUN PLAZA
NORTH SIDE

QUETZALPAPALOTL PALACE

ROOM COMPLEX
PATIO OF THE FOUR
SMALL TEMPLES

HOUSE OF THE PRIESTS

PALACE
OF THE
JAGUARS

SOUTH
COMPLEX

Antonio Cerda / Sep. 1971

FIGURE 14. Plans of excavated or partly excavated residential structures
on the "Street of the Dead" drawn to the same scale as the apartment compounds in Figure 13.

Around A.D. 600, Teotihuacán covered an area of 20 square kilometers, or 8 square miles (Map 18). The perimeter of the ancient city is very irregular. Map 18, for example, covers an area of 35 square kilometers in showing the 20 square kilometers of urban construction comprised in the ancient city. I have estimated the city's population in A.D. 600 to be not less than 75,000 and concluded that it was probably 125,000. The bases for these calculations are published elsewhere (R. Millon 1970b, 1973: 44–45). I now think my assumptions were too conservative, and that Teotihuacán's population may have reached 150,000 to 200,000, or perhaps even more. These estimates for the city at its height are considerably higher than the ones I made in 1966 (R. Millon 1967b). The newer figures are based on the map of the entire city.

The population of the city earlier in its history, around the first century A.D. (during the late First Intermediate period [Fig. 15]), is difficult to estimate. In 1970 I suggested a minimal estimate of 35,000, with "60,000 more likely" (R. Millon 1970a:41). I subsequently drew back from this estimate and took a more conservative position, suggesting that a population of 25,000 to 30,000 "would appear to be a reasonable estimate" and that "it might have been considerably more" (R. Millon 1973:52). Cowgill has now argued that even my earlier estimate may have been conservative and that the population of Teotihuacán in the late First Intermediate period (Fig. 15) may have been 50,000 to 60,000 (Cowgill 1974:385–87).

Although Teotihuacán was clearly subject to planning (Drewitt 1967, 1969), it is not clear whether it was built in accordance with a master plan established early in the city's history (Robertson 1963:35). Its buildup over a period of several centuries may have been the result of the gradual fulfillment of such a plan. But it may also have been the result of successive additions to a basic cruciform plan, that, when we see the completed whole, may give more of an impression of the realization of a master plan than actually was the case.

There is tenuous evidence for the existence of an "inner" and "outer" city in Teotihuacán (R. Millon 1973:43–44). If such a distinction did exist, it is probably significant that the only positively identified barrio of foreigners in Teotihuacán—the Oaxaca barrio (Map 18, no. 17)—would have been situated in the "outer city."

It has been clear for some time that Teotihuacán was a ritual and religious center of unequalled magnitude and importance in Mesoamerica

VALLEY OF TEOTIHUACAN CHRONOLOGY
Table of Concordances

Period (left)	Date	Phase Names [1]		Phase Numbers [2]	Period (right)
LATE HORIZON	A.D. 1500	Teacalco		Aztec IV	
	1400	Chimalpa		Aztec III	POST-
	1300				
	1200	Zocango		Aztec II	CLASSIC
SECOND INTER-MEDIATE PERIOD	1100	Mazapan		Mazapa	
	1000				PERIOD
	900	Xometla		Coyotlatelco	———— 900 A.D.
	800	Oxtoticpac		Proto-Coyotlatelco	
	700	METEPEC		Teotihuacán IV	CLASSIC
	600	XOLALPAN	Late	Teotihuacán IIIA	
MIDDLE HORIZON	500		Early	Teotihuacán III	PERIOD
	400	TLAMIMILOLPA	Late	Teotihuacán IIA-III	
	300		Early	Teotihuacán IIA	———— 300 A.D.
	200	MICCAOTLI		Teotihuacán II	TERMINAL
	100	TZACUALLI	Late	Teotihuacán IA	PRE-CLASSIC
	A.D. / B.C.		Early	Teotihuacán I	
	100	PATLACHIQUE	Chimalhuacán *		PERIOD
				Proto-Teotihuacán I	
FIRST INTER-MEDIATE PERIOD	200	Terminal Cuanalan; Tezoyuca	Cuicuilco *		LATE
	300	Late Cuanalan	Ticoman III *		PRE-CLASSIC
	400	Middle Cuanalan	Ticoman II *		PERIOD
	500	Early Cuanalan	Ticoman I *		
	600	Chiconauhtla	Middle		MIDDLE PRE-CLASSIC
	700		Zacatenco *		PERIOD
	B.C. 800				

(Vertical label along the left of the Phase Names column: TEOTIHUACAN)

[1] Phase names used by personnel of Teotihuacán Mapping Project (Millon and others) and by personnel of Valley of Teotihuacán Project (Sanders and others).

[2] Phase numbers used by personnel of the Proyecto Teotihuacán, of the Instituto Nacional de Antropologia e Historia (see Acosta 1964: 58-59).

* Pre-classic phases elsewhere in the Valley of Mexico.

NOTE : The absolute chronology shown is that used by the Teotihuacán Mapping Project. Terminology for the Teotihuacán phases is based on the Armillas classification (1950) with modifications.

TEOTIHUACAN MAPPING PROJECT
UNIVERSITY OF ROCHESTER

J.A.Cerda.

RENÉ MILLON
9/64
REVISED 5/72

FIGURE 15. Valley of Teotihuacán chronology.

during a large part of the first millennium A.D. The scope and nature of its influence in so much of civilized Mesoamerica are still only beginning to be understood. It is also becoming increasingly clear that Teotihuacán was a marketplace and trade center of great importance. It is my view of the evidence that the combined effects of ritual, marketplace exchange, craft production, and trade brought Teotihuacán to its position of pre-eminence. This process took place in a setting of strategic importance, in a valley rich in obsidian and potentially rich in cultivable land, and in a basin with a lake system whose resources and potential for communication were unparalleled in this part of the world.

At its height the city must have attracted thousands of outsiders to its temples and markets every day, and tens of thousands for major festivals. These would have included pilgrims, people attracted to the marketplace, merchants, petty traders, visitors, foreign dignitaries, religious personages, and probably a predictable group of thieves and con men (R. Millon 1967c:152). The economy of the city must have been based, in part, on servicing the needs of these visitors and on its attendant "tourist trade." The city's economic growth must have gone hand in hand with the growth of the city as a center of attraction for multitudes, both from surrounding and from far-off areas. Some of the outsiders coming to Teotihuacán must have had social ties with people living there, who would have provided them with places to stay. Unlike the case of Tenochtitlan (Calnek 1972a), we do not know what arrangements may have been made for those who had no such ties. What does seem clear is that the city must have been a metropolis that was so impellingly attractive, so alive, so much the center of things in so many ways that for hundreds of thousands of people it must have been the most important place in their world.

Other contemporary Mesoamerican centers during the Middle Horizon seem to have covered larger areas than Teotihuacán—for example, Tikal in the Petén area of Guatemala and Dzibilchaltún in northwestern Yucatán (W. R. Coe 1967, Haviland 1969, 1970, Andrews 1965, 1968). But so far as is now known, no other contemporary center seems to have been as highly urbanized as Teotihuacán. No other center of its time seems to have combined large populations, high population density, great size, one or more foreign enclaves, thousands of craft specialists, and a metropolitan urban environment in a marketplace and ritual center of monumental proportions. Teotihuacán seems, therefore, to have been the first great metropolitan urban center to develop in Mesoamerica, and nothing approaching it in the degree and nature of its urbanization seems to have arisen thereafter, until the much later rise of the Aztec island capital of Tenochtitlan during the latter part of the Late Horizon (Fig. 15).

THE TEOTIHUACÁN APARTMENT COMPOUND

The typical Teotihuacán apartment compound (Fig. 13) apparently did not appear until after the city had flourished and expanded for several hundred years. As mentioned earlier, the population of Tzacualli-phase Teotihuacán, around A.D. 100, was probably 30,000 or more. Temples during this period were built of stone and other permanent materials. But domestic structures (with the possible exception of structures near the great temple buildings) seem to have been built of relatively imperma-nent building materials, perhaps of adobe.

Our excavations and those of others indicate that the massive, perma-nent Teotihuacán apartment compounds did not come into being as standard residential architecture until the Tlamimilolpa phase (that is, until the third to fourth centuries A.D.) (Fig. 15). The beginning of what was to be a revolutionary change in settlement pattern in the city appears to coincide with a great expansion in the working of obsidian in Teoti-huacán. As I have previously noted (R. Millon 1968b:107), the Teoti-huacán apartment compound seems to have been designed for urban life, for life in a city that was becoming increasingly crowded, perhaps ap-proaching the chaotic, as obsidian working and other crafts grew more and more rapidly, and as more and more people came into the city.

But the Teotihuacán apartment compound is an unusual urban dwell-ing. It is unusual because of the relative inflexibility of its internal organi-zation, and it is unusual in being the standard residential structure in so large a city with so many buildings—what we are confronted with here are clusters of hundreds of apartment compounds in different parts of the city. The unusualness of the Teotihuacán apartment compound has not been sufficiently recognized, I think, for at least two reasons: (1) the fact that these compounds were not primarily residences of people of high status but rather were standard residential units numbering in the thou-sands was not known until we prepared a map of the entire city, and (2) in stressing the resemblances of Teotihuacán residential architecture to

Old World houses, with rooms arranged around interior patios, porticoes, and passageways, it is easy to overlook the important differences that exist between them.[2]

The standard Teotihuacán residential compound as revealed in excavation is not a *house* compound. It is, instead, an *apartment* compound—in other words, a compound with a great number of rooms and patios that could more or less readily have been divided into apartments (see Fig. 13). The layout of rooms, patios, and accessways implies that there must have been a number of households in a single compound. The amount of open space within the compounds is relatively small, sufficient to give most rooms some light from patios and light wells and to provide some privacy in a crowded environment. The importance of the privacy thus afforded should not be underestimated, but it should also be understood that it was a relative matter, for these compounds must have been crowded with people. My estimate, based on conservative judgments about the number of rooms in which people slept, is that a building 60 meters on a side would have held at least 60 and probably 100 or more people (R. Millon 1970b:1079–80, R. Millon 1973:45). This means that residential compounds of this size or larger probably housed social groups comprising a number of households.

Thus a standard-sized residential compound probably housed 100 or more people, and its rooms were probably grouped into clusters forming apartments. It is common for such compounds to have one or more prominently located temple platforms. I have previously stressed that the prominent placement of one or more such temple structures in residential compounds argues that the residents of the building participated in common rituals; to that extent, at least, they formed corporate groups, whose members may also have been related on the basis of kinship or occupation, or both (R. Millon 1967c:151, 1968b:113–14; see also Sanders 1965:173, 1967:125–29).

Because of his work on obsidian workshops, his interest in the organization of obsidian craft production, and his conviction that obsidian workers were men, Michael Spence (1971, 1974), through a study of anomalies in bone structure, investigated burials from several apartment compounds to see if he could find evidence of biological relationship among them. His results suggested that the men in one of the compounds (the only compound from which skeletons from many burials were available) were more closely related to each other than were the women to each other or to the men. His provisional conclusion from this was that after marriage, men may have tended to remain in the compounds where they were born, with women marrying in. His results do not necessarily tell us anything one way or the other about kinship organization in the compound, for we do not know what biological links might have been recognized in compound kinship organization, or indeed if those living in compounds were organized on the basis of kinship. His results suggest a possible pattern of residence, but they cannot tell us anything about how this may or may not have been conceptualized.

The Teotihuacán apartment compounds have two outstanding characteristics. First, most are so large as to be more than houses, yet, apart from the "Street of the Dead," most of those already excavated do not appear to be palaces or mansions. Second, they are so sharply bounded, so discrete, such clear entities. Each compound is a bounded unit surrounded by high windowless walls and most often separated from other such compounds by narrow streets. Apartment compounds vary in size, from 15 to 20 meters on a side to 50 by 150 meters. Most of the compounds fall between these two extremes and are very large residences. To my knowledge, such residential architecture extending over many square kilometers is unique in Mesoamerica and is, at best, unusual anywhere else. Recent research by Calnek (1972a, 1972b) on house plans in ancient Tenochtitlan has revealed nothing comparable to the Teotihuacán apartment compound. Instead, what he most frequently finds are individual house compounds occupied by some form of extended family, with a row of rooms often facing the street and another row of rooms connected to the first row at a right angle, forming an L-shaped unit, with a large, walled patio behind it. The patio often occupies at least as much space as the buildings themselves. They are house compounds, or patio houses, but they are not apartment compounds with many patios, as at Teotihuacán.[3]

If the Tenochtitlan evidence is not deemed relevant because it represents constructions on the peripheries of the Aztec capital rather than near its center, an inspection of the Teotihuacán map (Map 18) demonstrates that even on the peripheries, where limitations of space were not a factor, the Teotihuacanos built standard apartment compounds. What apparently was originally designed for crowded urban living evidently came to be regarded by the vast majority as the only way to build, whether one was in the crowded center of the city or on its outskirts (see peripheries of city on Map 18). The Teotihuacán village partly excavated by

Sanders north of Maquixco and due west of the western limit of Teotihuacán also seems to have been organized into residential compounds like
those of Teotihuacán, only much smaller (Sanders 1965:Fig. 12, 1967:
Fig. 3).

A Teotihuacán residential compound like the one named Zacuala Palace (Fig. 13) is a planned structure, laid out from the beginning with a
preconceived plan for the disposition of rooms, porticoes, patios, light
wells, accessways, entrances, and hallways. The same seems to be true
of Xolalpan, as well as of two other completely excavated apartment compounds at Teotihuacán, Yayahuala and Tetitla (Fig. 13). It even seems
to be at least partly true of so complex a structure as Tlamimilolpa (Fig.
13). Modifications were made in the plans of many of these compounds
over the years. However, except for apparent additions on the north side
of Tetitla, the basic plan seems to have remained substantially unchanged
even when the entire building or major sections of it were rebuilt, as usually happened several times in the history of an apartment compound
(Séjourné 1966:188).

The rebuilt structure maintained its same outer limits (the published
example from Tetitla includes its northern additions in both building levels shown in Séjourné's plans [1966]) and was itself a preconceived architectural whole from the outset of the rebuilding (compare Séjourné's
plans [1966:Fig. 22] of levels 2 and 3 of Tetitla and their respective and
differing drainage systems; see also Linné's [1934:43, 1942:110–11] cross
sections through Xolalpan and parts of Tlamimilolpa). Sections of two
levels at Tetitla and of their drainage systems evidently were rebuilt in
accordance with a preconceived plan. The fact that the drainage systems
for carrying off rainwater from interior patios in apartment compounds
ran underneath the lime-plastered "concrete" floors meant that the disposition of patios and accessways with drains had to be decided on at the
outset of building or rebuilding (Séjourné 1966:Fig. 22). This, in turn,
set limits on the disposition of rooms and porticoes that opened on these
patios or accessways and must have required the prior planning of most,
if not all, of the entire compound at one time.

The plan of Zacuala Palace conforms closely to multiples of what appears to be a basic Teotihuacán unit of measurement, slightly over 80
centimeters, found by Bruce Drewitt (personal communication, also
Drewitt 1969).[4] The same seems to be true of Tetitla, though not so
clearly as in the case of Zacuala Palace. Thus, it appears that most Teoti-

huacán apartment compounds so far excavated were built in accordance with preconceived plans, rather than gradually growing up in a "process of clustering among separate units around a common courtyard," as Kubler has argued (1964:355).

The only excavated buildings with plans that might be interpreted as representing growth by accretion rather than from a preconceived plan are Tlamimilolpa (Linné 1942) and La Ventilla B (Fig. 13). I do not think that these plans represent such a process of simple growth by accretion, but I do think it possible that they reflect something else of significance.

The lowest level at La Ventilla B appears to be the oldest apartment compound so far excavated at Teotihuacán outside the "Street of the Dead" area, dating to the Early Tlamimilolpa phase (about A.D. 250, near the beginning of the Middle Horizon) (Fig. 15). Our La Ventilla B data come from a salvage excavation in this building carried out by Juan Vidarte as part of the Mexican government's Teotihuacán Project in 1963 and 1964. For the most part the La Ventilla B plan represents the lowest building level on this site, most of the remains of upper building levels having been removed by bulldozers before the salvage excavation began. Because salvage excavation was carried out under great pressure of time, and because the building has since been bulldozed out of existence, problems in the data from it cannot be checked in the field. But given the data we have, its rooms do not appear to be as effectively or consistently organized around patios and light wells as they are in later buildings.

The problem here is whether the differences between the La Ventilla B plan and the plan of a compound such as Xolalpan (Fig. 13) are due to time or to social differences. La Ventilla B, while not far from the city's center, is at the same time close to the city's outer edge, because it is located where the edge of the city happens to be close to the center (Map 18, no. 20). Tlamimilolpa, on the other hand, occupies a clearly peripheral position (Map 18, no. 10), and while the organization of its rooms around patios more closely resembles the standard Teotihuacán apartment compound than the plan of La Ventilla B, Tlamimilolpa still has a crowded, cramped appearance when compared with other compounds.

Evidence from a number of burials at La Ventilla B, analyzed by Clara Millon for another purpose and referred to below, suggest that it was occupied by people of relatively low status. To a lesser extent the same can be said of the burial offerings at Tlamimilolpa. Even Burial 1 at Tlamimilolpa is impressive more for the quantity than for the quality of its offerings.

The plan of Tlamimilolpa as shown by Linné (Fig. 13) is the upper-most of three building levels, and dates to a period several hundred years later than La Ventilla B. Nevertheless, Linné's cross sections show that in the restricted area where he penetrated to the lowest building level, early room plans were continued into later periods without substantial modifications (Linné 1942:110–11, Figs. 182–88). Thus, in at least one part of the structure, the crowded plan of Tlamimilolpa appears to have been maintained throughout its history of several hundred years. Vidarte (personal communication) reports fragmentary evidence of the same kind at La Ventilla B. If this is so, it would suggest that apartment compounds on the peripheries may have been occupied by people of relatively low status who lived in crowded tenement-like quarters.

This evidence for architectural continuity suggests at least two possible explanations. First, the people living in peripheral apartment compounds may have continued to occupy a low status for the duration of the city's existence, for the compounds they lived in continued to be built following the same crowded, cramped plan. Or, alternatively, peripheral apartment compounds may have housed successive groups of low status, whose members moved to less cramped quarters when there was opportunity to do so. This would suggest that these compounds might have housed successive waves of people from the countryside or from other areas who were able to raise their status and move elsewhere. At this point there is not enough evidence to argue in behalf of either alternative, and more work will have to be done before we can test these possibilities.

Certainly it would not be surprising, from a comparative point of view, to find that the people with the highest status in Teotihuacán tended to live in the center of the city and that, moving out from the center to the peripheries, one would encounter people of lower and lower status. At the same time, it seems almost certain that we are not dealing with a simple linear decrease in status from center to periphery. There is strong evidence, for example, for differences in the status of the occupants of apartment compounds in neighboring barrios, arguing for a mosaic quality to the barrio structure of Teotihuacán rather than a simple gradient of status from center to periphery.

Since we do not have evidence for large, permanent residential compounds any earlier than the beginning of the Middle Horizon (the Early Tlamimilolpa phase, ca. A.D. 200 [Fig. 15]), we know little about the form and disposition of residential units before that time, with the possible exception of parts of the "Street of the Dead" area. I suspect, on the basis of tenuous evidence, that the antecedents of the apartment compound may have been smaller, simpler, adobe-walled compounds, consisting of partly open patios, with rooms opening on the patios on two or three sides. Testing will have to be done to see whether evidence for such an earlier form exists.[5]

A small part of the population seems to have lived in small, impermanent structures even when the city was at its height. As might be expected, there seem to be more of these on the peripheries of the city (see Map 18).

At this point I should emphasize that the internal arrangement of rooms and courts differs in each of the compounds so far excavated (Fig. 13). They do not have the appearance of structures built by the state to a uniform plan, and there is no special reason to think they were owned by the state. If rights to occupancy were governed by ascriptive criteria derived from membership in descent groups of some kind, the apartment compound would have been a relatively inflexible living unit. Why was it adopted, and why were thousands of them built? Does this argue for state intervention of some kind?

In my opinion, it would be an oversimplification to postulate that those who lived in the Teotihuacán apartment compounds were organized either solely on the basis of strong kin ties or solely on the basis of relatively impersonal landlord-tenant relations. A more complex model seems to be called for, one involving individual or corporate ownership of compounds, a variety of means of recruitment, and a variety of diffuse relationships of dependency that would be less than kinship yet more than landlord-tenant relations—perhaps something analogous to the social composition of the successive "circles" of the "family" in large landholdings in the traditional Japanese village in early Tokugawa Japan (Smith 1959:6).[6] The outermost "circle" of people in such a compound might have consisted of persons linked to each other by patron-client ties in a framework of ritual kinship. This model, however, will remain hypothetical until it can be tested in the controlled excavation of one or more apartment compounds. At the outset it may be possible to test only some of its dimensions. But it should be possible to avoid some of the pitfalls involved in such testing (Spence 1971, Binford and Binford 1968).

It is worth noting that the model for the population of the Teotihuacán apartment compound emerged from the study of comparative archaeological, ethnographic, and historic evidence from many parts of the New and Old Worlds[7]; this evidence disclosed no configurations even moderately resembling what exists at Teotihuacán—namely, hundreds of apartment compounds stretching over many square kilometers in an urban setting in which they served as the standard residential unit. The comparative study itself helped to define and bound the problem and to suggest a model for the archaeological evidence not found in the comparative urban evidence itself. It was not found in the comparative urban evidence because the evidence from Teotihuacán stands out as so unusual in comparative perspective, a fact that was not apparent when I started the comparative study. Thus, what emerges is a model for the Teotihuacán evidence to be tested in excavation that rests on comparative study, but at the same time does not replicate any particular evidence from any specific nonindustrialized urban setting examined elsewhere in the world.

The cohesiveness of groups living in apartment compounds presumably would have been enhanced if, in addition to participating in common ritual activities, its members also shared economic activities and interests. We have abundant evidence that similar economic activities were carried out by people living in the same compounds. Such mutual reinforcement of economic, ritual, and group ties might at least partially explain what appears to be archaeological evidence for the cohesiveness of groups in apartment compounds.

But, as pointed out earlier, this is not just a matter of opinion and fruitless discussion. It is subject to testing. Careful, controlled excavation of two or more Teotihuacán apartment compounds could disclose evidence for, first, minor yet distinctive customs associated with some parts of compounds where compound leaders might have lived, and, second, the sharing of highly localized idiosyncratic behavior such as might be expected among persons living in close proximity for long periods of time (Deetz 1968). Particular domestic practices can serve to set off one group from another, as appears to be the case with residents of the Oaxaca barrio vis-à-vis other Teotihuacanos. Much more difficult would be the isolation of micro-differences which might be expected to test the hypothesis that compounds were populated by successive "circles" of persons, with each successive "circle" less closely tied to compound leaders.

Still another independent and supplementary line of evidence might be obtained from a continuation of the line of investigation begun by

Michael Spence (1971, 1974)—the examination of skeletal material from one or more apartment compounds in an effort to determine, through anomalies in bone structure, the degree to which the inhabitants of an apartment compound may have been biologically related.

Teotihuacán must have had a particularly adaptable and flexible social organization to have been able to expand so rapidly and so successfully. Is this consonant with the existence of apartment compound populations of the kind we have been discussing? It would appear so, for if these groups were cohesive, with clearly defined social boundaries, their members need not have felt that their group identities were threatened by the incorporation of outsiders, either through adoption or through other fictive means. One might expect many such outsiders to have ties of one kind or another in the city that would identify and place them and provide a basis for their incorporation into a particular group within the city. In fact, when expansion of the group was economically or otherwise considered desirable, groups in a growing city might have welcomed and sought such additions. It is partly with this in mind that we drew the earlier analogy with rural Japan, for in parts of early Tokugawa Japan outsiders were readily incorporated through fictive and other means into kin groups in expanding rural households (Smith 1959:1–36).

As the city rapidly grew, as its economy and trade networks expanded, there might have been increasing demand for craftsmen and other workers. This demand may have attracted many people who, when they arrived in the city, were able to attach themselves by one means or another to already existing groups occupying compounds, perhaps through establishing or activating ties with specific individuals in these groups. The demand for apprentice craftsmen might have led to the practice of encouraging apprentices to marry women of the group to which they were economically (and probably also socially and ritually) attached. Such a situation occurred among West African glassworkers, whose numbers were rapidly expanding, in the Nupe capital of Bida in Nigeria (Nadel 1942: 278).[8]

In short, the internal composition of the apartment compound suggested here might have proved to be quite flexible and adaptable in a rapidly growing city; in fact, not only might it have contributed actively to the city's rapid growth, it might also have played a critical part in that growth. At the same time, we should realize that the relatively rapid transformation of the city into a city of apartment compounds (apparently begun on a large scale in the Tlamimilolpa phase) almost certainly would have been accompanied by major conflicts, antagonisms, and tensions. Enormous stresses were probably generated during the transformation itself, and to a lesser degree these stresses may have come to form a permanent part of compound life and urban life at Teotihuacán. This milieu of stress and conflict may have played a critical role in the growth of the city, and perhaps also in its eventual collapse.

With the passage of time some accommodation for increased size in domestic groups could have been made by subdividing existing apartments or individual rooms. There is fragmentary evidence for this in some Teotihuacán apartment compounds (for example, Xolalpan, Tlamimilolpa, and Tetitla [Linné 1934:43, 1942:110–11, Séjourné 1966: Fig. 22]). There is also evidence that some compounds were able to expand somewhat in one or more directions, thus providing accommodations for more people. The north side of Tetitla may have two or three such additions (Fig. 13). Without more excavation, however, we cannot know how common such internal changes and external additions may have been. I would suspect that such changes were commonly undertaken, but that in a rapidly growing city and over long periods of time, there must have been a significant number of other outlets for population growth. One part of a group might try to move to another building where some of its members could activate latent ties with other kinsmen; or they might move to a relatively less crowded part of the city and establish a new compound where there was still room and where they might have some social, or perhaps political, ties that could have facilitated or made possible such a move.

Another possibility is that outsiders moved into the city without previously existing ties there and formed their own local groups. This would presumably have required permission from whatever group (or person) controlled the land involved, and may have involved bureaucratic intervention as well.

As we have seen, the hypothesis about the nature of the groups occupying apartment compounds is subject to testing. Assuming that it has any validity, what implications would this have for the internal structure of the city? If the city's basic social unit was a cohesive, flexible, and adaptable group, capable of relatively rapid changes in size, it would seem well suited to the diversified craft economy that became increasingly important as the city grew, and that was itself probably a major contributing force to that growth.

We have already seen that many craft specialists tended to cluster in barrios. So did an ethnic group from Oaxaca (see Map 18, no. 17), and a possible merchants' group in the eastern part of the city (Map 18, no. 9). Other areas are so sharply defined that barrio boundaries are clear without any further evidence. The Tepantitla compound (Map 18, no. 12) lies on the southern edge of such a barrio. If apartment compounds were cohesive and organized, then so may have been the barrios into which they were grouped. Just as there may have been individuals who headed apartment compounds, so may there have been barrio leaders. The distinctive architecture of the Yayahuala compound (Fig. 13) may be an indication that this was a barrio temple, as suggested by Séjourné and Salicrup (1965). Unlike most other apartment compounds, Yayahuala seems open to the public, with a high, broad, public entrance on the west that leads directly into the compound's main patio, around which are disposed three relatively large temples. These temples occupy considerably more of the area of the Yayahuala compound than do the main temples in other excavated residential compounds at Teotihuacán. Thus, the Yayahuala compound stands out as being especially important in a ritual sense, yet the remainder of the compound is a crowded residential structure. For this reason, the suggestion that the Yayahuala compound may have been a barrio temple seems reasonable to me. It also seems likely, although Séjourné and Salicrup do not suggest this, that the compound housed the leader of the barrio, perhaps in the relatively large apartment immediately to the north of the compound's main temple (Fig. 13). (For a detailed plan of Yayahuala, see Séjourné 1966:Fig. 4, R. Millon 1967d:47.)

If barrio organization existed, based on economic, social, and ritual ties, it would have had important social consequences in the city as a whole, in addition to strengthening social and cultural integration within the barrio itself. Barrio organizations, if they existed, would have provided an important intermediate organizational level between the rulers of Teotihuacán and the level of the apartment compound. The apartment compound itself would have constituted a potential organizational level of major importance in the city, and it is difficult to imagine that the state would have been indifferent to its potential. The differing plans of individual compounds argue against state intervention in the layout of compounds. But there may have been a state decision involved when the "permanent" Teotihuacán apartment compound began to come into general use in the Tlamimilolpa phase, a decision involving the building of compounds as basic residential units, whatever their internal composition. In such a case, the state would have played a significant role in bringing into being the organizational level represented by the apartment compound.

STATUS DIFFERENCES IN TEOTIHUACÁN SOCIETY

While much has been written about the "theocracy" that dominated Teotihuacán, and how priest-ridden its society must have been, we know only a little more than what was known, say, ten years ago about those who ruled Teotihuacán.

When one has walked the "Street of the Dead" from the Ciudadela and the Great Compound in the center of the city north to the Plaza of the Moon (Map 18) it is difficult to avoid the conclusion that one of the purposes its architects had in mind was to overwhelm the viewer, to impress upon him the power and the glory of the gods of Teotihuacán and their earthly representatives. Whatever else the "Street of the Dead" may have been, it was a Via Sacra. This, together with the preponderance of religious themes and religious figures in Teotihuacán art, is the primary reason for concluding that Teotihuacán's polity and its supreme rulers were sacralized, a view that has received new support from the researches of Clara Millon on Teotihuacán mural art. In a recent paper she presents a persuasive case for the view that temple and polity were conceptualized as one by the Teotihuacanos (C. Millon 1973).

Whoever may have been at the apex of Teotihuacán society, the number and size of the clearly religious structures along the "Street of the Dead" alone would suggest the existence of hierarchies of priests of various grades and functions. Some of them probably were part of, or encompassed by, a state bureaucracy that also included a military component and that was responsible to the city's rulers for the administration of the state and the maintenance of order.

With the passage of time, as the city grew larger and its dominion spread over wider and wider areas, its social composition must have become increasingly diversified and complex. Differences in occupation, status, and origin were probably reflected in the formation of distinctive life-styles, each with differing modes of dress, housing, prerogatives, and cult practices. It must have been an inegalitarian, markedly stratified society, with a number of distinct social, economic, and cultural levels; in such a society, who a man was, how he earned his living, and where he lived and with whom were probably inextricably interwoven strands. Future careful excavation in apartment compounds and other residential structures should make it possible to test some of the dimensions of these hypotheses.

One way of approaching these questions on the basis of existing evidence is to examine that evidence for status differences that appear in the apartment compounds thus far excavated. In a study that Clara Millon and I are preparing together, she examined the available evidence from a number of apartment compounds with this problem in mind, using such variables as size of rooms, use of space, decoration, construction techniques, burials, offerings, and other relevant data. In so doing she was able to make a case for the existence of three status levels within the intermediate levels of Teotihuacán society. These three levels, from highest to lowest, are represented by the Zacuala Palace, Teopancaxco, and Xolalpan (Fig. 13).

Extending similar reasoning to other excavated structures, it is possible to distinguish what appear minimally to be six status levels. Two of these would be higher than those marking the occupants of the Zacuala Palace, while at least one would seem to be below the status level represented by the inhabitants of Xolalpan (see below). When more data are available and excavations are carried out with this problem in mind, it should be possible to go beyond gross distinctions of this kind and to arrive, perhaps, at a formulation of the composition and relative social position of at least some of the classes and status groups of which the city must have been composed.

While the data are not conclusive, and cannot be summarized here, there is some evidence from Clara Millon's analyses of burials to support the view that the crowded room arrangements in La Ventilla B and Tlamimilolpa are indicators of low status. Those who lived in these compounds may have occupied the lowest status so far identified in excavations at Teotihuacán. And since both compounds seem to have been occupied for several hundred years, they seem to have remained residences for people of low status throughout their history, as suggested previously.

SOCIAL, ECONOMIC, AND POLITICAL RELATIONS

The inhabitants of La Ventilla B and Tlamimilolpa may have lived in part or entirely by cultivating land, and there must have been a sizable number of Teotihuacanos who did so. While we cannot place an upper limit on how much of the population of Teotihuacán lived by engaging in craft activities, it seems probable at this writing that at least two-thirds of the people lived primarily through the cultivation of land—which means scores of thousands of people. It also means that for most of the year a large part of this population must have lived many miles from the fields they were cultivating, an inference that is supported by archaeological evidence from the eastern Valley of Mexico (J. R. Parsons 1968, 1971b). Why did they do so? Some of them may have come to the city voluntarily because they were attracted to the growing city and what it had to offer. But was there compulsion or the threat of force in this concentration? Adams reports that a similar concentration of population appears to have occurred in the "urban revolution" in southern Mesopotamia in Early Dynastic Uruk, as the Warka region was urbanized through the "depopulation of the countryside . . . , with whole districts seemingly abandoned as their inhabitants were persuaded or compelled to migrate to the cities" (Adams and Nissen 1972:87).

Whatever the reason may have been for this concentration of cultivators in the city and however it came about (on balance, some involvement by the state seems probable), the advantages to the Teotihuacán hierarchy of such an arrangement are obvious. With the majority of those who worked the land concentrated in the city, the state bureaucracy could have intervened in the agricultural sector of the economy with much greater ease than might otherwise have been the case. At a minimum, the administration of tax collection and the allocation of labor services would have been simplified.

Who owned the land these cultivators worked? Were there landholdings owned by corporate groups living in the city? Were there large estates? If so, who owned or controlled them? Who worked them? Related to these questions is the problem of the sources of stratification in Teotihuacán society and the relation of such processes to the formation of the Teotihuacán state. If, as seems probable, society-wide political institutions were sacralized, was the formation and consolidation of the Teotihuacán state related to processes of stratification involving differences in the size and productivity of landholdings and the formation of estates with large, dependent labor forces? If we reject as inadequate the model of Teotihuacán society suggested by the proponents of Wittfogel's (1957, 1972) "hydraulic" hypothesis, how do we try to investigate questions of the relation of the state to the ownership of land? Written records would be one obvious way, but so far we have none. One possible way of approaching this question archaeologically is to try to uncover ancient field boundaries bordering the city, perhaps through low altitude infrared or multispectral aerial photography, or related remote sensing techniques. Such techniques might not reveal such boundaries, of course, and even if they did, what they revealed probably would be subject to varying interpretations. Nevertheless, such a course of inquiry seems to me to be potentially the most productive for the immediate future in exploring questions of land tenure, stratification, and the state.

To take the most simplistic examples, consistently large fields might be taken as evidence of large landholdings, privately owned, or state owned, or both. Consistently small fields might be taken as evidence of many small, individual landholdings. Fields of intermediate size might be taken as evidence for landholdings by corporate groups, such as those that probably occupied the city's apartment compounds. Obviously, other interpretations would be possible, if not probable, even in such relatively simple situations. Almost certainly, field sizes would be very different in the irrigated lands of the lower Valley from those in lands depending solely on rainfall. In addition, it seems almost certain that even within lands of roughly the same potential, there would be significant differences in the plot sizes. But even if this should be the case, we would have some real data on which to begin the exploration of questions of land tenure in Teotihuacán times.

If remote sensing techniques should produce interesting results and not merely an uninterpretable palimpsest—or worse, nothing at all—the first step in the field would be to try to see if particular plots of land, especially on the southern and eastern borders of the city, could be related to nearby apartment compounds, perhaps through direct proximity, perhaps through the sharing of distinctive ritual or (less likely) technological complexes, or by other means. I am aware that the course of inquiry suggested may prove to be totally unproductive, or so equivocal as to be virtually meaningless. Nevertheless, it seems to me to be worth exploring in a pilot project designed to test its possibilities at low cost.

Adams contrasts "stratification as a mechanical, politically superimposed process on the African model and stratification as an organic process intimately related with agricultural management" (1966:119). He sees the first as applicable to late pre-Conquest central Mexico, the second, to early Mesopotamia. Conceivably, the exploration of patterns of land use, and the possible relation of these to specific apartment compounds, may help to clarify this problem at Teotihuacán. As for Adams's comments on the possible role of population growth in the "urban revolution" in Mesopotamia (1972a, 1972b:746, and as quoted in Spooner 1972:xxii–iii), the evidence from Teotihuacán does not support such an interpretation or is, at best, equivocal on this point (R. Millon 1973:50–52, 54, 59, G. L. Cowgill 1974, 1975a, 1975b). It seems equally important to keep in mind that Weberian "religious interests" may have played a significant role in the acceptance by the majority of Teotihuacanos of growing stratification and the differences in wealth and privilege this would have entailed among the rulers and the religious hierarchy, as well as the perhaps slowly growing civil and military hierarchy. Perceived "religious interests," both reinforced in some spheres and contradicted in others by "economic interests," may have provided significant motivation for the support of the growing differentiation and stratification of Teotihuacán society, even as that process may have been leading to greater and greater economic and political intervention and control in the affairs of Teotihuacán society by the minority that came to dominate it. These hypotheses are not necessarily contradictory, nor are they exhaustive. But more evidence is needed before the several hypotheses involved can be tested.

As we have seen, craft production was of great importance in the economy of Teotihuacán.[9] It appears from our survey and from our excavations that it was during the fourth and fifth centuries A.D.—during the latter part of the Tlamimilolpa phase—that the basis for Teotihuacán's expansion to so many parts of civilized Mesoamerica was established. As noted earlier, Teotihuacán was becoming a densely crowded city of closely spaced apartment compounds, while the production of obsidian implements was greatly expanding. Other crafts seem to have been growing at this time too, but they seem to reach a peak a little later, perhaps during the Xolalpan phase, in the middle of the Middle Horizon, in the sixth century A.D. (Fig. 15). By the fifth century A.D.—toward the end of the Tlamimilolpa phase—Teotihuacán had become so great a religious and commercial center that it began to attract foreigners not only temporarily (as pilgrims and traders) but permanently. This is when the Oaxaca barrio became established as a foreign enclave in Teotihuacán.

One of our excavations suggests that obsidian workers spent part of their time making implements of obsidian within a walled precinct west of and attached to the Moon Pyramid. Whether other craftsmen worked directly within the jurisdiction of a temple community is not known. Presumably the obsidian craftsmen who worked within the precinct west of the Moon lived immediately to the north, where many obsidian workers lived and where there were several barrios of obsidian workers.

It is possible that the involvement of a temple community associated with the Moon Pyramid in the production of obsidian implements may have been part of the larger involvement of the state in obsidian working, because it rapidly became the city's leading craft, or at least the leading craft with identifying evidence that survives the passage of time. The workshops where obsidian blades were produced cluster to the west of the Great Compound and its presumed marketplace (Map 18). Workshops where points and knives were chipped are scattered over the city. The blade workshops seem oriented to the marketplace; the others do not.

The state probably began to protect access to and, Michael Spence believes (personal communication), to bring under its control the major source of "green" obsidian in the early centuries of the Christian era. These "green" obsidian mines lie a short distance north of the Valley of Mexico in the modern state of Hidalgo, in a place called Cerro de las Navajas. This is the obsidian that is especially well suited to the production of fine blades. Cerro de las Navajas was one of the sources of the obsidian blades found by Michael Coe at the Olmec center of San Lorenzo in southern Veracruz in deposits dating prior to 1000 B.C. (Cobean et al. 1971). Obsidian from the same source has also been found by Robert Heizer at the Olmec center of La Venta (Stross et al. 1968). Cerro de las Navajas continued to be a major source for such blades in central Mexico to the time of the Aztecs (Hester, Heizer, and Jack 1971, Hester, Jack and Heizer 1971, 1972, Graham, Hester, and Jack 1972, Jack, Hester, and Heizer 1972).

The distribution of obsidian workshops of all kinds shows that there are major concentrations of such workshops immediately to the east of the Ciudadela, immediately to the west of the Great Compound, and immediately to the northwest of the Moon Pyramid. We have already seen that obsidian workers spent part of their time working inside a walled precinct west of the Moon Pyramid. Whether this or some other kind of relation existed between the state hicrarchy and obsidian workers in the center of the city—around the Ciudadela and the Great Compound—we do not know. But it is clear from these distributions that the Teotihuacán hierarchy was not indifferent to the working of obsidian.

There is some evidence that the Teotihuacán state intervened directly or indirectly in the exploitation of cinnabar mines in a barren area in the Sierra de Querétaro, over 100 miles north of the Valley of Mexico, late in the history of the city (Franco 1970a, 1970b, Minería Prehispánica 1970: 49). But the evidence for this is equivocal and by itself tells us little about the extent to which the state may have intervened in the economy of Teotihuacán at differing periods in its history.

While obsidian working appears to have been the city's major craft, investigators working on our project have tentatively identified 150 to 200 workshops in other materials. This number will doubtless increase as more of the analysis of these other workshops is completed. As of this writing, 100 to 150 ceramic workshops have been identified by Paula Krotser, many of them spanning the city's entire history, others concentrating on the mass production of a common cooking ware during the height of the city's existence. Warren Barbour has also identified more than 15 figurine workshops. There are, in addition, a still undetermined number of ground-stone workshops, plus a scattering of workshops where lapidaries lived and worked and where tools of basalt were made and ornaments of slate prepared and painted.

To this total must be added an unknown number of workshops in other materials—perishable materials that have left no traces, or at least none that we have been able to identify so far. For example, precious feathers, such as those of the quetzal, were highly prized by the Teotihuacanos, as their art demonstrates. At the time of the Aztecs, feather workers were among their most highly skilled artisans and occupied a status only a little below that of the nobility, the bureaucracy, and the military. They were called *Amanteca,* and their cultural origins may derive from Teotihuacán (Seler 1915:453–54).

Other perishable products of Teotihuacán artisans would have been cloth, basketry, matting, and objects of leather and wood. At least one extraordinarily finely worked, stucco-painted box of wood from Teotihuacán is in a private collection and is sufficient to demonstrate that this must have been an important craft. It is possible, however, that much of the cloth, basketry, and matting (mats were used for many purposes, including sleeping) was produced and used domestically. How important woven goods made for exchange would have been must remain an open question until we have more evidence. Still other artisans would have been engaged in crafts associated with construction—masons, carpenters, and plasterers—for the building and rebuilding that was constantly going on in the city. Some of these crafts need not have involved full-time specialization, and could have been combined with cultivating land or other pursuits. Others probably were full-time occupations, but only for some of the occupants of a compound.

Judging from this evidence, I would estimate that at least 400 of the city's 2,200 apartment compounds were occupied primarily by craftsmen and their households at any one time during the final several hundred years of Teotihuacán's history. In addition, there were perhaps another 200 or 300 apartment compounds, some of whose occupants were engaged in craft activities. Perhaps 25 percent or more of the city's population lived in the households of craftsmen. Craftsmen and the members of their households may therefore have exceeded 30,000 when the city was at its height.

Teotihuacán, like Tenochtitlan, seems to have been a craft and trading center without parallel for its time. Did merchants play as important a role and occupy as high a status in Teotihuacán society as they did among the Aztecs? Despite the fact that we have excavated in what we think was a merchants' barrio (Map 18, no. 9), our excavations have told us little about the "merchants" themselves. We did excavate in two buildings, in one of which we found some rooms of adobe that we think were probably used for storage, and we did find foreign pottery fragments in abundance in both buildings (principally from Veracruz and the Maya area). But our excavations were not extensive enough to tell us anything about the "merchants" themselves, if that is, in fact, what they were.

There is very scanty evidence suggesting that the Zacuala Palace compound was occupied by traders in maize. Another area that might have been occupied by traders is the Oaxaca barrio (Map 18, no. 17), but we have little evidence to support this. There is, however, some evidence that a pottery ware called "coarse thin orange" was being made in the Oaxaca barrio, as well as in workshops at the opposite end of the city, at its eastern extremity (in N1E7) (Evelyn Rattray, personal communication). The people of the Oaxaca barrio do not appear to have occupied a high status in the city; rather, they appear to fall in one of the lower two intermediate levels. They seem to have maintained cultural and other ties with Oaxaca, judging from the fact that in one of the apartment compounds in the barrio, several of them were buried in a Oaxaca-style tomb with a stela made from a reused Teotihuacán building stone and bearing a glyph and number in Oaxaca style (R. Millon 1968a, 1973:Figs. 60a, 60b). Two funerary urns—both made in Oaxaca—were also found in this apartment compound (R. Millon 1967e, 1968a, 1973:41, Figs. 58, 59). The people who lived in the barrio also continued to use domestic objects of Oaxaca style. While adopting many Teotihuacán customs, they seem to have remained an ethnic enclave until the fall of the city. The compounds in which they lived, while not especially well constructed, conformed to Teotihuacán building standards and to the Teotihuacán orientation of walls.

The Oaxaca barrio is probably not the only ethnic enclave in the city, but so far it is the only one for which there is unchallengeable archaeological evidence. Piña Chan (1963) has argued that the La Ventilla A compounds (Map 18, no. 19; Fig. 13) housed craftsmen from Veracruz. The evidence of craft activities is clear in at least one of the three La Ventilla A compounds. But the evidence for a Veracruz origin of the people living in these compounds is equivocal. Our map survey singled out at least two other areas that may prove to have housed other foreign enclaves, but more data are needed to determine whether this was indeed the case.

Who were Teotihuacán's architects and master builders? It is possible that early in the city's history those who designed some of its great buildings may have had special prestige, but even of this we cannot be sure. We have no information on the status of such individuals at any time in Teotihuacán's history.

Another unknown is the identity and status of the various practitioners of the arts in Teotihuacán society. Mural painting is the major art form that has survived, and it was most important during the last four or five centuries of the city's history. There must have been a substantial corps of artists, perhaps grouped into workshops where apprentices were trained.

Stucco-painted pottery vessels were probably also prepared in these workshops. Artists may have been traditionally associated with particular groups, much as craftsmen seem to have been, but we do not know whether artists occupied a higher status than craftsmen. Sculptors were important early in the city's history, although they seem to have been gradually supplanted by mural painters in the decoration of the city's temples and other public buildings.

Of the practitioners of the other arts—poets, dancers, singers, and musicians—we know virtually nothing. It is clear from artistic representations that they contributed to the rich ceremonial life of the city, and it is a fair guess that they were in demand in other celebrations as well. The inhabitants of entire compounds may have specialized in such arts, while others may have been scattered throughout the city and may have practiced these arts as a subsidiary specialty.

We know from murals and sculptures that a version of the Mesoamerican ball game was played at Teotihuacán (Angulo Villaseñor 1963, 1964:103, Aveleyra Arroyo de Anda 1963a, 1963b). It is possible that some aspects of the game and its attendant ritual were imported from the Gulf Coast and that people from coastal Veracruz came to live in the city, perhaps to work as craftsmen in stone and shell (Piña Chan 1963), as well as to participate in the ball game. But the Teotihuacán ball game as represented in the murals of Tepantitla was played with sticks rather than with parts of the body (Aveleyra Arroya de Anda 1963a:Fig. 12). Furthermore, judging from our survey for the map, it was not played on courts laid out like those found in other parts of central and southern Mexico and the Maya area. The game and its rituals, therefore, appear to have differed significantly from other games of its time. Possibly a variant of the game developed locally, out of Early Horizon or First Intermediate period antecedents (Fig. 15). Vidarte de Linares (1968) has suggested that it involved ritual reenactment of the myth of the Fifth Sun, an oft-recounted Aztec myth telling of the creation of the present world at Teotihuacán.

The work of Warren Barbour (1970) suggests that ritual specialists served as curers. These specialists, who may have been independent of the formal religious hierarchy, may have been called in to preside over difficult births and presumably on other occasions as well. As yet, however, there is no evidence as to their status.

There must have been many other groups of people contributing to the networks of activities involved in life in Teotihuacán. Among these must have been petty traders, vendors of foodstuffs and prepared foods, and others who plied their wares in the central marketplace in the Great Compound and elsewhere. There is some archaeological evidence for food preparation stands from our small excavation in the Great Compound. The city also probably had its prostitutes and, as noted previously, a complement of thieves, con men, and other such individuals.

Teotihuacán must have had thousands of very high-status people of second rank—people with higher status than the highest of the three intermediate status levels (the latter being represented by those who lived in the Zacuala Palace [Fig. 13]) but lower in status than those at the apex of Teotihuacán society. The sheer size of the metropolis and the religious and ritual matrix in which so many of its activities seem to have been embedded argues for a fairly numerous bureaucracy or bureaucracies, probably centered in the Great Compound (Map 18, no. 6). Both surface evidence and our recent excavation there lend support to the inference that the plaza of the Great Compound was the city's principal marketplace and the focal point of the city's economic life (R. Millon 1967c). One of the responsibilities of the bureaucracy might have been the regulation and administration of market activities. Other responsibilities might have included the collection and general administration of state income and of separate temple incomes, if such existed.

Most of the highest-ranking functionaries who did not live in the Great Compound probably lived close to the "Street of the Dead." It is surely no accident that the city's most luxurious buildings are located on the "Street of the Dead"—the partially excavated palaces in the Ciudadela north and south of the Temple of Quetzalcoatl, the Quetzalpapalotl Palace, and the Palace of the Sun (Map 18, nos. 4, 29, 39, Fig. 14). Among the thousands of high-status people of second rank probably should be included the most important priests of the city's great pyramids and pyramid complexes—the Sun Pyramid, the Moon Pyramid, the Moon Plaza pyramid complex, the Plaza of the Columns, the major pyramids in the "Street of the Dead" complex, and others.

Armillas (1964:307) argued many years ago that the rulers of Teotihuacán probably lived in the Ciudadela. Shortly after we began making our map of Teotihuacán, it became clear that the Ciudadela was in the center of the ancient city (Map 18, no. 3). The presence of the Great Compound opposite it and the use of space around the two giant precincts at the juncture of the city's major avenues lends even greater prominence to the Ciudadela than when Armillas wrote in 1964.

At the same time, it also seems clear that if the Ciudadela was the city's political center, it functioned as such in a sacred setting. The Temple of Quetzalcoatl and the many other temples in the Ciudadela make this clear. The Teotihuacán polity was undoubtedly sacralized. And, if David Drucker (1974) is right, the Ciudadela was the setting for the celebration of elaborate calendrical rituals. Did the sacralization of the Teotihuacán polity diminish with the passage of time? Was there, as often claimed, an increasing secularization, an increasing differentiation of the religious and the political in Teotihuacán's history? There is evidence for this, as noted below.

But what is of at least as much interest is that so much construction appears to have been lavished on the Ciudadela in the final phase of the city's existence as a great urban center (Drucker 1974). Among other things, this can be interpreted as an indication that the rulers of Teotihuacán were quite self-consciously seeking to emphasize the importance of the Ciudadela in the city's last years, and that whatever may have been happening in terms of social relations, in ideological terms Teotihuacán's rulers may have been trying to reemphasize the sacredness of the Teotihuacán political order. In other words, while there may have been an increasing separation between military and religious statuses in Teotihuacán society, there may also have been an attempt to deny this ideologically by reemphasizing the sacredness of the city's political center.

There are two large palace areas inside the Ciudadela, one to the north and one to the south of the Temple of Quetzalcoatl (Fig. 14). Only parts of each have been excavated. Since, as we have seen, it is reasonable to conclude that Teotihuacán's rulers lived in the Ciudadela, and since the Ciudadela contains twin palaces, each with the same ground plan, it is possible that Teotihuacán had twin rulers. There is precedent for this in later times in central Mexico (Carrasco 1971:372, 374). If the city's rulers were chosen on some hereditary basis, then these two palaces might have housed segments of two royal kin-groups. It is perhaps equally possible that they were chosen from an oligarchy, or—perhaps even more likely—through some complex combination of the two, as Calnek argues was the case in Tenochtitlan (Calnek 1969). It is also possible that the problem of succession was handled by selecting rulers alternately from one palace group, then the other.

Since the question of twin rulers for Teotihuacán has been raised, I should also point out that the Pyramid of the Sun probably once had twin temples on its top. One of our excavations in its uppermost tunnel disclosed that there was an earlier Sun Pyramid almost as tall as the present one, which almost certainly had twin temples on top of it (R. Millon 1973:Fig. 17b). We do not know whether this bears any relationship to the twin palaces in the Ciudadela or to the twin motifs on the Temple of Quetzalcoatl, but I mention it because it may.

Were Teotihuacán's rulers personifications of the Teotihuacán state? Or, to say the same thing in another way, was the Teotihuacán state personified in its rulers? Did they represent city and state to the outside world and the legitimate authority and repressive power of the state internally? When we have more evidence, the answers to some or all of these questions may be affirmative. But what will be more difficult to determine concerns one of the most interesting aspects of the Teotihuacán state, namely, the question of the degree to which it may have been thought of as occupying a position "above" all groups, classes, statuses, and sectors in Teotihuacán society, including those near or at the top. For example, Adams (1966:151–52), commenting on the formation of the state in early Mesopotamia and pre-Hispanic central Mexico, suggests that "perhaps the development of the state can best be described as fully consummated when it no longer represented solely the partisan interests of militaristic social strata but began at least to claim a position 'above' contending parties." But the example he then cites to illustrate his argument comes from a famous Mesopotamian text, and we have no such texts from Teotihuacán —at least not yet.

Clearly, it is not profitable to press these questions further here. Rather, they are questions whose dimensions we should be able to explore archaeologically, in excavations in the Ciudadela, the Great Compound, and elsewhere.

The Teotihuacán polity was undoubtedly sacralized. If the Ciudadela was a political center, it clearly functioned as such in a sacred setting. Certainly both the persons and the offices of the rulers would have been imbued and suffused with the sacred. They would have been the embodiment of the religion of Teotihuacán, and as such, the charisma of office would have hedged them with divinity.

This is not to deny the importance of the evidence from the Maya area that some Maya societies were governed by rulers whose secular attributes have recently been stressed (for example, see Proskouriakoff 1961). The importance of the work of Proskouriakoff and others in this regard cannot be overestimated. But one point should also be emphasized—the discovery that the Maya were, after all, not so different from other people is remarkable primarily because they had previously been described as so strange and unusual. The activities of individuals were thought to have been relatively unimportant among the Maya. Instead, it was believed that the Maya were obsessed with recording the passage of time and therefore centered much of their ritual and other religious activities around this obsession (for example, Thompson 1954). Thus, because of their past history, there is perhaps a tendency now in Mayan studies to overstress the secular. For it is, after all, a common phenomenon for the sacred and the secular to be fused in the single person of the ruler.

THE MILITARY IN TEOTIHUACÁN SOCIETY

The people of Teotihuacán must have faced many problems toward the end of the city's existence (R. Millon 1973:59–63). The source of some of these problems was probably ecological (Lorenzo 1968), while others may have been economic and social. There is some evidence, as we have seen, suggesting that late in the city's history the Teotihuacán state may have been intervening directly in economic affairs and in the exploitation of resources. Were the bureaucracy and the military becoming increasingly involved in matters that had previously been only peripherally within their jurisdiction? Was there a military-bureaucratic complex in Teotihuacán society? How important was the military? Probably in early times the highest military roles at Teotihuacán were fused with political and religious roles. At the same time, there is evidence that the military may have been assuming increasing importance in Teotihuacán society toward the end of its existence.

Within Teotihuacán itself there is very little direct evidence of military figures before the final phase of the occupation of Teotihuacán as an urban center—the Metepec phase, at the end of the Middle Horizon (Fig. 15). Armed figures in Teotihuacán murals and pottery seem to date to that phase or to the latter part of the Xolalpan or Teotihuacán III phase, that is, to the seventh century A.D. or later. We have several hundred figurines of military figures from various parts of the city, gathered during our surface survey for the map. But, according to Warren Barbour, who is studying the figurines from Teotihuacán, they do not appear in our stratigraphic excavations until the Metepec phase.

If the city's great expansion around A.D. 400 to 500 was at least partly due to conquest, as seems likely, there would have been an important military component in Teotihuacán society at least that early. It must have been still earlier, during the Tzacualli phase, when Teotihuacán's urban society exploded into being, or perhaps earlier still, that the military first became important in Teotihuacán's society. But they were not represented in murals, figurines, or sculpture until some five hundred years had passed.

One way of interpreting the representation of military figures in the last century or so of the city's existence is to see this as evidence for a militarization of Teotihuacán society, or, at the very least, for an increase in the importance of the military. There is other evidence from the Ciudadela itself, where defensive walls were built on its upper part late in the city's history. In the Tepantitla compound (Fig. 13), an armed Teotihuacán god appears in a late painting on its main temple.

There is evidence in murals, pottery, and figurines for the existence in Teotihuacán society of military orders whose emblems were animals. Other armed figures wear a tassel headdress. A hand-held shield or a hand in a shield, frequently with a spear or crossed spears behind it, is a military emblem. Military figures often wear cotton armor headdresses, or helmets enclosing the head and the lower part of the jaw. Inferences from murals in their architectural contexts provide a highly problematic argument for the existence, on the one hand, of professional or semiprofessional military groups and, on the other, of individuals who achieved a military status through exploits in combat or related activities.

In summary, there is sufficient evidence to argue that the military was assuming a greater importance in Teotihuacán society toward the end of its existence as a major urban center. Whatever the reasons for it, the Teotihuacán state seems to have become both more obtrusive and more defensive in its last hundred years. The military became prominent for the first time, the Ciudadela had defensive walls added to it, and at the same time there was great building activity in the Ciudadela, reemphasizing its importance as the sacralized political center of the city. Whether the state became more repressive in these final years and played a role in its own dissolution remains to be explored.

Partial answers to some of the questions raised about the Teotihuacán military and the Teotihuacán state are most likely to be found through careful, limited, problem-oriented excavations in the Ciudadela and the Great Compound. If the Teotihuacanos had any archives, this is where we might expect to find whatever may be left of them. This means, of course, that these areas must be excavated with the utmost care, so as not to destroy any codices that might be found there. But even in the absence of archives, these two great structures that formed the political, religious, bureaucratic, and, probably, military heart of the city represent the most logical place to search for clarification and eventual resolution of the various hypotheses propounded here concerning the Teotihuacán military and the Teotihuacán state.

URBANIZATION AT TEOTIHUACÁN[10]

Teotihuacán was unquestionably the preeminent ritual center of its time in Mesoamerica. It seems to have been the most important center of trade and to have had the most important marketplace. It was the largest and most highly differentiated craft center. In size, numbers, and density, it was the greatest urban center and perhaps the most complexly stratified society of its time in Mesoamerica. It was the seat of an increasingly powerful state that appears to have extended its domination over wider and wider areas. It became the most influential center in Mesoamerica. It rose in an area of relatively rich ecological potential, astride the major trade and access route into and out of the Valley of Mexico. The many differing manifestations of the intense process of urbanization that went on in Teotihuacán early in the Christian era, together with the unparalleled attraction Teotihuacán's shrines, temples, and marketplaces must have exerted over peoples from an increasingly wide area, appear to set Teotihuacán apart from other contemporary centers in Mesoamerica. Indeed, it appears to have been the most highly urbanized center of its time in the New World.

Stimulated by hypotheses put forward some time ago by Eric Wolf, Angel Palerm, and Julian Steward (Wolf and Palerm 1955, Steward 1955:62–63, Wolf 1959:17–18, 82–83), I have previously argued that the marketplace may have played an important role in the integration of Teotihuacán's complex urban society (R. Millon 1967c, 1968b:114). In essence the argument is that in an urban society as complex as Teotihuacán seems to have become, with so many outsiders attracted to the city by its marketplace(s), temples, and shrines, the institution of the marketplace would have provided a focal point for the competing and clashing interests of the various sectors of Teotihuacán society and of those outsiders attracted to it. Whatever may have been the differences among them, all would have had a stake in the maintenance of the "peace of the market." Given what we know of Teotihuacán society, it seems reasonable to hypothesize that the institution of the marketplace would have been sustained by the religion of Teotihuacán, by its prestige, by the meaning its rituals must have given to social life and the world, and by the loyalty and devotion its pervasive symbols must have evoked. In this context the two institutions would have nourished and supported one another, supporting and supported by the Teotihuacán state.

I have also suggested that the complex institutional web of temple and market, attracting pilgrims to shrines, and pilgrims and others to markets, may be represented in a mural painting from Teotihuacán—the "Offering Scene" from the Temple of Agriculture, discovered by Batres in the last century (Batres 1889, Gamio et al. 1922:1:125, lám. 33, R. Millon 1967c: 152). But since the original painting had been lost, it was difficult to know how much reliance should be placed on a copy. Now, however, we know what some parts of the mural looked like, thanks to an important discovery by Arthur Miller (1972, 1973:173–74) of fragments of this mural, which have been chronologically placed early in the history of mural painting at Teotihuacán (C. Millon 1972). Thus the "Offering Scene" may provide support for my hypothesis that there was an intimate relationship between temple and market in Teotihuacán. If this should be so, the relatively early date of the mural in Teotihuacán's history—the Tlamimilolpa phase (C. Millon 1972:86), early in the Middle Horizon—suggests that the relationship was already well established at that time.

As is obvious from the preceding discussions of the city's internal composition, what I have just outlined is, at best, a partial model for the integration of Teotihuacán society. Until we know more about the relations between Teotihuacán's rulers, its bureaucracy, and its military, on the,one hand, and other classes, status groups, and sectors in Teotihuacán society, on the other—and of the relations of the latter to each other— we shall have only an imperfect and partial view of what must have been some of the most critical social relations in Teotihuacán society.

We have already discussed the problems involved in exploring questions of land tenure in the ancient city, and of the nature and degree of involvement of the Teotihuacán state in the ownership of cultivable land. Of equally great importance is examining other economic activities in the city in terms of the degree to which they may have been subject to state control, as well as the degree to which those engaged in them may have had sufficient autonomy to participate directly in the expansion of Teotihuacán's economy. What were the relative degrees of autonomy in the economic activities of craftsmen, sellers, traders, and merchants? How were craftsmen internally organized? How was craft production organized? How did craftsmen exploit raw materials, and did they limit access to them? How was craft production related to marketplace trade? Under what motivations, restrictions, and compulsions did craftsmen produce and distribute what they made? How did traders and merchants, Teotihuacán and foreign, engage in their activities, particularly over long distances? And under what motivations, restrictions, and compulsions did they operate?

Did the growth potential represented by the activities of craftsmen in production, and craftsmen, sellers, traders, and merchants in marketplace and long-distance trade combine with the powerful religious attraction of Teotihuacán in a creative synthesis that provided the major impetus for the phenomenal growth of Teotihuacán's unique urban society and of its pervasive and heretofore unparalleled influence in Mesoamerica—economic, religious, cultural, and political? These are not easy questions to answer with archaeological evidence. It is difficult even to begin to explore some of the dimensions of these hypotheses. But the promise is there, and, with full recognition of the difficulties involved, this is the course of inquiry we are pursuing (R. Millon 1970b:1081–82).

An integral part of working out what may be unique aspects of Teotihuacán's urban society is that such an undertaking will simultaneously enrich our understanding of processes of urbanization in other times and places. The model or models growing out of this and other studies in progress may be more complex than those of the two most ambitious, recent comparative studies of urbanization (Adams 1966, Wheatley 1971), for they would encompass evidence either not available or not contemplated or envisaged when they were written—evidence not only from central Mexico and the Maya area, but also from elsewhere in Mesoamerica, and from such other parts of the world as Peru and the Near East. But what is a complication from one point of view may be a simplification from another. It does not seem overly optimistic to predict that current comparative studies of processes of urbanization and of the rise of complex societies will lead, in the near future, to new levels of understanding that will help us better to comprehend transformational social change and to come closer to developing a testable theory of such change.

TEOTIHUACÁN AND THE ECOLOGICAL APPROACH

The distinctiveness of Teotihuacán and of its pervasive and widespread influence has long demanded explanation, even before its great size and complexity as a city were appreciated. The most recent "explanation" proferred is basically ecological, grounded primarily on the presumed managerial requirements of the Valley of Teotihuacán's irrigation system and on the putative relationship of this to the centralization of authority in the incipient Teotihuacán state.

The Teotihuacán Valley is semiarid today. While rainfall may have been greater 2,000 years ago, its rich agricultural potential stems primarily from the springs that come together at the southwestern edge of the ancient city (S1W5 and the adjacent squares to the west and south) (Map 18). These springs supply water to irrigate the alluvial plain in the lower Teotihuacán Valley and to cultivate chinampas in the high-water-table area near the springs. Chinampas are highly productive when cultivated by intensive labor. During the Late Horizon they extended over large sections of the shallow lakes in the southern Valley of Mexico, supplying the urban markets of the Aztecs and their neighbors with produce (West and Armillas 1950, Palerm 1955, Sanders and Price 1968:148–49, 151, Armillas 1971). The potential of labor-intensive chinampa cultivation may have been first exploited in the small chinampa area of Teotihuacán (see also Lorenzo 1968:58, Fig. 13).

There is no direct archaeological proof for irrigation in the Teotihuacán Valley in Teotihuacán times. But there is persuasive indirect evidence. Ancient streams within and beyond the city were canalized, often in accord with Teotihuacán orientations (Maps 18, 19) (Drewitt 1967:80, 85–86, 88, Fig. 1). Excavations in pre-Hispanic watercourses indicate that irrigation in the Teotihuacán Valley goes back at least to the Second Intermediate period, about A.D. 1000 (R. Millon 1957). Canal irrigation predates Teotihuacán in nearby Puebla (MacNeish 1967, F. Johnson 1972)

and in Oaxaca (Flannery et al. 1967). Given this and the simple technology involved in the present system, it seems probable that the Teotihuacanos irrigated as large an area as the water flow permitted. This is my
view, and that of others (Sanders 1965, Adams 1966, Lorenzo 1968, J. R.
Parsons 1968, Price 1971).

The produce from an expanding irrigation system in the Teotihuacán
Valley probably contributed significantly to the support of the city when it
began to grow to great size. But the stimulus to the growth of the system
seems more likely to have come from the increasing requirements of
craftsmen and other specialists in the rapidly growing city, rather than the
reverse. Certainly, it is totally unwarranted to hypothesize that the "managerial requirements" of so small an irrigation system were a decisive factor in the explosive growth of the city, in its social, economic, or political
organization, or in the rise of the Teotihuacán state (see Wittfogel 1957,
1972, Sanders 1965, J. R. Parsons 1968, Sanders 1968, Sanders and Price,
1968, Price 1971).

Another major resource in the Teotihuacán Valley is its deposits of
obsidian. Obsidian working was the city's principal craft very early in its
history. Two of its most important plants—maguey and the nopal cactus
—thrive in semiarid conditions, and we know that both were grown in
Teotihuacán times.

In addition, the Teotihuacán Valley is on the north shore of the Valley
of Mexico's largest lake, Lake Texcoco, a location of strategic importance,
not only because of the potentialities for communication and transportation provided by the lake system, but also because the lakes themselves
were important economic resources.

The strategic importance of Teotihuacán's location in manufacturing,
commercial, and political terms must have become apparent quickly to
the early Teotihuacanos. Similarly, the potential of Teotihuacán as a religious center must have been viewed instrumentally soon after the site of
the later city was settled.

The first Teotihuacanos owed much to the builders of such centers as
Cuicuilco in the southern Valley of Mexico and early Cholula in the
neighboring Valley of Puebla, as may be seen in some of their customs and
beliefs. At the same time, Teotihuacán clearly rose to its position of pre-
eminence largely on its own. The great size of Teotihuacán in relation
to its valley very early in its history demonstrates that the rise of Teotihuacán, the economic center, cannot be understood apart from the simul-

taneous rise of Teotihuacán, the sacred center. "Explanations" of the rise of Teotihuacán that do not take this into account cannot do justice to the complexity of the problem.

The recently discovered sacred cave beneath the Pyramid of the Sun (Heyden 1975) might have provided the basis for the rise of a major pilgrimage center at Teotihuacán. But if its favored setting and the responsiveness of its social order to transformational change had not been exploited, Teotihuacán never could have become a critically important center of economic activity nor a political center of paramount importance, nor could it have developed the cultural magnetism of a metropolis. By the same token, Teotihuacán's key location, its access to resources of strategic potential, and an expanding market for its exports might have provided the basis for an important craft and marketplace center and a small city-state. But if its early shrines had not been exploited, it could never have become the most important ritual and pilgrimage center of its time.

The limitations of each of these formulations are not resolved by combining them. Clearly, there was more to the rise of Teotihuacán than this. What happened was a transformational change from an incipient city into a sacred metropolis—a metropolis teeming with religious, economic, and cultural activity, whose leaders extended its influence and domination widely and whose shrines and marketplaces exercised an unparalleled attraction for so many in so much of Mesoamerica. The processes of social change comprised in this phenomenal rise must have involved both synergism and antagonism. The outcome of the interplay of these processes was the transformation of provincial Teotihuacán into the metropolis revealed by archaeology.

Ecological analysis cannot explain such a transformation. Any attempt to explain it primarily in ideological terms would be just as inadequate. The transformation that led to Teotihuacán's urban civilization and to the revolutionary qualities of its city life demands for its understanding more than the ecological approach can supply. The limitations of ecological explanations will have to be recognized and transcended before progress can be made in understanding social changes such as occurred during the rise of Teotihuacán and in the rise of other great centers of civilization in Mesoamerica and elsewhere in the world.

Teotihuacán cannot be understood without understanding its ecological setting and the ways in which it was exploited. But any attempt to understand it solely or mainly with reference to that setting is doomed to

246

failure, for after the cultural ecology of Teotihuacán is analyzed and evaluated, critical problems of interpretation remain. And it is no solution to these problems to argue, as Kent Flannery does, that the "ecosystem approach" encompasses all and that "everything which transmits information is within the province of ecology" (1972:400). Ecology cannot be ignored, but neither can it be elevated to the status of the primary approach for the analysis of all societies at all times. To do this entails either reductionism or the encompassing of so much that the "explanations" offered are untestable.

NOTES

1. This is an abridged version of a manuscript being published elsewhere. The first three sections of the text—on the Teotihuacán apartment compound, on status differences, and on social, economic, and political relations—were presented in shortened and preliminary form at the Thirty-Ninth International Congress of Americanists, Lima, Peru, 1970. Subsequent research has greatly amplified and modified the version presented in Lima. The research discussed in the text was supported by the National Science Foundation (grant nos. G23800, GS207, GS641, GS1222, GS2204, and GS3137). Since 1973 our research facility at Teotihuacán has been supported by contributions from Brandeis University, the State University of New York at Buffalo, the University of Rochester, the University of Toronto, and the University of Western Ontario, as well as by donations from individuals and corporations.

2. I am not referring to Kubler's argument that Teotihuacán residential architecture differs fundamentally from the Old World atrium house (Kubler 1964:354–55). His interpretation is based on an unfortunate confusion between residential and temple architecture at Teotihuacán. He also fails to discriminate between those parts of Teotihuacán residential compounds that contain small temples or shrines around patios, and the domestic parts of those compounds that are organized quite differently. He compares the shrine architecture in part of a Teotihuacán residential compound with an atrium house, and it is not surprising that he finds them different. This is not to say that there are not important differences between the Teotihuacán apartment compound and the atrium house. What is important, however, is that, contrary to Kubler's argument, both were clearly preconceived architectural wholes.

3. Calnek (1973a) has also established that the so-called Maguey Plan, commonly used as a guide to residential architecture and other conditions in Tenochtitlan, is not a plan of any part of that ancient city.

4. Drewitt's calculations led him to believe that the unit he had found probably measured 0.805 meters (Drewitt 1969). David Drucker (1974:129–43) has since presented further evidence supporting Drewitt's calculations, and greatly strengthening the case for the 0.805-meter measurement.

5. The little evidence we have for the Tzacualli phase suggests houses or house compounds and nothing larger, but these examples are beyond the limits of the later city and may not be typical.

6. This model is not derived from urban data. Instead it stems from Smith's (1959) interpretation of Japanese rural data. Similar arrangements may well exist or have

existed in large social units in cities other than Teotihuacán—it would be surprising if they did not. But I am not aware of any urban setting where the model suggested by the Teotihuacán evidence would be typical, that is, would apply to the majority of the inhabitants of a city with a population of many tens of thousands.

7. The comparative evidence referred to has been omitted from this abridgment. Nowhere, except in ancient Rome, were large apartment houses found as planned, standard residential structures numbering in the thousands (in the case of Rome, in the tens of thousands). Rome, in this and many other respects, greatly surpassed Teotihuacán in complexity.

8. I am indebted to Warren Barbour for calling this situation to my attention. It is interesting to note that Spence's analysis of skeletal material from the La Ventilla B compound (Spence 1971, 1974:269–70) suggests that in one part of the compound some women appear to have remained in the compound after marriage to outsiders. Unfortunately, however, this does not support the expanding craft argument, since most of the inhabitants of La Ventilla B do not appear to have been craftsmen.

9. Michael Spence is studying the obsidian-working craft, its organization, the distribution of implements made by obsidian workers, obsidian sources, and the study of obsidian implements at Teotihuacán. He has published two preliminary papers on the subject (1967a, 1967b).

10. For a discussion on the rise of Teotihuacán, see R. Millon (1973:49–59).

11

Pre-Hispanic Relationships between the Basin of Mexico and North and West Mexico

RICHARD A. DIEHL

Department of Anthropology
University of Missouri–Columbia

INTRODUCTION

Anthropologists have long speculated about the relationships between the ancient civilizations of Mesoamerica and the less complex societies to the north, but the paucity of reliable archaeological and ethnographic data has impeded detailed reconstruction of these relationships. In this chapter, I will attempt to trace the pre-Hispanic relationships between societies in the Basin of Mexico and the northern portions of the Republic.[1] I have excluded the southwestern United States, not only because it is outside my competence, but because it has been dealt with recently by J. Charles Kelley (1966).

Our area contained the northern frontier of Mesoamerican civilization from the time of its inception until its demise in the sixteenth century. The actual frontier was probably never a fixed set of geographical points but rather, because of a combination of geographical, ecological, and cultural factors, was a constantly fluctuating zone with considerable inter-digiting of societies of varying complexity (Kirchhoff 1943). Furthermore, the frontier zone constantly advanced and retreated (Armillas 1964). The two basic culture types—the Mesoamerican and the Chichimec—which confronted each other in the frontier zone were strikingly different, as the following brief description will show.

Mesoamerican civilizations south of the frontier shared many characteristics that differentiated them from other New World cultures (Kirchhoff 1943). The most important were:

(1) Large populations living in towns, villages, and cities
(2) Agriculture
(3) A highly developed technology
(4) Elaborate economic institutions
(5) Social stratification
(6) Formalized religion with well-developed ritual, a well-defined pantheon, and a complicated calendar.

The domesticated plants included maize, various legumes, and chili peppers, as well as numerous vegetables and condiments. Several domesticated cactuses were grown in northern Mesoamerica, the most noteworthy being nopal, which produces the tuna fruit, and maguey, the source of pulque. Wherever possible, irrigation was practiced to increase productivity and crop security, but rainfall farming, terracing, swamp reclamation (the famous chinampa system), and intensively worked gardens called calmil plots were other characteristic agricultural techniques.

Mesoamerican settlement patterns varied considerably, depending on local ecological and social factors, but minimally they involved nucleated settlements containing elite residential compounds and ceremonial structures, along with smaller satellite communities located near the agricultural lands. True urban centers—for example, Teotihuacán, Tula, and Tenochtitlan—existed in some areas from the Middle Horizon on. Permanent buildings were constructed throughout the area. Public structures, such as temples, palaces, schools, ball courts, and marketplaces, were often arranged in ceremonial precincts around plazas. Residential architecture seems to have emphasized multifamily dwellings constructed of stone, adobe, and masonry, although many houses were built of less permanent materials. Residences characteristically included sleeping rooms, kitchens, storage areas, work zones, and small religious structures.

As might be expected, Mesoamerican technology was elaborate and specialized. Most cutting tools were made of obsidian, chert, or flint. Ground stone tools, such as food processing implements, were almost invariably made of volcanic stone. Ceramic objects included numerous pottery vessels, many with very specific functions; and small anthropomorphic and zoomorphic figurines.

Social organization in Mesoamerica was based on kin groups that were crosscut, at least in some cases, by incipient social classes. The elite had rights to commoner labor, taxes in goods, and tribute. Many social groups practiced specialized occupations—such as agriculture, trade, commerce, warfare, manufacturing, and societal leadership—or had tendencies in this direction.

Mesoamerican societies were politically organized with the area being divided into numerous small city-states (Bray 1972). Each claimed certain territories, collected taxes and drew labor from them, and attempted to defend them from outside incursion. At times these city-states were integrated into larger political units approximating empires. Religion was an important integrative factor. In the sixteenth century the people worshipped numerous deities with specialized functions, many of which can be traced far back into antiquity. The pantheon included deities related to agriculture, weather control and rainfall, warfare, and specialized crafts and occupations. Ritual activities were formalized and centered around a complex calendar used all over Mesoamerica.

The peoples beyond the pale of Mesoamerican civilization are commonly referred to as Chichimecs. The term, however, because of its various meanings and its indiscriminate use, has caused considerable confusion. It has been applied to nomadic hunters and collectors, to marginal agriculturalists on the southern fringe of the northern frontier, and to various ethnic groups. I will use "Chichimec" in a restricted sense, applying it only to the hunters and collectors of northern Mexico who practiced little or no agriculture.

The Chichimecs included numerous language groups that shared a basically similar culture (Beals 1932). Their culture type, which has been called the Desert Culture by numerous writers, has been best defined by Jennings (1957). The Chichimecs lived in bands of 50 to 100 people that often split up into smaller family groups. Because northern Mexico lacks both large concentrations of collectable foods and readily available water, they were thinly scattered over the landscape. Chichimec subsistence was based on a combination of wild plants (mesquite beans, cactus hearts, nuts, and seeds) and small game (rabbits, deer, rodents, and birds). The nomadic life of the Chichimecs made permanent structures superfluous. Although they occasionally occupied caves and rock shelters, they spent most of the time in open campsites, where wind breaks and crude shelters were the only protection from the elements.

Social organization among the Chichimec was a kin-based one in which all males in a band were related. Social differentiation followed age and sex lines; there were no social classes, specialized occupation groups, or associations. Each band had its own vaguely defined territory, but political integration and politically defined territories were absent. Very little is known about Chichimec religion, but we do know that it lacked temples, a hierarchically organized pantheon, full-time priests, and the Mesoamerican ritual calendar.

Chichimec technology was simple but adequate, with wood, vegetable fiber, and stone providing the basic materials for tools and other necessities. From wood, the Chichimecs made traps, bows, spears, and throwing sticks; from fibers, they fashioned sandals, baskets, aprons, string, and nets; and from stone (chert and flint), they made projectile points and cutting tools. Bone and antler were also used occasionally.

We now have a generalized picture of Chichimec life. Variations and differences existed among different groups; these are important for an accurate comprehension of pre-Hispanic life in northern Mexico, but are not relevant to the purposes of this chapter.

The following discussion is organized around four loosely defined geographical units: the Basin of Mexico; northeastern Mexico (northern Veracruz and Tamaulipas east of the crests of the Sierra Madre Oriental system); north central Mexico (the area north of the Basin between the crests of the Sierra Madre Occidental and the Sierra Madre Oriental); and northwestern Mexico (the area west and north of the Basin and west of the crests of the Sierra Madre Occidental).

The Lithic Period

The Tlapacoya excavations conducted by the Instituto Nacional de Antropología e Historia (INAH) in the southern Basin of Mexico show that humans reached central Mexico by at least 20,000 B.C. (Niederberger 1969). Although their ancestors must have passed through northern

Mexico at an earlier date, archaeological confirmation of this is not available.

The remains of preagricultural peoples in central and northern Mexico that postdate 10,000 B.C. indicate a basic Desert Culture pattern widespread in time and space. Included in these remains are the Infiernillo, Ocampo, Diablo, Lerma, and Nogales phases in Tamaulipas; the Ajuereado and El Riego phases in the Tehuacán Valley; and the Cienegas and Coahuila complexes in Coahuila (MacNeish 1958, Byers 1967, Taylor 1966). The basic similarities of these cultures are due, in part, to the exigencies of a foraging economy in an arid environment, but as our knowledge increases, we should be able to define regional variants of the Desert Culture theme, that is, variants related to environmental and social conditions. One might expect that areas which had extensive grasslands in Pleistocene times had significant megafauna populations, and that the people followed a way of life similar to that of the so-called Big Game Hunters of the midwestern and southwestern United States. The Basin of Mexico, the Bajío, and the Lake Chapala area would be likely spots to look for remains of such societies.

Initial Ceramic Period

Despite recent findings in Tehuacán and Guerrero (MacNeish, Flannery, and Peterson 1970, Brush 1964), the origins of Mesoamerican ceramics remain a mystery. I suspect that the idea of pottery making diffused into Mesoamerica from Central America and northern South America. The pottery found near Acapulco, in fact, may be the earliest yet known in Mesoamerica. From there the concept seems to have diffused northward into Central Mexico, where the earliest ceramics may be the Purrón pottery of the Tehuacán Valley. A ceramic figurine found at Tlapacoya in a level lacking ceramic pots was dated at 2200 B.C.— which presents a problem, since figurines did not appear in the Tehuacán Valley until Ajalpan times (about 1800 B.C.). The absence of figurines in Purrón deposits may be due to the small size of the Purrón samples. Thus the available data do not suggest that ceramic technology was invented independently in central or northern Mexico. We need many more data on the distribution of early ceramics before we can understand the acculturation processes at work during the crucial period of 2500–1500 B.C.

THE BASIN OF MEXICO

The Early Horizon

The earliest ceramic pots known in the Basin—the Ayotla, Justo, Bomba, Iglesia, and El Arbolillo phases (Tolstoy and Paradis 1970)— appear during the Early Horizon, a period which saw Olmec florescence on the Gulf Coast. Numerous Olmec influences were felt outside the homeland area—in fact, several Mesoamerican societies interacted with the Olmecs in varying degrees. The main foci of Olmec involvement in central Mexico were Morelos and Puebla, and only secondarily in the Basin.

The relationships between the Olmecs and such Basin centers as Tlatilco and Ayotla are unclear, despite much research on the subject. The Basin probably contained several small villages at the beginning of the Early Horizon (although their remains have not yet been discovered), which became involved in an expanding trade system at about 1200 B.C. The Tlatilco-Ayotla elite may have either dealt directly with Olmec traders or operated through intermediaries at Chalcatzingo, Las Bocas, San José Mogote, and other communities. The second possibility seems the more likely, and I see no convincing evidence that the Olmecs established colonies or ports-of-trade in the Basin. The manner in which Tlatilco has been excavated and reported prevents full comprehension of the situation there; too, further large-scale excavations are probably impossible since the site has been virtually destroyed. Future work at Ayotla could possibly clarify the Olmec-Basin relationships.

The goods and materials traded back and forth are, for the most part, unknown. Trace-element analysis of obsidian artifacts found at San Lorenzo demonstrates that the Olmecs maintained several long-distance procurement networks to obtain their raw material (Cobean et al. 1971). Teotihuacán Valley obsidian has been identified in the Chicharras phase (1350–1250 B.C.), and Pachuca obsidian was moderately abundant in San Lorenzo B phase deposits. It is interesting to note that although the Teotihuacán Valley is perhaps the most thoroughly surveyed area of its size in Mesoamerica (Sanders 1965), there is no evidence for Early Horizon occupation—which suggests that the area was virtually uninhabited and that the mines were exploited by small groups visiting them for short periods of time. Another interesting result of the trace-element analysis is that several major obsidian sources in Hidalgo, Querétaro, Michoacán, and Jalisco are not represented in the San Lorenzo obsidians. The reasons for this are not clear but may relate to the absence of substantial indigenous populations near the sources.

Goods exported from the Olmec heartland included pottery, jadeite, and ceramic figurines, and possibly rubber and feathers. The sociopolitical context of the trade is unclear, but Flannery's (1968b) reconstruction of the relationships between the Valley of Oaxaca and the Olmecs is quite plausible, and I suggest that relationships similar to those he describes also held in the Basin.

Life in central Mexico centered around small villages with total populations in the hundreds or, at most, a few thousand. There is no evidence for isolated ceremonial centers or even ceremonial precincts within communities, although Porter (1953) does mention clay-covered steps and terraces at Tlatilco. The dwellings seem to have been of wattle and daub; there is no evidence for adobe blocks in the area at this time. Data on subsistence activities are scanty, but the emphasis seems to have been on hillside cultivation rather than on exploitation of the bottomlands. If we project the Tehuacán Valley data to our area, the maize grown was probably Early Tripsicoid (Mangelsdorf, MacNeish, and Galinat 1966). Because of drought and frost problems, however, this variety may not have flourished in the Basin, and the resulting low productivity potential may be one reason for the sparse Early Horizon population. Terrestial and lacustrine hunting and collecting were important secondary subsistence activities.

Early Horizon social organization is unclear. The prevalence of female figurines has led several writers to suggest a matrilineal, matrilocal society participating in an Earth Mother–worship cult. However, evidence for this is unconvincing. The Tlatilco burials indicate that important social distinctions existed in the community. Sanders and Price (1968) have argued that these are distinctions of rank rather than social class and this seems to be a reasonable interpretation. Small elite groups were probably in charge of the trade and redistribution networks that linked central Mexico with its neighbors to the south, and ultimately, with the Olmecs. Sanders and Price further suggest that the Basin populations were organized into relatively small chiefdoms, a level of organization that has been questioned by one of its early proponents (Service 1971). I maintain that chiefdoms did exist, even if their evolutionary implications are open to question, and that chiefdom characteristics are evident in the Basin in the Early Horizon remains (Diehl, in press).

It can be assumed, though not demonstrated, that Tlatilco and Ayotla were the two dominant communities in the Basin, and that smaller communities were subordinate to them. These two major centers probably had proprietary rights over certain resources (such as obsidian mines), but there are no indications that they politically integrated large territorial domains or that they exacted considerable tribute from the smaller communities. The Tlatilco and Ayotla elite undoubtedly maintained marriage and economic relations with the elite of the smaller subordinate communities. These alliances, however, did not evolve into formal state organizations, perhaps because the total population of the area was too small to support such a structure, or perhaps because the necessary organizational techniques were not yet perfected.

Relations between the Basin societies and the Olmecs were finally broken, probably due to events in the Olmec homeland rather than in central Mexico. The nature of these events still eludes us, but military intrusion into the Olmec homeland from the Pacific slopes of Chiapas and Guatemala may have been a factor. In any event, with relations broken, Tlatilco lost whatever advantages it had held over its "subjects" and faded away, while Ayotla somehow remained a major center well into the First Intermediate period (Blanton 1972b).

The Olmec cultural contribution to the Basin of Mexico was considerable, particularly in the spheres of religion, elite practices, and the establishment of trade networks. But the Olmecs did not provide the pattern for future political and economic structures—these evolved as a result of local conditions during the following centuries.

The First Intermediate Period

The First Intermediate period was a crucial one in Mesoamerican prehistory. Processes and events took place which set the stage for the future in central Mexico and the Maya area. These culminated in the emergence of large, regional centers, some of which later evolved into full-fledged cities. It is becoming increasingly apparent that these two foci of later developments—central Mexico and the Maya area—were essentially isolated from one another at this time, each developing in its own unique directions within an overall framework that was the Olmec legacy. The absence of Izapa influence in central Mexico is one indication of this isolation. It is difficult, however, to assess the role that isolation played in the formation of the different kinds of societies which came to characterize the two areas in later times. I am not suggesting that the two areas were completely sealed off from one another, but rather that the contacts were ephemeral and inconsequential. This was the last time, incidentally, that such isolation existed within Mesoamerica.

We have considerably more data on the Basin societies for the First Intermediate than for previous periods. The First Intermediate sequence includes the Totolica-la Pastora, Atoto-Cuautepec and Ticomán phases in Tolstoy and Paradis's (1970) Basin-wide sequence. The Teotihuacán Valley sequence includes the Altica, Chiconautla, Cuanalan, Tezoyuca, Patlachique, Tzacualli, and Miccaotli phases (R. Millon 1967a).

Regional surveys by Blanton, Parsons, and Sanders have revealed many First Intermediate settlements in all areas surveyed to date. From the Totolica–la Pastora phase, such sites as El Arbolillo, Zacatenco, Tlatilco, and Tlapacoya have been excavated. These sites provided the major body of data on this period for many years, and we have only recently begun to realize the limitations of such a small data base and the false picture it presents. The Teotihuacán Valley Project located twenty-three Altica and Chiconautla phase sites (Sanders 1965), the Texcoco area survey found nineteen (J. R. Parsons 1971b), and four were identified in the Ixtapalapa survey (Blanton 1972b). The Teotihuacán Valley sites—all of which are hamlets or small villages lacking civic architecture—have a definite locational bias for the Piedmont slopes, with hillside swidden cultivation apparently having been the main subsistence base. The data suggest small isolated communities occupied by socially homogeneous groups that did not participate in the long-distance trade networks and elite practices common elsewhere in Mesoamerica.

The Texcoco region pattern was somewhat different. One nucleated settlement (Tx-MF-13) covered 45 hectares and contained at least two-thirds of the area's population. The remaining population lived in eighteen hamlets scattered throughout the Piedmont. Subsistence activities included hillside swidden agriculture, cultivation in high-water-table areas on the plain, perhaps simple canal irrigation, hunting, and lake exploitation for water fowl and turtles. As for the Ixtapalapa communities, they seem to have been involved in exploiting the Lakeside Plain, and all but one were small hamlets (Blanton 1972b).

The generalized picture of the Totolica–la Pastora phase is one of small hamlets occupied by agriculturalists who also practiced other subsistence activities. Evidence of social stratification, political integration, and trade is lacking, but future data from Tlatilco or Tlapacoya-Ayotla could alter the picture.

Tolstoy and Paradis's (1970) Atoto-Cuautepec phase is difficult to use in this synthesis for two reasons: it has only recently been defined, and the chronological framework used by the various survey projects is too gross to permit assignment of sites to this 100-year phase. El Arbolillo and Tlatilco were abandoned by the end of the phase, but Zacatenco continued to exist for perhaps an additional century. It is not known whether Tlapacoya-Ayotla continued to be occupied, though Blanton's evidence suggests that it did.

I will use Tolstoy and Paradis's Ticomán phase to cover the time span from 350 B.C. to A.D. 1. Although numerous sites have been excavated, only some—Teotihuacán, Tlapacoya, Cuicuilco, Ticomán, and Cuanalan—can be considered here. The first three were major centers, while the last two were hamlets on the order of El Arbolillo and Zacatenco in earlier times.

The site of the future city of Teotihuacán had been settled during Totolica–la Pastora (Cuanalan) times, but its first real growth spurt occurred during the Patlachique phase (Ticomán in the Basin-wide sequence). The Patlachique-phase settlement covered at least 6 square kilometers and had a minimal population of 5,000 to 10,000 people. The reasons for Teotihuacán's relatively rapid emergence as an urban center during this period are not yet clear. R. Millon (1973) suggests that it was related to the proliferation of the obsidian processing industry based on nearby raw material sources, in conjunction with other secondary factors. Sanders and Price (1968) feel that the managerial requirements of a major irrigation system begun at this time provided the impetus to state formation and urbanization. Neither hypothesis, however, seems completely adequate. My own feeling is that emerging cities very quickly begin to generate their own growth through elaboration of the nonagricultural economic sphere (Jacobs 1969); my biases, therefore, tend to favor Millon's interpretations. Social stratification and expansion of the state territory all grew simultaneously with the city, so that by the end of the Patlachique phase, the city of Teotihuacán may well have controlled the entire Teotihuacán Valley and nearby areas.

But Teotihuacán did not grow in a sociopolitical vacuum. Two potential rivals existed—Tlapacoya and Cuicuilco—and there may have been others. One of the major structures excavated at Tlapacoya (Barba de Piña Chan 1956) revealed a complex temple base that contained several elite burials. Neither Tlapacoya nor neighboring Tlaltenco seems comparable to Patlachique-phase Teotihuacán in size or degree of urban development (Blanton 1972b).

Cuicuilco is famous for its crudely constructed circular temple base (Cummings 1933, Heizer and Bennyhoff 1958). Because an eruption by the volcano Xitle covered the area with a thick lava mantle, thus eliminating Cuicuilco, the community's extent is unknown; however it may well have rivaled Teotihuacán. Cuicuilco was undoubtedly an independent community with a politically integrated hinterland. We do not know if the same was true of Tlapacoya and Tlaltenco; the size differences between these two communities and their spatial proximity, in fact, may indicate that Tlapacoya was subordinate to Tlaltenco. And conceivably, both might have been under Cuicuilco's domination. Whatever, Cuicuilco and Patlachique-phase Teotihuacán undoubtedly competed with one another, probably utilizing a combination of military, economic, and social techniques. When Cuicuilco's development was terminated by Xitle's eruption, the entire Basin was left open to Teotihuacán domination in the succeeding Tzacualli phase, a domination that was facilitated by two factors: Teotihuacán's earlier experiences at organizing territories and people, and the disparity between its total military and economic resources and those of its less highly organized neighbors.

The Tzacualli and Miccaotli phases at Teotihuacán, at the conclusion of the First Intermediate period, were a time of tremendous growth and change in the city. The occupied area expanded to approximately 20 square kilometers. Population growth was also pronounced, the Tzacualli figure numbering between 30,000 and 50,000 people. The obsidian processing industry developed considerably, and raw materials were brought from as far away as Pachuca, Hidalgo. An unbelievable quantity of civic architecture was erected—the Sun and Moon Pyramids, the Ciudadela, and the Temple of Quetzalcoatl, in addition to scores of structures along the "Street of the Dead." This period saw the basic cruciform plan of the city laid down. Too, Teotihuacán's foreign contacts were expanded considerably, with Teotihuacán goods reaching Altun Ha, on the eastern fringe of the Maya area (Pendergast 1971).

The Middle Horizon

During the Middle Horizon period, Teotihuacán rose to a power position never again equaled by a Mesoamerican center. Since the history of the city has been dealt with elsewhere in this volume (Chapter 9), I will not discuss Teotihuacán at length.

One fact, however, seems obvious: for the first time, the entire Basin was a politically and socially integrated unit, controlled by a single center and a single elite. The Basin was the power base from which Teotihuacán operated, giving it a social, political, economic, religious, and military advantage which no Mesoamerican center had ever possessed before or would thereafter.

The Second Intermediate Period

Synthesis of the Second Intermediate period is a frustrating endeavor, primarily because the archaeological data are relatively scarcer than for other periods, and much of what we do have is of poor quality. This period (which is often called the Toltec Era because the Toltecs of Tula exercised political domination over the northern half of Mesoamerica, and perhaps over some southern portions as well) begins with the final collapse and abandonment of Teotihuacán. The ensuing sociopolitical vacuum was soon filled by at least two, and possibly four, centers. Tula and Cholula seem to have exerted direct political control over much of the Basin during at least part of this period. The roles that Xochicalco and Tajín played in central Mexican politics are unclear, except that both reached their highest developments at this time.

Teotihuacán's collapse brought the once-great city down to the status of a town with a few thousand inhabitants. Sanders (1965) shows that Teotihuacán Valley population was concentrated in two areas during Early Toltec times: the edge of the lower Valley plain where the Xometla phase has been defined, and the ancient Classic city where some old buildings were still in use during the Oxtotipac phase. The chronological relationship between the two phases is unclear; they may or may not be contemporaneous. Sanders suggests that they are, and that the Oxtotipac materials represent remnants of the former Teotihuacán culture; furthermore, he theorizes, the Xometla ceramic users may have moved into this unoccupied area from somewhere else in the Basin and perhaps owed political and social allegiance to Tula rather than to Teotihuacán. After the city's collapse, the Teotihuacán Valley went through a period of pronounced ruralization, with small hamlets and villages located near prime agricultural resources the only settlement types present.

In the Texcoco and Ixtapalapa areas populations increased over the Middle Horizon levels, but once again the settlement patterns have a pronounced rural cast—there were many villages and small towns, and only a few centers with populations in excess of ten thousand.

Tula Toltec society was involved in many of the events and processes in the Basin and in northern and western Mexico at this time. The INAH, under the direction of Jorge R. Acosta, conducted excavations at Tula from 1940 until 1955 (Acosta 1957) and has recently initiated new explorations under Eduardo Matos Moctezuma. The research has dealt primarily with excavation and restoration of large civic buildings. Since 1970 the University of Missouri Tula Archaeological Project, under my direction, has been conducting residential zone excavations and a survey of the ancient city. At this writing, we are terminating our third and final field season and have not yet begun analysis of the materials from 1970 and 1971. Thus, many of my ideas about Tula are still tentative and subject to revision.

Tula's occupational history is still unclear. Acosta (1957) defined three periods at the site: Coyotlatelco, Tula-Mazapan, and Aztec. This tripartite division is basically sound, although it will undoubtedly be modified by new data. Tula's early history is a particularly thorny problem, because while most archaeologists agree that Tula had a hand in Teotihuacán's downfall, there is no evidence that Tula was occupied until after Teotihuacán's collapse. Despite this present lack of evidence, I am tempted to propose that Tula was a relatively small late Middle Horizon regional center that grew and eventually turned on Teotihuacán with the aid of other regional centers. Analysis of the material collected on the 1972 urban survey should settle this question one way or the other.

We know relatively little about Tula during Coyotlatelco times. Occupation was apparently spread along the ridge that forms the backbone of the city for at least 2 kilometers, but the intensity of the occupation is not known. We do know that many areas with dense Mazapan occupation lack Coyotlatelco debris, indicating that the city reached its areal and demographic climax in Mazapan times. The extent of Aztec or Late Horizon occupation is also unknown, but it seems to have been considerable. Several semihistorical, semilegendary accounts of Toltec history recorded after the Spanish Conquest (*Anales de Cuauhtitlan, Historia Tolteca-Chichimeca*) tell of Tula's destruction and abandonment. And while it has generally been accepted that the city was sacked and burned by invaders, then abandoned, and later reoccupied by users of Aztec II ceramics, I will not be surprised if our data show that Tula's occupation was continuous from Coyotlatelco times into the Colonial period. I suspect the city went through two cycles of growth and decline (Toltec and Aztec), all the while maintaining a respectable population even after having lost its political and military hegemony over neighboring areas.

Our survey has demonstrated that the ancient city covered at least 12 square kilometers, and, according to our estimates, contained a maximum population of about 60,000 people. It is located on the top and sides of a long north-south mesa and the lower slopes of several surrounding hills. Its position commands the junction of the Tula and Rosa rivers, which seems to be a strategic position for controlling movements of goods and people up and down the river valley and may, in fact, have been a spur to Tula's early growth.

The legally defined archaeological zone of Tula contains the Main Ceremonial Precinct, which is part of what we call the Acropolis. The Acropolis, a large, partly artificial and partly natural eminence bounded by steep masonry walls, contained at least two large temple mounds (mounds B and C) with such associated structures as the Palacio Quemado, as well as two ball courts, a long linear structure that Mayanists would call a range building, and several smaller temples and elite residences. A second, smaller ceremonial precinct called Tula Chico (Matos Moctezuma 1970, personal communication) is located approximately 2 kilometers to the north. Several other smaller precincts have also been identified. All in all, the arrangement of Tula's ceremonial architecture is more reminiscent of Classic Maya ceremonial centers than that of Teotihuacán, in that there is no overall plan to the city comparable to that of Teotihuacán. The difference between Tula and Maya centers is that Tula's population was densely packed in the areas between the ceremonial structures, with houses built literally one against another over the entire occupied zone.

Only six or seven of Tula's several thousand houses have been excavated. The residences uncovered at the northern edge of the city (by the University of Missouri project) were multifamily units constructed of stone and adobe walls occasionally covered with lime plaster; they had compacted earth or plaster floors and probably had flat roofs resting on horizontal beams. Room complexes were arranged around enclosed patios or courtyards that contained small adoratorios. There is a considerable range in quality of house construction and materials, undoubtedly reflecting socioeconomic differences among different families and kin groups. We also excavated a small temple dedicated to Tlaloc, which probably functioned as a religious focus for the surrounding neighborhood. It seems comparable to the Aztec calpulli temples in Tenochtitlan.

Considerable evidence exists for trade and contact between Tula and other areas of Mesoamerica. Here we will mention only the evidence at Tula itself. Several figurines found in our excavations seem to have come from western Mexico but have not yet been positively identified. Pacific Ocean marine shells have also been uncovered in the excavations, along with others from the Gulf of Mexico (Feldman 1971, personal communication).

Foreign pottery definitely identified at Tula includes Papagayo polychrome from Costa Rica or Nicaragua, considerable quantities of Plumbate from the coastal zone of Chiapas and Guatemala, and a few sherds of Tres Picos ware from Central Veracruz. Fine Orange ware has not been identified either by Acosta or by us, although Beatriz Braniff (1966, personal communication) informed me that a few sherds are known from the site. From J. Charles Kelley (1972, personal communication), I learned that Bertha Dutton found at least one definite sherd of Mercado Red-on-Brown at Tula, a ware apparently imported from the Rio Colorado Valley in Zacetecas.

The factors behind Tula's demise as a political center remain a puzzle. There is evidence of burning in the Acropolis structures, but at least some of them were rebuilt and enlarged in later times. As previously mentioned, Tula continued to have a respectable population through the Late Horizon and into the Colonial period.

The Late Horizon

The nature of the data for the Late Horizon is different from that for previous times. Although the published archaeological data are relatively scanty, they are supplemented by numerous ethnohistorical materials, such as pre-Columbian books, accounts by the conquistadores, and a multitude of sixteenth-century Spanish documents.

The basic picture in the Basin is one of numerous moderate-sized communities competing among themselves for control over land, peoples, and tribute. Three victors emerged: Tenochtitlan-Tlatelolco, Texcoco, and Tlacopan, which together formed a political alliance that was eventually dominated by Tenochtitlan-Tlatelolco. The processes by which Tenochtitlan-Tlatelolco, a small, island community in a marshy lake surrounded by hostile neighbors, became the politically dominant center in Mesoamerica north of the Isthmus of Tehuantepec are a mystery, particularly if one is as suspicious of the Aztec histories as I am. And since Tenochtitlan-Tlatelolco was destroyed by the Spaniards, who then built Mexico City on its ruins, it will always be difficult—but not impossible—to study this process archaeologically. If research on Aztec mainland and lakeshore sites is conducted before these areas disappear under the burgeoning sprawl of Mexico City, it should provide some data on the process.

NORTHEAST MEXICO

Why northeast Mexico is one of the poorest known areas of Mesoamerica is not clear, but the reasons are probably related to the area's marginality to the remainder of Mesoamerica. This lack of information is unfortunate, because a look at Ignacio Marquina's "Arquitectura Prehispánica" or an automobile trip along any highway in the area will show that there are many impressive ruins and that the aboriginal population was obviously dense. The main bodies of data on the ancient cultures in this area come from the work of Ekholm in the Pánuco area, MacNeish in Tamaulipas and the Pánuco area, and Du Solier in several places (summarized in Marquina 1964). The paucity of data virtually forces us to think of northeastern Mexico as a recipient of outside influences rather than as an innovator, but this could change radically with more information. We will first analyze the data from the Gulf Coast lowlands, then look at MacNeish's material from the mountains of Tamaulipas.

We have no archaeological evidence, controlled or otherwise, on the Lithic and Initial Ceramic periods. This does not mean that the area was unoccupied; it undoubtedly did have a population.

Pre-Hispanic Relationships between the Basin and Mexico

The Early Horizon

In central and northern Veracruz, several Early Horizon sites and phases have been identified—the earliest levels at El Trapiche, and the Pavón and Ponce periods in the Pánuco Basin (García Payón 1966, MacNeish 1954). The area was presumably well settled, but local populations seem to have maintained only fleeting relationships with the Olmecs. A few possible trade ceramics and figurines have been identified at Trapiche, but such hallmarks of the Olmec trade system as jadeite statuettes are conspicuously lacking. This is very puzzling, because the Pánuco River Basin provides a setting very similar to that of the Coatzacoalcos and Tonalá basins. I suggest that future research in the middle reaches of the Pánuco will produce remains of many Early Horizon villages, but not a civilization comparable in complexity to the Olmecs.

The First Intermediate Period

MacNeish's (1954) Chila and El Prisco–Tancol periods (Ekholm's [1944] Periods I and II) belong to the First Intermediate period. Chila sites have truncated conical mounds that lack stone veneers and staircases and are not found in plaza groups; these may be burial mounds, but none have been excavated. Plaster-surfaced mounds placed in plaza groups occur in the El Prisco-Tancol period. Numerous sites of these two periods—El Ebano, Tancanhuitz, and Tamposoque in San Luis Potosí, and Huejutla, Hidalgo (Marquina 1964)—have been described in the literature, but not in detail. Most contain structures that are architecturally similar to the Cuicuilco mound, although the actual historical relationships between the two areas are obscure, if indeed any existed.

The Middle Horizon

Periods III and IV in Ekholm's sequence are coeval with Teotihuacán's rise and florescence. The ceramics that Ekholm recovered show virtually no Teotihuacán influence but rather seem related to types at Tajín. (Some figurines, however, do have similarities with Teotihuacán types.) Little is known about architecture, but conical structures with asphalt surfaces were discovered at the Pavón site.

The lack of Teotihuacán influence is puzzling. It is probably more apparent than real, particularly if the Teotihuacán influence was centered on one or two unstudied major communities. Were it not for a series of fortuitous events that led to the excavation of Mounds A and B at Kaminaljuyú, we would have a very misleading impression of Teotihuacán's penetration into the Guatemala highlands, and the same could be true of the Huasteca. An alternative explanation is that the Teotihuacán influence was centered on Tajín, which was closer to Teotihuacán and may have provided it with all the Gulf Coast exotic goods it needed, thus reducing the value of the Huasteca.

The Second Intermediate Period

The Huasteca was perhaps more closely integrated with central Mexico during the Second Intermediate period than at any other time in its history. This is Period IV, or Las Flores, in the Ekholm sequence. Although many communities are known to have existed we will consider only the best-known ones here. Mound A at Las Flores near Tampico, for example, was one of many on the site, and the ancient community was apparently large. The excavated building was a circular temple base with numerous Las Flores–phase superimposed reconstructions; six stairways and twenty-six floors were identified. Covering the mound was a lime plaster stucco. The nature of the temple superstructures is not clear, but they were probably built of pole and thatch.

Las Flores–phase artifacts include the usual Mesoamerican ceramics and lithics. Among the ceramics are Las Flores Red-on-Buff, Las Flores Incised, Las Flores Relief Ware, Heavy Plain Ware, Pánuco Metallic, ladles, and handled incensarios, all of which have close relationships to Tula types. Few of the illustrated human figurines show much similarity to Tula types, but the wheeled animal effigies are strikingly similar to examples from Tula. Some Las Flores spindle whorls are identical to Tula pieces, and the tobacco pipes are similar, but not identical. Interestingly, Ekholm did not find Plumbate at Las Flores, although it is common at Tula.

266

Tamuin, San Luis Potosí, has been excavated by Du Solier (1946) and Stresser-Péan (1972), but the published reports are sketchy. The ancient community was apparently a large one, the ceremonial precinct covering at least 16 hectares (Marquina 1964) and consisting of large mounds grouped around plazas. Du Solier uncovered a large rectangular mound with two conical altars in front of it. The temple base and altars had elaborate polychrome friezes similar in style and iconography to contemporaneous central Mexican art and seemingly related to the Quetzalcoatl cult.

Near Tamuin is Tantoc, a site with large temples; the major mound measures 450 meters on a side and 70 meters high. Its date is uncertain, but Marquina suggests that the structure is pre-Toltec. Numerous Second Intermediate buildings have been identified at Tantoc; they include circular and rectangular temple bases decorated with friezes.

The Late Horizon

Ekholm's Period VI is coeval with the Aztec ascendancy in the Basin. Huastec Black-on-White, a very distinctive ceramic type, was invented and became extraordinarily popular. It was traded into the Basin and even appears in village refuse at places like Cuanalan (Diehl 1962, personal observation). Huastec stone sculpture was highly developed—in fact, the famous Adolescent sculpture from Tamuín now in the Museo Nacional de Antropología probably dates from this period. The Aztecs apparently exerted sufficient control over portions of the Huasteca to exact tribute from as far north as Tochpa (Tuxpan), and there are indications of an expansion of Nahua speakers into the area at this time (Barlow 1949, Stresser-Péan 1972).

TAMAULIPAS

MacNeish's work in Tamaulipas provides long sequences for the Sierra de Tamaulipas and the Sierra Madre Oriental, which are particularly important because they deal with marginal areas where constant acculturation-deculturation processes were at work. Many Mesoamericanists are reluctant to work in such areas, but the payoff in unusual types of data and insights into the nature of the frontiers of civilization clearly outweighs the absence of spectacular remains. I will combine the two distinct local sequences into one, following MacNeish (1972).

The Lithic Period

The Lithic period includes the Diablo Complex and the Lerma, Nogales, La Perra, Infiernillo, Ocampo, and Flacco phases. Materials from dry cave deposits indicate a gradual change from a subsistence based primarily on hunting to one based on plant collection and domesticated plants. By 2000 B.C. domesticated plants—pumpkins, peppers, beans (*Phasaeolus vulguris*), gourds, and Early Nal-Tel maize—comprised 15 to 20 percent of the diet. The artifacts included dart points, gouges, scrapers, nets, mats, and baskets. Ceramics and settled villages, however, were not present.

The Initial Ceramic Period

In this time period appear the Almagre and Guerra phases. "Initial Ceramic" is a misnomer in Tamaulipas, however, because ceramics did not appear until well after 1400 B.C. But the number of domesticated plants increased, as did their overall importance in the diet (30 percent domesticated plants, 10 percent hunting, and 60 percent collecting). Small villages that were at least semipermanent became common.

The Early Horizon and First Intermediate Period

These two periods are considered jointly because the data do not suggest any significant separation between the two. The phases included are Mesa de Guaje, La Florida, and Laguna. Agriculture continued to increase in importance at the expense of plant collection, while hunting may have been relegated to the status of a pleasurable pastime. Villages became permanent settlements, with small temples constructed and arranged around plazas. Ceramics appeared for the first time; fired clay was used for pots, figurines, whistles, and ladles. This was obviously a period of accelerated acculturation, and we can only guess at the changes in social organization and people's attitudes and world views. New demands on time for agricultural activities and construction tasks must have caused more than one old-timer to look back wistfully to the days when a man could go up into the mountains to collect wild millet whenever he pleased.

The Middle Horizon

The Eslabones and Palmillas phases represent the cultural climax in the Sierras. Domesticated plants made up 45 percent of the diet, and 50 percent came from wild plant collecting. Several large communities existed, consisting of hundreds of house platforms in addition to pyramids, ball courts, and other civic structures. The larger communities were commonly found on hilltops, while smaller villages and campsites were scattered throughout the hinterland. Material culture, particularly ceramics, reached the zenith of its complexity. In short, the Sierra societies were full-fledged though provincial participants in Mesoamerican culture. Definite evidence of sustained contact with other societies is absent, although some individuals must have traveled to the Pánuco Basin to enjoy the markets, festivals, and fleshpots.

The Second Intermediate Period

Agriculture decreased slightly in importance during the La Salta and San Lorenzo phases. Permanent houses with stone bases were still in use, but the communities were small and lacked ceremonial structures. The ceramics seem impoverished compared with their Eslabones-phase predecessors. The general picture is that of a deculturation process in motion and a diminution of Mesoamerican influence. The factors behind this situation are unknown, but they may relate to a general retraction of the Mesoamerican northern frontier at this time.

The Late Horizon

Agriculture continued to decrease in importance during the Los Angeles and San Antonio phases. Communities contained only a few families, and rock shelters once again became foci of habitation. The quality of ceramics declined further. By this time, the Sierra population had become more Chichimec than Mesoamerican.

NORTH CENTRAL MEXICO

The Early Horizon

Our ignorance of pre–First Intermediate period cultures in northern and western Mexico is abysmal—correcting this, in fact, should be a primary goal of future Mesoamerican research. We do not know where the Mesoamerican boundary was in these early times, how far north agriculture diffused, or what role the area played in the formation of sedentary village life in the southwestern United States.

The Bajío—The First Intermediate Period

The best-known remains of this time period belong to the Chupícuaro ceramic style, which was concentrated in southern Guanajuato, Querétaro, Michoacán, and northern Estado de Mexico. The style is named after an archaeological site now covered by waters behind the Solís Dam. During the 1940s INAH personnel excavated 390 burials at Chupícuaro (Porter 1956), all of which exhibited considerable variation in mode of interment and quantity of grave goods (one burial contained 48 items, while 71 lacked offerings of any kind). Numerous structural remnants encountered in the excavations suggest that the burials were placed under house floors, but the report is not clear on this point.

The most salient characteristic of the pottery is the tremendous range of vessel shape and decoration within a few basic forms and styles. Virtually every vessel illustrated by Porter (1956) and by Matos Moctezuma (1968) from nearby Jerécuaro is slightly different from other vessels. Potters were obviously not restricted by mass-production methods and rigidly defined artistic canons. Porter seriated the ceramics into three phases: Early, Transitional, and Late. Absolute dates are lacking, but she equates the Early Phase with Ticomán III (Late Cuanalan) in the Teotihuacán Valley sequence and the Late Phase with Miccaotli. I see no reason to question this assignment. Chupícaro ceramics have been found at numerous sites north of the Basin—Tepejí del Río, San Juan del Río, Celaya, León, Zinapécuaro, Zacapú, Pureparo, and Jerécuaro—but none have been adequately investigated. Many questions remain about the Chupícuaro complex. Were the pots specialized burial offerings, or did they also have utilitarian functions? What social, economic, and political relationships existed between these communities and their contemporaries in the Basin? Were the Chupícuaro communities somehow related to the earlier Olmec influence in the Basin? What role did Chupícuaro people play in transmitting Mesoamerican culture to groups further north and west? These questions can only be answered by future research.

Recent investigations in various parts of Guanajuato have provided interesting new data on that area (Braniff de Torres 1972). The earliest materials discovered to date belong to the Morales phase, which is related to Ticomán I–III and the Early Phase at Chupícuaro. The people were sedentary farmers living in small villages, but indications of social stratification, urbanism, or complex religion are absent in the sites studied thus far.

The Bajío—The Middle Horizon

The only Middle Horizon materials known from the Bajío belong to San Miguel phase defined by Braniff de Torres (1972). The San Miguel phase, which is contemporaneous with Miccaotli, has been placed at A.D. 200. There is a surprising lack of Teotihuacán influence in the area at this time, but R. Millon (1973) mentions a possible Teotihuacán cinnabar mine in Queretaro. Two ceramic traditions that were later important at Tula are characteristic of the San Miguel phase: Tula water-colored (Blanco Levantado) and Red-on-Buff. Both occur on domestic kitchen wares rather than ceremonial ceramics.

The succeeding Tierra Blanca and Agua Espinosa phases are poorly known, but the former is related to Metepec (A.D. 600–750) and the latter to Oxtotipac at about A.D. 800.

The Bajío—The Second Intermediate Period

The Second Intermediate period includes two apparently contemporaneous phases in different parts of the state: Coporo Tardío and Carabino. The Carabino phase contains many items identical to those of the Mazapan phase at Tula, including such ceramics as Wavy-Line Mazapan, Blanco Levantado, Naranja Sobre Blanco, Red-on-Buff tripod bowls, *molcajetes*, tobacco pipes, comals, and figurines. The shared traits involve utilitarian objects rather than the elite objects and architecture of the Toltec "Great Tradition." Second Intermediate sites are apparently

271

numerous, and all seem to have been simple villages lacking ceremonial structures. The data suggest either that Tula was settled by migrants from the north or that it was the one community in the entire cultural configuration which became a great urban center. I prefer the latter interpretation.

Numerous "Toltec" sites have been reported in Querétaro and San Luis Potosí, but the published data are skimpy.

Braniff de Torres reports that, despite extensive survey, Late Horizon sites have not been found in Guanajuato. In the sixteenth century the general Bajío area was inhabited by Tarascos, Guachichiles, Guamares, and Pames (Jiménez Moreno 1943). The Tarascos were civilized agriculturalists, while the other peoples were nomadic hunters and collectors. Thus, there is clear evidence for a retraction of the Mesoamerican frontier after about A.D. 1100 to 1200 in the Bajío area.

Zacatecas and Durango—the Middle Horizon

Recent research by personnel from Southern Illinois University has shown that Mesoamerican culture expanded to its northern limits during the Middle Horizon and that several communities formerly thought to be post-Classic were actually occupied during this period. Chalchihuites, recently renamed Alta Vista, has been known for many years, but recent research by Kelley and his associates has resolved many problems about the site (Kelley 1971, Kelley and Kelley 1971).

The Suchil River Basin was first occupied by agriculturalists during the Canutillo phase (about A.D. 200). Canutillo farmers, who occupied small villages located near good farmland, utilized *temporal* hillside cultivation in high-water-table areas, as well as small-scale irrigation. The well-developed ceramic complex emphasized red and red-on-cream wares and figurines. Houses of perishable materials placed on stone-walled platforms were arranged around open courtyards with centrally located altars. Temple bases have not been identified, and there are no other indications of a local elite or the hieratic aspects of Mesoamerican culture.

The Alta Vista phase (A.D. 300–500) was a time of radical innovation and culture change, with most, if not all, of the new features coming from the south. Settlement pattern data indicate a population maximum at this time—although people still lived in scattered hamlets, many more communities existed. Ceramics became more diversified, and several pottery types may have had special functions related to elite activities. Possible elite functions are also indicated by other artifact classes: animal effigy axes; turquoise beads, pendants, and mosaics; and conch trumpets and shell beads. This period saw the construction of the Alta Vista ceremonial center, containing temples and numerous special-purpose structures.

The sudden burst of prosperity in Alta Vista times was apparently a result of mining activities. Several hundred mine pits dating from the latter part of the Canutillo phase and into the Alta Vista phase have been identified by Weigand (1968). The materials extracted from the mines are still unknown; a white variant of chalchihuitl (jadeite) is the most likely possibility, but turquoise may also have been mined (Kelley 1972, personal communication). Workshop areas where the raw materials were processed into artifacts have not been located and the ultimate consumers are unknown, but the market must have been to the south and may well have been Teotihuacán.

Was the Chalchihuites area an integral part of Mesoamerica, or was it an island of civilization surrounded by Chichimec nomads? The former theory seems most probable at the moment, but only future investigation will decide the issue.

The Calichal (A.D. 500–650) and Retoño (A.D. 650–750) phases were a time of cultural regression—most communities (including the Alta Vista ceremonial center) were abandoned, and out-migrations seem to have taken place. Mining activities ceased. Ceramics became simpler, and the former elite wares were no longer manufactured. Indeed, during these phases, there are virtually no archaeological indications of a social or political elite. This deculturation process was completed by A.D. 750, although a few population remnants continued in nearby areas until A.D. 950.

The factors behind this cultural collapse are unclear. Were the mines exhausted? Did climatic fluctuations make agriculture untenable? Did the water table drop sufficiently to prevent successful temporal cultivation for many years? Did Chichimecs interrupt the trade networks sufficiently to destroy the base of the prosperity? How did Teotihuacán's collapse fit into the problem? Was the loss of such resource areas as the Chalchihuites zone the opening act of the decline, or was it an aftereffect? What effect did migrating Chalchihuitecos have on societies further south? We hope to have the answers to some of these questions in the near future.

The evidence at hand suggests that people migrated northward from the

Chalchihuites area to an area near modern Victoria de Durango in the Guadiana Valley, where two Second Intermediate phases have been defined: Las Joyas (A.D. 700–950) and Rio Tunal (A.D. 950–1150). In the Guadiana Valley archaeologists have identified two major sites—Schroeder Ranch and Navacoyan. The Schroeder Ranch site was a ceremonial center with an attached residential zone, while Navacoyan was a cemetery and perhaps a ceremonial center. At the Schroeder Ranch site, there is a pyramid, a ball court, and several courtyards surrounded by houses on raised platforms. The precise dates of the structures are unknown, so they may or may not belong to the Second Intermediate Period. The ceramics and architecture strongly resemble the Chalchihuites culture of Zacatecas and seem to be derived from it.

In the Las Joyas phase considerable construction activity occurred. Ceramics were well developed, and trade wares included Lolandis Red Rim ware from the west coast. In Rio Tunal times the Chalchihuites culture sphere extended as far north as Zape, Durango. New construction activities slowed down at the Guadiana sites, but many structures were remodeled. The ceramics became less complex, but Guasave and other Sinaloa polychromes were imported from the west coast. Other artifacts include spindle whorls, elbow tobacco pipes, and various copper objects such as bells, needles, awls, rings, and pendants.

La Quemada, Zacatecas, is one of the most famous sites in northern Mexico. Extending from A.D. 400 to 1200 (with the major occupation taking place at A.D. 900–1000), the site is located on a partially fortified hill and was connected with smaller satellite communities by numerous long causeways. La Quemada itself, which seems to have been a ceremonial center without a substantial resident population, contained courtyards surrounded by buildings, steep-sided pyramid bases, causeways, terraces, colonnaded porticoes, and perhaps an I-shaped ball court. The masonry structures, built of tabular stone laid horizontally without mortar, were originally covered with stucco. This construction is not common in Mesoamerica, but structures of this type can be seen at Calixtlahuaca and Malinalco, Estado de México; Tzintzuntzan and Ihuatzio, Michoacán; and Ajacuba, Hidalgo. In all cases the structures probably postdate A.D. 1000. The significance of this is unclear, and the relationship between these sites and La Quemada is unresolved. At the end of its occupation La Quemada was burned, but we do not know if it was done by invaders, by the departing inhabitants, or even by later peoples who arrived after the community was abandoned.

Explorations at Casas Grandes, Chihuahua, by the Amerind Foundation have produced evidence of an interesting culture with a unique blend of Mesoamerican, American Southwestern, and Chichimec elements (Di Peso 1966). The site's long occupational history has been divided into three periods (Viejo, Medio, and Tardío), each with several phases. The Tardío period is the most important one for this discussion because there is evidence of strong Mesoamerican contacts. The Pacquime phase of the Tardío period saw a marginal southwestern village changed into a community of 5,000 people who lived in multistoried houses centered around plazas, and who built ceremonial structures and ball courts. Many trade goods from Mesoamerica and the southwestern United States have been identified, for example, ceramics, copper objects, and bird remains. Although La Quemada seems to have functioned as a major way station for trade between Mesoamerica and the Southwest, the archaeological remains seem more southwestern than Mesoamerican.

Coahuila

The archaeology of central and northern Coahuila provides examples of a Chichimec way of life essentially untouched by Mesoamerican influence. From the end of the Pleistocene until Colonial times, culture change was virtually absent. The people of Coahuila were nomadic collectors and hunters, with primary emphasis on wild plant foods (Taylor 1966). They occupied caves and rock shelters but spent most of their time in open campsites. Coahuilan technology emphasized fiber, wood, and stone, in order of importance. Organized political structures, elaborate religions, and social differentiation did not exist.

Although cultural stability was the rule, some change did occur. Indeed, there was a dynamic side to Chichimec culture history, as evidenced by the Jora and Mayran complexes after A.D. 1000. The Jora complex contained several new traits related in subsistence—arrow points, self-pointed wooden arrows, ceramics, and new types of food processing implements. Many of these items, however, probably diffused into Coahuila from Texas, and therefore do not represent Mesoamerican influences. The Mayran complex was a mortuary cult whose best-known remains have been found in Candelaria and Paila caves (Aveleyra Arroya de Anda, Maldonado-Koerdell, and Martínez del Río 1956). With the cadavers, which were wrapped in cotton textiles, a variety of unusual artifacts have been found. Mesoamerican influence cannot be detected in these materials either.

WEST MEXICO

Because northwest Mexico has not received the attention it deserves from archaeologists, the prehistory of the area is extremely difficult to reconstruct. For example, we do not have a complete record of human occupation for any portion of the area. Recent articles in the *Handbook of Middle American Indians* provide good regional summaries, but no attempt has been made to prepare a coherent overall picture of the area. In view of these deficiencies, the best approach seems to be an analysis of the few areas for which we do have adequate data. I will use a modified version of the "archaeological provinces" defined by Lister (1955) and incorporate data that have appeared since his publication. The provinces are (1) Sonora and Sinaloa, (2) Nayarit, Jalisco, and Colima, (3) Lake Chapala, (4) Lake Pátzcuaro, (5) Apatzingán, and (6) the Toluca Valley.

Sonora and Sinaloa

This province is a relatively long, narrow zone crossed by numerous river valleys containing short, rapidly running streams. General aridity increases to the northeast until the Sonoran Desert is reached.

A. E. Johnson (1966) has summarized the scant archaeological data on Sonora. According to his studies, Mesoamerican contacts and influences never reached this area, and all outside ties were with the southwestern United States—a fact that is indicated by the architecture, projectile points, ceramics, and food-grinding implements. The post–A.D. 1000 societies should probably be classified as marginal southwestern rather than peripheral Mesoamerican.

Although little archaeology has been done in Sinaloa since World War II, recent research in Durango, Mexico, has substantiated the early findings of Isabel T. Kelly (Kelley and Winters 1960, Meighan 1971).

The earliest known sites in this province belong to the Middle Horizon (Chametla being the only one that has been excavated [Kelly 1938]).

However, we believe that earlier remains must exist. The Tierra del Padre phase, which is contemporary with Tlalmimilolpa at Teotihuacán, is followed by the Baluarte phase, which correlates with Xolalpan and Metepec. Although neither of these phases has been dated at Chametla, cross dating with sites in Durango confirms their placement (Kelley and Winters 1960). Large architectural remains and other indicators of societal complexity are absent, but the ceramics indicate that Chametla was within the Mesoamerican sphere; however, there is no evidence of relationships with the Central Highlands.

Three Second Intermediate sites have been reported: the Lolandis, Acaponeta, and El Taste phases at Chametla (Kelly 1938); the Acaponeta and La Divisa phases at Culiacán (Kelly 1945a); and the Huatabampo and Guasave phases at Guasave (Ekholm 1942). The Aztatlán horizon, best known for its elaborate engraved and polychrome ceramics, was widespread at this time, with copper, silver, and gold objects apparently in abundance. The Aztatlán ceramics indicate relationships with the Mixteca-Puebla area, although some vessel forms seem more closely related to contemporary Maya pottery. The metallurgy may be related to the poorly understood inception and florescence of this craft in Michoacán and Guerrero at about this time. The total picture for the Second Intermediate period seems to be one of a regional florescence based on local indigenous events and processes, rather than on wholesale importation of cultural norms and techniques from the south. Ekholm (1942) has suggested a somewhat different reconstruction, placing greater emphasis on the Mixteca-Puebla contribution to Guasave-phase ceramics.

At Culiacán the Yebalito and La Quinta phases and the latter portion of the Guasave phase extend into the Late Horizon; it is questionable, however, whether a distinction should be made between the two periods in this area. Ethnohistorical materials compiled by Sauer and Brand (1932) indicate that the area had a dense population organized into numerous small states in the sixteenth century.

Nayarit, Jalisco, and Colima

Nayarit. A University of California, Los Angeles, project under the direction of C. W. Meighan conducted surveys in the southern lowlands and coastal region of Nayarit during the early 1960s and excavated the sites of Peñitas and Amapa. The project results have been summarized by

Bell (1971). Three phases were defined at Peñitas: Tamarindo (A.D. 200, duration unknown), Chala (A.D. 300–600), and Mitlán (A.D. 1050–1300). Central Mexican relationships are not evident in the materials recovered. At Amapa (located near the mouth of the Rio Santiago) two periods have been defined: Early (A.D. 250–700) and Late (A.D. 900–1520). Excavations at the site, which covers approximately one and one-half square kilometers and contained perhaps 200 mounds of various types, revealed a ceremonial complex, a ball court, a residential area, and a cemetery. Early Period pottery found in the ceremonial complex is similar to the Tierra del Padre material at Chametla, but not to that of Central Mexico. The Late Period materials include Aztatlán ceramics similar to those from Guasave, Plumbate, Mazapan trade figurines and lòcal imitations of them, and numerous copper objects. The I-shaped ball court, constructed during the Late Period, shares several architectural features with Tula ball courts.

The cultures of southern highland Nayarit are much better known from looted grave goods than from scientific archaeology. Virtually all the large hollow figurines and village models for which the area is famous lack archaeological provenience, although recent work by Furst (1965) and Bell (1971) has begun to relate them to a controlled archaeological framework. Las Cebollas tombs containing shell trumpets and pyrite-encrusted mirrors seem to belong to the Middle Horizon, and Furst (1966) sees strong ties between Teotihuacán and the Nayarit highlands.

Ixtlán del Río is the only highland site with major architecture. Stratigraphic excavations have not been conducted at Ixtlán, but Gifford's (1950) survey in the area led him to propose Early, Middle, and Late phases. The site itself seems to belong to the Middle and Late periods, which probably postdate A.D. 1000. A few Mazapan figurines represent the only sure ties with central Mexico, although some of the pottery Gifford uncovered appears similar to Tula types. Additional work is badly needed at this important site

Jalisco. None of the Jalisco sites have produced long sequences (Bell 1971: Chart 1). The Las Cuevas site and the San Sebastian and El Arenal tombs, all in the Magdalena Lake region near the Nayarit border, belong to the early part of the Middle Horizon, while several sites and phases in the Autlan-Tuxcacuesco area and the Magdalena Basin pertain to the Second Intermediate period. Kelly (1945b) illustrates several sherds and artifacts from the Autlan zone that are reminiscent of Tula types—Autlan Red-on-Brown, fragments of large-knobbed incensarios, and two Mazapan-like figurines. The same is true of the Tuxcacuesco materials. La Loma Red-on-Brown has Coyotlatelco-like designs, the Colima shadow-striped pottery is identical to Tula water-colored, and several Mazapan figurines are illustrated.

Colima. Colima archaeology is best known for its large anthropomorphic and zoomorphic figurines placed in tombs. The tomb offerings have been seriated into four ceramic complexes by Kelly (1944, 1948), but stratigraphic proof of the seriation is lacking (except for cross ties with excavated materials at Tuxcacuesco, Jalisco). Although Kelly's Ortices-Chanchopa phase probably belongs to the First Intermediate period, several of her phases (Armeria, Colima, and Periquillo) postdate A.D. 1000. Recent work by University of California, Los Angeles, crews at Morett near the Jalisco border has produced evidence of occupation from 200 B.C. to A.D. 800, but this material has not been published in detail. None of the Colima assemblages show relationships with central Mexico.

Lake Chapala

Two sites have been excavated and reported for the Lake Chapala area: Cojumatlan (Lister 1949) and Tizapan el Alto (Meighan and Foote 1968). At each site two occupation phases were defined. The combined sequence includes the Chapala (A.D. 600–900), Cojumatlan (A.D. 900–1100), and Tizapan (A.D. 1100–1250) phases. These chronological assignments are based on Meighan and Foote's reinterpretation of Lister's Cojumatlan report.

Clear evidence exists for relationships and communication between Cojumatlan-phase societies and Tula. Of the thirty Cojumatlan burials uncovered at Tizapan, most were in a seated position, which is generally unusual in Mesoamerica, but common at Tula. And, in addition to the numerous Mazapan-like figurines found in midden deposits, spindle whorls from the excavations are strikingly similar to those of Tula. Several pottery types are similar to Tula types: plain ware comals, Chapala Red-on-Brown, Chapala Red-Rim, a Tlaloc incensario, and perhaps others. Plumbate was not found at Tizapan but is present at Cojumatlan.

Meighan and Foote suggest that the Lerma-Santiago river system was the major route through which communications were maintained with central Mexico.

Lake Pátzcuaro

The Tarascan homeland is virtually unknown archaeologically, despite the Tarascans' successful defense of their territory against the Aztecs and their notable achievements in architecture, lapidary techniques, and metallurgy. Major excavations at Tzintzuntzan and Ihuatzio have been limited to clearing yacatas (temple bases incorporating both rectangular and circular buildings). An extremely tentative chronology proposed by Rubín de la Borbolla (1948) has not yet been improved. He defined three phases: Lacustre Inferior (late Middle Horizon?), Lacustre Medio (Second Intermediate), and Lacustre Superior (Late Horizon). During recent visits to the area, my students and I ascertained that both Tzintzuntzan and Ihuatzio have reasonably extensive occupation zones, but nothing is known of the community patterns. Historical records indicate and archaeology confirms the lack of peaceful interaction between the Tarascans and the Aztecs. However, strong ties seem to have existed between the Tarascans or their predecessors and Tula—a fact that is reflected in the Chac Mool sculptures at Tzintzuntzan and Ihuatzio, ceramic figurines, and tobacco pipes. The relationships may have been mediated through the Toluca Valley societies based at Malinalco and Calixtlahuaca.

Apatzingán

Apatzingán, located in the Rio Tepalcatepec drainage of lowland Michoacán, has been excavated by Kelly (1947) and surveyed by Goggin (1943), providing us with the bulk of the data on the area. Three Middle Horizon phases—Chumbicuaro, Delicias, and Apatzingán—have been defined, but the artifacts show no relationships with central Mexico.

The Tepetate and Chila phases belong to the Second Intermediate period in Apatzingán. Mazapan-like figurines are present but rare, and the common burial position is the flexed seated type found at Tizapan el Alto and at Tula. In general, central Mexican ties were tenuous, and relationships with the Lake Pátzcuaro area seem to have been stronger than those with the Basin.

The Toluca Valley

García Payón's (1956–57a, 1956–57b) excavations at Tecaxic-Calixtla-huaca and Malinalco produced data on Second Intermediate and Late Horizon architecture and ceramics. Hints of earlier occupations exist in both areas, but these occupations are poorly known; we do know, however, that Matlatzinca speakers occupied the Toluca Valley at the time of the Conquest. Both Tecaxic-Calixtlahuaca and Malinalco were subject to the Triple Alliance and were buffer states between it and the Tarascans (Barlow 1949).

Aztec trade ceramics have been found on both sites, but in surprisingly small quantities. The famous rock-cut temple at Malinalco was built between A.D. 1501 and 1515 by stone workers from Tenochtitlan under orders from Ahuitzotl and Motecuhzoma Xocoyotzin. The structure's possible dedication to the Military Orders of the Eagle and Tiger Knights may be a reflection of Tarascan military pressure on the empire's western frontier.

SUMMARY AND CONCLUSIONS

The relationships between Basin societies and their northern neighbors were constantly changing. We will review them here, period by period, emphasizing the major features.

The Lithic and Initial Ceramic Periods

The paucity of archaeological data forces us to see the early post-Pleistocene period as a time of cultural uniformity. Future research, however, should define significant regional differences based on the varying nature of available natural resources. The Basin probably had significantly larger game populations than the Tehuacán Valley—the Bajío, in fact, must have been a hunter's paradise, which undoubtedly influenced the nature of the individual societies. Gulf Coast populations may already have begun to exploit the abundant aquatic resources for which the area is famous. In addition, botanical and archaeological evidence suggests that maize was domesticated in the southern highlands and that its cultivation diffused into the Basin after a considerable time lag. The same is true of ceramics; while the origin of Mesoamerican ceramics is unresolved, present evidence indicates introduction into the Basin from the south. Ceramics and agriculture, then, probably diffused northward and westward from the Basin, although as this is written, Kelly (1970) reports early ceramics at Capacha, Colima (1450 B.C.). This confirms the antiquity of the potters' art in this area, and the vessels in question are not fumbling first attempts at ceramic manufacture. Many surprises may await us when we finally learn the complete history of Mesoamerican ceramics.

The Early Horizon

Olmec influence in the Basin is indisputable, but its nature has been interpreted in various ways. Following Flannery's (1968b) proposal for Oaxaca, I interpret the situation as one of economic exchange between local elites in several areas, without Olmec conquest, permanent Olmec settlements, or conscious missionization. I do not deny that Olmec societies were more highly developed and complex than their Basin contemporaries, nor do I think Olmec influence on Basin societies was negligible. The Olmecs obviously initiated enduring patterns in religious belief and practices, ways of validating rank and privilege, and interregional exchange. But they did not introduce urbanism, a characteristic trait of later Basin societies.

The First Intermediate Period

Basin societies seem to have turned in upon themselves during this crucial period. The only foreign relationships for which evidence exists are a few hints of ties to the northeast and the west. Thus, the organizational "quantum jump" from ranked to fully stratified urban societies must have resulted from local processes and events, not nebulous and ill-defined "foreign influences." To date, we have had only partial success in identifying these processes and events, because we have not fully understood what data are needed and how to collect and interpret them. This is not a criticism of the investigators working on this problem; in fact, Mesoamericanists are closer to understanding the nature of the "Urban Revolution" than are prehistorians working in most other parts of the world. It is precisely the advances made during the past two decades that have pushed us into unexplored methodological and theoretical territories. The next decade will undoubtedly be very fruitful for studies of the origins of Mesoamerican urbanism and state organizations.

Once Teotihuacán passed the urban threshold, it did not delay long in turning its interests outward—by Miccaotli times it had established connections with the most distant parts of the Maya world. Future investigations in north-central and west Mexico may give substance to presently vague indications of early Teotihuacán's influences on local societies. As it is, Teotihuacán's trade routes to the south seem to duplicate those established by the Olmecs, and I wonder if connections between the Basin and southern Mesoamerica before A.D. 100 were as insignificant as they seem at present.

The Middle Horizon

Teotihuacán seems to have achieved a dominance over Mesoamerica that was never again equaled. Virtually every region in Kirchhoff's (1943) sixteenth-century Mesoamerica—and some outside it—interacted with the Basin metropolis. Its relationships with the Maya area are obvious at Kaminaljuyú, Bilbao, Tikal, Uaxactun, and possibly Uxmal and Chichén Itzá. Ties between the Maya and Teotihuacán may have been so strong that relationships between the Maya and societies in northern Central America broke down for the first time in almost a millennium (Baudez 1970). Although the north Gulf Coast seems to be outside the interaction sphere, future work in the Pánuco drainage may uncover a site similar to Matacapan, Cerro de las Mesas, or Kaminaljuyú. Teotihuacán's relationships with distant societies were undoubtedly based on contacts between the Teotihuacán state bureaucracy and local elites, with minor influences on the lower social levels. The situation is somewhat similar to earlier Olmec influence on foreign societies, but Teotihuacán seems to have moved substantially larger quantities of goods than the Olmecs. Teotihuacán exerted true political control over the foreign societies, which was not true of the Olmecs.

Traditionally, the Middle Horizon has been characterized as a time of peace. But Sanders (1965), in view of new data from Teotihuacán, has recently criticized this characterization. However, I think both points of view contain an element of truth. Peace did reign within the Teotihuacán Empire because the city had sufficient economic and military strength to maintain it, a situation somewhat analogous to the Roman Empire. War came to the Basin only when Teotihuacán was unable to keep it away, the result being the final defeat that turned the city into an archaeological site. The factors and peoples behind Teotihuacán's downfall are still mysteries, but, if I correctly interpret the recent explorations as demonstrating a cultural decline after A.D. 700 (Marquina 1970), Tula-based Toltecs were not involved, nor was Cholula. Internal organizational problems may have weakened Teotihuacán to the point where it could not defend itself against invaders from several directions. Whatever happened, Teotihuacán's fall and its repercussions had a profound effect on populations to the east, north, and west. Migrations of hunters and collectors, marginal farmers, occupational specialists, and other people must have resulted, but the size and significance of these migrations is yet to be resolved.

The Second Intermediate Period

After A.D. 700, the focus of political power in western Mesoamerica shifted, for the first time in 1,000 years, to outside the Basin. Tula, Cholula, Xochicalco, and Tajín all attempted to assume Teotihuacán's mantle, but none were successful. There were too many powerful competitors, too many pretenders to the throne. Each eventually settled for a portion of the prize, but when none could hold onto it permanently, political power soon reverted to a Basin community. Tula, which is the only one of these four states relevant to this study, seems to have been the first central Mexican state to maintain relationships with the north Gulf Coast and with west Mexico. The nature of these relationships, however, must have varied considerably with time and place, and it is still possible to argue about which way the influences went. Until there is evidence to the contrary, I will assume that Tula was the dominant party in the relationships, although this does not necessarily mean that Tula politically controlled the distant areas; I doubt that it effectively integrated much more than the northern Basin, Hidalgo, the Bajío, and perhaps isolated areas in the Lerma-Santiago drainage. Its control to the east probably did not extend much beyond the crests of the Sierra Madre Oriental.

The Toltec trade goods found in many sites are different from those noted in Teotihuacán times. Such utilitarian goods as cooking and storage vessels are in evidence, in addition to ceremonial objects such as tobacco pipes, Mazapan figurines, and knobbed incensarios. Many of the objects may have been manufactured at places other than Tula. Tula Water-Colored (Blanco Levantado) ceramics have a long history in the Bajío, and they may or may not be Tula exports. Yet to be explored is Tula's possible role as a port of entry for eastern Mesoamerican goods, such as Plumbate pottery and perishable goods. Except for Plumbate, eastern Mesoamerican trade goods are virtually absent in west Mexico, but major centers (for example, Ixtlán del Río) have not been explored, and such goods may be restricted to these centers. It is interesting to note the lack of Toltec influence on the numerous western and northwestern Mexico polychrome ceramics. In fact, the only central Mexican influence on polychrome ceramics is the Mixteca-Puebla stylistic similarities with Aztatlán ceramics. Equally interesting is the apparent complete absence of west Mexican polychromes at Tula.

The Late Horizon

The Aztecs attempted to emulate the Teotihuacán pattern of expansion to the south and east, neglecting north and west Mexico. This was related in part to a general retraction of the northern Mesoamerican frontier and in part to the military expansion of the Tarascan state. Parts of the north Gulf Coast were conquered, and, if the Spaniards had not intervened, Nahua infiltration into the area might eventually have led to a duplication of the Second Intermediate period relationships.

The brittleness of the Aztec empire was apparent to the Spaniards, who successfully played Indian groups off against each other. I wonder how we would view the Aztec Empire if we had only archaeological data at our disposal. Conversely, could a group of foreign invaders have conquered the Teotihuacán Empire with equal ease 1,000 years earlier? I am not suggesting that this in fact happened, but only that the Teotihuacán and

Aztec political structures were probably very similar and that students of culture process and culture history must be constantly aware of the limitations imposed by their particular methodology and techniques.

NOTE

1. I wish to thank Jeffrey R. Parsons and William T. Sanders for discussing with me certain points covered in this chapter. I have profited from discussions with all members of the Santa Fe conference and with the personnel of the 1972 Field Season Crew of the University of Missouri Tula Archaeological Project. I am also in debt to the authors of regional syntheses published in the *Handbook of Middle American Indians* (vols. 4, 10, and 11). I particularly wish to thank J. Charles Kelley, who kindly spent part of a very busy day discussing the Zacatecas-Durango data with me. None of these individuals, however, are responsible for the opinions I express in this chapter.

12

The Internal Structure of Tenochtitlan[1]

EDWARD E. CALNEK

Department of Anthropology
University of Rochester

According to the traditional Aztec histories, Tenochtitlan was founded on a small island near the western shore of Lake Texcoco in the Basin of Mexico in A.D. 1325.[2] After achieving political independence for the first time in about 1427, it commenced a vigorous career of military expansion that continued until the Spanish invasion in 1519. The entire process of its urban development, therefore, spanned slightly less than two centuries. At the end of this period Tenochtitlan was unquestionably the largest and most highly urbanized city in the New World. It was also the political center of an empire that extended from the Gulf Coast to the Pacific, and southward, at some points, to the modern frontier between Mexico and Guatemala.

The internal political history of the Aztec state is complicated by the existence of a second settlement, Tlatelolco, founded by a dissident faction on another island a short distance to the north in A.D. 1337. Since Tlatelolco was conquered and annexed by its more powerful sister-city in 1473, it is discussed here as though it were a simple subdivision of Tenochtitlan. Certain anomalies resulting from this division are discussed below. It should be kept in mind, nonetheless, that there were important differences in the growth patterns of each city. Commerce played a key role in the early development of Tlatelolco, while other types of occupational specialization may have been more highly elaborated in Tenochtitlan. A detailed examination of similarities and differences would, however, carry us far beyond the scope of this chapter.[3]

Reliable quantitative evidence relating to urban growth rates is not available. The historical sources suggest moderate but continuous increases in Tenochtitlan's urban population throughout the preimperial period—in part stimulated by state initiatives designed to induce outsiders to settle and marry within the city (Durán 1951, vol. I:60–61). When Chimalpopoca assumed the throne in 1415, the city had begun to take on a more conventionally urban aspect, as the surrounding marshlands were converted to residential space, and well-built houses of stone and adobe replaced the *chozas* (huts) of earlier times (Durán 1951, vol. I:62). The wealth and prestige that resulted from even the early military successes during the Imperial period evidently began to attract immigrants in significantly larger numbers. During the reign of Motecuhzoma Ilhuicamina (1440–67), vigorous state intervention was required to suppress internal disorders and to reorganize a population that included numerous foreigners, as well as descendants of the city's founders (Durán 1951, vol. I:213–14). By 1519 the area of more or less continuous urban habitation can be estimated at between 12 and 15 square kilometers, and the total population as in the vicinity of 150,000 to 200,000 inhabitants (Calnek 1970, 1972a).

Information summarized elsewhere (Calnek 1972b) suggests that the transition from an essentially rural to a highly urbanized economic base was achieved after A.D. 1385, and that it was closely linked to rapid demographic growth—achieved in large part by absorbing immigrants into the urban labor force. At the present time, it is not possible to determine whether the still higher growth rates sustained during the Imperialist period (following 1427) occurred in spurts or whether they were more or less continuous up to the time of the Spanish Conquest. Whatever the answers to these and related questions, it is clear that Tenochtitlan's population multiplied several times over during the two centuries of its existence, and that population growth was associated with a series of important changes in the city's internal structure over time.

288

The Internal Structure of Tenochtitlan

Before attempting to describe Tenochtitlan's internal organization at the time of the Conquest, it is useful to consider several characteristics of population growth that have not been sufficiently emphasized by previous investigators. The existence of a large immigrant population from comparatively early times has already been noted. This included organized craft groups such as the lapidaries, who originated in Xochimilco but retained important ritual links to their homeland even though they appear to have been wholly absorbed into the politico-administrative system of the host city (Sahagún 1950–69, Bk. 9:80, Torquemada 1723, vol. II: 60). Acosta Saignés (1945:39–41) suggests that the *pochteca* (merchants) were linked ethnically to populations residing near the Gulf Coast, while Sahagún's informants date their appearance to the reign of Cuacuauhpitzauac of Tlatelolco—that is, the late fourteenth or early fifteenth century (1950–69, Bk. 9:1). The manuscript painters (*tlacuiloque*) were probably descendants of the Tlailotlaca, a Mixtecan group that arrived in the Basin of Mexico in the fourteenth century and then dispersed to centers where their particular skills were needed and wanted (Robertson 1959:13, 138–39.

Other sources of immigration included war refugees. A large group from Huexotzinco, for example, settled temporarily in Tenochtitlan when their homeland was devastated by the Tlaxcallans (they returned when peace was restored between the two former allies) (Durán 1951, vol. I: 476–77, Tezozomoc 1944:460–70). The Cuauhquecholteca—also victims of Tlaxcallan attacks—remained in the city, where many of them owned houses near the great market of Tlatelolco (Sahagún 1950–69, Bk. 12: 103). Population movements of this type were by no means unusual, nor was Tenochtitlan-Tlatelolco the sole beneficiary of political disruptions in other city-states. The Aztecs themselves, for example, had dispersed widely after a military defeat at Chapultepec in the late thirteenth century. A large group of refugees settled at Colhuacan, where they immediately began to intermarry and mingle with the local population (García Icazbalceta 1941:225–26, Durán 1951, vol. I:33, Torquemada 1723, vol. I:91). Of these refugees a good many apparently remained in Colhuacan, even after the founding of Tenochtitlan, since several barrios calling themselves Mexica later moved from Colhuacan to Texcoco (Ixtlilxochitl 1952, vol. I:295, vol. II:74).

When Colhuacan was totally abandoned in the late fourteenth century, a part of its population settled in one of the southeastern districts of Tenochtitlan (García Icazbalceta 1941:228). Others, as noted above, went to Texcoco, to Cuauhtitlan (Velázquez 1945:29 ff.), and doubtless to many other localities. On the eve of their great rebellion against Azcapotzalco in 1426 or 1427, the Aztecs are said to have seriously considered moving en masse to that city, where their presence would scarcely be noted because of its great size—or so the Tenochcan leaders thought (Durán 1951, vol. I:70, Tezozomoc 1944:27).

From these and similar references, it is clear that the city-states that began to emerge during the thirteenth and fourteenth centuries were heterogeneous with respect to ethnic composition and highly unstable insofar as political loyalties were concerned. Colhuacan played a key role in defeating the Aztecs at Chapultepec, for example, but within a few years, Aztec warriors were fighting side-by-side with their former enemies against the armies of Xochimilco (Dibble 1963:31 ff.). Too, there is no indication that Mexica barrios in Texcoco retained sentiments of political solidarity with their cousins in Tenochtitlan. All in all, then, the ease with which political loyalties could be manipulated and transferred is a background factor of major importance in explaining the rapidity with which individual city-states grew and declined throughout the chaotic era that preceded Tenochtitlan's rise as an imperial power.

It must be remembered, however, that this was also a period characterized by generally rising populations and the gradual intensification of land use throughout the Basin of Mexico. As long as cultivable land was available, it was relatively easy to move large groups from one place to another. But by the mid fifteenth century, this was no longer the case, and we observe instead the opposite process—the recolonization of temporarily abandoned regions and the construction of relatively large-scale hydraulic systems designed to improve agricultural productivity (Palerm 1955, Armillas 1971, Calnek 1972b). The situation at Tenochtitlan-Tlatelolco differed from that elsewhere mainly in the degree to which the labor force consisted of full-time occupational specialists rather than peasant farmers. Since the ability to absorb immigrants depended on the availability of jobs rather than land, it is not surprising that Tenochtitlan had outstripped even its most powerful rivals (for example, Texcoco) by the end of the fifteenth century.

Viewed from this standpoint, Tenochtitlan and Tlatelolco may already have been more *cosmopolitan* in structure and outlook than any of their neighbors at the beginning of the Imperial Period. The emphasis on trade and craft production required the development of political strategies aimed at securing markets and sources of raw material, for example, rather than the planning and execution of large-scale irrigation systems, as was the case at Texcoco (Palerm and Wolf 1954–55).[4]

The cosmopolitan quality of urban life was further enhanced by the presence of literally thousands of visitors who came to buy and sell in the market (Conquistador Anónimo 1941:43, Cortés 1963:72), to deliver tributes, and to perform labor services, as well as for a great variety of other purposes. In some cases large groups had to be accommodated for periods of days or even weeks. Visiting dignitaries received the hospitality of the royal court, where they were supported with revenues provided by the king's personal estates (Carrasco 1967:149, Durán 1951, vol. I:101). The rulers of many subject states, along with their personal retinues, were required to spend a part of each year at the imperial court, and at least some of these rulers maintained personal residences in Tenochtitlan (Cortés 1963:75, Díaz del Castillo 1960:176, Gómara 1943, vol. I:228. The pueblo of Cuitlatenamic either owned a house in Tenochtitlan or maintained a permanent relationship with an Aztec household where its men stayed when they brought tributes or had other business there (AGN Tierras, vol. 34, exp. 4, fols. 2, 32, 82). Casual visitors could purchase cooked foods at the urban markets and stay overnight in hostels scattered throughout the city (Díaz del Castillo 1960:159, Anglerius 1912, vol. II:109).

There is, in short, substantial evidence for fluidity and movement between cities and other localities in the Basin, ranging from permanent immigration to brief visits. Although the internal organization of cities is necessarily based on the permanent resident population, it is evident that Tenochtitlan, from comparatively early times, had developed sufficient internal flexibility not only to integrate a heavy flow of outsiders who intended to remain, but also to accommodate the large transient populations that had become a virtually permanent feature of urban life.

These and related points require a more detailed examination than can be attempted in this chapter. They are emphasized here only to suggest aspects of the quality and complexity of urban life at Tenochtitlan which do not emerge with any clarity from analytic studies of groups defined in terms of territory, kinship, occupation, and other types of relatively permanent affiliation.

In the remainder of this chapter, I will attempt to define the principal types of permanent social groupings that can be identified from descriptions of the city as it existed at the time of the Conquest, and that can also be linked to potentially identifiable architectural markers. This is, of course, only one of a variety of procedures that might be adopted to organize data relating to Tenochtitlan's social organization. It is adopted here with the intent of clarifying the relationship between social structure and settlement pattern, thereby facilitating comparisons between the Aztec capital and other early cities, such as Teotihuacán, for which there is little or no direct historical evidence.

The most serious difficulty resulting from this procedure is that good physical descriptions are available for only a small number of the more monumental types of public buildings and, because they were the subject of frequent lawsuits in the Colonial Period, a few of the simpler types of domestic architecture (Calnek 1972a). It is frequently possible to link groups or activities to definitely named structures mentioned in the chronicles, but we lack sufficiently precise information to permit definitive identifications, even if an example were to be encountered in archaeological context. At the present time, archaeological evidence relating to urban settlement pattern and architecture is extremely limited.[5] The justification for this obviously imprecise procedure is, quite simply, that there appears to be no other workable alternative, if our objective is to begin a comparative study of ancient Mesoamerican cities.

It is convenient to begin by examining the principal territorial divisions of the city (Map 20), because they can be described with considerable precision on the basis of written documents and colonial period maps. The largest unit—the city (*hueialtepetl*)—originally consisted of two autonomous states: Tenochtitlan and Tlatelolco. Both were founded at about the same time, and both were closely linked by geographic proximity, a common history before their foundation, and a strong sense of cultural and ethnic identity. Both groups regarded themselves as Mexica, maintaining an exceptionally close ceremonial and economic relationship both before and after the annexation of Tlatelolco by its more powerful sister-city in 1473 (see, for example, Durán 1951, Tezozomoc 1944, Toscano, Berlin, and Barlow 1948). The fact that both cities originated and developed as separate political units is reflected in the duplication of large, walled ceremonial precincts, associated with a *tecpan* (administrative palace) and a market in both cities. Together, these constituted a monu-

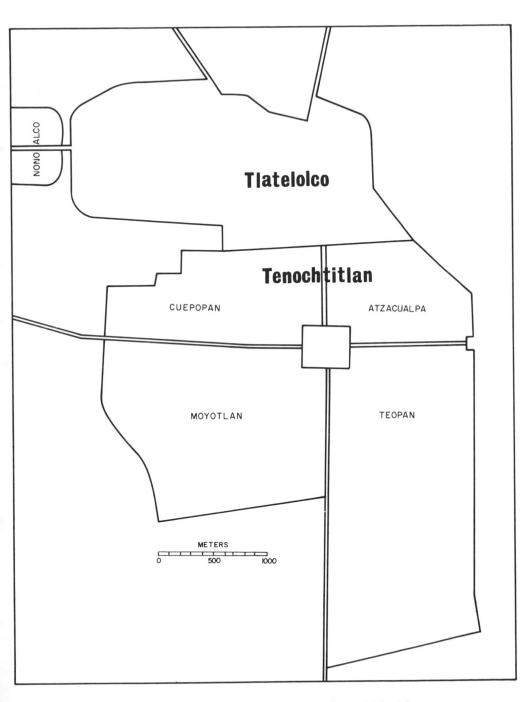

MAP 20. Map showing the relative locations of Tenochtitlan and Tlatelolco and the four Great Quarters of Tenochtitlan.

mental and, in principle, easily identifiable architectural complex that functioned as the focal point of government, religion, and economic life.

At Tenochtitlan (and probably at Tlatelolco, although good descriptions of the *tecpan* there are not available), there was a strict segregation of the architectural components associated with each branch of civic organization. The ceremonial precincts, which were walled in, included temples dedicated to the most important deities, as well as residential complexes occupied by members of well-organized temple communities (Durán 1951, vol. I:82–83). The precinct, in turn, was sharply differentiated from the palace, which functioned as the seat of secular government. The *tecpan*, in common with all other households in the city, included a personal shrine of the ruler and his household but otherwise lacked definable architectural characteristics relating to the state religion. It corresponded, therefore, to the predominantly secular character of kingship and civil administration, as described by both the Aztec and the Spanish chronicles. Although there are repeated references to the personal divinity of the king (Durán 1951, vol. I:162, 292, 421), it is notable that there were the barest beginnings of organized cult activities devoted to the ruler during his lifetime or after his death.

The physical differentiation of sacred and secular localities was partially bridged by the fact that the king and other noblemen were also high priests (Durán 1951, vol. I:196; Ixtlilxochitl 1952, vol. II:305–6). Explicitly ecclesiastical functions, however, were performed at temples and sacred localities outside the *tecpan*, and were marked by the adoption of entirely different personal regalia in each setting (Durán 1951, vol. I:196). In short, the duality of roles linked the palace to the temple, but within carefully organized and sharply differentiated social and architectural contexts. The king, for example, worshiped privately at the Tlillancalco ("House of Darkness"). He assumed the role of high priest mainly when the ceremonies were visible to the public at large. Otherwise, the day-to-day routines of ritual life were entrusted to a full-time priesthood, which appears to have exercised relatively little influence over governmental affairs.

The generally greater importance of governmental officials, who were titled noblemen of the highest rank, is most effectively demonstrated by Durán (1951, vol. II:124–25), who observes that men who had already demonstrated their probity, personal worth, and piety within the priesthood could be promoted to offices of great honor and authority within the state ("los sacauan a dignidades y cargos honrrossos en las republicas"). The ceremonial precinct, therefore, was symbolically identified with the city and the state. Nonetheless, it was clearly subordinate to the palace insofar as the distribution of political and even ecclesiastical authority was concerned.

This type of organization is evidently reflected in the greater architectural prominence and independence of the *tecpan* with respect to the sacred precinct, and possibly in the closed-in character of the latter, as compared with Teotihuacán. Large, complex, and even luxurious residential quarters adjoin religious structures at Teotihuacán, but they are clearly subordinated to an architectural design that emphasizes the temple pyramids of the "Street of the Dead" as the dominant component. No palace thus far identified at Teotihuacán approaches the size and independence of Motecuhzoma's palace, as described by such early chroniclers as Cortés (1963:77–79). This structure occupied an area of about 2.4 hectares—approximately double the combined areas of three closely related residential complexes adjoining the Temple of Quetzalcoatl in the Ciudadela at Teotihuacán (R. Millon, personal communication). The secular component of the urban center also included large palaces formerly occupied by Axayacatl, the father of Motecuhzoma Xocoyotzin, and by the Cihuacoatl—a dignitary whose rank was second only to that of the king himself (see Marquina 1960:Lam.2).

In addition, while the great temples occupied the highest rank within the inventory of religious structures of the city as a whole, they did not stand at the apex of a hierarchically organized system of temple communities. The individual temples located in the ceremonial precinct outranked those associated with the great quarters and the barrios (see below), but in this case rank order did not correspond to a rigidly organized chain of command. The palace occupied by a reigning monarch, in contrast, included numerous functionally differentiated halls and patios —each concerned with clearly defined administrative, military, or judicial functions, which ultimately engaged much wider groups by the delegation of authority through officials of progressively lower rank (Sahagún 1950– 69, Bk. 8:41–45, Durán 1951, vol. II:161–66). The barrio headmen, for example, assembled each day at the *calpixcalli*, where they awaited orders from the king or other high officials, and then transmitted them to lower officials who supervised their execution (Durán 1951, vol. I:323–24, vol. II:165, Torquemada 1723, vol. II:544–45). Separate courts existed to hear cases brought by noblemen or commoners. The judges controlled a staff of lower officials who maintained order, made arrests, recorded decisions, and carried them out (Motolinía 1903:303–12, Sahagún 1950–69, Bk. 8:41–42, Torquemada 1723, vol. II:351–53). The great military councils deliberated at the palace: thereafter, the army was mobilized by great quarters and then by barrios, by officers whose rank was linked to each level of the military chain of command (Sahagún 1950–69, Bk. 8:51, Tezozomoc 1944:273, 284, 403, 437).

Tenochtitlan (but not Tlatelolco) was divided into four great quarters, marked off by four avenues that extended in the cardinal directions from the gates of the ceremonial precinct (see Map 20). A large temple or temple complex was located in each of the great quarters, but nothing whatever is known of their actual size or architectural character (Códice Franciscano 1941:6). Tezozomoc mentions structures called *huehuecallis* (1944:399), occupied by officials described as the absolute lords (*señores absolutes*) or chiefs (*caudilles*) of the quarters (1944:284, 315–16, 399–400, 437). The *huehuecallis* may have adjoined the temples and plazas associated with the great quarters to replicate, on a smaller scale, the pattern already described for the urban center.

In late pre-Hispanic and early colonial texts, the great quarters were subdivided into barrios called *tlaxillacallis*. The *tlaxillacallis* bore the same names as were employed to identify units called calpullis. An examination of the contexts in which each term occurs in the Sahagún texts suggests that *calpulli* referred to a certain kind of corporate, localized social group, while *tlaxillacalli* was most frequently employed as a locational reference.[6] It would appear, consequently, that individuals were members of a named calpulli, but they resided in a *tlaxillacalli* or barrio bearing the same name. Although it is impossible to summarize the full range of documentary source materials regarding this question, it is likely that calpulli membership was closely related to occupation and to personal membership in certain types of ritual groups (Monzón 1949:47–51).

The territorial framework provided by the *tlaxillacalli* may have been exploited as a primary component for the internal administrative organization of the Aztec state. That the two types of affiliation did not result in entirely coterminous social groups is at least suggested by Durán's reference to the possibility that marriages could occur between members of different barrios (1951, vol. II:228–29), and as well as by the occurrence of several cases of uxorilocal residence in early colonial archival texts.

Thus, according to our literature, a certain *platero* (goldsmith or silversmith), who resided with his wife's family in the barrio named Zacatlan in the great quarter of Atzacualpa, acknowledged the authority of the lords (*principales*) of the *plateros'* guild (which was centered in the barrio of Yopico in Moyotlan) up to the time of his death in 1543. He himself employed an apprentice from Copolco in Cuepopan, who appears as a craftsman in his own right at a later date (AGN Tierras, vol. 30, exp. 1, fols. 14–16, 64). Although little more than two decades had elapsed since the Conquest, there is no indication that this arrangement was considered unusual.

The barrios—conceived as territorial units—were marked by a structure that housed the patron deities of the group (Durán 1951, vol. II:148, Sahagún 1950–69, Bk. 2:16, 39). This structure was evidently a part of a larger complex that also included a *telpochcalli* (young men's house) (Sahagún 1950–69, Bk. 3:58, Durán 1951, vol. I:216–17), and in most or all cases, a plaza or market (Cortés 1963:72, Gómara 1943, vol. I:236). The architectural characteristics of these units cannot be adequately defined at present, but they should have formed a distinctive type of complex, which could be easily distinguished from those marking the great quarters and the city in overall scale. The calpulli temple, as illustrated by Sahagún (1950–69, Bk. 2:Fig. 51), does not seem to have been a large pyramid-temple, but is shown as an almost houselike structure, constructed over a low, stepped platform; it was within a small, walled enclosure that included other buildings as well. In addition to providing the locus for public and private rituals dedicated to local deities, the temple was also the meeting place for barrio elders and the focal point for large ceremonials organized by occupationally specialized groups (see Sahagún 1950–69, Bks. 2, 3, 9). It provided, in short, a kind of civic center in relation to which the social identities of the greater part of the urban population were most immediately expressed, and, additionally, where a great variety of activities essential to the urban neighborhoods were conducted.

Although each barrio was divided into groups of houses or households for administrative purposes (Durán 1951, vol. I:323–24), there are no references to distinctive architectural features occupying an intermediate position between the calpulli center and the individual residential sites. Domestic architecture represents an entirely distinct level of organization, directly below the *tlaxillacalli*. In this chapter I will merely sketch out a few of domestic architecture's salient characteristics and their relation to the internal organization of household groups—primarily because of the great importance of these data for comparison with, and interpretation of, settlement patterns at Teotihuacán and other earlier cities. Fortunately, there is a good deal of detailed archival evidence relating to residential sites and to household organization, including genealogies and census data that, in some cases, can be followed over periods ranging up to five or six generations—that is, over time periods long enough to yield important insights into developmental cycles at the level of the elementary household or domestic group.

A number of typical residential sites at Tenochtitlan have been illustrated in Fig. 16. All have been drawn to the same scale from early ground plans or written descriptions that include the dimensions of basic site components. Residential sites characteristically took the form of walled compounds that enclosed a number of separately entered dwelling units and faced inward on an open patio space. Each compound was normally occupied by a bilateral joint family—most frequently, a group consisting of an elderly couple, their married children (including daughters, although virilocal residence was most common), and grandchildren, or some derivative unit at later stages in the normal cycle of family development. Each married couple occupied a single one- or two-room dwelling or, in some cases, a single floor within a two-story house. If sufficient space were available, a new dwelling might be constructed to accommodate a child at the time of his or her marriage. There are also cases where childless couples invited a nephew or other close kinsman to occupy a vacant house at their site.

Conversely, corporate family organization appears to have been successful only when the joint family was based on parents and children, siblings, or first cousins. We know of several cases in which the death of the last male in a generation of siblings or first cousins was followed by a dispute and the physical subdivision of the original site. An interesting result of this process was that households occupying only a fraction of what had been much larger sites frequently became as large as those existing before the division, and this in the space of a generation or two. Very small sites, which are likely to have resulted from this type of subdivision, appear most frequently toward the center of the city—a fact that possesses considerable demographic interest if we observe that the depth of occupation there is likely to have been four or more generations, as

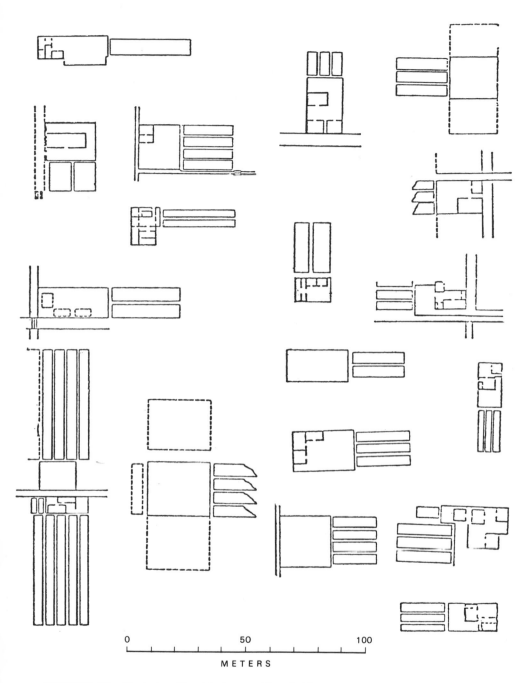

0   50   100

M E T E R S

FIGURE 16. Typical residential sites at Tenochtitlan.

against the two or three generations that would be more probable in peripherally located districts.

The Tenochtitlan household compound most closely resembles the individual apartments within the Teotihuacán apartment compounds in scale (see R. Millon 1970b:1079–80), but it was an architecturally free unit, in the sense that each compound at Tenochtitlan enjoyed direct access to streets and canals and was related to neighboring sites mainly by physical juxtaposition, rather than by assimilation to large unitary structures of the Teotihuacán type. This, in turn, may reflect a greater freedom in the organization of productive activities and interpersonal or interhousehold bonds, as well as greater possibilities for upward mobility based on wealth or personal achievement than was characteristic of Teotihuacán society. Even commoners could achieve high rank through military service or the acquisition of great personal wealth (Durán 1951, vol. I:239 ff., vol. II:124, 164–65, Sahagún 1950–69, Bk. 9). The architectural segregation of relatively small residential compounds permitted the public display of status markers—most commonly architectural ornamentation—to distinguish individual compounds from even their immediate neighbors (Tezozomoc 1944:144).

The organization of residential neighborhoods in Tlatelolco was essentially the same as in Tenochtitlan, but the higher-level administrative divisions followed a different pattern. The quadriform layout, as already noted, was absent in Tlatelolco. Instead, there were fifteen to twenty *barrios grandes*, each subdivided into a number of *barrios menores*. San Martin Atezcapan, for example, included the *barrios menores* named San Martin Tlilhuacan, Pochtlan-Telpochcaltitlan, Zacatlan, and others. Early archival texts designate both units with the term *tlaxillacalli*, and administrative functionaries at both levels as *tlaxillacaleque*. Unfortunately, I know of no archival materials in which the term *calpulli* occurs, with the result that the articulation between the two kinds of units cannot be established at the present time. Similarly, we lack precise information that would clarify the relation between each of these divisions and architectural markers of the type described above for Tenochtitlan. That the *barrios grandes* included a large temple complex is suggested by the symmetrical arrangement of colonial period churches in relation to the ceremonial precinct of Tlatelolco—a point first noticed by Barlow (1947). It is highly probable that Barlow was correct, but the point as yet lacks direct archaeological or historical verification.

300

The Internal Structure of Tenochtitlan

The quality of the information available for a study of Tlatelolco's internal organization is, in general, greatly inferior to that which exists for Tenochtitlan. It is highly probable that the large and small barrios of Tlatelolco were integrated to a chain-of-command structure culminating in the local *tecpan*, and ultimately in the palace at Tenochtítlan—at least following Tlatelolco's conquest in 1473. After 1473 the monarchy at Tlatelolco was abolished and replaced with a system of military governors (*cuauhtlatoani*) appointed by the ruler of Tenochtitlan (see, for example, Sahagún 1950–69, Bk. 9:2).

In any event, it would be relatively easy to conclude from the architectural and settlement pattern evidence that what might be called "Greater Tenochtitlan" incorporated two major subdivisions, with the internal structures of each differing in significant respects. It might, on the other hand, be extremely difficult to determine the precise political relationship between the two foci of political and religious organization at the time of the Spanish Conquest. Tangible indications of Tlatelolco's subordination are not clearly represented in the material summarized to this point, and one might easily conclude that we are dealing with a dual system, established early in the history of the city and maintained unchanged throughout its subsequent development.

Whatever the answers to these and similar questions, it is evident that a clear understanding of the urbanization process and its consequences for the development of particular types of internal structure requires that we exploit every available source of archaeological and ethnohistorical information. The advantages of working from historical texts, as compared with purely archaeological inference, are virtually self-evident in the case of Tenochtitlan-Tlatelolco. The disadvantages resulting from the scarcity of archaeological information are relatively minor as compared with the opposite situation as it exists at Teotihuacán. In the case of Tenochtitlan, for example, it is not necessary to develop complex procedures designed to clarify the nature of social groups in residence in particular types of residential structures. In a substantial number of cases, the question is answered by documents that give us the names and genealogies of individual household members.

Although no attempt has been made in this chapter to make a detailed survey of the similarities and contrasts in settlement pattern and social organization at Tenochtitlan and Teotihuacán, enough has been said to show that a comparison of the physical layouts of the two cities can be illuminating when interpreted in the light of relevant historical information. Further work in this direction must, of course, await not only the completion of research relating to Tenochtitlan, Teotihuacán, and other large Mesoamerican cities, but also fuller publication of the results than has been possible up to the present time.

NOTES

1. This is a substantially revised and expanded version of a paper entitled "The Internal Structure of Cities in America: The Case of Tenochtitlan" presented at the Thirty-Ninth International Congress of Americanists in Lima, Peru, in 1970. I am indebted to René and Clara Millon for valuable comments on the earlier version. The archival investigations cited here were supported by research grants from the National Science Foundation and the University of Rochester.

2. The interpretation of fourteenth-century dates as expressed in the Aztec calendar system remains uncertain. The traditional chronology, in which the year 2 Calli is equated to A.D. 1325, is employed in this chapter and is valid for all fifteenth- and sixteenth-century dates. Fourteenth-century dates, however, may be too early by as much as twenty to forty years. See Kirchhoff (1950), Jiménez Moreno (1954–55), and Caso (1967) for more detailed discussions of this problem.

3. Archival evidence that I have obtained but have not yet adequately studied may permit a more detailed description of Tlatelolco's internal structure at a later time.

4. It is worth noting that the larger hydraulic enterprises undertaken by the Aztecs were carried out under the direction of specialists from Texcoco. This suggests a lack of both interest and experience on the part of the Aztecs.

5. Archaeological evidence obtained during the excavations at the Plaza de las Tres Culturas in Tlatelolco and the recent Metro constructions may contribute significantly to our knowledge, but the data have not yet been analyzed or published in sufficient detail.

6. See Carrasco (1971:364) for a somewhat different interpretation.

References

ABECEDARIO
1905   *See* Paso y Troncoso 1905a.

ACOSTA, JORGE R.
1957   "Interpretación de algunos de los datos obtenidos en Tula relativos a la época Tolteca," *Revista Mexicana de Estudios Antropológicos* 14(2):75–110.
1964   *El palacio del Quetzalpapalotl*, Memorias del Instituto Nacional de Antropología e Historia, no. 10 (Mexico City).

ACOSTA SAIGNÉS, MIGUEL
1945   "Los Pochteca: ubicación de los mercaderes en la estructura social Tenocha," *Acta Antropológica*, época I, vol. 1, no. 1 (Mexico City: Sociedad de Alumnos, Escuela Nacional de Antropología e Historia).

ADAMS, ROBERT M.
1966   *The Evolution of Urban Society* (Chicago: Aldine Publishing Co.).
1972a "Demography and the 'Urban Revolution' in Lowland Mesopotamia," in *Population Growth: Anthropological Implications*, ed. Brian Spooner (Cambridge, Mass.: M.I.T. Press), pp. 60–63.
1972b "Patterns of Urbanization in Southern Mesopotamia," in *Man, Settlement and Urbanism*, ed. Peter J. Ucko, Ruth Tringham, and G. W. Dimbleby (London: Duckworth & Co.), pp. 735–49.

ADAMS, ROBERT M. AND HANS J. NISSEN
1972   *The Uruk Countryside* (Chicago: University of Chicago Press).

ALLAN, WILLIAM
1965   *The African Husbandman* (New York: Barnes and Noble).

ANDREWS, E. WYLLYS IV
1965   *Dzibilchaltún, Yucatán, Mexico: Map of the Central Area* (New Orleans: Middle American Research Institute, Tulane University).
1968   "Dzibilchaltún: a Northern Maya Metropolis," *Archaeology* 21(1):36–47.

ANGLERIUS, PETRUS MARTYR (PIETRO MARTIRE D'ANGHIERA)
1912   *De Orbe Novo: The Eight Decades of Peter Martyr d'Anghiera*, trans, and ed. Francis A. MacNutt, 2 vols. (New York and London: G. P. Putnam).

303

ANGULO VILLASEÑOR, JORGE
1963 "Teotihuacán tiene un juego de pelota," *Siempre*, no. 526, July 24.
1964 "Teotihuacán: un autoretrato cultural" (Master's thesis, Escuela Nacional de Antropología e Historia, Mexico City).

ARCHIVO GENERAL DE LA NACIÓN (AGN)
n.d. Unpublished manuscripts: cited by *ramo*, *parte*, and *expediente* (Mexico City).

ARMILLAS, PEDRO
1948 "A Sequence of Cultural Development in Meso-America," in A *Reappraisal of Peruvian Archaeology*, ed. Wendell C. Bennett, Memoirs of the Society for American Archaeology, vol. 13, no. 4 (Menasha, Wisconsin: Society for American Archaeology), pp. 105–11.
1949 "Notas sobre los sistemas de cultivo en Mesoamérica," in *Anales del Instituto Nacional de Antropología e Historia*, vol. 3 (Mexico City: Instituto Nacional de Antropología e Historia), pp. 85–113.
1950 "Teotihuacán, Tula y los Toltecas," *Runa* 3(1–2):37–70.
1951 "Tecnología, formaciones socio-económicas y religión en Mesoamérica," in *The Civilizations of Ancient America*, Twenty-Ninth International Congress of Americanists, ed. Sol Tax (Chicago: University of Chicago Press), pp. 19–30.
1964 "Northern Mesoamerica," in *Prehistoric Man in the New World*, ed. Jesse D. Jennings and Edward Norbeck (Chicago: University of Chicago Press), pp. 291–329.
1971 "Gardens in Swamps," *Science* 174(4010):653–61.

ARMILLAS, PEDRO, ÁNGEL PALERM, AND ERIC R. WOLF
1956 "A Small Irrigation System in the Valley of Teotihuacán," *American Antiquity* 21(4):296–99.

ARNOLD, ROSEMARY
1957 "A Port of Trade: Whyda on the Guinea Coast," in *Trade and Market in the Early Empires*, ed. Karl Polanyi, Conrad M. Arensberg, and Harry W. Pearson (Glencoe, Ill.: Free Press), pp. 154–76.

AVELEYRA ARROYO DE ANDA, LUIS
1963a *La estela Teotihuacana de La Ventilla*, Cuadernos Museo Nacional de Antropología no. 1 (Mexico City: Instituto Nacional de Antropología e Historia).
1963b "An Extraordinary Composite Stela from Teotihuacán," *American Antiquity* 29(2):235–37.

AVELEYRA ARROYO DE ANDA, LUIS, MANUEL MALDONADO-KOERDELL, AND PABLO MARTÍNEZ DEL RÍO
1956 *Cueva de la Candelaria*, Memorias del Instituto Nacional de Antropología e Historia, vol. 5 (Mexico City: Instituto Nacional de Antropología e Historia).

BAKER, H. G.
1965 *Plants and Civilization* (Belmont, Calif.: Wadsworth Publishing Co.).

BARBA DE PIÑA CHAN, BEATRIZ
1956 *Tlapacoya: un sitio preclásico de transición*, Acta Antropológica, época 2, vol. 1, no. 1 (Mexico City: Sociedad de Alumnos, Escuela Nacional de Antropología e Historia).

BARBOUR, WARREN
1970 "Pregnant Figurines and Their Association at Teotihuacán," paper presented at the Thirty-Fifth Annual Meeting of the Society for American Archaeology, Mexico City.

References

BARLOW, ROBERT H.
1947   "Las ocho ermitas de Santiago Tlatelolco," *Memorias de la Academia Mexicana de la Historia*, vol. 6, pp. 183–88.
1949   *The Extent of the Empire of the Culhua Mexica*, Ibero-Americana no. 28 (Berkeley: University of California Press).

BARRAU, JACQUES
1961   *Subsistence Agriculture in Polynesia and Micronesia*, Bernice P. Bishop Museum Bulletin no. 223 (Honolulu: B. P. Bishop Museum).

BATRES, LEOPOLDO
1889   *Teotihuacán; or the Sacred City of the Toltecs*, Monographs of Mexican Archaeology (Mexico).

BAUDEZ, CLAUDE
1970   *The Ancient Civilization of Central America* (London: Barrie and Jenkins).

BEALS, RALPH L.
1932   *The Comparative Ethnology of Northern Mexico Before 1750*, Ibero-Americana no. 2 (Berkeley: University of California Press).

BELL, BETTY
1971   "Archaeology of Nayarit, Jalisco, and Colima," in *Archaeology of Northern Mesoamerica*, part 2, *Handbook of Middle American Indians*, vol. 11, ed. Gordon F. Ekholm and Ignacio Bernal (Austin: University of Texas Press), pp. 694–753.

BENSON, ELIZABETH (ED.)
1968   *Dumbarton Oaks Conference on the Olmec* (Washington, D.C.: Dumbarton Oaks Research Library and Collection and Trustees for Harvard University).

BERNAL, IGNACIO
1968   *The Olmec World* (Berkeley and Los Angeles: University of California Press).

BERRY, B. J. L.
1967   *Geography of Market Centers and Retail Distribution* (Englewood Cliffs, N.J.: Prentice-Hall).

BINFORD, SALLY R. AND LEWIS R. BINFORD (EDS.)
1968   *New Perspectives in Archaeology* (Chicago: Aldine Publishing Co.).

BLANTON, RICHARD E.
1972a "Prehispanic Adaptation in the Ixtapalapa Region, Mexico," *Science* 175 (4028):1317–26.
1972b *Prehispanic Settlement Patterns of the Ixtapalapa Region, Mexico*, Pennsylvania State University Occasional Papers in Anthropology, no. 6 (University Park, Pa).
1975   "The Cybernetic Analysis of Human Population Growth," in *Population Studies in Archaeology and Biological Anthropology: A Symposium*, ed. Alan Swedlund, Memoir of the Society for American Archaeology no. 30 (Washington, D.C.: Society for American Archaeology).

BOSERUP, ESTER
1965   *The Conditions of Agricultural Growth: The Economics of Agrarian Change Under Population Pressure* (Chicago: Aldine Publishing Co.).

BRANIFF DE TORRES, BEATRIZ
1972   "Secuencias arqueológicas en Guanajuato y la Cuenca de México: intento de

correlación," in *Teotihuacán, XI Mesa Redonda*, vol. 2 (Mexico City: Sociedad Mexicana de Antropología), pp. 273–323.

BRAY, WARWICK
1972   "The City-State in Central Mexico at the Time of the Spanish Conquest," *Journal of Latin American Studies* 4(2):161–85.

BRUSH, CHARLES F.
1964   "Pox Pottery: Earliest Identified Mexican Ceramic," *Science* 149:194–95.

BYERS, DOUGLAS S. (ED.)
1967   *Environment and Subsistence, The Prehistory of the Tehuacán Valley*, vol. 1 (Austin: University of Texas Press).

CALDWELL, JOSEPH
1964   "Interaction Spheres in Prehistory," in *Hopewellian Studies*, Illinois State Museum Scientific Papers, vol. 12, pp. 133–43.

CALNEK, EDWARD E.
1969   "Dynastic Succession in Tenochtitlan," paper presented at the Meeting of the Ethnohistorical Association, Ithaca, New York.
1970   "The Population of Tenochtitlan in 1519," paper presented at the Sixty-Ninth Annual Meeting of the American Anthropological Association, San Diego, California.
1972a "The Internal Structure of Cities in America. Pre-Columbian Cities: The Case of Tenochtitlan," in *El Proceso de Urbanización en América Desde sus Orígenes Hasta Nuestros Días, Actas y Memorias*, vol. 2, *XXXIX Congreso Internacional de Americanistas*, Lima, 1970 (Lima, Peru: Instituto de Estudios Peruanos), pp. 347–58.
1972b "Settlement Pattern and Chinampa Agriculture at Tenochtitlan," *American Antiquity* 37(1):104–15.
1973a "The Localization of the Sixteenth-Century Map Called the Maguey Plan," *American Antiquity* 38(2):190–95.
1973b The Organization of Urban Food Supply Systems: the Case of Tenochtitlan," *Revista de Indias* (in press).

CARNEIRO, ROBERT L.
1967   "On the Relationship between Size of Population and Complexity of Social Organization," *Southwestern Journal of Anthropology*, 23(3):234–43.
1970   "Theory of the Origin of the State," *Science* 169(3947):733–38.
1974   "The Four Faces of Evolution," in *Handbook of Social and Cultural Anthropology*, ed. J. J. Honigmann (New York: Rand McNally), pp. 89–110.

CARRASCO, PEDRO
1967   "Relaciones sobre la organización social indígena en el siglo XVI," in *Estudios de Cultura Nahuatl*, vol. 7 (Mexico City: Instituto de Investigaciones Históricas, Universidad Nacional Autónoma de México), pp. 119–54.
1971   "Social Organization of Ancient Mexico," in *Archaeology of Northern Mesoamerica*, part 1, *Handbook of Middle American Indians*, vol. 10, ed. Gordon F. Ekholm and Ignacio Bernal (Austin: University of Texas Press), pp. 349–75.

CARTER, WILLIAM E.
1969   *New Lands and Old Traditions: Kekchi Cultivators in the Guatemalan Lowlands*. Latin American Monographs, no. 6 (Gainesville: University of Florida Press).

References

CASO, ALFONSO

1967 *Los calendarios prehispánicos* (Mexico City: Instituto de Investigaciones Históricas, Universidad Nacional Autónoma de México).

CHAPMAN, ANNE C.

1957 "Port of Trade Enclaves in Aztec and Maya Civilizations," in *Trade and Market in Early Empires,* ed. Karl Polanyi, Conrad M. Arensberg, and Harry W. Pearson (Glencoe, Ill.: The Free Press), pp. 114–53.

CHARLTON, THOMAS H.

1969 "Texcoco Fabric-Marked Pottery, Tlatels, and Salt-Making," *American Antiquity* 34(1):73–76.

1972a "Population Trends in the Teotihuacán Valley, A.D. 1400–1969," *World Archaeology* 4(1):106–23.

1972b *Post-Conquest Development in the Teotihuacán Valley, Mexico. Part 1: Excavations,* Office of the State Archaeologist Report no. 5 (Iowa City: University of Iowa).

1973 "Texcoco Region Archaeology and the Codex Xolotl," *American Antiquity* 38(4):412–23.

CHILDE, V. GORDON

1936 "Changing Methods and Aims in Prehistory," *Proceedings of the Prehistoric Society for 1936,* pp. 1–15.

1951 *Social Evolution* (London: Watts).

CHRISTALLER, WALTER

1966 *Central Places in Southern Germany* (Englewood Cliffs, N.J.: Prentice-Hall).

COBEAN, R. H., MICHAEL D. COE, EDWARD A. PERRY, JR., KARL K. TUREKIAN, AND DINKAR P. KARKAR

1971 "Obsidian Trade at San Lorenzo Tenochtitlan, Mexico," *Science* 174 (4010): 661–71.

CÓDICE FRANCISCANO

1941 *Nueva colección de documentos para la historia de México,* vol. 2, ed. J. García Icazbalceta (Mexico City: Hayhoe).

COE, MICHAEL D.

1962 *Mexico* (New York: Frederick A. Praeger, Ancient Peoples and Places Series).

1965 *The Jaguar's Children: Preclassic Central Mexico* (New York: Museum of Primitive Art).

1968 "San Lorenzo and the Olmec Civilization," in *Dumbarton Oaks Conference on the Olmec,* ed. E. P. Benson (Washington, D.C.: Dumbarton Oaks Research Library and Collection and Trustees for Harvard University), pp. 41–71.

1969 "The Archaeological Sequence at San Lorenzo Tenochtitlan, Mexico," paper presented at the Annual Meeting of the Society for American Archaeology, Milwaukee, Wis.

COE, MICHAEL D. AND R. H. COBEAN

1970 "Obsidian Trade at San Lorenzo Tenochtitlan, Mexico," paper presented at the Twenty-Fifth Annual Meeting of the Society for American Archaeology, Mexico City.

COE, MICHAEL D. AND KENT V. FLANNERY

1967 *Early Cultures and Human Ecology in South Coastal Guatemala,* Smithsonian Contributions to Anthropology, vol. 3 (Washington, D.C.: Smithsonian Institution).

COE, WILLIAM R

1967   *Tikal: A Handbook of the Ancient Maya Ruins, with a Guide Map* (Philadelphia: University Museum, University of Pennsylvania).

COMISIÓN HIDROLÓGICA DE LA CUENCA DEL VALLE DE MÉXICO

1968   *Boletín hidrológico resumen, no. 1* (Mexico City: Secretaría de Recursos Hidrológicos).

CONQUISTADOR ANÓNIMO

1941   *Relación de algunas cosas de la Nueva España y de la gran ciudad de Temestitan. Escrito por un compañero de Hernan Cortés.* (Mexico City: Editorial América).

COOK, SCOTT

1970   "Price and Output Variability in a Peasant-Artisan Stoneworking Industry in Oaxaca, Mexico: An Analytic Essay in Economic Anthropology," *American Anthropologist* 72(4):776–801.

COONTZ, SIDNEY H.

1968   *Population Theories and the Economic Interpretation* (London: Routledge and Kegan Paul).

CORTÉS, HERNÁN

1963   *Cartas y Documentos* (Mexico City: Editorial Porrúa).

COWGILL, GEORGE L.

1974   "Quantitative Studies of Urbanization at Teotihuacán," in *Mesoamerican Archaeology: New Approaches,* ed. Norman Hammond (London: Duckworth & Co.), pp. 363–96.

1975a   "Population Pressure as a Non-Explanation," in *Population Studies in Archaeology and Biological Anthropology: A Symposium,* ed. Alan C. Swedlund, Memoir 30, *American Antiquity* 40, part 2 (April 1975): 127–31.

1975b   "On Causes and Consequences of Ancient and Modern Population Changes," *American Anthropologist* 77(3):505–25.

COWGILL, URSULA M.

1961   "Soil Fertility and the Ancient Maya," in *Transactions of the Connecticut Academy of Arts and Sciences,* vol. 42, pp. 1–56.

1962   "The Agricultural Study of the Southern Maya Lowlands," *American Anthropologist* 64(2): 273–86.

CUMMINGS, BYRON C.

1933   *Cuicuilco and the Archaic Culture of Mexico,* Bulletin of the University of Arizona, vol. 4, no. 8 (Tucson).

DALTON, GEORGE

1964   "The Development of Subsistence and Peasant Economics in Africa," *International Social Science Journal* 16(3):378–89.

DEETZ, JAMES

1968   "The Inference of Residence and Descent Rules from Archaeological Data," in *New Perspectives in Archaeology,* ed. Sally R. Binford and Lewis R. Binford (Chicago: Aldine Publishing Co.), pp. 41–48.

DÍAZ DEL CASTILLO, BERNAL

1910   *The True History of the Conquest of New Spain,* vol. 2, trans. and annotated A. P. Maudslay (London: Hakluyt Society).

References

1960   *Historia de la Conquista de la Nueva España* (Mexico: Editorial Porrúa).

DIBBLE, C. E. (ED. AND TRANS.)

1963   *Historia de la Nación Mexicana. Reproducción a todo color del Códice de 1576 (Codice Aubin)*, Collección Chimalistac, no. 16 (Madrid: Ediciones José Porrúa Turanas).

DIEHL, RICHARD A.

n.d.   *An Evaluation of the Mesoamerican Formative*, Pennsylvania State University Occasional Papers in Anthropology (University Park, Pa.) (in press).

DI PESO, CHARLES C.

1966   "Archaeology and Ethnohistory of the Northern Sierra," *Archaeological Frontiers and External Connections, Handbook of Middle American Indians*, vol. 4, ed. Gordon F. Ekholm and Gordon R. Willey (Austin: University of Texas Press), pp. 3–25.

DIXON, KEITH A.

1959   *Ceramics from Two Preclassic Periods at Chiapa de Corzo, Chiapas, Mexico*, New World Archaeological Foundation Papers, no. 5 (Provo, Utah: Brigham Young University).

DREWITT, BRUCE

1967   "Planeación en la antigua ciudad de Teotihuacán," in *Teotihuacán: XI Mesa Redonda*, vol. 1 (Mexico City: Sociedad Mexicana de Antropología), pp. 79–94.

1969   "Data Bearing on Urban Planning at Teotihuacán," report presented at the Annual Meeting of the American Anthropological Association, New Orleans, La.

DRUCKER, DAVID

1974   "Renovating a Reconstruction: The Ciudadela at Teotihuacán, Mexico: Construction Sequence, Layout and Possible Uses of the Structure" (Ph.D. diss., University of Rochester).

DUMOND, DON E.

1965   "Population Growth and Culture Change," *Southwestern Journal of Anthropology* 21:302–24.

1972a   "Demographic Aspects of the Classic Period in Puebla-Tlaxcala," *Southwestern Journal of Anthropology* 28(2):101–30.

1972b   "Population Growth and Political Centralization," in *Population Growth: Anthropological Implications*, ed. Brian Spooner (Cambridge, Mass.: M.I.T. Press), pp. 286–310.

DUMOND, DON E. AND FLORENCIA MULLER

1972   "Classic to Postclassic in Highland Central Mexico," *Science* 175:1208–15.

DURÁN, DIEGO

1951   *Historia de las Indias de Nueva España y Islas de Tierra Firme*, 2 vols. (Mexico City: Atlas).

DU SOLIER, WILFREDO

1946   "Primer fresco mural Huasteco," *Cuadernos Americanos* 5(6): 151–59.

EARLE, TIMOTHY

1971   "Nearest Neighbor Analysis in Archaeology, with Reference to Settlement Pattern Studies in the Formative Period in Mexico" (unpublished).

EKHOLM, GORDON F.

1942 "Excavations at Guasave, Sinaloa, Mexico," *American Museum of Natural History Anthropological Papers,* vol. 38 (New York: American Museum of Natural History), pp. 23–139.

1944 "Excavations at Tampico and Pánuco in the Huasteca, Mexico," *American Museum of Natural History Anthropological Papers,* vol. 38 (New York: American Museum of Natural History), pp. 319–509.

FELDT, ALLAN

1965 "The Metropolitan Area Concept: An Evaluation of the 1950 SMA's," *Journal of the American Statistical Association* 60:617–36.

FLANNERY, KENT V.

1968a "Archaeological Systems Theory and Early Mesoamerica," in *Anthropological Archaeology in the Americas,* ed. Betty J. Meggers (Washington, D.C.: Anthropological Society of Washington), pp. 67–87.

1968b "The Olmec and the Valley of Oaxaca: a Model of Inter-Regional Interaction in Formative Times," *Dumbarton Oaks Conference on the Olmec,* ed. E. P. Benson (Washington, D.C.: Dumbarton Oaks Research Library and Collection and Trustees for Harvard University), pp. 119–30.

1970 "Preliminary Archaeological Investigations in the Valley of Oaxaca, Mexico, 1966–1969," report presented to the National Science Foundation and the Instituto Nacional de Antropología e Historia.

1972 "The Cultural Evolution of Civilization," *Annual Review of Ecology and Systematics* 3:399–426.

FLANNERY, KENT V., ANNE V. T. KIRKBY, MICHAEL J. KIRKBY, AND AUBREY W. WILLIAMS, JR.

1967 "Farming Systems and Political Growth in Ancient Oaxaca," *Science* 158 (3800):445–54.

FLANNERY, KENT V. AND J. SCHOENWETTER

1970 "Climate and Man in Formative Oaxaca," *Archaeology* 23(2):144–52.

FORGE, ANTHONY

1972 "Normative Factors in the Settlement Size of Neolithic Cultivators (New Guinea)," in *Man, Settlement and Urbanism,* ed. Peter Ucko, Ruth Tringham, and G. Dimbleby (London: Duckworth & Co.), pp. 363–76.

FRANCO, JOSÉ LUIS

1949 "Algunos problemas relativos a la cerámica Azteca," *El México Antiguo* 7:162–208.

1970a "Material recuperado," in *Minería Prehispánica en la Sierra de Querétaro* (Mexico City: Consejo de Recursos Naturales No Renovables, Secretaría del Patrimonio Nacional), pp. 27–44, láms. de color 2, 4, láms. 15–67.

1970b "Trabajos excavaciones arqueológicos," *Minería Prehispánica en la Sierra de Querétaro* (Mexico City: Consejo de Recursos Naturales No Renovables, Secretaría del Patrimonio Nacional), pp. 23–26, láms. de color 1, 3, láms. 1–14, 68–69, plano 1.

FURST, PETER T.

1965 "West Mexican Tomb Sculpture as Evidence for Shamanism in Prehispanic Mesoamerica," *Antropológica* 15:29–81.

1966 "Shaft Tombs, Shell Trumpets, and Shamanism: A Culture-Historical Ap-

References

proach to Problems in West Mexican Archaeology" (Ph.D. diss., University of California, Los Angeles).

GAMIO, MANUEL
1922   *La población del Valle de Teotihuacán*, 3 vols. (Mexico City: Secretaría de Agricultura y Fomento).

GARCÍA ICAZBALCETA, JOAQUÍN
1941   *Nueva collección de documentos para la historia de México*, 5 vols., 2d ed. (Mexico City: Hayhoe).

GARCÍA PAYÓN, JOSÉ
1956–57a "Síntesis de las excavaciones estratigráficas en Tecaxic-Calixtlahuaca," *Revista Mexicana de Estudios Antropológicos* 14(2):157–60.
1956–57b "Síntesis de las excavaciones en Malinalco," *Revista Mexicana de Estudios Antropológicos* 14(2):161–67.
1966   *Prehistoria de Mesoamérica: excavaciones en Trapiche y Chalahuite, Veracruz, Mexico, 1942, 1951, y 1959*, Cuadernos de la Facultad de Filosofía, Letras y Ciencias, no. 31 (Xalapa, Mexico: Universidad Veracruzana).

GEERTZ, CLIFFORD
1963a   *Agricultural Involution: The Processes of Ecological Change in Indonesia* (Berkeley and Los Angeles: University of California Press).
1963b   "Two Types of Ecosystems," in *Environment and Cultural Behavior*, ed. Andrew P. Vayda (Garden City, N.Y.: Doubleday & Co., Natural History Press), pp. 3–28.

GIFFORD, E. W.
1950   *Surface Archaeology of Ixtlán del Río, Nayarit*, University of California Publications in American Archaeology and Ethnology, vol. 43, no. 2 (Berkeley: University of California Press).

GOGGIN, JOHN M.
1943   "An Archaeological Survey of the Rio Tepalcatepec Basin, Michoacán, Mexico," *American Antiquity* 9:44–58.

GÓMARA, FRANCISCO LÓPEZ DE
1943   *Historia de la Conquista de México*, 2 vols. (Mexico City: Robredo).

GORDUS, A. A., W. C. FINK, M. E. HILL, J. C. PURDY, AND T. R. WILCOX
1967   "Identification of the Geologic Origins of Archaeological Artifacts: An Automated Method of Na and Mn Neutron Activation Analysis," *Archaeometry* 10:87–96.

GRAHAM, JOHN A., THOMAS R. HESTER, AND ROBERT N. JACK
1972   "Sources for the Obsidian at the Ruins of Seibal, Peten, Guatemala," in *Studies in the Archaeology of Mexico and Guatemala*, ed. John A. Graham, Contributions of the University of California Archaeological Research Facility no. 16 (Berkeley), pp. 111–16.

GRIFFIN, JAMES B. AND ANTONIETA ESPEJO
1947   "La alfarería correspondiente al último periodo de ocupación nahua del Valle de México," *Memorias de la Academia Mexicana de la Historia* 6(2):131–47.

GROVE, DAVID C.
1968a   "Chacaltzingo, Morelos, Mexico: A Reappraisal of the Olmec Rock Carvings," *American Antiquity* 33(4):486–91.

1968b "The Morelos Preclassic and the Highland Olmec Problem: An Archaeological Study" (Ph.D. diss., University of California, Los Angeles).

1968c "The Pre-Classic Olmec in Central Mexico: Site Distribution and Inferences," *Dumbarton Oaks Conference on the Olmec*, ed. E. P. Benson (Washington, D.C.: Dumbarton Oaks Research Library and Collection and Trustees for Harvard University), pp. 179–85.

1970 "The San Pablo Pantheon Mound: A Middle Pre-Classic Site in Morelos, Mexico," *American Antiquity* 35(1):62–73.

HAGGETT, PETER

1966 *Locational Analysis in Human Geography* (New York: St. Martin's Press).

HARDING, THOMAS G.

1967 *Voyagers of the Vitiaz Strait*, American Ethnological Society Monograph no. 44 (Seattle: University of Washington Press).

HASSAN, F. A.

1973 "On Mechanisms of Population Growth during the Neolithic," *Current Anthropology* 14:535–42.

HAVILAND, WILLIAM A.

1969 "A New Population Estimate for Tikal, Gutemala," *American Antiquity* 34(4):429–33.

1970 "Tikal, Guatemala and Mesoamerican Urbanism," *World Archaeology* 2(2): 186–97.

HEIZER, ROBERT F. AND JAMES BENNYHOFF

1958 "Archaeological Investigations of Cuicuilco, Valley of Mexico," *Science* 127:232–33.

HERODOTUS

1954 *The Histories*, trans. Aubrey de Sélincourt (Harmondsworth, Eng.: Penguin Books).

HESTER, JOSEPH A.

1952 "Agriculture, Economy, and Population Density of the Maya," in *Annual Report of the Director of the Department of Archaeology, Carnegie Institution of Washington* (Washington, D.C.), pp. 289–92.

HESTER, THOMAS R., ROBERT F. HEIZER, AND ROBERT N. JACK

1971 "Technology and Geologic Sources of Obsidian from Cerro de las Mesas, Veracruz, Mexico, with Observations on Olmec Trade," in *Contribution of the University of California Archaeological Research Facility* no. 13 (Berkeley), pp. 133–41.

HESTER, THOMAS R., ROBERT N. JACK, AND ROBERT F. HEIZER

1971 "The Obsidian of Tres Zapotes, Veracruz, Mexico," in *Contribution of the University of California Archaeological Research Facility* no. 13 (Berkeley), pp. 65–131.

1972 "Trace Element Analysis of Obsidian from the Site of Cholula," in *Studies in the Archaeology of Mexico and Guatemala*, ed. John A. Graham, Contribution of the University of California Archaeological Research Facility no. 16 (Berkeley), pp. 105–10.

HEYDEN, DORIS

1975 "An Interpretation of the Cave underneath the Pyramid of the Sun in Teotihuacán, Mexico," *American Antiquity* 40 (2, part 1):131–47.

References

HILL, JAMES N.
1970   *Broken K Pueblo: Prehistoric Social Organization in the American Southwest*, University of Arizona Anthropological Paper no. 18 (Tucson: University of Arizona Press).

IXTLILXOCHITL, FERNANDO DE ALVA
1952   *Obras Históricas*, ed. Alfredo Chavero, 2 vols. (Mexico City: Editora Nacional).

JACK, ROBERT N., THOMAS R. HESTER, AND ROBERT F. HEIZER
1972   "Geologic Sources of Archaeological Obsidian from Sites in Northern and Central Veracruz, Mexico," in *Studies in the Archaeology of Mexico and Guatemala*, ed. John A. Graham, Contribution of the University of California Archaeological Research Facility no. 16 (Berkeley), pp. 117–22.

JACOBS, JANE
1969   *The Economy of Cities* (New York: Random House).

JENNINGS, JESSE D.
1957   *Danger Cave*, Memoir of the Society for American Archaeology no. 14 (Salt Lake City: University of Utah Press).

JIMÉNEZ MORENO, WIGBERTO
1943   "Colonización y evangelización de Guanajuato en el siglo XVI," in *El Norte de México y el Sur de los Estados Unidos* (Mexico City: Sociedad Mexicana de Antropología), pp. 17–40.
1954–55 "Síntesis de la historia precolonial del Valle de México," *Revista Mexicana de Estudios Antropológicos* 14:219–36.

JOHNSON, ALFRED E.
1966   "Archaeology of Sonora, Mexico," in *Archaeological Frontiers and External Connections, Handbook of Middle American Indians*, vol. 4, ed. Gordon F. Ekholm and Gordon R. Willey (Austin: University of Texas Press), pp. 26–37.

JOHNSON, FREDERICK (ED.)
1972   *Chronology and Irrigation. The Prehistory of the Tehuacan Valley*, vol. 4 (Austin: University of Texas Press).

JOHNSON, GREGORY A.
1973   *Local Exchange and Early State Development in Southwestern Iran*, University of Michigan Museum of Anthropology, Anthropological Paper no. 51 (Ann Arbor).

KASARDA, J. D.
1971   "Economic Structure and Fertility: A Comparative Analysis," *Demography* 8:307–16.

KATZ, SOLOMON H.
1972   "Biological Factors in Population Control," in *Population Growth: Anthropological Implications*, ed. Brian Spooner (Cambridge, Mass.: M.I.T. Press), pp. 351–69.

KELLEY, J. CHARLES
1966   "Mesoamerica and the Southwestern United States," in *Archaeological Frontiers and External Connections, Handbook of Middle American Indians*, vol. 4, ed. Gordon F. Ekholm and Gordon R. Willey (Austin: University of Texas Press), pp. 95–110.

1971 "Archaeology of the Northern Frontier: Zacatecas and Durango," in *Archaeology of Northern Mesoamerica*, part 2, *Handbook of Middle American Indians*, vol. 11, ed. Gordon F. Ekholm and Ignacio Bernal (Austin: University of Texas Press), pp. 768–803.

KELLEY, J. CHARLES AND ELLEN ABBOTT KELLEY
1971 *An Introduction to the Ceramics of the Chalchihuites Culture of Zacatecas and Durango, Mexico, Part I: The Decorated Wares*, Southern Illinois University Museum Mesoamerican Studies, no. 5 (Carbondale).

KELLEY, J. CHARLES AND HOWARD D. WINTERS
1960 "A Revision of the Archaeological Sequence in Sinaloa, Mexico," *American Antiquity* 25(4):547–61.

KELLY, ISABEL T.
1938 *Excavations at Chametla, Sinaloa*, Ibero-Americana, no. 14 (Berkeley: University of California Press).
1944 "West Mexico and the Hohokam," in *El norte de México y el sur de los Estados Unidos* (Mexico City: Sociedad Mexicana de Antropología), pp. 206–22.
1945a *Excavations at Culiacan, Sinaloa*. Ibero-Americana no. 25 (Berkeley: University of California Press).
1945b *The Archaeology of the Autlan-Tuxcacuesco Area of Jalisco, I: The Autlan Zone*, Ibero-Americana no. 26 (Berkeley: University of California Press).
1947 *Excavations at Apatzingan, Michoacán*, Viking Fund Publication in Anthropology no. 7 (New York: Wenner-Gren Foundation for Anthropological Research).
1948 "Ceramic Provinces in Northwestern Mexico," in *El Occidente de México* (Mexico City: Sociedad Mexicana de Antropología), pp. 55–71.
1970 "Vasijas de Colima con Boca de Estribo," *Boletín del Instituto Nacional de Antropología e Historia* 42:26–30.

KELLY, ISABEL T. AND ÁNGEL PALERM
1952 *The Tajin Totonac: Part 1. History, Subsistence, Shelter and Technology*, Smithsonian Institution, Institute of Social Anthropology Publication no. 13 (Washington, D.C.: U.S. Government Printing Office).

KIRCHHOFF, PAUL
1935 See Kirchhoff 1959.
1943 "Mesoamérica: sus límites geográficas, composición étnica y carácteres culturales," *Acta Americana* 1:92–107.
1950 "The Mexican Calendar and the Founding of Tenochtitlan-Tlatelolco," *Transactions of the New York Academy of Sciences*, series 2, 12(4):126–32.
1959 "The Principles of Clanship in Human Society," in *Readings in Anthropology*, ed. Morton H. Fried (New York: Thomas Y. Crowell), 2:259–70.

KIRKBY, ANNE V. T.
1973 "The Use of Land and Water Resources in the Past and Present, Valley of Oaxaca, Mexico," in *Prehistory and Human Ecology of the Valley of Oaxaca*, ed. Kent V. Flannery, Memoirs of the University of Michigan Museum of Anthropology, vol. 1, no. 5 (Ann Arbor).

KLUCKHOHN, CLYDE
1940 "Conceptual Structure in Middle American Studies," in *The Maya and Their Neighbors*, ed. C. L. Hay et al. (New York: Appleton-Century), pp. 41–51.

References

KUBLER, GEORGE
1964 "Polygenesis and Diffusion: Courtyards in Mesoamerican Architecture," in *Actas y Memorias del XXV Congreso Internacional de Americanistas, 1962* (Mexico City), 1:345–57.

LEE, RICHARD B.
1972 "Work Effort, Group Structure and Land Use in Contemporary Hunter-Gatherers," in *Man, Settlement and Urbanism*, ed. Peter Ucko, Ruth Tringham, and G. Dimbleby (London: Duckworth Co.), pp. 177–86.

LINNÉ, S.
1934 *Archaeological Researches at Teotihuacán, Mexico*, Ethnographic Museum of Sweden, new series, Publication 1 (Stockholm).

1942 *Mexican Highland Cultures: Archaeological Researches at Teotihuacán, Calpulalpan, and Chalchicomula in 1934–35*, Ethnographic Museum of Sweden, new series, Publication 7 (Stockholm).

LISTER, ROBERT
1949 *Excavations at Cojumatlán, Michoacán, Mexico*, University of New Mexico Publications in Anthropology, no. 5 (Albuquerque).

1955 *The Present Status of the Archaeology of Western Mexico*, University of Colorado Studies, Series in Anthropology, no. 5 (Boulder).

LORENZO, JOSÉ LUIS
1968 "Clima y agricultura en Teotihuacán," in *Materiales para la Arqueología de Teotihuacán*, ed. José Luis Lorenzo, Serie Investigaciones, Instituto Nacional de Antropología e Historia no. 17 (Mexico City), pp. 51–72.

LUNDELL, CYRUS L.
1937 *The Vegetation of the Peten*, Carnegie Institution of Washington Publications, no. 478 (Washington, D.C.).

MACKAY, DONALD M.
1964 "Communication and Meaning—A Functional Approach," in *Cross-Cultural Understandings: Epistemology in Anthropology*, ed. F. S. C. Northrop and Helen H. Livingston (New York: Harper and Row), pp. 162–79.

MACNEISH, RICHARD S.
1954 "An Early Archaeological Site near Pánuco, Vera Cruz," *Transactions of the American Philosophical Society* 44:593–641.

1958 "Preliminary Archaeological Investigations in the Sierra de Tamaulipas, Mexico," *Transactions of the American Philosophical Society* 48:1–209.

1962 *Second Annual Report of the Tehuacan Archaeological Botanical Project* (Andover, Massachusetts: Phillips Academy).

1964 "Ancient Mesoamerican Civilization," *Science* 143(3606): 531-37.

1967 "A Summary of the Subsistence," in *Environment and Subsistence, The Prehistory of the Tehuacan Valley*, vol. 1, ed. Douglas S. Byers (Austin: University of Texas Press), pp. 290–309.

1972 "Archaeological Synthesis of the Sierra," in *Archaeology of Northern Mesoamerica*, part 2, *Handbook of Middle American Indians*, vol. 11, ed. Gordon F. Ekholm and Ignacio Bernal (Austin: University of Texas Press), pp. 573–81.

MACNEISH, RICHARD S., FREDERICK A. PETERSON, AND KENT V. FLANNERY
1970 *Ceramics, The Prehistory of the Tehuacan Valley*, vol. 3 (Austin: University of Texas Press).

MANGELSDORF, PAUL C., RICHARD S. MACNEISH, AND WALTER C. GALINAT
1966 "Prehistoric Wild and Cultivated Maize," in *Environment and Subsistence, The Prehistory of the Tehuacan Valley*, vol. 1, ed. Douglas S. Byers (Austin: University of Texas Press), pp. 178–200.

MARQUINA, IGNACIO
1960 *El Templo Mayor de México* (Mexico City: Instituto Nacional de Antropología e Historia).
1964 *Arquitectura Prehispánica*, Memorias del Instituto Nacional de Antropología e Historia, vol. 1, 2d ed. (Mexico City).

MARQUINA, IGNACIO (ED.)
1970 *Proyecto Cholula*, Instituto Nacional de Antropología e Historia, Serie Investigaciones, no. 19 (Mexico City).

MARUYAMA, MAGOROH
1963 "The Second Cybernetics: Deviation-Amplifying Mutual Causal Processes," *American Scientist* 51:164–79.

MATOS MOCTEZUMA, EDUARDO
1968 "Piezas de saqueo procedentes de Jerecuaro, Guanajuato," *Boletín del Instituto Nacional de Antropología e Historia*, no. 33, pp. 30–35.

MAYER-OAKES, W.
1960 "A Developmental Concept of Pre-Spanish Urbanization in the Valley of Mexico," in *Middle American Research Records*, vol. 2, *Middle American Research Institute* (New Orleans: Middle American Research Institute, Tulane University), pp. 165–76.

MEGGERS, BETTY J.
1956 "Environmental Limitation on the Development of Culture," *American Anthropologist* 56:801–24.

MEIGHAN, CLEMENT W.
1971 "Archaeology of Sinaloa," in *Archaeology of Northern Mesoamerica*, part 2, *Handbook of Middle American Indians*, vol. 11, ed. Gordon F. Ekholm and Ignacio Bernal (Austin: University of Texas Press), pp. 754–67.

MEIGHAN, CLEMENT W. AND LEONARD J. FOOTE
1968 *Excavations at Tizapan el Alto, Jalisco*, University of California, Los Angeles, Latin American Studies, vol. 11.

MILLER, ARTHUR G.
1972 "A Lost Teotihuacán Mural," *Boletín Bibliográfico de Antropología Americana* 35:61–83.
1973 *The Mural Painting of Teotihuacán* (Washington, D.C.: Dumbarton Oaks Research Library and Collection and Trustees for Harvard University).

MILLER, JAMES G.
1965 "Living Systems, Basic Concepts," *Behavioral Science* 10(3):193–257.

MILLON, CLARA
1972 "Commentary about 'A Lost Teotihuacan Mural' by Arthur G. Miller," *Boletín Bibliográfico de Antropología Americana* 35:85–89.
1973 "Painting, Writing, and Polity at Teotihuacán, Mexico," *American Antiquity* 38(3):294–314.

References

MILLON, RENÉ

1954 "Irrigation at Teotihuacán," *American Antiquity* 20(2):177–80.
1957 "Irrigation Systems in the Valley of Teotihuacán," *American Antiquity* 23(2): 160–66.
1967a "Cronología y periodificación: datos estratigráficos sobre períodos cerámicos y sus relaciones con la pintura mural," in *Teotihuacán, XI Mesa Redonda* (Mexico City: Sociedad Mexicana de Antropología), 1:1–18.
1967b "Extensión y población de la ciudad de Teotihuacán en sus diferentes períodos: un cálculo provisional," in *Teotihuacán, XI Mesa Redonda* (Mexico City: Sociedad Mexicana de Antropología), 1:57–78.
1967c "El problema de integración de la sociedad teotihuacana," *Teotihuacán, XI Mesa Redonda* (Mexico City: Sociedad Mexicana de Antropología). 1:149–55.
1967d "Teotihuacán," *Scientific American* 216(6):38–48.
1967e "Urna de Monte Albán IIIA encontrada en Teotihuacán," *Boletín del Instituto Nacional de Antropología e Historia*, no. 29, pp. 42–44.
1968a "Teotihuacán: primera metrópoli prehispánica," *Gaceta Médica de México* 98(3):339–50.
1968b "Urbanization at Teotihuacán: The Teotihuacán Mapping Project," in *Actas y Memorias, International Congress of Americanists, 1966* (Buenos Aires), 1:105–20.
1968c "Urban Revolution II: Early Civilizations in the New World," in *International Encyclopedia of the Social Sciences* (Glencoe, Ill.: Free Press), 16:207–17.
1970a "Progress Report on the Teotihuacán Mapping Project for the Departamento de Monumentos Prehispánicos," no. 10, Instituto Nacional de Antropología e Historia, Mexico City (unpublished).
1970b "Teotihuacán: Completion of Map of Giant Ancient City in the Valley of Mexico," *Science* 170(3962):1077–82.
1973 *Urbanization at Teotihuacán, Mexico.* Vol. 1, *The Teotihuacán Map, Part One: Text* (Austin: University of Texas Press).

MILLON, RENÉ, BRUCE DREWITT, AND JAMES BENNYHOFF

1965 "The Pyramid of the Sun at Teotihuacán: 1959 Investigation," *Transactions of the American Philosophical Society* 55(6):3–93.

MILLON, RENÉ, BRUCE DREWITT, AND GEORGE L. COWGILL

1973 "Urbanization at Teotihuacán, Mexico," in *The Teotihuacán Map, Part Two: Map* (Austin: University of Texas Press).

MILLON, RENÉ, CLARA HALL, AND MAY DÍAZ

1962 "Conflict in the Modern Teotihuacán Irrigation System," *Comparative Studies in Society and History* 4(4):494–521.

MINERÍA PREHISPÁNICA

1970 *Minería prehispánica en la Sierra de Querétaro* (Mexico City: Consejo de Recursos Naturales No Renovables, Secretaría del Patrimonio Nacional).

MOLÍNS FÁBREGA, N.

1954-55 "El Códice Mendocino y la economía de Tenochtitlan," *Revista Mexicana de Estudios Antropológicos* 14(1): 303–35.

MONZÓN, ARTURO

1949 *El calpulli en la organización social de los Tenochca,* Publicaciones del Instituto de Historia, ser. 1, no. 6 (Mexico City: Universidad Nacional Autonoma de México and Instituto Nacional de Antropología e Historia).

MOTOLINÍA, TORIBIO DE BENAVENTE
1903 *Memoriales*, ed. Luis García Pimentel, *Documentos Históricos de Méjico*, vol. 1 (Mexico City: Luis García Pimentel).

MULLER, FLORENCIA
1970 *La cerámica de Cholula*, Proyecto Cholula, Serie Investigaciones, no. 19 (Mexico City: Instituto Nacional de Antropología e Historia).

NADEL, SIEGFRIED F.
1942 *A Black Byzantium: The Kingdom of Nupe in Nigeria* (London: Oxford University Press for the International African Institute).

NAROLL, RAOUL
1956 "A Preliminary Index of Social Development," *American Anthropologist* 58:687–715.

NETTING, ROBERT M.
1972 "Sacred Power and Centralization: Aspects of Political·Adaptation in Africa," in *Population Growth: Anthropological Implications*, ed. Brian Spooner (Cambridge, Mass.: M.I.T. Press), pp. 219–44.

NIEDERBERGER, CHRISTINE
1969 "Paleoecología humana y playas lacustres post-Pleistocénicos en Tlapacoya," *Boletín del Instituto Nacional de Antropología e Historia*, no. 37, pp. 19–24.

ODUM, EUGENE
1971 *Fundamentals of Ecology*, 3d ed. (Philadelphia: W. B. Saunders).

ODUM, HOWARD T.
1971 *Environment, Power, and Society* (New York: John Wiley & Sons).

PALERM, ÁNGEL
1952 "La civilización urbana," *Historia Méxicana* 2(2):184–209.
1954 "La distribución del regadío en el área central de Mesoamérica," *Ciencias Sociales* 5(25, 26):2–15, 64–74.
1955 "The Agricultural Bases of Urban Civilization in Mesoamerica," in *Irrigation Civilizations: A Comparative Study*, by Julian H. Steward, Robert M. Adams, Donald Collier, Ángel Palerm, Karl A. Wittfogel, and Ralph L. Beals, Pan American Union Social Science Monograph no. 1 (Washington, D.C.: Pan American Union), pp. 28–42.
1961 "Sistemas de regadío prehispánico en Teotihuacán y en el Pedregal de San Ángel," *Revista Interamericana de Ciencias Sociales*, época 2, vol. 1(2):297–302.
1973 *Obras hidráulicas prehispánicas en el sistema lacustre del Valle de México* (Mexico City: Instituto Nacional de Antropología e Historia).

PALERM, ÁNGEL AND ERIC R. WOLF
1954-55 "El desarrollo del área clave del imperio texcocano," *Revista Mexicana de Estudios Antropológicos* 14(1):337–49.
1957 "Ecological Potential and Cultural Development in Mesoamerica," in *Studies in Human Ecology*, Anthropological Society of Washington and Pan American Union Social Science Monograph no. 3 (Washington, D.C.: Pan American Union), pp. 1–37.

PARSONS, JEFFREY R.
1968 "Teotihuacán, Mexico, and Its Impact on Regional Demography," *Science* 162(3856):872–77.

References

1970 "An Archaeological Evaluation of the Códice Xolotl," *American Antiquity* 35(4):431–40.

1971a "Pre-Hispanic Settlement Patterns in the Chalco Region, Mexico, 1969 Season," report presented to the Instituto Nacional de Antropología e Historia, Mexico City.

1971b *Pre-Hispanic Settlement Patterns in the Texcoco Region, Mexico*, Memoirs of the University of Michigan Museum of Anthropology, no. 3 (Ann Arbor).

1973 *Reconocimiento superficial en el Sur del Valle de México, temporada 1972.* Report presented to the Instituto Nacional de Antropología e Historia, Mexico City.

1974 "The Development of a Prehistoric Complex Society: A Regional Perspective from the Valley of Mexico," *Journal of Field Archaeology* 1:81–108.

n.d.a "The Functions of Texcoco Fabric-Marked Pottery," *Revista Mexicana de Estudios Antropológicos* (in press).

n.d.b National Science Foundation Project on Settlement Surveys in the Zumpango Region.

PARSONS, LEE A.

1969 *Bilbao, Guatemala: An Archaeological Study of the Pacific Coast Cotzumalhuapa Region*, vol. 2. Milwaukee Public Museum Publications in Anthropology, no. 12 (Milwaukee).

PARSONS, LEE A. AND BARBARA J. PRICE

1971 "Mesoamerican Trade and Its Role in the Emergence of Civilization," in *Observations on the Emergence of Civilization in Mesoamerica*, ed. Robert F. Heizer and John A. Graham, Contribution of the University of California Archaeological Research Facility no. 11 (Berkeley), pp. 169–95.

PARSONS, MARY HRONES

1972a "Aztec Figurines from the Teotihuacán Valley," in *Miscellaneous Studies in Mexican Prehistory*, University of Michigan Museum of Anthropology, Anthropological Papers, no. 45 (Ann Arbor), pp. 81–125.

1972b "Spindle Whorls from the Teotihuacán Valley, Mexico," in *Miscellaneous Studies in Mexican Prehistory*, University of Michigan Museum of Anthropology, Anthropological Papers, no. 45 (Ann Arbor), pp. 45–80.

PASO Y TRONCOSO, F. (ED.)

1905a *Papeles de Nueva España*, vol. 1, section 1, *Abecedario de las Visitas de los Pueblos de la Nueva España* (Madrid: F. Paso y Troncoso).

1905b *Papeles de Nueva España*, vol. 6, section 12 (Madrid: F. Paso y Troncoso), pp. 209–36.

PENDERGAST, DAVID M.

1971 "Evidence of Early Teotihuacán–Lowland Maya Contact at Altún Ha," *American Antiquity* 36(4):455–60.

PIÑA CHAN, ROMÁN

1958 *Tlatilco* (Mexico City: Instituto Nacional de Antropología e Historia).

1963 "Excavaciones en el Rancho 'La Ventilla,'" in *Teotihuacán: Descubrimientos, Reconstrucciones*, ed. Ignacio Bernal (Mexico City: Instituto Nacional de Antropología e Historia), pp. 50–52.

PIRES-FERREIRA, JANE WHEELER

1973 "Formative Mesoamerican Exchange Networks" (Ph.D. diss. University of Michigan).

POLGAR, STEVEN
1971 "Culture History and Population Dynamics," in *Culture and Population: A Collection of Current Studies*, ed. Steven Polgar (Chapel Hill, N.C.: Carolina Population Center), pp. 3–8.

PORTER, MURIEL N. (see also WEAVER, MURIEL PORTER)
1953 *Tlatilco and the Pre-Classic Cultures of the New World*, Viking Fund Publications in Anthropology, no. 19 (New York: Wenner-Gren Foundation for Anthropological Research).
1956 *Excavations at Chupícuaro, Guanajuato, Mexico*, Transactions of the American Philosophical Society, vol. 46, no. 5.

POSPISIL, LEOPOLD
1963 *The Kapauku Papuans of West New Guinea* (New York: Holt, Rinehart and Winston).

PRICE, BARBARA J.
1971 "Prehispanic Irrigation Agriculture in Nuclear America," *Latin America Research Review* 6(3):3–60.

PROSKOURIAKOFF, TATIANA
1961 "The Lords of the Maya Realm," *Expedition* 4(1):14–21.

RAPPAPORT, ROY A.
1968 *Pigs for the Ancestors* (New Haven, Conn.: Yale University Press).
1971 "The Flow of Energy in an Agricultural Society," *Scientific American* 225(3): 117–32.

RATTRAY, EVELYN
1966 "An Archaeological and Stylistic Study of Coyotlatelco Pottery," *Mesoamerican Notes* 7–8:87–193.
1972 "El complejo cultural Coyotlatelco," *Teotihuacán, XI Mesa Redonda* (Mexico City: Sociedad Mexicana de Antropología), 2:201–9.

REINA, R. E.
1967 "Milpas and Milperos: Implications for Prehistoric Times," *American Anthropologist* 69:1–20.

RELACIÓN DE TECCIZTLÁN
1905 See Paso y Troncoso 1905b.

ROBERTSON, DONALD
1959 *Mexican Manuscript Painting in the Early Colonial Period*, The Metropolitan School, Yale Historical Publications, History of Arts XII.
1963 *Pre-Columbian Architecture* (New York: George Braziller).

ROWE, JOHN HOWLAND
1960 "Cultural Unity and Diversification in Peruvian Archaeology," in *Men and Cultures, Selected Papers of the Fifth International Congress of Anthropological and Ethnological Sciences*, Philadelphia, September 1956, ed. Anthony Wallace (Philadelphia: University of Pennsylvania Press), pp. 627–31.

ROWE, JOHN HOWLAND AND DOROTHY MENZEL (EDS.)
1967 *Peruvian Archaeology: Selected Readings* (Palo Alto, Calif.: Peek Publications).

RUBÍN DE LA BORBOLLA, DANIEL F.
1948 "Arqueología Tarasca," in *El Occidente de Mexico* (Mexico City: Sociedad Mexicana de Antropología), pp. 29–33.

References

SAHAGÚN, BERNARDINO DE
1950–69 General History of the Things of New Spain; Florentine Codex, ed. and trans. Arthur J. O. Anderson and Charles E. Dibble, 13 parts, School of American Research Monograph no. 14 (Santa Fe, N.M.: School of American Research, and Salt Lake City: University of Utah Press).

SAHLINS, MARSHALL D.
1958 Social Stratification in Polynesia (Seattle: University of Washington Press).
1960 "Political Power and the Economy in Primitive Society," in Essays in the Science of Culture in Honor of Leslie White, ed. Gertrude E. Dole and Robert L. Carneiro (New York: Thomas Y. Crowell), pp. 390–415.
1965 "On the Sociology of Primitive Exchange," in The Relevance of Models for Social Anthropology, ed. Michael Banton (London: Tavistock Publications), pp. 139–236.
1972 Stone Age Economics (Chicago: Aldine-Atherton).

SANDERS, WILLIAM T.
1952 "El mercado de Tlatelolco: un estudio de economía urbana," Tlatoani, 1(1): 14–16.
1953 "The Anthropogeography of Central Veracruz," in Huastecos, Totonacos, y sus vecinos, ed. Ignacio Bernal and Eusebio Dávalos Hurtado (Mexico City: Sociedad Mexicana de Antropología), pp. 27–78.
1956 "The Central Mexican Symbiotic Region," in Prehistoric Settlement Patterns in the New World, ed. Gordon R. Willey, Viking Fund Publications in Anthropology, vol. 23 (New York: Wenner-Gren Foundation for Anthropological Research), pp. 115–27.
1965 Cultural Ecology of the Teotihuacán Valley: A Preliminary Report of the Results of the Teotihuacán Valley Project (University Park: Department of Sociology and Anthropology, Pennsylvania State University).
1967 "Life in a Classic Village," Teotihuacán, XI Mesa Redonda (Mexico City: Sociedad Mexicana de Antropología), 1:123–48.
1968 "Hydraulic Agriculture, Economic Symbiosis and the Evolution of States in Central Mexico," in Anthropological Archaeology in the Americas, ed. Betty J. Meggers (Washington, D.C.: Anthropological Society of Washington), pp. 88–107.
1970 "Resource Utilization and Political Evolution in the Teotihuacán Valley" (in press).
1971 "Chiefdom to State: Political Evolution at Kaminaljuyú, Guatemala" (unpublished).

SANDERS, WILLIAM T., ANTON KOVAR, THOMAS H. CHARLTON, AND RICHARD DIEHL
1970 "The Natural Environment, Contemporary Occupation, and Sixteenth-Century Population of the Valley," The Teotihuacan Valley Project: Final Report, vol. 1, Pennsylvania State University Occasional Papers in Anthropology, no. 3 (University Park, Pa.).

SANDERS, WILLIAM T. AND BARBARA J. PRICE
1968 Mesoamerica: The Evolution of a Civilization (New York: Random House).

SAUER, CARL AND DONALD BRAND
1932 Aztatlan: Prehistoric Mexican Frontier on the Pacific Coast, Ibero-Americana no. 1 (Berkeley: University of California Press).

SEELE, ENNO
1973 "Restos de milpas y poblaciones prehispánicas cerca de San Buenaventura Neal-
tican, Puebla," in *Proyecto Puebla-Tlaxcala Comunicaciones*, no. 7, ed. Wil-
helm Lauer and Erdmann Gormsen (Puebla, Mexico: Fundación Alemana de
la Investigación Científica), pp. 77–86.

SÉJOURNÉ, LAURETTE
1966 *Arquitectura y Pintura en Teotihuacán* (Mexico City: Siglo XXI Editores).

SÉJOURNÉ, LAURETTE AND GRACIELA SALICRUP
1965 "Arquitectura y arqueología," *Revista de la Universidad de México* 19(7):4–8.

SELER, EDUARD
1915 "Die Teotiuacan Kulter des Hochlands von Mexiko," *Gesammelte Abhand-
lungen zur Amerikanischen Sprach-und Alterthumskunde* (Berlin: Behrend
und Co.), 5:405–585.

SERVICE, ELMAN R.
1971 *Cultural Evolutionism: Theory in Practice* (New York: Holt, Rinehart and
Winston).

SMITH, THOMAS C.
1951 *Agrarian Origins of Modern Japan* (Stanford, Calif.: Stanford University
Press).

SPENCE, MICHAEL W.
1967a "The Obsidian Industry of Teotihuacán," *American Antiquity* 32(4):507–14.
1967b "Los talleres de obsidiana de Teotihuacán," *Teotihuacán, XI Mesa Redonda*
(Mexico City: Sociedad Mexicana de Antropología), 1:213–18.
1971 "Skeletal Morphology and Social Organization in Teotihuacán, Mexico" (Ph.D.
diss., Southern Illinois University).
1974 "Residential Practices and the Distribution of Skeletal Traits in Teotihuacán,
Mexico," *Man* 9(2):262–73.

SPENCE, MICHAEL, AND JEFFREY R. PARSONS
1972 "Pre-Hispanic Obsidian Exploitation in Central Mexico: A Preliminary Synthesis," in *Miscellaneous Studies in Mexican Prehistory*, by Michael W. Spence,
Jeffrey R. Parsons, and Mary Hrones Parsons. University of Michigan Museum
of Anthropology Anthropological Papers, no. 45 (Ann Arbor), pp. 1–44.

SPOONER, BRIAN (ED.)
1972 *Population Growth: Anthropological Implications* (Cambridge, Mass.: M.I.T.
Press).

STADELMAN, RAYMOND
1940 *Maize Cultivation in Northwestern Guatemala*, Contribution to American
Anthropology and History no. 33, Carnegie Institution of Washington Publication no. 523 (Washington, D.C.: Carnegie Institution).

STEGGERDA, MORRIS
1941 *Maya Indians of Yucatan*, Carnegie Institution of Washington Publication no.
531 (Washington, D.C.: Carnegie Institution).

STEWARD, JULIAN H.
1937 "Ecological Aspects of Southwestern Society," *Anthropos* 32:87–104.
1949 "Cultural Causality and Law: A Trial Formulation of the Development of
Early Civilizations," *American Anthropologist* 51(1):1–27.
1955 *Theory of Culture Change* (Urbana: University of Illinois Press).

References

STEWARD, JULIAN H., ROBERT M. ADAMS, DONALD COLLIER, ÁNGEL PALERM, KARL A. WITTFOGEL, AND RALPH L. BEALS
1955 *Irrigation Civilizations: A Comparative Study*. Pan American Union Social Science Monograph no. 1 (Washington, D.C.: Pan American Union).

STRESSER-PÉAN, GUY
1972 "Ancient Sources on the Huasteca," in *Archaeology of Northern Mesoamerica*, part 2, *Handbook of Middle American Indians*, vol. 11, ed. Gordon F. Ekholm and Ignacio Bernal (Austin: University of Texas Press), pp. 582–602.

STROSS, F. H., J. R. WEAVER, G. E. A. WYLD, ROBERT F. HEIZER, AND JOHN A. GRAHAM
1968 "Analysis of American Obsidians by X-Ray Fluorescence and Neutron Activation Analysis," in *Papers of Mesoamerican Archaeology*, Contributions of the University of California Archaeological Research Facility, no. 5 (Berkeley), pp. 59–79.

STRUEVER, STUART
1968 "Woodland Subsistence-Settlement Systems in the Lower Illinois Valley," in *New Perspectives in Archaeology*, ed. Sally R. Binford and Lewis R. Binford (Chicago: Aldine Publishing Co.), pp. 143–50.
1971 "Comments on Archaeological Data Requirements and Research Strategy," *American Antiquity* 36:9–19.

TAYLOR, WALTER W.
1966 "Archaic Cultures Adjacent to the Northeastern Frontiers of Mesoamerica," in *Archaeological Frontiers and External Connections, Handbook of Middle American Indians*, vol. 4, ed. Gordon F. Ekholm and Gordon R. Willey (Austin: University of Texas Press), pp. 59–94.

TEZOZOMOC, HERNANDO ALVARADO
1944 *Crónica Mexicana*, ed. Manuel Orozco y Berra (Mexico City: Editorial Leyenda).

THOMPSON, J. ERIC S.
1954 *The Rise and Fall of Maya Civilization* (Norman: University of Oklahoma Press).

TOLSTOY, PAUL
n.d. "The Archaeological Chronology of Western Mesoamerica before 900 A.D.," in *Chronologies in New World Archaeology*, ed. C. W. Meighan (New York: Seminar Press, in press).

TOLSTOY, PAUL AND LOUISE I. PARADIS
1970 "Early and Middle Preclassic Culture in the Basin of Mexico," *Science* 167 (3971):344–51.

TORQUEMADA, JUAN DE
1723 *Primera (Segunda, Tercera) Parte de los Veinte i un Libros Rituales i Monarchia Indiana*, 2d ed., 3 vols. (Madrid).

TOSCANO, SALVADOR, HEINRICH BERLIN, AND ROBERT H. BARLOW (EDS.)
1948 *Anales de Tlatelolco: unos anales históricos de la nación Mexicana y Códice de Tlatelolco, fuentes para la historia de México*, vol. 2 (Mexico City: Antigua Librería Robredo de José Porrúa e Hijos).

323

TOWNSEND, WILLIAM H.
1969 "Stone and Stone Tools Used in a New Guinea Society," *Ethnology* 8(2)199–205.

TOZZER, A.
1921 *Excavations at a Site at Santiago Ahuitzotla, Mexico, D.F.*, Bureau of American Ethnology Bulletin no. 74 (Washington, D.C.: Smithsonian Institution).

VAN ZANTWIJK, RUDOLF
1973 "Politics and Ethnicity in a Pre-Hispanic Mexican State between the Thirteenth and Fifteenth Centuries," *Plural Societies* 4(2):23–52.

VAPNARSKY, CESAR A.
1969 "One Rank-Size Distributions of Cities: An Ecological Approach," *Economic Development and Cultural Change* 17(4):584–95.

VAYDA, ANDREW P. AND ROY A. RAPPAPORT
1963 "Island Cultures," in *Man's Place in the Island Ecosystem*, ed. F. R. Fosberg (Honolulu: B. P. Bishop Museum Press), pp. 133–44.
1967 "Ecology, Cultural and Non-Cultural," in *Introduction to Cultural Anthropology*, ed. James A. Clifton (Boston: Houghton Mifflin Co.), pp. 477–97.

VELÁSQUEZ, PRIMO FELICIANO (TRANS.)
1945 *Códice Chimalpopoca: Anales de Cuauhtitlan y Leyenda de los Soles* (Mexico City: Instituto de Historia, Universidad Nacional de México, Imprenta Universitaria).

VIDARTE DE LINARES, JUAN
1968 "Teotihuacán, la ciudad del quinto sol," *Cuadernos Americanos*, yr. 27, 158(3):133–45.

WEAVER, MURIEL PORTER (see also PORTER, MURIEL N.)
1972 *The Aztecs, Maya, and Their Predecessors: Archaeology of Mesoamerica* (New York: Seminar Press).

WEIGAND, PHIL C.
1968 "The Mines and Mining Techniques of the Chalchihuites Culture," *American Antiquity* 33(1):45–61.

WEST, M.
1965 "Transition from Preclassic to Classic at Teotihuacán," *American Antiquity* 31(2):192–202.

WEST, ROBERT C. AND PEDRO ARMILLAS
1950 "Las chinampas de México," *Cuadernos Americanos* 50(2):165–82.

WHEATLEY, PAUL
1971 *The Pivot of the Four Quarters: A Preliminary Enquiry into the Origins and Character of the Ancient Chinese City* (Chicago: Aldine Publishing Co.).

WHITE, BENJAMIN
1973 "Demand for Labor and Population Growth in Colonial Java," *Human Ecology* 1(3):217–36.

WICKE, CHARLES
1971 *Olmec, An Early Art Style of Precolumbian Mexico* (Tucson: University of Arizona Press).

WILLEY, GORDON R.
1953 *Prehistoric Settlement Patterns in the Viru Valley, Peru*, Bureau of American

References

Ethnology Bulletin no. 155 (Washington, D.C.: U.S. Government Printing Office).

1962 "The Early Great Styles and the Rise of the pre-Columbian Civilizations," *American Anthropologist* 64(1):1–14.

WILLEY, GORDON R., GORDON F. EKHOLM, AND RENÉ MILLON

1964 "The Patterns of Farming Life and Civilization," in *Natural Environment and Early Cultures, Handbook of Middle American Indians*, vol. 1, ed. Robert C. West (Austin: University of Texas Press), pp. 446–98.

WITTFOGEL, KARL A.

1931 *Wirtschaft und Gesellschuft Chinas* (Leipzig: C. L. Hirschfeld).

1938 *New Light on Chinese Society* (New York: Institute of Pacific Relations).

1957 *Oriental Despotism* (New Haven, Conn.: Yale University Press).

1972 "The Hydraulic Approach to Pre-Spanish Mesoamerica," in *Chronology and Irrigation, The Prehistory of the Tehuacan Valley*, vol. 4, ed. Frederick Johnson (Austin: University of Texas Press), pp. 59–80.

WOLF, ERIC R.

1959 *Sons of the Shaking Earth* (Chicago: University of Chicago Press).

WOLF, ERIC R. AND ÁNGEL PALERM

1955 "Irrigation in the Old Acolhua Domain, Mexico," *Southwestern Journal of Anthropology* 11(3):265–81.

WOODBURN, J.

1972 "Ecology, Nomadic Movement, and the Composition of the Local Group among Hunters and Gatherers: An East African Example and Its Implications," in *Man, Settlement and Urbanism*, ed. Peter Ucko, Ruth Tringham, and G. Dimbleby (London: Duckworth & Co.), pp. 193–206.

WRIGHT, HENRY T.

1969 *The Administration of Rural Production in an Early Mesopotamian Town*, University of Michigan Museum of Anthropology, Anthropological Papers, no. 38 (Ann Arbor).

1970 "Toward an Explanation of the Origin of the State," in *Explanation of Prehistoric Change*, ed. J. N. Hill (Albuquerque: University of New Mexico Press, in press).

WRIGHT, HENRY T. AND GREGORY A. JOHNSON

1975 "Population, Exchange, and Early State Formation in Southwestern Iran," *American Anthropologist* 177(2):267–89.

WRIGLEY, E. A.

1969 *Population and History* (New York: McGraw-Hill).

Index

Index

Index

Index

Index

Index

DATE DUE

MAY 2 1984			
FEB 2 7 1985			